Foundations of Health Service Psychology

Foundations of Health Service Psychology

An Evidence-Based Biopsychosocial Approach

Second Edition

Timothy P. Melchert
Department of Counselor Education and Counseling Psychology,
Marquette University,
Milwaukee, Wisconsin,
United States

ELSEVIER
ACADEMIC PRESS
An imprint of Elsevier

Academic Press is an imprint of Elsevier
125 London Wall, London EC2Y 5AS, United Kingdom
525 B Street, Suite 1650, San Diego, CA 92101, United States
50 Hampshire Street, 5th Floor, Cambridge, MA 02139, United States
The Boulevard, Langford Lane, Kidlington, Oxford OX5 1GB, United Kingdom

Library of Congress Cataloging-in-Publication Data
A catalog record for this book is available from the Library of Congress

British Library Cataloguing-in-Publication Data
A catalogue record for this book is available from the British Library

ISBN: 978-0-12-816426-6

For information on all Academic Press publications visit our website at https://www.elsevier.com/books-and-journals

Publisher: Nikki Levy
Editorial Project Manager: Barbara Makinster
Production Project Manager: Bharatwaj Varatharajan
Cover Designer: Matthew Limbert

Typeset by TNQ Technologies

Contents

Preface

The field of psychology has entered an exciting period. In fact, one can argue that it recently took one of its most significant steps since it emerged as an academic discipline nearly a century and a half ago. It will be explained in Chapter 1 how psychology recently became a unified, paradigmatic science that is now fully consistent with the rest of the natural sciences. For the first time in its history, psychology can now be considered one of the natural sciences. This is an historic achievement that also increases the potential of the field to strengthen its effectiveness as a health care profession. This likewise strengthens the potential of the field to help improve the behavioral health of the population in general.

As a result of these developments, the title of the first edition of this book (*Foundations of Professional Psychology: The End of Theoretical Orientations and the Emergence of the Biopsychosocial Approach*) needed to be changed for the current edition. *Health service psychology* is now becoming preferred over the older term *professional psychology* when referring to clinical services provided in the context of behavioral health care (Health Service Psychology Education Collaborative, 2013). The subtitle of the second edition also needed to be changed because an evidence-based biopsychosocial approach has now become widely accepted as the basic framework for conceptualizing education and practice in the field. As explained in Chapters 1 through 3, the age of competing theoretical orientations for case conceptualization in behavioral health care has largely come to an end. In its place, a science-based approach has emerged that integrates the biological, psychological, and sociocultural influences on human psychology and provides a unified, evidence-based framework for practicing behavioral health care. Some would argue that it is premature to discard other epistemological approaches to understanding human psychology, but most of them would probably also agree that a science-based biopsychosocial approach is necessary for practicing health service psychology in a responsible, ethical manner alongside the other health care professions. Human psychology cannot be understood without an integrated scientific understanding of the biological, psychological, and sociocultural influences on individuals' development, and so a biopsychosocial approach is necessary as the underlying framework for understanding health service psychology.

This volume attempts to provide a comprehensive description of the evidence-based biopsychosocial approach to behavioral health care. After reviewing the basic underlying scientific and ethical foundations of the field, it illustrates a comprehensive perspective for understanding the populations we work with. It then goes on to describe the behavioral health treatment process, from intake through outcomes assessment and follow-up, along with a public health perspective on behavioral health. The discussion of topics is firmly evidence-based and grounded in the research literature. There is sufficient depth and detail so the reader will gain a solid introduction to the issues involved, and key references are provided for those who want to pursue greater depth.

The intended audience for this volume is graduate students and practitioners in health service psychology. It is presumed that readers will have had a grounding in the discipline of psychology. Although this book is aimed at students in doctoral programs in health service psychology, it is applicable for students in all graduate programs in behavioral health care and even for higher-level undergraduate students who are being challenged to learn about the field at a higher level.

This volume is organized into four parts that describe the conceptual framework for understanding health service psychology from a science-based biopsychosocial approach. The first part of the book is comprised of four chapters that address the conceptual foundations needed for learning and practicing the profession. Chapter 1 provides an overview of these foundations and argues that recent scientific progress in the field compels a paradigm shift away from outmoded practices and toward a solidly scientific approach to clinical practice. Chapter 2 then reviews the complicated historical development of theory and research in psychology and the scientific reasons for the irreconcilable differences between the traditional theoretical orientations and schools of thought in psychology. The chapter then goes on to explain some of the essential characteristics of an integrated science-based approach to understanding human psychology and behavioral health care. Chapter 3 provides an overview of the unified scientific explanation of human development, functioning, and behavior change. Chapter 4 then explains why professional ethics need to be added to the basic conceptual foundations of behavioral health care. The chapter also provides an overview of the current scientific perspective on moral reasoning and behavior, the critical role that ethics play in health care and in human behavior, and then summarizes the most influential approach designed specifically to guide the practice of health care.

Part 2 of the volume includes four chapters. The first three of these provide an overview of the psychological, sociocultural, and physical health of the American public. This is followed by a fourth chapter that provides the developmental perspective that integrates the factors discussed in the previous three chapters. Human development obviously occurs across time, and so development becomes a necessary dimension for the integration of the biological, psychological, and sociocultural influences on human psychology. These four dimensions (i.e., the three biopsychosocial dimensions plus time/development) are so fundamental for understanding human psychology that they are compared to the three spatial dimensions (i.e., up-down, left-right, and forward-backward) plus time that are fundamental for understanding the physical world (Melchert, 2011, 2015). Human psychology and behavioral health care cannot be understood from a scientific perspective without considering how biopsychosocial factors interact across time and development.

Part 3 of this volume describes the process of applying the scientific and ethical foundations of the biopsychosocial approach in behavioral health care. The four chapters in this part of the book address the four general phases of the treatment process: assessment, treatment planning, implementing treatment, and evaluating its effectiveness. The boundaries between these phases of treatment are often unclear. The treatment process begins with assessment, but assessment continues throughout, and assessing the effectiveness of treatment is the last phase of the ongoing assessment that continues across the therapeutic relationship. Treatment also occurs throughout, from the beginning of the development of a therapeutic relationship during the initial interactions with patients on through the discussion of treatment termination at the end. However, there are normally clear shifts in purposes and activities across the four phases of treatment, and the science-based biopsychosocial approach has specific implications for each of them.

Part 4 of this volume addresses additional implications of the evidence-based biopsychosocial approach for behavioral health care. Chapter 13 presents an overview of a public health and integrated care perspective on behavioral health. The health and well-being of a population cannot be understood without this perspective and it should receive more attention in behavioral health care education, practice, research, and policy. Finally, Chapter 14 discusses several conclusions and implications that derive from the evidence-based biopsychosocial approach to behavioral health care along with several exciting possibilities that are more likely to result from taking a unified science-based biopsychosocial approach.[1]

Before moving on to other topics, some of the terminology used in this book is briefly explained. The individuals served by behavioral health care professionals are often referred to as clients, patients, or sometimes consumers or even customers. The term *patient* is used throughout this handbook, however, for multiple reasons. The term *patient* is firmly ingrained in health care generally and it is important that behavioral health care professionals use the same term if health service psychology is to become better integrated into health care generally. The term *client* has the advantage of avoiding the connotations of the "sick role" in the traditional medical model where ill patients were expected to be relatively passive recipients of services provided by experts as opposed to being active participants in the treatment process. But the term *client* also evokes a business relationship where individuals purchase a desired or needed service and where the ethical obligations of the seller are normally viewed as being lower than they are in behavioral health care. As explained in Chapters 1 and 3, professional ethics play a critical role in health care, and referring to the individuals who we serve as patients helps convey the importance of that role. The recent policy statement by the American Psychological Association (APA) recommending that psychologists use the term *patient* instead of client when referring to those cared for by health service psychologists also reflects these concerns (APA, 2018).

[1] Part 4 of the book only includes two chapters, whereas the other parts of the book all have four chapters. The repetition of *four* in the organization of the book is entirely coincidental but nicely highlights the four naturally occurring dimensions (biopsychosocial plus time) that explain human development and the four basic phases of the treatment process (assessment, treatment planning, providing treatment, and outcomes assessment).

This volume also refers to *behavioral health* rather than *mental health* because the former term generally has a broader meaning. Mental health historically has focused on intrapersonal psychological issues. Substance use disorders, health psychology, family functioning, and other topics often fell outside the main focus of mental health, whereas behavioral health normally included all of those issues. This volume is specifically focused on the broad range of behavior and psychological functioning and their interactions with physical health and social functioning. Consequently, this volume focuses on behavioral health and biopsychosocial functioning broadly. As noted earlier, the term *health service psychology* is now generally preferred to the term *professional psychology* for referring to the work of psychologists who provide behavioral health care (Health Service Psychology Education Collaborative, 2013). The term *professional psychology* had a specific meaning within psychology, but was imprecise and easily misunderstood outside the field. Psychologists who provide health services are regulated and licensed similar to the way other health care professionals who provide health services are, whereas other types of applied psychologists who provide professional services in non–health care settings often are not (e.g., educational, industrial-organizational, many consulting psychologists). The term *professional psychologist* does not adequately differentiate between different types of applied psychologists or even between applied and other types of psychologists. After all, *all* psychologists are expected to be *professional*; there should be no such thing as a nonprofessional psychologist.

Timothy P. Melchert
Department of Counselor Education and Counseling Psychology,
Marquette University,
Milwaukee, Wisconsin,
United States

Part One

Conceptual foundations of the biopsychosocial approach to behavioral health care

The foundational framework for understanding human psychology and behavioral health care

1

The discipline of psychology works to understand human behavior and the nature of the human mind and brain. For many people, there is no more interesting subject of study. The complexity, sensibilities, and creativity of the human mind seem endless. We are awestruck by its amazing abilities and soaring intellect, and our personal experiences with others and when alone can bring us great contentment, joy, and sometimes even exhilaration. Humans, of course, are also capable of very hurtful and even depraved behavior, and many people suffer greatly due to a wide variety of mental health problems. Psychological questions absorb and fascinate us from childhood through to our last breaths, and religious and political leaders, philosophers, and sages throughout history have attempted to understand how we are capable of such extremes of behavior. The scientific study of these topics is, of course, fascinating as well.

Until relatively recently, however, human psychology was not well understood from a scientific standpoint. The tremendous complexity involved was simply greater than what the available scientific methods and techniques were able to uncover and explain. Scattered scientific knowledge as well as a variety of diverse theoretical orientations were available for understanding aspects of human psychology, but these were widely acknowledged as being incomplete and/or inaccurate. Because these orientations conflicted with one another, most of them (and perhaps all of them) had to be at least partially wrong. (These issues are all discussed more extensively below.)

For most of the history of the field, traditional approaches to education and practice in health service psychology and the other behavioral health care fields generally involved learning one or more of the well-accepted theoretical orientations and then applying that approach to conceptualize clinical cases and deliver treatment. Individual graduate programs often emphasized a particular orientation, while the various mental health specializations tended to support certain orientations. In the first half of the 20th century, American psychiatry came to strongly endorse psychoanalytic approaches, and later a biological approach in the 1980s, while clinical psychology often adopted behavioral and later cognitive approaches. Counseling psychology was heavily influenced by humanistic theories, as was mental health counseling. Social work and marriage and family therapy were heavily influenced by systemic approaches, while the substance abuse treatment field often relied on mutual aid support groups. The practice of adopting one or more theoretical orientations to guide one's clinical work is still generally considered part of required training in the field. For example,

Foundations of Health Service Psychology. https://doi.org/10.1016/B978-0-12-816426-6.00001-3

in health service psychology the Application for Psychology Internship, the standard application form used by the Association of Psychology Postdoctoral and Internship Centers, includes the following required essay question: "Please describe your theoretical orientation and how this influences your approach to case conceptualization and intervention" (APPIC, 2018). The American Psychological Association (APA) Assessment of Competency Benchmarks Work Group (Fouad et al., 2009) noted the following as an "essential component" for demonstrating treatment planning skills: "Formulates and conceptualizes cases and plans interventions utilizing at least one consistent theoretical orientation" (p. S19).

One's adopted theoretical orientation naturally had a strong influence on case formulation and treatment. If one ascribed to cognitive therapy, a patient's depression was likely to be conceptualized as being caused by depressogenic cognitions or irrational beliefs, and treatment would probably involve replacing those cognitions and beliefs with more rational ones. If one ascribed to a biological psychiatry model of depression, one was likely to conceptualize the same depressive symptoms as resulting from a serotonin deficiency in the brain and the treatment plan would probably include antidepressant medication that blocks the reuptake of serotonin in the synaptic spaces between neurons. If one ascribed to psychodynamic theory, one was likely to focus on the patient's developmental history, while solution-oriented therapists would have much less interest in identifying the causes of one's problems than in identifying solutions to those problems. Behavioral, feminist, family-systems, client-centered, or eye movement and desensitization and reprocessing therapists would focus on still other issues. (Maslow (1966) famously noted that if all you have is a hammer, then everything looks like a nail, or as Kaplan (1964, p. 28) put it, "Give a small boy a hammer, and he will find that everything he encounters needs pounding.")

This situation caused great confusion for those within the field as well as for health care systems and the general public. There was often deep disagreement and conflict between the theoretical camps regarding the nature of healthy personality functioning, the development of psychopathology, and the appropriate methods for alleviating distress and changing maladaptive behavior. It was widely recognized that the fundamental differences between psychodynamic, behavioral, humanistic, systemic, biological, and postmodern constructivist approaches could not be reconciled (Messer & Winokur, 1980; Wood & Joseph, 2007). These perspectives also could not all be correct, many had not been empirically evaluated, and they all appeared to be incomplete as well. And although integrative and eclectic approaches seemed to offer a solution to the problem, combining some number of the existing theoretical orientations, when each appeared to be incomplete or only partly valid, did not represent a scientifically acceptable solution, either.

The behavioral sciences have now reached a very different point in their understanding of human psychology. A great deal is now known about biological, psychological, and sociocultural influences on human growth and development. Much obviously remains to be learned, but enough is now known that behavioral health care education and practice can be informed by a unified scientific perspective on human psychology. All the sciences have made dramatic progress recently and the behavioral sciences have made especially rapid progress. New scientific tools have been developed that allow observations of the living human brain, the unconscious mind, the genome, and other phenomena. In the past, scientists could speculate about the nature of these phenomena, but discovering even whether particular mechanisms existed had to wait for the development of more precise and powerful scientific tools.

Although we are still at the early stages of scientifically understanding many aspects of the human mind and brain, explanations are continuing to grow in comprehensiveness and detail. Hypotheses about the nature of many psychological processes that in the past had to remain speculations can now be experimentally tested. Many of Freud's notions about the nature and role of the subconscious in mental life could not be directly tested for nearly a century, but subconscious mental activity is now being experimentally examined from multiple perspectives. Advances like these are allowing behavioral health care to be practiced on the basis of scientific knowledge that was simply unavailable in the past. Indeed, recent progress in the scientific understanding of the human mind and brain is so great that one is reminded of the quantum revolution that physics underwent a century ago that led to a far more detailed understanding of the physical world.

Health service psychology and the other behavioral health care fields have not yet made a full break with traditional approaches to mental health education and practice, but the transition is now well underway. This volume is based on the view that there is now overwhelming support for a unified scientific understanding of human psychology, and it is time for the field to systematically transition to this new scientific framework. As a science-based clinical profession, it is essential that behavioral health care update its theoretical and conceptual foundations so they are consistent with the latest science on human psychology. In many ways, this new scientific understanding of human psychology is far more complex and fascinating than traditional views of human nature, and so behavioral health care education and practice are entering a very exciting era. This volume attempts to describe what a thoroughly science-based approach to health service psychology education and practice might look like.

The foundational structure of biopsychosocial behavioral health care

The basic conceptual foundations of the approach described in this volume are not controversial. At the most basic level, it is argued that behavioral health care must be conceptualized as being squarely founded on science and ethics. Neither science nor ethics alone is sufficient for structuring humane, respectful, ethical, and effective behavioral health care. Scientifically based health care that is not ethically based is simply not acceptable and, in today's world, health care interventions that are not based on scientific knowledge and tested for safety and effectiveness are also not acceptable. Both perspectives are simply necessary.

Until recent decades, scientific knowledge of human behavior had not progressed sufficiently for health service psychology to proceed under a unified conceptual framework. But psychological science and professional ethics are now both sufficiently well developed to allow the field to proceed using a solid, well-grounded framework for understanding human psychology and behavioral health care practice. Neither scientific nor ethical knowledge is fully developed—far from it! Although we have come a great distance in both areas, there is no question that much, much more needs to be learned (these issues are discussed more fully in the coming chapters). Nonetheless, research and theory in both these areas have progressed sufficiently to provide firm conceptual foundations for the practice of behavioral health care.

Several aspects of the basic conceptual foundations of behavioral health care are now clear. First, behavioral health care focuses on meeting the behavioral health needs of the population just as physical health care focuses on meeting individuals' medical needs. But behavioral health and functioning are necessarily intertwined with sociocultural and biological functioning, and so behavioral health care does not focus solely on mental health, but it also aims to promote and enhance biopsychosocial functioning generally. The following definition captures these basic definitional issues:

> *Behavioral health care involves the clinical application of scientific knowledge and professional ethics to address behavioral health needs and promote biopsychosocial functioning.*

This conceptualization of behavioral health care is depicted graphically in Fig. 1.1. This figure portrays an edifice representing the practice of behavioral health care that

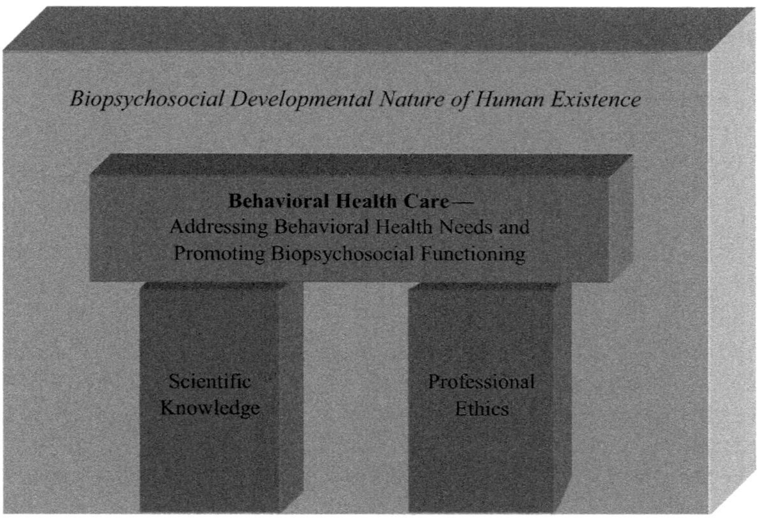

Figure 1.1 Behavioral health care rests on the pillars of scientific knowledge and professional ethics, all of which exist within the context of the biopsychosocial developmental nature of human existence.

rests on two pillars representing scientific knowledge and professional ethics. Together, science and ethics form the foundation for the practice of behavioral health care; if either one is removed, the structure immediately fails. In addition, behavioral health care along with the underlying scientific knowledge and professional ethics all must be understood within the context of the biopsychosocial developmental nature of human existence.

Science based

There is now widespread agreement regarding the general scientific framework for understanding human development and functioning. It can be argued, however, that confidence in such a framework was not possible until relatively recently. Applied psychology was always committed to basing clinical and applied practice on science, but a major obstacle for achieving that goal was the limited scientific knowledge for understanding human development and behavior. The original founders of the field clearly recognized this problem. Wilhelm Wundt, the German scientist generally acknowledged as the founder of psychology as an experimental science, allowed his graduate students to investigate only elemental processes involved in sensation, perception, and attention, not because he believed that higher levels of consciousness were unimportant, but because he believed the scientific tools for reliably investigating such complex phenomena were simply unavailable at the time (Benjamin, 2014). William James was also well aware of the limitations of experimental techniques for investigating the tremendous depth and complexity of human experience (e.g., the constantly changing stream of human consciousness; James, 1890). As will be discussed in the next chapter, Sigmund Freud, John Watson, Carl Rogers, and others soon proposed a diverse array of alternative explanations for human psychology. Each of their theories contributed important insights into the human condition, but they all were eventually found to be incomplete and unable to withstand scientific scrutiny as comprehensive explanations of human development and functioning.

The behavioral and biological sciences have advanced greatly in recent decades and there is now widespread agreement regarding the broad outlines of the scientific understanding of human psychology. There are, of course, disagreements about details and new findings that are not yet well established, but the main findings are not controversial. As a result, the era of many conflicting and competing theoretical orientations for explaining human development and functioning can now be left behind.

At the most general, metatheoretical level, the basic biopsychosocial framework for understanding human development and functioning has been widely accepted ever since George Engel (1977) proposed it nearly a half century ago. There is no disagreement that the scientific understanding of human psychology requires a comprehensive framework that recognizes the interactions between the biological, psychological, and sociocultural levels of natural organization. The evidence for this basic framework is overwhelming. In fact, it may be impossible to find an introductory psychology textbook that does not discuss the interacting psychological, biological, and social bases of human behavior. Conceptualizations of development, personality, intelligence, psychopathology, adjustment, behavior change, and other important psychological constructs that are not based on all three of these interacting levels of natural organization are simply not supported by the evidence. These same three dimensions are involved in determining the experience and life course of all organic life, though of course the biological, neural, and environmental factors involved in simple life forms can be relatively uncomplicated. No other organism comes close to the biopsychosocial complexity involved in human beings.

The biopsychosocial approach had a major influence on education in the health and human service professions in the first decade of the 21st century in particular. During that time, the biopsychosocial framework was incorporated into medical education throughout the U.S. and Europe (Frankel, Quill, & McDaniel, 2003). It was incorporated into the accreditation standards for master's and doctoral education in the mental health specializations (e.g., the biological, psychological, and social bases of behavior had to be covered in APA-accredited doctoral programs, and the accreditation standards for mental health counseling incorporated the biopsychosocial perspective; APA Commission on Accreditation, 2009; Council for the Accreditation of Counseling and Related Educational Programs, 2009). It was adopted by several of the clinical specializations in professional psychology (e.g., child, school, health, and addiction psychology; neuropsychology; and geropsychology; see Martin, Weinberg, & Bealer, 2007; Seagull, 2000; Shah & Reichman, 2006; Suls & Rothman, 2004; Williams & Evans, 2003). It was also endorsed by 23 different health care and human service professional organizations in the U.S. (APA, 2006).

The basic notion behind the biopsychosocial approach can be illustrated graphically by a cube representing the three intertwined psychological, sociocultural, and biological dimensions of influence on human psychology (see Fig. 1.2). In addition, human development and functioning necessarily take place across time: human beings are living, adapting organisms that continually change and evolve across the life span. We also have the longest maturation period of any animal, and we

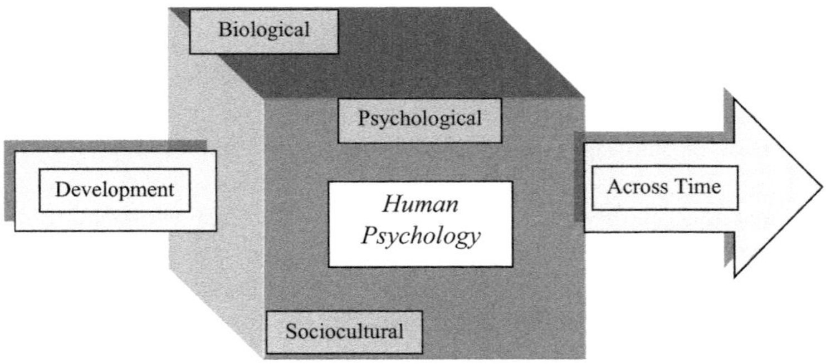

Figure 1.2 Understanding human psychology requires a perspective that integrates the inextricably intertwined biopsychosocial dimensions across time.

are exceedingly dependent and malleable as infants and children before reaching maturity, a characteristic that has profound implications for children and all the people in their environment. Therefore, a fourth dimension representing time can be depicted by an arrow running through the biopsychosocial cube. The fourth dimension of time was not part of Engel's (1977) original conceptualization of the biopsychosocial approach, but it is obvious that time must be included in any conceptualization of living organisms or, indeed, any phenomenon in the universe. The cube with the arrow through it also represents the inextricably intertwined nature of these dimensions that cannot be disaggregated without destroying the holistic nature of the living, adapting organism. This conceptualization of human psychology is so important for understanding human psychology that it is analogous to the three spatial dimensions plus the dimension of time that are necessary for conceptualizing the entire physical world (Melchert, 2011, 2016).

An essential characteristic of the biopsychosocial developmental framework is its holistic, fully interconnected nature. The biological, psychological, sociocultural, and time dimensions cannot be meaningfully separated but are inextricably intertwined, and the individual cannot be understood without reference to the whole. Biology affects psychology and culture; culture affects psychology and biology; some effects are short lived while others last a lifetime; and so on through all the permutations of these four dimensions. They do not function as independent domains but continually interact over the life span. In a sense, the person dies if any of the biological, psychological, sociocultural, or time dimensions ceases functioning.

People sometimes assume a reductionist perspective whereby an individual's psychology can be explained by underlying biological processes. Particularly in American culture, since the 1980s it has been widely believed that chemical imbalances in the brain account for the psychological syndromes manifest in one's emotion, cognition, and behavior (e.g., the dopamine hypothesis for schizophrenia or serotonin hypothesis regarding depression). A century ago, popular cultural and eugenics ideas supported the notion that biological factors were responsible for differences between racial groups, the genders, and those belonging to different religions and social classes. But research clearly does not support these assumptions. We now know that experience and behavior frequently change brain function and even structure. Likewise, changes in the biology of the brain can also change behavior and experience. Of course, brain activity is correlated with behavior: if particular behaviors, thoughts, and emotions are not also observable in the brain, they did not happen! The brain mediates behavior because we are biological organisms, and cognition, emotion, and behavior are mediated by the nervous system. But that does not imply causation—it is simply correlation—and much more research is needed to clarify the causal interactions between biological, psychological, and sociocultural factors across development as well as the constraints imposed at each of the levels. These issues are discussed more extensively in Chapters 2 and 3 below.

It is critical to distinguish the science-based biopsychosocial developmental approach from traditional views on eclecticism and theoretical integration that have been very popular in behavioral health care. Some have argued that the biopsychosocial approach is vague and unspecified and consequently supports eclecticism because it provides no rationale for selecting one theory or behavioral health care treatment over another (e.g., Ghaemi, 2010; McLaren, 2007). Eclecticism in mental health treatment has been defined as selecting what is likely to work best for a particular person and problem, based primarily on what has worked best in the past for others with similar problems and characteristics (Lazarus, Beutler, & Norcross, 1992). But in addition to this common-sense, trial-and-error approach to treatment selection, eclecticism can also be uncritical, unsystematic, arbitrary, and based on personal preference rather than scientific research and theory (e.g., Eysenck, 1970). Finding what works best in a particular situation in a trial-by-error manner can be a very effective strategy: across human history, this was often very effective for responding to life's challenges and opportunities. But it is not based on scientific understanding and is vulnerable to massive errors, particularly with regard to processes that cannot be readily observed (e.g., the understanding of infectious disease or psychological disorder). When science advances to the point at which phenomena can be explained and the safety and effectiveness of health care interventions can be systematically evaluated and improved through the application of experimental methods, then eclecticism is no longer justified.

The science-based biopsychosocial approach is also quite different from traditional approaches to theoretical integration in health service psychology. Integration applied to the merging of different beliefs in religion or politics is referred to as *syncretism*, in which discrete traditions or perspectives are amalgamated or assimilated to allow different groups to compromise and find a way to move forward together (e.g., the ancient Greeks and Romans commonly integrated local deities from the areas they governed into their divine pantheons). In those realms, it may be a very effective approach to dealing with the challenges of collective life and competing cultures. Like eclecticism, however, it is not a science-based approach. Combining two or more of the traditional psychological theoretical orientations, when each is based on assumptions or a worldview instead of the ability to scientifically explain particular phenomena, is more similar to religious or political syncretism than it is to science.

Eclecticism and integration (and syncretism) may have been essential to human survival and progress in the past and were perhaps the main approaches to medical and mental health care throughout human history until just recently. But those approaches are no longer satisfactory. Science now provides verified explanations of many aspects of human development and functioning, from our evolutionary origins to specific psychological, biological, and sociocultural processes and mechanisms. Of course, a huge amount remains to be learned, but we now understand many aspects of development, functioning, and behavior change, and this knowledge can be used to improve the safety and effectiveness of behavioral health care intervention and enhance biopsychosocial functioning. These issues are all discussed in more detail in the chapters that follow.

Ethics based

Health service psychology and the other health care fields are clinical professions, and it is essential to appreciate the applied nature of these professions. In clinical professions, science provides the understanding of health and biopsychosocial functioning, but science does not necessarily explain *how* to apply that understanding appropriately in terms of clinical care, prevention, and health care policy. The proper application of scientific knowledge and tools with human beings in the context of their families, communities, society, and governmental and health care systems fundamentally requires an ethical perspective to balance all the interests involved. As will be discussed in Chapter 4, science and ethics both are fundamentally important in health care because science is needed for understanding *health* and ethics for understanding *care*. Science alone cannot answer many questions related to the respectful, compassionate, fair, and appropriate way to care for the health needs of individuals and the general public, and ethics alone cannot answer many questions related to understanding health, illness, and dysfunction. When the two realms of *health* and *care* are combined in the provision of modern health care, then science and ethics both are essential for the appropriate and responsible practice of health care.

No one disputes that professional ethics and related legal issues are critical throughout human service fields as well as in health care specifically. Science informs many important issues in education, criminal justice, public health, social services, and health care, but ethical issues regarding how individuals are treated in all these arenas are essential as well. Not infrequently, the ethical and legal issues are more difficult than the scientific ones, and they can be particularly complicated in behavioral health care. When emergencies occur in medicine, ethical obligations to provide care to prevent harm or death are usually straightforward; patients may have limited ability to make informed decisions and may even be unconscious, but the ethics surrounding the provision of emergency care are often relatively straightforward. When mental health emergencies occur, on the other hand, the ethics involved can be quite complicated. Mental health emergencies often involve situations in which someone is suicidal or a risk to others, and decisions about detaining and controlling individuals against their will can be very difficult when they have committed no crimes but there is an interest in minimizing risks of harm to self or others.

Observing ethical obligations to respect people's autonomy and privacy, to not cause harm, to prevent and remove harms, and to do this all in a manner that is fair to the individual and others is a very complicated process that requires the balancing of numerous ethical and legal considerations. Science alone is insufficient for the decision-making involved in clinical work. Therefore, professional ethics have always been fundamental to clinical training and practice in the field. Research on the fallibility, irrationality, and complicated biopsychosocial nature of moral reasoning and behavior also needs to be considered to understand people's ethical feelings, decisions, and behavior. This is true when considering one's own ethical feelings and behavior as well as those of colleagues and patients (see Chapter 4). Health care practice, education, research, prevention, and policy all must be grounded solidly in ethics.

Translating science and ethics into behavioral health care: evidence-based practice

The aforementioned framework addresses the most general metatheoretical level for conceptualizing the practice of behavioral health care. Basing behavioral health care on science and professional ethics provides the foundation for conceptualizing practice, research, education, and policy, but additional frameworks are needed to translate those basic foundations into practice. The most current and widely accepted approach for conceptualizing the next level of practice involves the principles of evidence-based practice. This approach is often referred to as a "three-legged stool" which cannot stand without all three legs (see Fig. 1.3). The legs of the stool represent: (1) the best available research evidence, (2) clinical expertise, and (3) patient characteristics, culture, and preferences (APA Presidential Task Force, 2006).

Evidence-based practice has become well established in behavioral health care and across the health service professions. Archibald Cochrane (1972) was an early advocate for the view that empirical evidence about the most effective treatments should guide health care and that the most reliable evidence comes from randomized controlled trails (the very influential Cochrane Collaboration in the United Kingdom was named in honor of his work and influence). Interest in these issues grew substantially in the U.S. after the Institute of Medicine studied the problems of uneven quality and effectiveness and high cost in American health care. In their landmark report, *Crossing the Quality Chasm: A New Health System for the 21st Century*, the Institute of Medicine (2001) identified safety and effectiveness as core needs in health care. It further concluded that clinical decision-making should be based on research evidence as well as being customized according to individual patient needs, values, and preferences. The APA soon after adopted a policy of evidence-based practice in psychology that endorsed the same principles. Their 2005 policy included the following definition: "*Evidence-based practice in psychology* (EBPP) is the integration of the best available research with clinical expertise in the context of patient characteristics, culture, and preferences" (APA Presidential Task Force, 2006, p. 273).

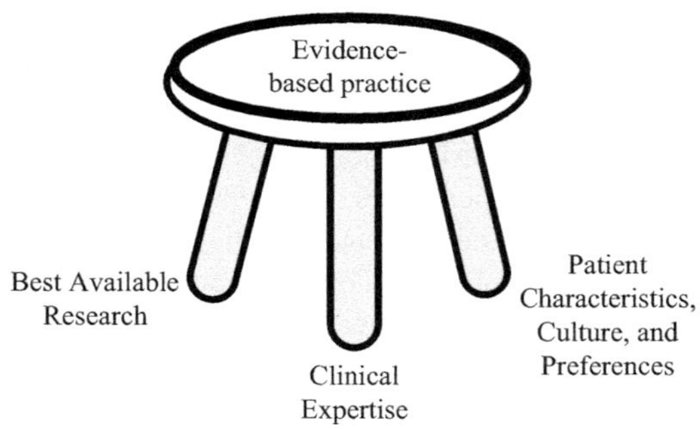

Figure 1.3 The evidence-based practice "three-legged stool."

The purpose and intent of evidence-based practice are straightforward and very widely accepted. They involve "the conscientious, explicit, judicious use of current best evidence in making decisions about the care of individual patients" (Sackett, Rosenberg, Gray, Haynes, & Richardson, 1996). But each of the three components of evidence-based practice (the three-legged stool) involves a variety of complicated considerations (Spring, 2007). The first leg is perhaps the most straightforward and focuses on the best available research evidence regarding whether and why a treatment works. The methodological issues involved in clinical research can be extremely complicated, but methods for analyzing and synthesizing the available research evidence are becoming well established. There are many types of research designs and all have advantages and disadvantages. Randomized clinical trials provide some of the least biased and most reliable evidence about the effectiveness of treatments for the average person receiving a treatment. But systematic reviews are also necessary for synthesizing the findings from all the available research regarding the effectiveness of particular treatments (e.g., see the Institute of Medicine, 2011, report "Finding What Works in Health Care: Standards for Systematic Reviews" for an excellent discussion of these issues).

The second leg of the evidence-based practice stool has less precise meaning. Clinical expertise is based on one's clinical experience and judgment regarding an individual patient's health, diagnoses, and circumstances, along with the risks and benefits of potential interventions in specific case. Individuals' lives are complicated and it takes great skill to effectively integrate all the relevant considerations. The expertise necessary for doing this effectively relies on a range of clinical skills, including communication, relationship building, assessment, and diagnostic skills, as well as the skills needed to implement treatments effectively. Learning all these skills is ambitious and a top priority of graduate education in health service psychology and all the behavioral health care fields.

The third leg of the stool involves client preferences, values, characteristics, and circumstances. These considerations are critical for engaging patients in treatment and the self-management of their behavioral health issues and their overall health and well-being. Some patient characteristics or preferences have very clear and straightforward effects on treatment, such as the lack of health insurance coverage or the desire for psychotherapeutic over pharmacological treatment of a mood disorder. Other patient circumstances are very complicated, and assessment and treatment planning can be very challenging as a result (e.g., consider the man who sought treatment for substance abuse and posttraumatic stress disorder after being diagnosed with cancer, who also found out that his wife was having an affair and was losing her job and the family's health insurance, and their teenage daughter had become pregnant and wanted to keep the child while she finished high school). Nonetheless, in all cases, patients' personal, family, and cultural values and characteristics must be considered along with the best available research evidence in the context of the clinician's expertise. Integrating knowledge of all these factors will maximize the likelihood that treatment will be effective.

The principles of evidence-based practice are critical to health care precisely because knowledge of human health and functioning is still limited. Knowledge of physical and behavioral health may one day become so extensive that the diagnosis and etiology of dysfunction and disease can be clearly established, the mechanisms that explain why treatments work are clearly identified, and patient characteristics, circumstances, and preferences that affect treatment effectiveness can all be accounted for and matched with appropriate treatments. At that point, perhaps computer programs could integrate all the patient history and current status information important in an individual case, and then search through the treatment outcome research literature and identify the most effective treatment options given the specifics of the case. Perhaps the program could provide a list of indicated treatments, each with the percentage likelihood of the patient returning to normal functioning, including at 1-, 5-, and 10-year follow-up periods. Patient and therapist factors that contribute to variability and outliers could also be identified and planned for. Research on the feasibility of using "big data" analytics for treatment matching and other aspects of clinical decision-making has begun (Raghupathi & Raghupathi, 2014), although a huge amount of additional research is needed before these systems will be available for complicated behavioral health issues.

Until this research can be done, health care providers must do the best we can with the knowledge we have. At this point, the first leg of the three-legged stool (best available research) may not be as strong as we would like, and so it is especially important that the second leg (clinical expertise) be as strong as possible. This is the nature of the first version of evidence-based practice ("EBP 1.0") that we have embarked on. The depiction of evidence-based practice as a three-legged stool is useful because the absence of any one of the three legs in clinical practice means the stool falls down. The seat of the stool (representing evidence-based practice) can stand firm only as long as all three legs are solid. In clinical practice, one leg of the stool does not trump the others. All three are necessary.

It is important to note that the approach advocated in this volume is entirely consistent with approaches across the basic and applied sciences and with practices used across health care professions. To appreciate this, first consider the nature of the underlying science that is foundational to this approach.

The scientific foundations of the biopsychosocial developmental approach are based on levels of natural organization where knowledge is consistent across levels and builds in a cumulative, integrative manner. At the lowest microlevels, knowledge from biochemistry and molecular biology is used to understand the functioning of organelles, cells (neurons in the case of the brain), and tissues that comprise organs and organ systems (including the brain and nervous system). Knowledge of these organ systems is integrated to understand the functioning of the whole organism, and this knowledge is integrated with knowledge of social behavior to understand groups, populations, and culture. Understanding the interactions between human populations and the natural environment further leads to understanding the ecosystem and ultimately the biosphere. These levels must be appreciated to understand the interactions with and constraints imposed by adjacent levels (e.g., human behavior is highly constrained by lower level biological processes as well as higher level ecosystemic processes).

More is known about many lower level processes but knowledge about human psychology and higher level phenomena is steadily building as explanations grow in precision and detail and as processes are linked across levels of natural organization. For example, linking the biological operation of the brain with the conscious and subconscious operation of the mind has resulted in findings with great explanatory power (see Chapter 3). The famous biologist E. O. Wilson (1998) described the elegant and exquisite interconnectedness of scientific knowledge across levels of natural organization as "consilience." Accumulating scientific knowledge shows how the physical and living worlds are thoroughly linked, from the smallest level of particle physics to the level of atomic physics and biochemistry and on through the level of human experience on this planet, and then on to the level of our solar system and ultimately the entire cosmos. The consilience of scientific knowledge truly is a grand and wonderful enterprise!

The relationship between science and practice in behavioral health care also functions the same way as it does in other clinical and applied sciences. Consider the relationship between biology and medicine. Biological knowledge regarding many aspects of health and disease is far from complete, but medicine and public health nonetheless use the knowledge that is available to provide many safe and effective interventions and preventive measures for a wide variety of health problems. For example, little is known about some aspects of heart disease and cancer; especially at the level of the individual, only a limited amount is known about which nonsmokers will get heart disease or cancer and which smokers will not. Nonetheless, medicine is very useful for treating heart disease and cancer as well as a wide range of other medical problems, curing some, although only partially ameliorating symptoms in others. Despite limited knowledge of many medical issues, very few individuals will choose not to rely on modern public health and medicine to manage disease, injury, and other physical health problems.

Evidence-based medicine and behavioral health care both also take very similar approaches to clinical practice. In medicine, physicians practice in an evidence-based manner when conducting examinations, identifying diagnoses, and then developing treatment plans. This can be a quick and easy process for straightforward problems (e.g., a single episode of ear infection) but can be very complex for more serious problems. Consider cardiovascular disease, the leading cause of morbidity and mortality in the U.S. and increasingly throughout the world (see Chapter 7). After arriving at a diagnosis, physicians consider the relevant efficacy research, combine that with knowledge gained from prior clinical experience, and then discuss that information with the patient in the context of the patient's preferences, values, overall health, behavior, and lifestyle. A variety of medications are available to treat heart disease (e.g., anticoagulants, beta blockers, diuretics, statins), along with a variety of surgeries (e.g., angioplasty, bypasses, stents) and implantable devices (e.g., pacemakers, defibrillators). Lifestyle changes are typically prescribed as well (e.g., diet, exercise and physical activity, stress management, smoking or alcohol use reduction). Even though a massive amount of research on heart disease has been conducted, predicting the onset and course of major heart disease for an individual, or how an individual will respond to treatment after he or she develops disease, is often highly imprecise, and effect sizes for many treatments are small or moderate (Leucht, Helfer, Gartlehner, & Davis, 2015; Meyer et al., 2001). To minimize risks, a stepped approach is often used, in which less intensive and invasive treatments are tried first (Bonow, Mann, Zipes, & Libby, 2012). Competent, ethical physicians do not recommend treatments eclectically without sound evidence and rationales, nor do they base recommendations on personal preferences regarding theoretical orientation or other factors unrelated to evidence-based practice—doing so obviously raises concerns about malpractice. Instead, they develop treatment plans that minimize risks while maximizing the likelihood of successful outcomes.

The diagnosis and treatment of mental illness is essentially similar. A significant amount is known about many psychotic, mood, substance use, and other disorders, and many treatments have been shown to be quite effective (see Chapter 11). Nonetheless, predictions about which individuals will respond successfully to treatment (i.e., without reoccurrence of the problem) are frequently imprecise. After conducting an assessment and diagnosis, psychologists practicing in an evidence-based manner will consider the knowledge of the relevant efficacy research in the context of knowledge about the individual patient (e.g., his or her values, preferences, characteristics, circumstances). Based on their clinical experience and judgment about all the relevant factors (including seriousness of the disorder, any cooccurring disorders, precipitating events, family history, trauma history, current social support, level of functioning, mental status, cultural factors, other risk and protective factors), they then develop treatment recommendations that they discuss with the patient. A variety of treatment options is typically available, some of which will fit much better for patients with particular characteristics and preferences. As in the case of medicine, these are often considered in a stepped fashion with the aim of minimizing risks while maximizing the likelihood of successful outcomes over the short and long term. (These issues are discussed in detail in Chapters 9 through 12.)

Medicine and behavioral health care are also similar in that both were not practiced in an evidence-based manner in the past. Centuries ago, the practice of medicine was sometimes effective because some effective treatments were discovered through trial by error and others were effective due to the placebo effect. Science did not inform diagnosis and treatment, however, until just the past century or two. The tipping point when medicine in the U.S. began a clear transition from being primarily an art to a science-informed practice was reached in 1910, when Abraham Flexner submitted his report on the state of medical education in North America. In the preceding decades, biology had been making important advances, such as Pasteur's introduction of the germ theory of infection in 1878 (which explained the nature of infectious disease). Sterilization of medical instruments had been introduced and was becoming common toward the end of the century (before the use of antiseptic methods, death rates following amputations, for example, were very high; one Parisian surgeon noted that his death rate was 100%; Porter, 1997). Out of concern that American medical education was not keeping up with the science, Flexner visited and rated nearly every one of the 168 medical schools in the U.S. and Canada. His highly influential report included his ratings and often scathing criticisms of individual schools, and several closed soon after as a result. Over the next decades, 42% of medical schools closed, and the remaining schools significantly increased their admission standards and laboratory and clinical training requirements (Hiatt & Stockton, 2003). Very little was known at the time about many medical interventions that we now take for granted (e.g., the first antibiotic, penicillin, was not even discovered until 1928 and was not mass produced until the end of World War II). By today's standards, medical knowledge was in a state of infancy. Nonetheless, transitioning to a science-based approach to medical education and practice was viewed as not just appropriate, but necessary.

Psychology as both a basic and an applied science has evolved in a similar manner, although a unified scientific perspective was reached later (largely due to the extraordinary complexity of the phenomena involved; see Chapter 2).[1] Enough was discovered in physics, chemistry, and biology that those fields long ago reached the point at which a substantial body of scientific explanations had been experimentally verified and accepted. To be valid, those explanations also needed to be consistent with explanations of phenomena at other levels of natural organization. Knowledge was obviously seriously incomplete or nonexistent regarding many phenomena, but enough was known that the applied fields of engineering and medicine could be practiced in an increasingly safer and more effective manner.

Psychology has now reached a similar point, where clinical practice can be based on a unified body of scientific knowledge. In the past, the traditional theoretical orientations offered explanations of various psychological processes, but they could not survive scientific scrutiny as comprehensive explanations consistent with biological (lower) and sociocultural (higher) levels of natural organization. As a result, those orientations have now been replaced by scientific explanations that have been experimentally verified and are consistent with biology and the rest of the sciences. The practice of selecting from a diverse array of competing "prescientific" theoretical orientations for guiding one's clinical practice is no longer necessary or sufficient. Instead, clinicians can now practice informed by a unified and steadily growing body of scientific knowledge of human development, functioning, and behavior change.

Since 2000, a wide variety of health professions have officially endorsed the evidence-based approach to clinical practice. This was a historic and emblematic step marking the transition to a solidly science-informed approach to health care.

[1] The term "psychology" is used to refer to the broad field of psychology, in both its basic and its applied forms, and "psychologist" is used to refer to both scientists and practitioners. This causes some confusion that is avoided in other fields, such as engineering, which is the application of physics and the other natural sciences, or the field of medicine, which is the application of biology and related fields. Using the term "health service psychology" to refer to the applied specialty of psychology that focuses on behavioral health care helps reduce that confusion.

This in no way implies that we now have final answers or a complete understanding of physical or mental health—although this is obvious, it is important to be reminded of how easy it is to be overconfident about what we think we know. For example, there are widespread concerns about the safety of many medical and psychological interventions and the overuse of tests, medicines, and other interventions that may cause more harm than benefit (e.g., Frances, 2009; Goldacre, 2012; Healy, 2012; Institute of Medicine, 2000; Lilienfeld, Lynn, & Lohr, 2015; U.S. Preventive Services Task Force, 2019; Whitaker & Cosgrove, 2015; see also Chapter 4 of this volume). Much, much more needs to be learned about biopsychosocial functioning, health, and well-being. But enough is now known that all areas within health care can be practiced in an evidence-based manner.

A very exciting time for psychology

Psychology has been remarkably successful over its relatively short history as both a basic and an applied science. It grew quickly in size and influence and has had a large impact on the behavioral sciences, health care, education, human services, business and industry, and even culture generally. Unfortunately, the field was also marked by major competition and conflict between different theoretical orientations and schools of thought for explaining various psychological phenomena. But those conflicts and competition are becoming outdated because a unified scientific perspective has emerged that successfully explains a wide variety of psychological phenomena. There is still much to be learned, but the field has advanced dramatically in recent decades and has entered an exciting period when its potential and promise are greater than ever.

Leaving behind the conflicts and competition of the past will be very helpful for professional psychology. These conflicts and competition caused a great deal of inefficiency and distraction. Large amounts of time, energy, and effort were spent developing, promoting, and defending the various theoretical orientations, and therapists were sometimes unable to even comprehend the language and concepts used by therapists who practiced different orientations. It was also obviously very hard to explain that system (or "nonsystem") to other scientists, health care providers, insurers, regulators, health system managers, or the general public.

Moving forward under a unified scientific framework will allow professional psychology to be conceptualized in a straightforward manner as a health care profession that can become integrated into the rest of health care much more easily. A generation ago, psychotherapy was still often conceptualized similar to a service industry, where clients interested in obtaining psychotherapy would choose a therapist whose orientation and methods fit their preferences and needs. The services that were offered might or might not have been tested for safety and effectiveness; in either case, it was often not considered a major priority. Health care professions, however, generally carry higher expectations and responsibilities for providing safe and effective care. Insurers, health care systems, legal and regulatory systems, and the public generally hold higher expectations for clinical sciences than for service industries and expect that interventions are informed by science and that treatments have been tested for safety and effectiveness.

The chapters that follow discuss how behavioral health care can be conceptualized from the perspective of a unified clinical science. In addition to explaining the scientific and ethical foundations of professional psychology, all three legs of the evidence-based practice stool are discussed as well as more detailed issues involved in translating these issues into clinical practice. The scientific foundations of professional psychology are addressed in Chapter 3 and the ethical foundations in Chapter 4. But before those foundations can be properly understood in context, the complicated historical development of psychology as a scientific discipline and field of professional practice needs to be appreciated.

The evolution of psychology as a science and field of professional practice

2

Psychology as a scientific and clinical discipline is a relatively young field, but has already been remarkably successful. Since its emergence at the end of the 19th century, the field has become very popular and influential. For example, there was no college course in psychology offered in the U.S. in the early 1870s when the field was first getting established, and now psychology is the fourth most popular undergraduate college major (Snyder, de Brey, & Dillow, 2016). Psychotherapy was invented around the same time, in the late 1800s, and gradually grew to become very popular as well. The number of licensed psychologists in the U.S. grew from zero in 1945, when the first psychology licensure law was enacted, to nearly 90,000 just a half-century later (Manderscheid & Henderson, 2004). Psychological research has revolutionized our understanding of the human mind and brain and has had a profound impact across the social sciences and humanities as well as in the economy, society, and culture generally.[1]

Although psychology has been a fascinating and successful academic discipline, it has also been known for major conflict and divisiveness between theoretical camps and between scientists and practitioners. The field experienced serious conflict and confusion throughout its history and, until recently, there was little consensus on many basic issues. At times, psychologists wondered if the conflicts and divisiveness were so serious that the field would not be able to continue as a single, unified discipline (e.g., Benjamin, 2001; Sternberg, 2005). These conflicts and controversies have subsided substantially in recent years but the field is still not fully unified around a

[1] I will usually refer to the mind and the brain as a single phenomenon in this volume. For centuries many philosophers believed that the mind was a separate and distinct phenomenon (or even substance) from the human brain (e.g., Descartes' dualism), but contemporary scientific psychology and neuroscience do not make those distinctions. Although the word "brain" tends to refer to the biological organ and the word "mind" tends to refer to the outputs of that organ, the mind obviously is not distinct from nor functions separately from the brain. Outputs of the "mind" are inputs into the subsequent operation of the "brain" and the two are inseparable. The brain is merely the final common pathway where all the influences on cognition, emotion, and behavior converge to create mind and behavior. Nonetheless, the complexity involved is simply stupendous and is only beginning to be fully understood. To illustrate, when the corpus callosum is cut in the treatment of some cases of severe epilepsy, the person ends up with two consciousnesses, one in each hemisphere, that do not communicate directly with each other (Gazzaniga, 2011). It is possible that the more rational and reality-based right hemisphere may ignore the sometimes massive errors and confabulations of the left hemisphere because it cannot understand what the left hemisphere says when it talks (because speech is generated in the left hemisphere and the right hemisphere is mute in most people; Ramachandran, 2011). It will take years of research before these complicated processes become well understood.

Foundations of Health Service Psychology. https://doi.org/10.1016/B978-0-12-816426-6.00002-5

common conceptual framework for understanding the scientific foundations underlying the practice of psychology. This volume is an attempt to help rectify that problem.

This chapter outlines the development of psychology as a scientific discipline and field of professional practice, with emphasis on its underlying scientific foundations. The strength and even the nature of the scientific foundations of the field have been in question over much of the history of the field, but now these issues are being resolved. Throughout its history, psychology, and especially health service psychology, relied on a diverse array of conflicting and competing theoretical orientations as explanatory frameworks. But psychology has reached a historic point at which we now have a solid scientific understanding of human development and functioning that is, for the first time, thoroughly consistent with the rest of the natural sciences. This transition has occurred in just the last couple decades and has tremendous implications for understanding human nature as well as the practice of behavioral health care.

To understand the complex historical development of psychology as a discipline, several issues regarding epistemology and scientific method need to be appreciated. This chapter includes a discussion of the nature of science so one can appreciate the evolution of psychology from a preparadigmatic scholarly field into a scientific discipline grounded firmly in scientific findings and consistent with the rest of the natural sciences. The chapters that follow then show how the current science of psychology informs the different aspects of behavioral health care. To introduce the subject of this chapter, the importance of science in general to the human experience is highlighted.

Science, the most successful invention ever

Human beings were very impressive animals right from the start. By about 1.5 million years ago, *Homo erectus* had already developed the hand ax, a stone tool much more advanced than the tools used by earlier hominins and other primates. *Homo erectus* also controlled the use of fire as a vital aid for comfort and survival. *Homo sapiens* evolved about 200,000 to 300,000 years ago and developed sophisticated art and technology tens of thousands of years ago. In addition to beautiful cave drawings, *Homo sapiens* made jewelry, fishing gear, animal traps, clothing, tents, and huts. They developed long-distance transport of valued materials, held ceremonies and conducted rituals, and domesticated the dog well before 35,000 years ago (Stringer, 2012a).

Although humans produced many remarkable works of art, technology, engineering, and civilization across our history, our greatest achievement of all has been the invention of science. Uncovering how nature works has fundamentally changed our understanding of the universe and everything in it. Applying that knowledge has thoroughly changed the material and psychological conditions of our existence. Although *Homo sapiens* were technologically adept tens of thousands of years ago, far beyond their evolutionary ancestors, their lives changed very little over the eons. Inventions such as the controlled use of fire, stone tools, clothing, and huts came along so infrequently that life surely seemed to never change at all—during a lifetime, one was likely to never see an invention that changed your existence in a significant way. For most of human existence, across hundreds of generations, life stayed pretty much the same as it always had been.

There have been many important transitions over the course of human evolution, but one that had an especially large impact on modern human experience occurred about 2500 years ago, just 125 generations ago. This was the pivotal period when the modern world that we are familiar with was invented. This was when dramatic advances in philosophy, religion, government, technology, and engineering were made simultaneously in several areas of the ancient world, and the great ancient civilizations arose in China, India, and the Eastern Mediterranean. Between roughly 500 and 300 BCE, agricultural and economic advances provided a new level of security and prosperity that dramatically transformed society and culture. This truly remarkable period saw the emergence of several of the world's great religions and philosophies within just a few centuries of one another, including Taoism, Confucianism, Hinduism, Buddhism, Zoroastrianism, Second Temple Judaism, and classical Greek philosophy and drama (Jaspers, 1953). What an incredible time to be alive if you could have traveled and met Confucius, Buddha, Pythagoras, Aeschylus, and the Hebrew prophets, whose lives actually overlapped with one another. Everyday life changed dramatically with the rise of these civilizations, for common people and certainly for the ruling, scholarly, artistic, and priestly classes. The German philosopher Karl Jaspers described it as the time when "Man, as we know him today, came into being" (1953, p. 1).

Despite the dramatic changes that occurred in psychological life and physical conditions during the Axial Age, people's understanding of their world was far different from our modern understanding. What changed society, culture, and daily life even more dramatically than the religion, philosophy, and technology of the ancient world was the rise of science. Societies before the Scientific Revolution in the 17th century clearly developed great literature, art, architecture, technology, and engineering, but the emergence of science changed human experience more fundamentally still. Knowledge began to be based on a scientific understanding of the way nature works, which had dramatic effects in terms of not only basic and applied science but also human psychological experience.

The historian David Wootton (2015) noted that an educated Englishman in 1600, before the Scientific Revolution, would have understood the world as follows:

> *He believes witches can summon up storms that sink ships at sea ... He believes in werewolves, although there happen not to be any in England—he knows they are to be found in Belgium. He believes Circe really did turn Odysseus's crew into pigs. He believes mice are spontaneously generated in piles of straw. He believes in contemporary magicians ... He has seen a unicorn's horn, but not a unicorn.*
>
> *He believes that a murdered body will bleed in the presence of the murderer ... He believes that the shape, colour and texture of a plant can be a clue to how it will work as a medicine because God designed nature to be interpreted by mankind. He believes that it is possible to turn base metal into gold, although he doubts that anyone knows how to do it. He believes that nature abhors a vacuum. He believes the rainbow is a*

> *sign from God and that comets portend evil. He believes that dreams predict the future, if we know how to interpret them. He believes, of course, that the earth stands still and the sun and stars turn around the earth once every twenty-four hours.*
>
> *Wootton (2015, pp. 6–7).*

One and a third centuries later, however, an educated person from England would believe none of those things. Modern science had emerged and the understanding of life and the world changed fundamentally and forever—indeed, the intellectual world of the educated elite changed more rapidly during that time than in all previous human history (Wootton, 2015). Chemistry was still in its infancy and biology did not yet exist, and so bleeding, purges, emetics, and other prescientific interventions were still used to cure disease. But human intellectual and emotional life had fundamentally changed. Not only was this an escape from ignorance about how the world worked, but it was also an escape from superstition, terror, and "a kind of collective paranoia" (Scott, 2010, p. 20) whereby weather and astrological events (e.g., storms, lightning, thunder, shooting stars, eclipses) were considered signs of God's displeasure, and witches, demons, and omens foreshadowing danger were present virtually everywhere.

Science has been a tremendously successful human invention. It has a record of continual success over the past four centuries in explaining an ever-growing range of phenomena, and these have led to technological improvements that have radically transformed virtually all life on earth. Science and the technology derived from it have so thoroughly transformed our existence that most people in developed countries have always lived in homes with central heat, electricity, indoor plumbing, and, in many places, even air conditioning. We also now have Internet access to most of the world's libraries, museums, universities, and travel destinations, something we now take for granted but that was not even part of the most fantastical fiction writing from previous generations. The level of security, health, and comfort in which we live our lives is beyond what people from prior generations could even imagine. Science has had a greater impact on life in this world than any other human invention.[2]

The nature of science

What is it about science that made it so tremendously successful, arguably the greatest of all inventions in human history? In the most basic sense, science is merely the refining of reason to understand natural phenomena. It is an informed, honest, and critical approach to explaining how the world works. One might think this would not be threatening or controversial, but it always has been. One of the first modern scientists, Galileo (1564–1642), sometimes called the "father of science," was found guilty of heresy by the Catholic Church for verifying a scientific understanding of the

[2] Some also consider science to be the only universal contribution of Western civilization to the rest of the world (Rosenberg, 2012). Although many civilizations achieved great technological and engineering success, the invention of the scientific method (in terms of experimental or pure as opposed to applied science) was developed most extensively in Europe. Virtually all societies, nations, and populations that learned about this European invention adopted it wholeheartedly.

solar system in which planets revolved around the sun rather than the Church's preferred view that the moon, sun, and stars all revolved around the earth. He was forced to recant the theory and was placed under house arrest for the rest of his life. Over the ensuing centuries, this basic method of pursuing and telling the truth about how nature works has frequently faced criticism and even condemnation by some political and religious authorities who saw it as a threat to their power.

Viewing science as a threat or malevolent force lessened as Enlightenment values increasingly took hold in the world, but even today it faces criticism. For example, some on the far right see science as a threat to their religious beliefs or family and community values and do not want their children to be taught about topics such as evolution. Some on the far left view science not as a tool for understanding the world and improving human existence but as a means for the white male patriarchy to dominate others (Cohen, 2007; Hicks, 2004).

Psychologists have always viewed their discipline as being grounded in science, but there always was also heated debate about the scientific validity of many of the traditional theoretical orientations in the field. Underlying these debates were often disagreements about the epistemologies that can lead to reliable knowledge for understanding human psychology (e.g., realism, constructivism, pragmatism). Indeed, even the existence of such a diverse array of divergent theoretical orientations raised questions about whether psychology was actually based on a body of coherent scientific knowledge about human development and functioning.

One needs to understand the nature of science to appreciate why science has been so successful and to appreciate the criticisms levied against it. This understanding is also necessary to appreciate the conflicts between the traditional theoretical orientations in psychology as well as the current scientific foundations of the field and how to practice behavioral health care in a responsible evidence-based manner. Several perspectives are critical for appreciating the nature of science. Some of these emanate from the philosophy of science, the philosophy subfield that attempts to understand the nature and methods of science. Others come from history and other fields. First, however, it is critical to appreciate the nature of the phenomena that psychology attempts to understand.

Complexity of the phenomena

Before considering specific historical and scientific reasons for the complicated development of the discipline of psychology, it is important to note that probably the most important underlying reason is the extraordinary complexity of the subject matter. The human mind and brain are often referred to as the most complicated system known to exist. As the famous biologist E.O. Wilson (1998) put it, "... the most complex systems known to exist in the universe are biological, and by far the most complex of all biological phenomena is the human mind" (p. 81).[3] Understanding human nature

[3] For example, research suggests that psychological traits and disorders are highly polygenetic and could be influenced by thousands of DNA variations known as single-nucleotide polymorphisms. This contrasts with physical traits and chronic diseases, which tend to be far less polygenetic (Zhang, Qi, Park, & Chatterjee, 2018).

is also very complex because we humans are so varied in our natures. No other animal pursues such a variety of interests and skills (from fishing and farming to cabinetry, cooking, healing, writing, acting, science, athletics, and warfare). Understanding human nature has been so complicated, in fact, that it has only recently begun to be understood with comprehensive scientific explanations that are integrated and fully consistent with the rest of the natural sciences. Before recent decades, different theoretical camps offered dramatically varied and irreconcilable explanations for psychological phenomena. There were also many philosophical, religious, popular folk, and "pseudoscience" explanations for human nature. But comprehensive scientific explanations have emerged only relatively recently.

The complexity of human psychology also accounts for other things. One is that human life itself is only a very recent development in earth's history because it takes so long for highly complex organic systems to evolve. The physical world is very old: our universe formed roughly 13.8 billion years ago and our earth evolved 4.5 billion years ago (Tyson, 2017). The earliest single-celled life formed about 4 billion years ago and multicellular life emerged about 1 billion years ago (Dawkins, 2004). The earliest animals appeared approximately 600 million years ago, mammals about 220 million years ago, and primates around 75 million years ago. The first bipedal human-like apes appeared relatively recently, only 4 million years ago, and anatomically modern human beings, *Homo sapiens*, evolved just 200,000–300,000 years ago.[4] The Cognitive Revolution, which accounts for the rise of modern language, tool use, and art, occurred perhaps 70,000 years ago, and the last major evolutionary transition that gave rise to modern human life was the Neolithic Revolution (the new Stone Age), which occurred only approximately 10,000 years ago in the Middle East (Dunbar, 2016). This last transition included the development of agriculture and the social and cultural mechanisms (especially doctrinal religions) that allowed large numbers of individuals to live together cooperatively (e.g., in cities many times larger than hunter–gatherer groups). Modern human life is indeed a very recent phenomenon, a mere instant old relative to simpler life forms. It took a very long time for the tremendous social and cognitive complexity of modern human psychology to evolve. A timeline is depicted in Fig. 2.1 to illustrate the scale of these developments.

The complexity of human psychology also accounts for why psychology is such a young field compared with the physical and biological sciences. Philosophers, theologians, artists, and writers have contemplated human nature for thousands of years, and people undoubtedly contemplated the nature of mental life ever since we developed the ability to talk (since the Cognitive Revolution about 70,000 years ago). But the systematic study of psychology using experimental scientific methods is not even a century and a half old. The birth of psychology as a science is usually given as 1879, when Wilhelm Wundt established the first scientific laboratory devoted to the study of psychology at the University of Leipzig in Germany. Psychology is thus much younger than physics, which got underway more than two millennia ago and was approached

[4] Recent paleoanthropological findings are pushing some of these dates back somewhat as earlier skeletal remains are discovered.

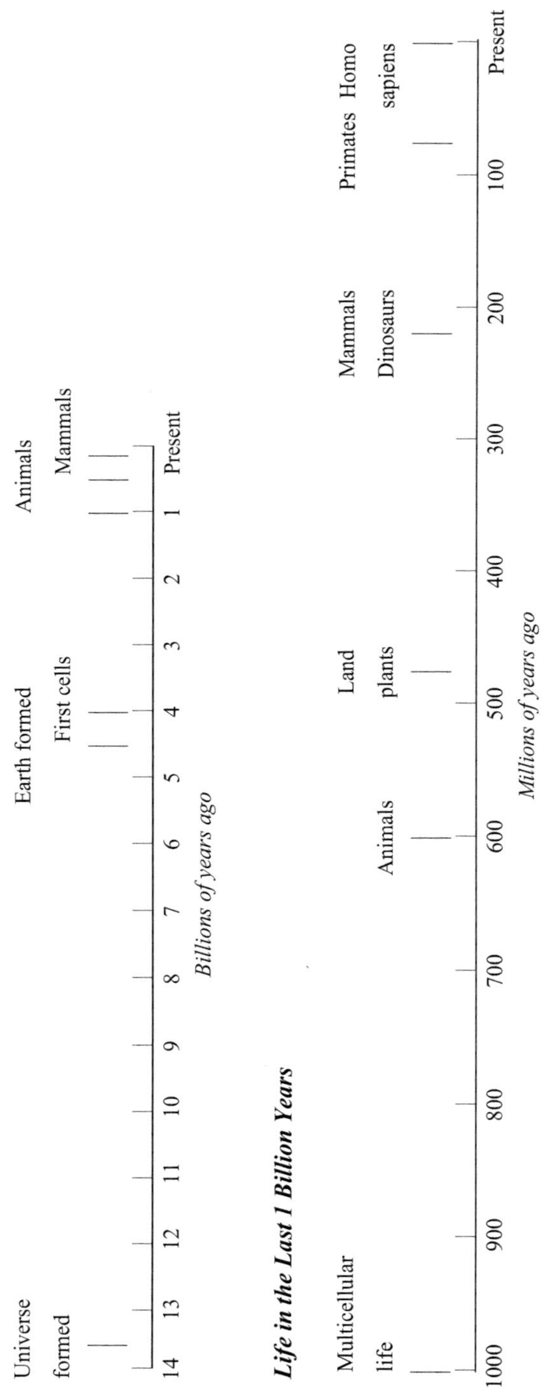

Figure 2.1 Timeline of the history of the universe and emergence of life on earth.

in a systematic scientific manner starting in the 1600s. Physics was followed by chemistry in the 1700s and biology the century after that. Uncovering the tremendous complexity of psychological phenomena is extremely difficult and so it took longer for scientific theory and methods to develop to the point at which they could tackle the subject. The "soft" sciences are *very hard*! Von Foerster (1972) noted that it is harder to explain phenomena in the so-called "soft sciences" (i.e., the social sciences) than it is in the "hard sciences" (i.e., the physical sciences).

Positivism

The modern approach to scientific explanation began with Galileo (1564–1642), Isaac Newton (1643–1727), and others who initiated the Scientific Revolution in the 17th century. Newton, believed by some to be the greatest scientist who ever lived, sought a small number of mathematical laws that accounted for the regularities that could be observed in nature. Through the use of three laws of motion and a law of gravity, he showed how laws could precisely account for the movement of the bodies in our solar system. Critics noted that Newton failed to identify any mechanism that explained gravity and "action at a distance," an unobservable mechanism that seemed to operate magically. Newton (1713) famously replied "Hypotheses non fingo," or "I frame no hypotheses." He refused to speculate on the nature of gravity beyond what he could establish through precise and meticulous reasoning. This was a radical departure from conventions and norms that had been in place for millennia whereby the understanding of how things worked relied heavily on appeals to authority (typically religious) rather than to logic and data (Deutsch, 2011).

Auguste Comte (1798–1857) developed a more extreme form of this type of thinking that became known as positivism. Comte and his followers claimed that science worked because it remained as close as possible to observable facts and as far as possible from hypothetical explanations. The primary purpose of science therefore was *description*, not explanation. From accurate descriptions of natural phenomena, it was then possible to make *predictions* of future observations of those phenomena, which in turn made *control* possible. Roughly a century later, in psychology, the behaviorists were very successful in utilizing this approach for decades. Comte also argued that societies proceed through three stages in their quest for truth, from the theological (i.e., explanations provided by divinities) to the metaphysical (e.g., speculations on the nature of being or existence beyond objective experience) and finally to the positive (i.e., knowledge obtained through use of the scientific method).

Logical positivism and the deductive–nomological approach

The positivists identified the three functions of science as description, prediction, and control, but viewed the investigation of *explanation*, or answers to "*why*" and "*how*" questions, as indulging in theological or metaphysical speculation. Logical positivism is often seen as taking the same view as the positivists, that science should never refer to anything unobservable, but it extended the positivist position to incorporate the function of *explanation*. This was accomplished by emphasizing that scientific findings needed to be verifiable. An influential description of this approach was provided by Carl Hempel and colleagues (Hempel & Oppenheim, 1948), who argued that explanations are deductions from scientific laws, and so their approach is often called the deductive–nomological model of explanation ("nomos" is Greek for law). It is also called the *covering law* model because it argues that a scientific explanation demonstrates how an event is "covered" by a set of scientific laws. This approach avoided reference to the specific notion of causation, which was still considered suspect due to its metaphysical connotations.

The covering law model views prediction and explanation, however, as essentially the same thing. The appearance of Haley's Comet in 1986 may be "explained" or deduced from various scientific laws, but the next appearance of the comet can be predicted to occur a few decades from now using the same deduction; both the explanation of the past occurrence and the prediction of a future occurrence essentially involve the same explanation. Instead, we typically want to understand the factors involved that *caused* the appearance of the comet (e.g., the nature of gravity), not just an explanation of what happened before and will occur again. From a causal perspective, the positivists are too reliant on adhering only to the facts, are too fearful of engaging in metaphysics, and miss the importance of explaining causation (Salmon, 1984). This perspective is particularly relevant in psychology, in which we often want to know the causes of behavior, not just predictions that particular behaviors will occur (cf., past behavior is often the best predictor of future behavior, but this explains little about why the past behavior occurred in the first place or under what conditions it is likely to happen again).

Reductionism

The term "reductionism" has been used in multiple ways but usually refers to "reducing" the explanation of a phenomenon to the operations of lower, more basic processes or entities connected to it (Ruse, 2005). For example, Nagel (2012, p. 4) refers to "psychophysical reductionism" as the reduction of psychological phenomena to chemistry and physics. This implies that a system is nothing but the sum of its parts. This is in contrast to a systemic view that a system is composed entirely of its parts, but the system also has features that arise from the operation of those parts and which none of the parts themselves have.

Issues related to reductionism have been debated since the times of Plato and Aristotle. One of the most famous arguments against reductionism involves the mind–body dualism provided by René Descartes (1596–1650). Descartes argued for a separation of the material world governed by the laws of physics from that of the nonphysical world of the mind, consciousness, and free will. He argued that the mind is independent of the physical world and cannot be understood through knowledge of the operations of the body. Reductionist thinking and methods have clearly been highly successful in the natural sciences, however, and no one disputes that chemistry is rooted in physics, that molecular biology is rooted in chemistry, that the function of bodily organs (including the brain) is rooted in molecular biology, and so on. Nonetheless, reductionism applied to the social sciences has been controversial. Although psychology clearly has roots in biology (e.g., our genetic inheritance, the biological basis of development, emotion, and cognition), reducing mental life to biological operations alone is obviously problematic.

The emergence of systems thinking largely resolved the historical concerns about reductionism. Higher level systems clearly influence lower ones and complex systems are characterized by feedback loops of many kinds. For example, the Nobel laureate Anderson (1972) noted that although the sciences are arranged according to increasing levels of natural organization (particle physics, physics, chemistry, molecular biology, physiology, psychology, etc.), and although the processes at one level obey the laws of the science preceding lower in the hierarchy, this does not imply that one science is merely the applied version of the science that preceded it. Anderson (1972) wrote, "At each stage, entirely new laws, concepts and generalizations are necessary ... Psychology is not applied biology nor is biology applied chemistry" (p. 393).

It is also important to note that the behavior of higher level phenomena is semiautonomous, a relationship known as *emergence* (Carroll, 2016; Deutsch, 2011). It is certainly true that automobiles and brains are composed of atoms, but knowledge of atomic physics will not explain why a car will not start or why someone has volatile relationships with family members and coworkers. Phenomena at higher levels of organization must be explained at the appropriate level, and *all* human behaviors are emergent phenomena. Explanations of that behavior must be consistent with processes at lower levels of organization, but low-level processes cannot explain human behavior at higher emergent levels. For example, the morality of a person's behavior cannot be determined by analyzing his or her biology.

Kuhn's historical perspective

Thomas Kuhn's 1962 book, *The Structure of Scientific Revolutions*, was very influential in psychology for its social and cultural perspective on the work of scientists. Rather than emphasizing the roles of observation and logic, Kuhn emphasized the culture and worldview of scientists working within a scientific discipline. Kuhn argued that the practice of science occurs within a paradigm, a worldview agreed upon by the scientists working within a particular subject area.

Kuhn argued that the evolution of scientific fields tends to follow a five-stage pattern. The first stage is characterized by many conflicting views and competing explanations. Kuhn noted, for example, that during the first half of the 18th century "there were almost as many views about the nature of electricity as there were important electrical experimenters ... all were components of real scientific theories ... Yet though all the experiments were electrical and though most of the experimenters read each other's works, their theories had no more than a family resemblance" (Kuhn, 1962, pp. 13–14). He called this first stage *preparadigmatic* because what is lacking is a paradigm, a major scientific achievement that convincingly explains phenomena and unites the scientific community within an area. Once a school of thought or paradigm is found to explain phenomena in an area better than alternative explanations, Kuhn argued that the field reached the second stage, which he called *normal science*. A great deal of time is then spent testing deductions made within the paradigm and making minor improvements. If anomalies are discovered that can be accounted for by the existing theories, the paradigm is strengthened. If not, a third stage is reached. Kuhn called this the *crisis* stage, which involved a period of "pronounced professional insecurity" (pp. 67–68) because no accepted explanation can account for the anomalies. Kuhn proposed a fourth stage (*revolutionary science*) in which an active struggle ensued between defenders of the old paradigm and proponents of a new paradigm, with each camp attempting to solve the greatest number of anomalies with their theories. Kuhn proposed a final stage (*resolution*) in which one paradigm becomes dominant, which then generates a new period of *normal science* (stage 2).

As a young field investigating tremendously complicated phenomena, many areas within psychology were preparadigmatic in the way Kuhn described. Particularly within health service psychology, numerous theoretical camps proposed a remarkably diverse array of processes for understanding personality, psychopathology, and behavior change (e.g., developmental fixations, one's learning history, imposed conditions of worth, depressogenic cognitions, a constructed phenomenological worldview). Often these camps defended their proposals in a parochial manner that reminds one of competing political parties or religions rallying for the superiority of their views more than a critical, evidence-based analysis designed to uncover the true nature of particular psychological phenomena.

Psychologists often referred to Kuhn's model when explaining the complicated, preparadigmatic nature of theory and research during the first century in the history of the field, but the model is not useful for explaining the recent evolution of the discipline. In fact, Kuhn's model is not useful for explaining the evolution of the sciences in general (Rosenberg, 2012). Some have doubted whether revolutions in science have actually occurred (e.g., Gutting, 1980), and Kuhn himself later backed away from his claims regarding these revolutions (Kuhn, 1977). Kuhn's perspective was also taken to a postmodernist, relativistic extreme in which individuals can apply whatever standards of evidence or justification that suit them in never-ending contests between paradigms (e.g., Feyerabend, 1975). Such a perspective varies so widely from the demonstrated reliability of cumulative scientific knowledge that it is viewed as "patent preposterousness" (Rosenberg, 2012, p. 273).

Popper and falsification

Karl Popper moved beyond positivism to help establish the modern view of scientific theory that is particularly relevant for the social sciences. Popper noted that some of the traditional theoretical orientations in psychology suffered from a critical weakness. These theories proposed a diverse array of processes and mechanisms to explain different aspects of personality, psychopathology, and psychotherapy. The explanations varied widely and conflicted with one another, and so they could not all be correct. Many of them were also untested by careful experimental research. Their proponents nonetheless viewed them as providing valid explanations for essentially all outcomes that occur in individual cases (e.g., from the most saintly to the most heinous, from the behavior of Mother Theresa to that of Hitler). It was consequently difficult to disprove that any particular theory could account for any particular outcome

(Popper, 1963). But evaluating these theories on the basis of scientific analysis and empirical support was not necessarily a requirement. Instead, students learning the profession were often advised (and sometimes still are) to choose a theoretical orientation that best fits with their personality and personal worldview. This practice diverges dramatically from the scientific approach that requires experimental scrutiny to establish the validity of theoretical claims.

Popper made a critical observation that resolved this problem. As a young student in Vienna in 1919, Popper heard Einstein as well as psychoanalysts present their work. He was very impressed with both, but noticed a fundamental difference between them (Popper, 1963). Freud presented his theory in terms that made it amenable to confirmation, whereas Einstein's theory had testable implications, which, if demonstrated to be false through careful experimentation, would prove the theory wrong. Popper noted that many psychological theories were amenable only to confirmation and could not be refuted, and he therefore judged them to be poor theories. As Popper helped point out, a theory that appears to explain everything is a poor theory—in fact, it actually explains nothing. Popper argued that scientific theories must be falsifiable and that genuine tests of theories are attempts to refute them. Popper's critique has been very influential throughout the social and natural sciences, and scientists generally recognize the necessity of falsifiability as a prerequisite for the possibility of scientific claims to be valid.

Postmodernism

Postmodernism has been very influential recently in the humanities and social sciences. It was originally developed by several French intellectuals in the 1960s and 1970s who were critical of Enlightenment principles such as *reason* and *objectivity*. These included Lyotard, who expressed skepticism about "grand narratives" such as Christianity, Marxism, and even science in general, and argued that knowledge is constructed in language games and is linked to power. Foucault similarly argued that it was meaningless to speak of knowledge, reason, or truth because "power-knowledge" was determined by those in dominant roles in society. Derrida deconstructed language and concluded that meaning was arbitrary and unattainable. Baudrillard argued that society had moved beyond meaning and was descending into simulation and artificiality (Hicks, 2004; Pluckrose, 2018). Rorty abandoned the possibility of truth or objectivity, although he hoped that we would pursue "intersubjective agreement" among "members of our own tribe" (Rorty, 1991, pp. 22–23, 29).

The postmodernists were dismissive of the idea that an objective reality exists that is independent of human interpretation (Duignan, 2017; Hicks, 2004). In its extreme form, the dismissal of the notion of an objective natural reality and the assertion that all knowledge is constructed by humans means that there are no such things as objective facts or truths; reason and logic are merely conceptual constructs that are valid only within the intellectual traditions that use them. This perspective is consistent with Kuhn's (1962) argument that scientific paradigms do not represent objectively accurate explanations about the world but are temporary explanations that are overturned once enough dissatisfaction arises regarding an old paradigm and enough scientists support a new one.

Many postmodernists made subjectivity and relativism so prominent that they essentially dismantled notions of knowledge, reason, language, society, and even the individual (Cohen, 2007; Hicks, 2004). After this, there was little more for postmodernists to do, and some view these early forms of postmodernism as having basically died out as a result (Pluckrose, 2018). Postmodernist ideas also conflicted so completely with the ability of science to explain the physical and organic worlds that few scholars outside the humanities and social sciences took them seriously. A leading philosopher of science, Alex Rosenberg, concluded that "We can therefore reduce the threat of relativism to levels that can be safely ignored" (2012, p. 282). In addition, it is now widely understood that theoretical perspectives based on relativism and subjectivity are self-refuting. If one claims that all viewpoints are relative or subjective, then that claim too represents merely another relative or subjective viewpoint, and there is no reason to consider it more valid than any other viewpoint (Deutsch, 2011; Hicks, 2004; Pinker, 2018). Feeling deeply the "truth" of one's political, artistic, religious, or idiosyncratic personal perspective is clearly an important part of human experience, but that does not make it true—people frequently feel or believe false things about other individuals, other groups, the world in general, and even themselves (e.g., millions of people believe President Obama was not born in the U.S., aliens live among us, or the world was created roughly 6000 years ago). These feelings can be explained by a scientific understanding of psychology, but sometimes these feelings have limited or even no relationship with reality.

Nonetheless, the first generation of postmodernist ideas were picked up by several academics and activists in the 1970s and 1980s who politicized and focused them on various identity groups. These developed into postcolonial studies (e.g., Edward Said, *Orientalism*, 1978), gender theory and queer theory (e.g., Judith Butler, 1990, *Gender Trouble*), and intersectional and critical race theory (Crenshaw, 1991, "Mapping the margins: intersectionality, identity politics, and violence against women of color"). Some within these movements went beyond the notion that knowledge is relative and endorsed the view that science is a tool used by the Caucasian, male patriarchy to concentrate and maintain its power (Cohen, 2007; Hicks, 2004). Few of those who do science subscribe to these views, and these views have had negligible impact within the natural sciences as a result.[5] These movements nonetheless became prominent in women's and cultural studies, English, and education departments in American, Canadian, and English higher education, and are endorsed by several psychologists as well. The current sensitivity around politically correct speech,

[5] Just as there are some creationists in the natural sciences, there are undoubtedly postmodernist scientists as well, and certainly numerous academics in the social sciences subscribe to postmodernist views. But it is difficult to know how to categorize their research if they deny part, or all (in the case of those with more extreme views), of the findings or methods of science. Emmanuel Kant started the postmodernist enterprise to defend religion against scientific reasoning and evidence (Hicks, 2004), and many contemporary postmodernists similarly use an antiscience and antirealist epistemology to defend their sociocultural and political perspectives. Religious and postmodernist arguments are similar in that regard.

controversies surrounding the rise of far left as well as far right groups based on identity politics, and concerns about the emergence of a "posttruth" society are manifestations of how influential and widespread these views have become.

Science as "the view from nowhere"

A proposal that avoids concerns about a purported lack of objectivity in science argues that the human perspective be removed entirely when considering scientific findings (Nagel, 1986). In its quest to find purely objective knowledge about the nature of phenomena, human subjectivity should not play a role in how that knowledge is interpreted or explained. There is no doubt that human consciousness is subjective, but scientific knowledge should not rely on human consciousness and interpretation but instead should omit all subjectivity from its methods and explanations. From this perspective, science describes the world from no perspective at all, as if there were no people in it. The prominent philosopher Thomas Nagel described this perspective in his 1986 book titled *The View from Nowhere*:

> *The world described by this objective conception is not just centerless: it is also in a sense featureless. While the things in it have properties, none of these properties are perceptual aspects. All of those have been relegated to the mind .... The physical world as it is supposed to be in itself contains no points of view and nothing that can appear only to a particular point of view (p. 15).*

Although it is difficult to imagine generating scientific knowledge in a place with no people in it, Nagel offered a useful analogy for how science should be conducted. Science must operate in ways that minimize human subjectivity, bias, and error. (The noted physicist Richard Feynman said of science that "The first principle is to not fool yourself—and you are the easiest person to fool.") Of course, fallible humans conduct science and we are error prone, but a critical characteristic of science is that it is self-correcting. The validity of scientific propositions is not dependent on the authority or identity of the person stating them (or even an alien stating them; scientific knowledge is universal throughout the cosmos). Instead, their validity derives from logic and data. Two plus two equals four, regardless of who makes the claim. Evolution by natural selection is a fact, whether it is stated by an African American biologist or a liberal female Christian minister, or is being refuted by a white male fundamentalist Christian. Claims that are considered valid by only one individual or group are not scientific. They may be religious, political, personal, or even delusional, but they are not scientific claims.

Improvements in scientific technology

An essential perspective for understanding the nature, achievements, and progress of science involves a technical rather than philosophical perspective. This perspective has long been appreciated in the physical and biological sciences but was applied relatively infrequently in the behavioral sciences until recently.

It has long been known that the power and precision of scientific tools limits the types of discoveries that are possible in the natural sciences. Scientific progress is highly dependent on these tools and some of the most important ones have been *conceptual* rather than technological. For example, mathematics in Europe was largely written out in words prior to the introduction of the Hindu–Arabic numeral system by the Italian Fibonacci in 1202. The new numeral system allowed vastly more complex calculations to be performed, and science and commerce were transformed as a result. Four centuries later, Newton's invention of calculus proved to be so useful that science was again transformed. The use of calculus quickly led to major advances in understanding the nature of gravity, heat, light, sound, fluid dynamics, electricity, and magnetism (Crump, 2001). The later development of regression, correlation, other statistics and advanced mathematical modeling more recently again transformed the types of phenomena that can be scientifically investigated and explained. Gauge theory in physics represents another new and powerful conceptual advance for explaining physical phenomena.

Scientific progress is also dependent on the development of technological tools. For example, Copernicus hypothesized that the earth revolved around the sun in 1543, but his hypothesis could not be confirmed until Galileo started building telescopes in 1609. Galileo's first telescope had about 3× magnification, but he kept on perfecting his instruments and by December of that year had achieved 20× magnification. This allowed him to be the first person to observe that the Milky Way consisted of thousands of stars (at minimum), the known planets are nearby, they reflect sunlight, the earth rotates around the sun, and several additional discoveries that completely transformed the understanding of the cosmos (Crump, 2001). Each further advance in telescope technology over the centuries, such as the Hubble Space Telescope more recently, has led to significant advances in understanding the universe.

The microscope has been one of the most versatile and transformative scientific instruments ever invented. Van Leeuwenhoek (1632–1723) made the best early instruments, capable of 270× magnification, and became the first person to observe protozoa, bacteria, blood corpuscles, and blood circulation through capillaries. He was the first person to observe sperm and then found them in the males of all species that reproduce sexually. Biology was transformed as a result. The next revolutionary advance in microscopes occurred in the 1930s when beams of electrons replaced beams of light, allowing very small objects such as viruses, chromosomes, and nucleic acids (including DNA) to be observed. Biology was transformed once again. The rise of fluorescence microscopy is currently leading to further important advances in biology.

A recent technological advance that has been particularly important in psychological research is functional magnetic resonance imaging (fMRI). Before the development of clinically useful fMRI in the early 1990s, the electroencephalogram, which uses electrical leads placed on the outside of the skull, had been the primary tool available for measuring what was happening inside living human brains. Although its temporal resolution was very good (within milliseconds), its spatial resolution was poor, such that it could place neural events only to within centimeters, which can be the difference between different lobes within the brain. The higher spatial resolution of fMRI allows for far more precise observations of brain activity. Further improvements in scanning technology are leading to even more precise measurements of neuronal activity. For example, magnetoencephalography (MEG) has high spatial resolution (millimeters) as well as very high temporal resolution (less than a millisecond)—the difference between MEG and older generation fMRI has been described as analogous to watching brain activity with a high-resolution video camera compared with a series of poorly focused still photos. The ability to observe and measure the activity of the brain with ever-increasing precision is allowing tremendous advances in our understanding of emotion, cognition, and behavior.

The importance of philosophical and historical perspectives in psychology

Many of the philosophical critiques outlined above have been critical for creating stronger confidence in the methods and findings of science. This is particularly important in the behavioral and social sciences due to the pervasive effects of subjectivity and bias inherent in human psychology. A critical, analytical perspective is especially important when studying human behavior because we humans have great difficulty thinking objectively about ourselves and others. Science is inherently a critical enterprise but is carried out by highly fallible human beings. Therefore, it is essential that psychologists remain ever vigilant in taking a critical, logical, and well-informed approach to observation, analysis, and interpretation. This is true when we conduct research or when practicing psychology as an applied science. There have been many times when scientific knowledge has been applied inappropriately and unethically (e.g., when eugenics became very popular in the U.S. and several other countries in the first half of the 20th century). Applied sciences are also expected to be based on the scientific understanding of phenomena, not on pseudoscience, "folk" or intuitive theoretical orientations, personal perspective, or poor-quality data or analysis. Psychologists need to be especially vigilant about these issues because their knowledge, skills, and interventions are applied directly in the lives of individuals, families, communities, and society.

The aforementioned philosophical critiques were very important in the historical development of the sciences, but they now play a smaller role. This is largely due to dramatic advances in science over the past century. It is easy to see why questions about epistemology and the basis for knowledge were so prominent several decades ago. For example, before the atom was discovered in the early 1900s and the gene discovered in the 1950s, both were presumed to exist based on inferences from theory and research, but neither had ever been directly observed. Now that so many previously invisible entities and processes have been observed, concern about epistemology has lessened. The same is true in psychology as well. Imaging machines such as fMRI have been used to observe subconscious mental processes in the human brain since the 1990s and the human genome was first sequenced just at the beginning of this century. These technologies are now providing verifiable observations of mental events and processes that until recently could only be inferred.

In other ways, however, philosophical and especially ethical questions are becoming much more important as science advances. This too is due in part to the advance of science. For example, medicine can now maintain comatose individuals in a persistent vegetative state on ventilators and feeding tubes, and may soon allow parents to genetically edit babies and choose particular desired characteristics while deleting others. This raises very difficult questions about how these technologies should be used. Likewise, if research finds that it is possible to prevent the onset of mental disorders through the use of various prevention and intervention measures, what are the ethical implications of not using (and using) those measures? Rosenberg (2012) defined philosophy as the study of "questions that science—physical, biological, social, behavioral—cannot answer now and perhaps may never be able to answer" (p. 3). This perspective is absolutely critical in the human realm due to the role of *values* and questions about *how* scientific knowledge and technology should be used. These questions are not answerable by science, at least not now. That is why philosophical and ethical perspectives are absolutely critical to the appropriate and responsible application of psychology, in clinical practice as well as in research, education, policy, and other areas of application.

The invention of science has been a revolutionary development in human history that has greatly benefited psychological experience as well as the material conditions of human beings. Nonetheless, it has been contested throughout. A variety of criticisms have been levied against it, including creationist and postmodernist critiques. Proposals based on relativism and subjectivity are conceptually self-refuting, however, and vary so greatly from the way science is done that they do not play significant roles in the physical, biological, or behavioral sciences (Deutsch, 2011; Pinker, 2018; Rosenberg, 2012). Philosophical perspectives are nonetheless absolutely critical in the practice of behavioral health care, and especially in terms of the foundational role played by ethics.

Historical development of research and theory in psychology

Relying on the aforementioned perspectives for understanding the nature of science, we can turn our attention to understanding the nature of psychological science. Theory and research in the field developed in a very complicated and confusing manner but are now taking a qualitatively different approach. Appreciating these developments is critical for understanding contemporary psychology and health service psychology in particular.

Historically, the standard approaches to learning about and understanding personality, psychopathology, and psychotherapy within the field were based on the traditional theoretical orientations. Textbooks that covered this material frequently took a chronological approach to reviewing the most important of these orientations, starting with Freudian theory and progressing through a selection of psychodynamic, behavioral, humanistic, cognitive, systemic, multicultural, postmodern, and eclectic and integrative approaches. Some theories focused primarily on the development of personality and psychopathology with little emphasis on the process of psychotherapy (e.g., existentialism, multicultural approaches), while others focused primarily on therapy process and methods (e.g., interpersonal therapy, eclectic approaches). The number of theories that were proposed was simply staggering; Corsini and Wedding (2008) counted more than 400 different theoretical perspectives. The earliest of these, Freudian psychoanalysis, still remains the most comprehensive of these attempts to explain personality, psychopathology, and psychotherapy. Indeed, Freud's theory was the basis for one of the most influential intellectual movements of the past century. But it also ended up being the most controversial of the theoretical orientations in psychology.

It is obviously not possible to learn a large number of these theories in detail. Learning one or more of them was nonetheless considered required training in the field. And this is still generally the case. For example, the Application for Psychology Internship, used by nearly all psychology internship programs in the Association of Psychology Postdoctoral and Internship Centers, still requires that applicants complete the following essay question: "Please describe your theoretical orientation and how this influences your approach to case conceptualization and intervention" (APPIC, 2018). The conclusions of the American Psychological Association Assessment of Competency Benchmarks Work Group (Fouad et al., 2009) also support this approach. They noted the following as an "essential component" for demonstrating clinical intervention planning skills: "Formulates and conceptualizes cases and plan interventions utilizing at least one consistent theoretical orientation" (p. S19).

Given the central role that the traditional theoretical orientations played in behavioral health care education and practice (and still do to an extent), it is certainly remarkable how very controversial they were throughout the history of the field. The criticisms and weaknesses of these various orientations are well known: standard undergraduate and graduate textbooks routinely discuss them when presenting the theories. Even what is currently the single most influential approach, cognitive behavior therapy, is considered inadequate as an explanation for psychotherapy change (e.g., Kazdin, 2007). Its corollary in experimental psychology, the cognitive psychology movement that started in the 1960s, is likewise considered inadequate as a scientific explanation for psychological development and functioning (Bargh, 2017).

This is an odd situation to be in for a field that purports to be based on science. The traditional theoretical orientations in behavioral health care are widely considered to provide incomplete explanations of personality, psychopathology, and behavior change, but they continue to play important roles in the field nonetheless. Indeed, it would be difficult for many faculty, students, and practicing psychologists to imagine case conceptualizations that are not based on these orientations. The appropriateness of this practice from a scientific perspective, however, is clearly questionable. If these orientations have not received experimental validation and are widely viewed as incomplete or erroneous, is it appropriate for clinicians to select one or more of them to understand behavioral health and guide their approach to clinical practice? As an applied clinical science, it is critical that behavioral health care update its basic theoretical foundations as scientific knowledge of human psychology accumulates.

Theoretical proliferation and confusion in the discipline

There are clear scientific and historical reasons for the complicated development of research and theory in psychology. These reasons must be understood to appreciate the theoretical confusion that has characterized much of the history of the field and to evaluate the current status of psychological theory and research that can guide clinical practice.

Right from the founding of psychology as a scientific discipline, there was controversy regarding the appropriate approaches to understanding psychology. The founding of the field is usually credited to Wilhelm Wundt, who established the first scientific psychology laboratory in 1879 at the University of Leipzig, Germany. Wundt argued that higher cognitive processes should not even be investigated because they were simply too complex to investigate and explain using the available experimental methods of the time (Benjamin, 2014). He therefore allowed his students to study only elemental experiences such as basic sensations, associations, and feelings.[6]

During the same time that many American graduate students went to Liepzig to study with Wundt, Sigmund Freud began advocating for a radically different approach to understanding human psychology. Instead of focusing on conscious phenomena, Freud realized the unconscious mind is very large, complicated, and important and continually interacts with the conscious mind, often outside our awareness. He also realized that it therefore must have a cognitive and emotional structure. He proceeded to build a very impressive, complex model of the interacting subconscious, preconscious, and conscious minds. Although no one else has ever developed a more complex and wide-ranging model of human psychology, and very few other individuals had as large an impact on Western culture in the 20th century, unfortunately, Freud's model was intuitively developed and was ultimately unscientific. Despite his remarkable insights into human development and functioning, many of his specific proposals have not withstood scientific scrutiny.

In 1913, John Watson presented another radically different perspective on psychological science, urging his colleagues to abandon their interest in consciousness and instead focus on behavior. Watson's arguments were very persuasive in American psychology at the time and many psychologists over the next half century were convinced that behavior was mostly determined by the reinforcements and punishments we experienced and, therefore, we were largely the products of our environment. Behaviorists consequently viewed free will and even consciousness as illusions or epiphenomena that might seem very real and vitally important to us but actually play a small role in our lives.

The rise of psychoanalysis and behaviorism caused two fundamentally important psychological processes, the conscious and subconscious minds, to be largely

[6] Wundt's contributions to psychology are often underappreciated. He researched a remarkably wide range of phenomena and his productivity was simply staggering. Over his career, he published 58,735 pages across 68 years, an average of 2.2 published pages per day (Benjamin, 2014). This is as much as many people read per day!

excluded from most experimental research in the U.S. for the next 50 years. A leading psychologist, Woodworth (1921), described this situation this way: "First psychology lost its soul, then it lost its mind, then it lost consciousness; it still has behavior, of a kind" (p. 2).[7] This was considered a colossal error by Koestler (1967), who noted that psychology was making fundamental errors and floundering at the same time the other sciences were shooting ahead and making tremendous advances.

A new theoretical perspective replaced behaviorism in American universities in the 1960s. Cognitive psychology went to the other extreme and argued that our behavior, thoughts, and emotions are very much under our intentional, conscious control and are rarely triggered by environmental stimuli. Cognitive psychology, along with the very influential cognitive therapies developed by Albert Ellis (1957) and Aaron Beck (1967), argued that behavior is not determined by environmental contingencies but by our own thoughts and beliefs. They argued that humans do indeed have free will and we are very much in charge. As we will see in the next chapter, however, research has shown that this perspective went too far as well.

Remarkably varied alternative approaches to understanding human psychology continued to proliferate within health service psychology and other behavioral health fields. These included a wide variety of humanistic, systemic, cognitive, and postmodern orientations. Indeed, new theoretical systems for understanding personality, psychopathology, and psychotherapy still continue to be developed (e.g., Thought Field Therapy (Callahan & Callahan, 2000), coherence therapy (Ecker & Hulley, 2006), a "new unified theory of psychology" (Henrique, 2011), a new "unifying" approach to psychotherapy (Magnavita & Anchin, 2014)). In addition, none of these individual approaches has become dominant. Surveys typically find that the largest number of adherents to any one orientation, even an eclectic or integrative approach, still remains a minority, usually less than one-third of the sample (Prochaska & Norcross, 2018). Although the intensity of conflict between the theoretical camps has diminished in recent years, concern has grown regarding the use of discredited or potentially harmful therapies. Norcross, Koocher, and Garofalo (2006) conducted a survey listing dozens of treatments and asked experts about the degree to which they believed each of them had been discredited. The experts rated 25 of the treatments as somewhere between "probably discredited" and "certainly discredited" (e.g., sexual reorientation therapy, rebirthing therapies, Thought Field Therapy, reparenting therapy). (For more examination of this issue, see Lilienfeld, Lynn, & Lohr, 2015.)

Despite irreconcilable conflicts between the traditional theoretical orientations in psychology, their sheer number and remarkable ability to proliferate, as well as the paucity of experimental research conducted on most of them, most practicing psychologists have tended to accept the existence of a diverse array of theoretical orientations as a normal state of affairs. One was simply expected to choose one or more of these orientations for conceptualizing one's approach to practice. This was basically viewed as a natural characteristic of the field, similar to the way in which politicians of

[7] More recently, it was similarly said that psychiatry, in its swing from embracing psychoanalysis to psychopharmacology, went from brainless to mindless (author unknown).

different parties or clergy from different religions are frequently able to accept fundamental differences between their groups but still find common ground on other issues. The validity of these orientations was frequently based on the intuitions and convictions of their authors and their ability to cultivate followers, and many of these orientations did not undergo any rigorous experimental testing. The natural sciences clearly operate very differently; they do not offer an array of unverified theoretical orientations for understanding the night sky, the similarities and differences between species, or the causes of infection and disease. Explanations in the sciences must also survive the most rigorous tests one can think of to falsify them and prove them wrong.

In hindsight, the scientific and historical reasons for this very confusing situation are obvious. As mentioned previously, the complexity of the subject matter was very difficult to handle. Two geniuses who played central roles in founding the field, William James and Wilhelm Wundt, both appreciated the astounding complexity of the human mind and were skeptical about the ability of science at the time to explain it. Sigmund Freud also appreciated that human psychology was far more complex than what was commonly believed, but he went ahead confidently asserting his theoretical speculations and applying them in practice before their validity could be established through scientific experimentation. It took a long time before the necessity of falsifiable theory in the behavioral sciences became widely appreciated.

Another reason for the problems with many of these theoretical orientations involves their underlying assumptions. This issue plagued the field since the beginning. The two primary historical forerunners of scientific psychology were physiology and philosophy. Physiology became increasingly focused on the nervous system after discoveries such as Helmholtz's measurement of the speed of nerve conduction in 1849. Discoveries like this caused scientists to realize that the physiology of the brain could be measured precisely and the operation of the mind and brain consequently could be studied empirically. The other forerunner of psychology was mental philosophy, including the works of John Locke, David Hume, and John Stuart Mill (Benjamin, 2014). The field of physiology was strongly empirical and directly connected with the biological sciences, while mental philosophy largely was not, and many areas within psychology up to the 21st century took the latter of these approaches.

The assumptions underlying many of the historically important theoretical orientations in health service psychology were well known. Many of these orientations were based on foundational assumptions or first principles that take widely varying perspectives on human nature (e.g., biologically based drives in Freudian theory, the *blank slate* of nearly complete malleability in behaviorism, an optimistic self-actualizing tendency in humanistic theories, a postmodern constructivism in solution-focused therapy). But these philosophical starting points had not been scientifically validated. They also conflicted with one another in fundamental ways that led to irreconcilable differences in the understanding of human psychology and behavior change (Messer & Winokur, 1980; Wood & Joseph, 2007). Therefore, adherence to these orientations necessarily involved accepting their underlying philosophical assumptions or worldview as opposed to being convinced by the weight of the scientific evidence.

As a result, disagreements between adherents of the different theories frequently resembled philosophical, political, or religious disputes more than scientific ones.

As will be discussed in the next chapter, evolutionary theory had not developed far enough to explain social behavior until the latter part of the 20th century. Humans are highly social animals and biological explanations for social behavior were not uncovered until relatively recently. The ability of evolutionary theory to explain the behavior of social animals was necessary for psychology to become integrated with the rest of the natural sciences.

Current scientific status of psychology

The scientific status of the field of psychology has evolved dramatically in recent decades. At the turn of the 21st century, psychology had reached a crossroads. Serious weaknesses in many of the traditional theoretical orientations were apparent at the same time that evolutionary theory was explaining larger amounts of social behavior and mental activity. Medicine was no longer being practiced as an art, and society increasingly was expecting health care to be delivered in an evidence-based, safe, and effective manner. New research technologies such as fMRI and genomic sequencing had become more precise and powerful, and were being used to investigate mental processes that had never been observed before and simply had to remain hypotheses in the past. Structural equation modeling and other computational methods had become very sophisticated and could analyze data in much more powerful ways. Psychology was becoming a full-fledged science whereby scientific explanations were becoming consistent with the rest of the natural sciences. This was a historic achievement! Even the most complex of natural phenomena, the human mind and brain, was giving way to a scientific approach to understanding its development, structure, and function. The field is still in its early stages as one of the natural sciences, but there is no turning back once a sufficient number of verifiable scientific explanations emerge.

Psychology has now entered the paradigmatic stage in its development in which knowledge is cumulative, untested theoretical hypotheses and models are being dropped, and expectations to practice in an evidence-based manner are widely accepted. Psychology has become a mature science and is now widely considered one of the natural sciences.

Scientific foundations: understanding human nature

3

Given the tremendous complexity of the subject matter, it is not surprising that the behavioral sciences took a meandering journey to reach a scientifically integrated perspective on human psychology. But many aspects of that perspective are now well established. A comprehensive understanding of human psychology requires knowledge of all the relevant levels of natural organization involved. These include numerous lower level and higher level biological, psychological, and sociocultural factors. For example, the sociocultural dimension includes both proximal environmental factors (e.g., family, school, work, and neighborhood) as well as distal ones (e.g., community, society, and cultural and historical context). Omitting any relevant levels of influence can result in seriously incomplete explanations of personality, psychopathology, intellectual functioning, neuropsychological and physical dysfunction, and all the other aspects of biopsychosocial development and functioning that are important in behavioral health care. Health service psychology often focused primarily on psychosocial issues in the past, but it is now clear that a comprehensive, integrative biopsychosocial perspective is necessary for a scientific understanding of human psychology.

Another very basic but important perspective for understanding the complexity of human psychology was made by Clyde Kluckhohn and Henry Murray (1953), who observed that "Every man is in certain respects[:] a. like all other men, b. like some other men, c. like no other man." They further explain "He is like all other men because some of the determinants of his personality are universal to the species." This is, of course, true with regard to the mind and brain as well; if a person, for any reason, fails to possess an adequate number of the universal structures and functions of the human brain, the person cannot live. But humans also share features that characterize groups, often in terms of personality, interests, abilities, psychopathology, ethnicity, and sociocultural factors. And, "Finally, there is the inescapable fact that a man is in many respects like no other man. Each individual's modes of perceiving, feeling, needing, and behaving have characteristic patterns which are not precisely duplicated by those of any other individual." This is true of the physical brain as well: just like with one's body, each individual's brain is unique in terms of its structure and function as a result of his or her unique genetic inheritance, experience, and biopsychosocial life history. Some people overemphasize individuals' uniqueness so much that they miss group and universal characteristics. Prejudice and discrimination can occur when people overemphasize group characteristics and minimize the importance of the other two levels.

These basic observations regarding the nature of human psychology suggest many useful starting points for learning the complex scientific literature regarding human psychology. But perhaps the most logical place to start is with evolutionary theory. If one wants to understand why any animal is structured, functions, and behaves the way it does, evolutionary theory is simply necessary. As the biologist Theodosius

Foundations of Health Service Psychology. https://doi.org/10.1016/B978-0-12-816426-6.00003-7

Dobzhansky (1973) noted, "Nothing in biology makes sense except in the light of evolution" (p. 125). We now understand that the same observation applies to human psychology as well.[1]

Evolutionary theory is necessary in the biological as well as the behavioral sciences because it explains the origins and functions of behavior; that is, it can explain why organic life is designed in the manner it is. The renowned ethologist Niko Tinbergen (1963) noted that the study of animal behavior focuses on different levels of questions, from *ultimate* explanations regarding the origins and functions of behavior to *proximate* explanations regarding the operation of specific mechanisms underlying behaviors. Evolutionary theory is necessary for explaining both these types of questions. In behavioral health care, clinicians often focus on the level of proximate mechanisms involving emotion, cognition, or behavior because facilitating changes at this level can lead to desired outcomes in terms of decreased symptomatology and improved functioning. Focusing only on this level, however, misses larger questions involving how and why particular psychological mechanisms and behavior patterns developed, the adaptive value they may have, and which interventions are more likely to be successful in achieving desired outcomes. A full understanding of human development and functioning requires both ultimate and proximate explanations of behavior. Evolutionary theory is the only perspective that provides explanations at both these levels, and human psychology does not make sense without it.

Another benefit of evolutionary theory as the starting point for understanding human psychology is that it links psychology with the rest of the natural sciences. Most of the traditional theoretical orientations in psychology were not directly connected to the biological sciences. This was a very different relationship from what is found in the natural sciences. As science developed over the past three centuries, new subfields generated knowledge in a cumulative manner that was thoroughly consistent with knowledge from other disciplines. As noted in the discussion on reductionism in the previous chapter, all levels of natural organization function consistent with the operation of processes at lower levels on the hierarchy. E. O. Wilson (1998) referred to this as *consilience*, the seamless convergence and unity of all knowledge across scientific disciplines regarding all levels of natural organization. In the past, many theoretical explanations in psychology were not supported by or consistent with scientific knowledge regarding processes at other levels of natural organization. But evolutionary theory shows how biological, psychological, and sociocultural processes interact in producing psychological characteristics. It not only connects all the subdisciplines within psychology (e.g., neuroscience, developmental, personality, cognitive, social, clinical, educational), but also "integrates psychology theoretically with the rest of the natural sciences in a unified causal framework" (Buss, 2005b, p. xxv). Since the turn of the 21st century, psychology has become thoroughly connected with the rest of the life sciences and thereby with the physical sciences as well. As a

1 After all, psychological science is continuous with biology; it is another one of the life sciences. The boundaries that academic disciplines place between levels of natural phenomena are artificial, although very useful for practical reasons. But nature does not include these same boundaries; they are a human construction.

result, psychology is now often referred to as one of the natural sciences and a STEM field (i.e., science, technology, engineering, and mathematics; Bray et al., 2009).

Evolution is also critical for understanding human nature because it provides a *deeply* historical perspective. It was noted in Chapter 1 that the scientific perspective for understanding human psychology requires a fourth dimension, *time*, in addition to the biological, psychological, and sociocultural dimensions. At the level of the individual, one's personality, intellectual functioning, coping style, psychopathology, and other important psychological characteristics cannot be understood without considering her or his development across time. Likewise, at the level of human nature, or people in general, the structure and functioning of biological, psychological, and sociocultural characteristics cannot be understood without considering the development of human beings across our history. For clinicians, three timescales are typically important: the short term (e.g., why is the person seeking treatment at this time?), the life span (e.g., what happened that caused the personality characteristics and psychopathology?), and the extremely long term, which includes the evolution of psychological mechanisms (e.g., are the psychological mechanisms involving fear, anger, sadness, happiness, attachment, etc., functioning adaptively or maladaptively in this case?). Neither individual patients nor human beings in general can be understood without taking into account the dimension of time.

Psychologists understood that humans were evolved organisms since the beginning of the discipline (Darwin's *On the Origin of Species* was published two decades before, in 1859), but the significance of that fact was not fully appreciated for nearly a century. For much of the 20th century, evolution was thought to play only a minor role in the development of important human psychological characteristics because humans seemed so different from other species and culture plays a hugely important role in our mental life and development (Mameli, 2007). Evolution was seen as responsible for basic innate mental abilities, such as sensation, perception, classical and operant conditioning, imitation, and basic logical and probabilistic reasoning. Humans may have inherited from our evolutionary ancestors these basic mental abilities, but their operation within the context of human culture and civilization led to psychological and social characteristics that were viewed as categorically different from basic animal abilities. As a result, evolution was viewed as largely irrelevant for understanding human psychology and received little attention in the social sciences.

That era has passed. It is now perfectly clear that evolution is essential to understanding the structure and function of human psychology just as it is for understanding human biology. None of the biopsychosocial levels of human functioning can be scientifically understood (or even make sense) without an evolutionary perspective. This is true from the level of genetics to the level of attachment style to the level of the cultural and political conflicts that perennially divide society and the human community.[2] Evolution consequently provides perhaps the best starting point for understanding the vast scientific literature regarding human psychology. Health

[2] The evolutionary perspective is also essential for understanding the nature of the universe—cosmology makes no sense except in light of the evolution of the universe.

service psychology has not yet thoroughly integrated evolutionary theory even though nearly all psychologists would probably agree that it is necessary. This and the next chapter attempt to rectify that issue. The discussion begins with an overview of the evolution of human beings.

The evolutionary origins of humans and human psychology

The story of life on earth begins with LUCA, our last universal common ancestor. One of the truly remarkable findings of science is that not only are all animals that have ever lived on earth related to one another, but all living organisms, plant and animal, are related as well. Life's smallest components, such as proteins and nucleic acids, are actually universal components of all plant and animal life on earth. The genetic code is written the same way across living organisms, and all branches of life share the same organelles (i.e., subparts of cells that perform specialized functions) and associated enzymes. Darwin (1859) predicted that every living creature could trace its lineage back to one source, and that remarkable hypothesis has now been verified to an extremely high degree of certainty (Theobald, 2010). There are no fossil remains of LUCA, but scientists believe that it was very similar to a modern bacterium, lived about 3.5 billion years ago, and later split into microbes and, after 2.5 billion years, into multicellular organisms (eukaryotes). After another 400 million years, multicellular organisms began evolving into the amazing range of animals and plants that now exist. We share these basic components of life with every other living thing that has ever lived, no matter how large or small, whether still living or extinct, all the way back to the point of our common origin 3.5 billion years ago.

We carry within each of us many other developments in the evolution of animals on earth. In *Your Inner Fish: A Journey Into the 3.5-Billion-Year History of the Human Body*, Neil Shubin (2008) describes how we in fact carry the whole history of evolution within our bodies. It has long been known that our basic skeletal structures are similar to our mammalian, reptilian, and amphibian forebears: all have the same basic skeletal structures featuring a head at the end of a spine, limbs involving first one large bone followed by two smaller bones, then a bony clump and then small bones. Even insects like the common housefly share some of these same structural features. Very similar structural elements also appear in ancient and modern fish, although it was not known until recently how their fins (which also feature one large bone, two smaller bones, and a clump followed by small bones) evolved into legs strong enough to support animals on dry land. In 2004, Shubin and his colleagues discovered a 375-million-year-old fossil creature in northern Canada that had evolved strong fins that enabled it to leave the water and walk on land. This discovery provided the link that had been missing in the fossil record between fish and four-legged animals. Even fish, it turns out, are among our very distant relations.

Our own species made its debut much more recently. As illustrated in Fig. 2.1 in the previous chapter, *Homo sapiens* made their appearance on the world stage right at the far right end of the timeline illustrating life on earth. A large number of ape species had been flourishing during the Miocene era beginning about 20 million years ago. But this was followed by a gradual cooling and drying of the earth's climate about 10 million years ago, which greatly reduced the number of ape species that were living in the great tropical forests of Africa and Asia. One African ape lineage survived and became the common ancestor of the great apes that are still alive in the world (e.g., gorillas, chimpanzees, orangutans, humans). Around 8 million years ago, the gorilla lineage split off and about 6 to 7 million years ago the ancestor that became modern humans split off from the human–chimpanzee ancestor. The human–chimpanzee ancestor, however, became extinct. The bipedal early human ancestor moved out of the tropical forest because it was better suited to survival in the savannahs that had appeared in Africa (Dunbar, 2016; Johanson & Wong, 2009; Stringer, 2012a). Arboreal chimpanzees are well adapted to climbing and scrambling through the trees of rain forests, while humans are suited to walking on the ground, scavenging, and hunting in open grasslands.

Many hominin lines then evolved in Africa over the past 6 million years. Although the early lineages were bipedal, they were very close in brain size and other aspects to the apes (Dunbar, 2016). The first more modern species was *Homo erectus*, which evolved about 2 million years ago and dominated Africa for a very long time, about 1.5 million years. They dispersed out of Africa about 1.7 million years ago in an event that has become known as "Out of Africa 1" (Stringer, 2012a). Although they had successfully made the transition to life in the open, scavenging and later hunting over long distances, none of that species lived on into the modern era. The Neanderthals split off from *Homo erectus* about 300,000–400,000 years ago and lived north of the Mediterranean Sea, but then disappeared about 30,000 years ago.

Homo sapiens, or anatomically modern humans, are the only hominins that have survived to the modern era. By sequencing the DNA of current humans, it is actually possible to trace our genetic history to a small population of about 5000 females who lived about 200,000 years ago in southern Africa. Most of the lineages of these women died out over time (due to famine, disease, infertility, warfare, etc.), resulting in a truly extraordinary circumstance. Analyses of mitochondrial DNA, which is passed down intact from mothers to daughters, indicate that all living *Homo sapiens* now alive on earth are descendants of a single mother (nicknamed "Mitochondrial Eve") who lived in East Africa about 200,000 years ago (Cann, Stoneking, & Wilson, 1987). The common male ancestor of all human beings (dubbed "Y-chromosomal Adam") is estimated to have lived more recently, about 142,000 years ago in central or northwestern Africa (Cruciani et al., 2011). This is likely due to the practice of polygamy, whereby fewer males than females end up passing along their genes to their offspring (i.e., some males in polygamous groups do not get the opportunity to reproduce, and so the effect of those who do reproduce is larger).

One group of *Homo sapiens* began growing rapidly in number about 100,000 years ago and expanded out of Africa to the southern coastline of Asia by 70,000 years ago and Australia by 60,000 to 40,000 years ago (Dunbar, 2016; Stringer, 2012a; Wade, 2006).[3] They did not enter Europe until about 35,000 years ago, but when they did

[3] Some new fossil finds have pushed the estimates for when the first migrations of *Homo sapiens* left Africa further back (Bae, Donka, & Petraglia, 2017).

they replaced the Neanderthals who were living there at the time. The sequencing of an intact sample of Neanderthal DNA made possible the discovery that about 2.5% of the DNA in all modern humans living outside of Africa comes from Neanderthal genes. This indicates that there was intermating between the Neanderthals and *Homo sapiens*, although researchers note that it is unlikely that the very small amount of Neanderthal DNA that remains in our genomes is responsible for our current appearance or traits (Stringer, 2012b). *Homo sapiens* also migrated to the Americas 20,000−16,000 years ago (during the last Ice Age, when the oceans were much lower and Asia and Alaska were connected by land). Remarkably, they colonized both North and South America all the way to the southern tip within just dozens of generations. Once *Homo sapiens* developed language and advanced social abilities, they quickly became a remarkably successful species that soon colonized the entire planet (except for the continent of Antartica).

The community of *Homo sapiens* that had left Africa was small, perhaps only 4000 individuals. This accounts for why the genetic variation of the peoples who ended up outside of Africa is relatively small as well (Johanson & Wong, 2009; Stringer, 2012a; Wade, 2006). For example, there is great genetic variation in the heights of the various groups who live in Africa (e.g., between the very tall Maasai and the very short pygmies), while groups living in the rest of the world are similar in height. Because *Homo sapiens* evolved relatively recently, humans around the world are actually quite similar genetically; in fact, we are 99.9% genetically identical. Of the small amount of variance that remains between individuals, very little is attributable to one's continent of origin (Bonham, Warshauer-Baker, & Collins, 2005). Only about 2.8% of the remaining variance is attributable to the continents where one's ancestors lived, while another 2.5% is attributable to large groups within continents. The vast majority of our genetic differences, as much as 95%, is actually attributable to differences between local populations.

These findings have major implications for understanding the complicated and contentious issue of race. Race is typically defined in terms of skin color that is then used as an identifier of one's continent of origin, but this is a cultural definition that has little biological meaning (Montagu, 1942; Omi, 2001). As was just mentioned, there is great genetic variation between local populations within Africa that is actually far greater than what is found in all the rest of the world (Tishkoff & Kidd, 2004). As a result, some Africans are genetically much more similar to Europeans than they are to other Africans. And skin color has little to do with this. Instead, humans need dark skin to survive in equatorial regions of the earth to avoid dying from skin cancer (e.g., albinos in Nigeria seldom live more than 30 years; Yakubu & Mabogunje, 1993). On the other hand, those living far from the equator need to have light skin to avoid dying from a lack of vitamin D. In other words, skin color is not associated with one's continent of origin but with the distance one lived from the equator. In the first few centuries of Europeans living in the Americas, individuals taken from Africa and turned into slaves of course had dark skin, but such a large difference in skin color between slaves and their owners was often not the case. One of the saddest characteristics of human beings across history is that slavery has been practiced by all civilizations around the world (Patterson, 1985). But slaves were frequently taken from nearby tribes and so were very similar in appearance to those who took them.[4]

Reproduction is our most important biological priority and also involves some of our most intense and significant human experiences. It too requires an evolutionary perspective to understand. For example, the biological anthropologist Helen Fisher (2016) argues that humans evolved three systems that enable mating and reproduction. The first system involves the sex drive (lust), which evolved so that humans initiate mating; this system is associated with testosterone in both women and men. The second involves intense romantic love (infatuation) to focus one's mating energy on one partner at a time; this is associated primarily with dopamine. The third system involves feelings of deep attachment, produced principally by oxytocin and vasopressin, that evolved to encourage pair bonding so parents can raise children together as partners. Fisher argues that human beings would not exist today if not for these survival mechanisms and stated that "I ... propose that these brain systems for lust, romantic love and attachment began to take their human forms soon after our forebears descended from the fast-disappearing trees of Africa to walk on two feet instead of four and form pair-bonds to rear their helpless young at least through infancy as a team" (Fisher, 2016, p. 151).

One of the most critical evolutionary transitions that is central to modern human experience evolved relatively recently: the development of language. Social bonding is an essential need for all the great apes. Grooming, primitive language, play, laughter, and perhaps even singing and dancing were essential forms of social behavior that allowed slightly larger social groups to form within various hominid lines as well as among early *Homo sapiens* (Stringer, 2012a). But major changes occurred by 50,000 to 70,000 years ago. The size of our social groups (i.e., the number of people in individuals' social networks or community) grew significantly during this time to an average of 150 individuals, the size it remains today (Dunbar, 2016). It appears that modern human language that also developed during this time was critical for facilitating this change. The cognitive ability to use verbal symbols to stand for everyday concepts is the foundation of language, and other forms of symbolism and increased cognitive complexity emerged during this time as well, such as artwork (e.g., necklaces, small statutes, cave paintings), more complex cave dwellings, and much more complex stone and bone tools. This is when behavioral modernity emerged, a transition referred to as the *Human Revolution* (Mellars & Stringer, 1989). (The more popular term for referring to this development is the *Cognitive Revolution.*) The archeologist Richard Klein (2000) suggested that brain mutations were the likely cause of changes in brain function that allowed language and more complex cognition to emerge around 70,000 years ago, because brain size did not increase. Although the

[4] Regardless of whether slaves were taken from close or far away places, they were always dehumanized (Patterson, 1985). For example, the Roman emperor Cicero, who lived in the 1st century BCE, wrote that the Britons who could be bought for slavery were not worth it because they were not smart enough to make good slaves (http://www.bradford-delong.com/2009/06/cicero-the-britons-are-too-stupid-to-make-good-slaves.html). Several centuries later, some of the descendants of these British slaves themselves became slave owners in the American South and held similar disparaging views of others who had been forced into slavery.

details require further research to untangle (Stringer, 2012a), clearly our behavioral evolution made great advances during this time while our morphological evolution did not—we are physically very similar to early *Homo sapiens* but the evolution in our behavior and culture accelerated rapidly from the Cognitive Revolution on. Although anatomically modern humans emerged by 200,000–300,000 years ago, it was much more recently (only about 70,000 years ago) that behaviorally modern humans emerged.

Later developments resulted in fundamental changes in human behavior and culture as well. One of the most important was the invention of agriculture, which of course resulted in many changes in the way people lived, but had major implications for relations between the sexes in particular. In hunter and gatherer cultures, women typically did most of the gathering, while men did most of the hunting. The plant food gathered mostly by women actually often provided most of the calories consumed by the community; although meat is often prized, it is typically harder to acquire and made a smaller contribution to the overall diet (Lieberman, 2013). In these communities, women's power and status were relatively high as well, and most hunting–gathering societies were relatively egalitarian. But this situation changed dramatically after agriculture was discovered. In cultures in which people garden with a hoe, women typically do most of the cultivating and are often relatively powerful as well (Whyte, 1978). But the invention of the plow around 6000 BCE fundamentally changed women's role. As Fisher (2016) noted, "There is probably no single tool in human history that wreaked such havoc between women and men or stimulated so many changes in human patterns of sex and love as the plow" (p. 284). Controlling a plow is physically difficult and men's advantage in size and strength made cultivation their responsibility. Women no longer played the major role as provider of most of the calories consumed by the community, as most calories were now provided by men. Women lost much of their social power as a result and often began to be considered property, like chattel, up until recent centuries (Bullough, 1976). With the modern emergence of the "knowledge economy," where intellectual abilities rather than muscular power provide the means to earning income, women are now returning to much more egalitarian roles in families and society after a hiatus of several thousand years.

More recent cultural and technological developments are dependent on underlying evolutionary processes as well. The *Axial Age*, which occurred about 300–500 BCE simultaneously in China, India, and the Eastern Mediterranean, was described in the previous chapter. This was when the great civilizations and religions of the ancient world arose, including Taoism, Confucianism, Hinduism, Buddhism, Second Temple Judaism, and classical Greek philosophy and government. During this period, the intellectual life that we are more familiar with arose and "Man, as we know him today, came into being" (Jaspers, 1953, p. 1). The emergence of these movements in far-flung regions of the world cannot be explained by military or political conquest or even by scientific discoveries or inventions; instead, they resulted from evolutionary processes. During this era, there was a sharp uptake in *energy capture*, an estimate of affluence that is measured in calories (kcal) per capita per day (from 4000 kcal for hunter–gatherer societies to 15,000 kcal for large-scale civilizations like Ancient Egypt and Sumer to over 20,000 kcal in the three particularly prosperous regions of the Axial Age; Baumard, Hyafil, Morris, & Boyer, 2015). (The level of energy capture in the

West rose to about 30,000 kcal/cap/day by 1 CE, where it stayed until 1600 CE. It then rose slightly over the next 2 centuries before undergoing explosive growth starting in 1800 and rising to 230,000 kcal/cap/day in the U.S. by 2000; Morris, 2013.) The level of energy capture reached during the Axial Age allowed for the rise of larger cities, the support of a scholarly and priestly class, and a reorientation of priorities from short-term "fast-life" strategies (resource acquisition and coercive interactions with others aimed at survival) toward long-term "slow-life" strategies (self-control techniques and cooperative interactions). These developments are prime examples of how culture has become much more influential than biology in human evolution since the Cognitive Revolution and especially since the rise of agriculture and civilization.

The evolutionary origins and functions of a wide range of psychological characteristics are now well documented. Among these are speech and language acquisition; social cognition and behavior; empathy, cooperation, and prosocial behavior; decision-making; reproductive behavior; parenting and family life; physical health and disease; aggression and violence; and even the development of religion, art, music, and literature. All these topics are important for understanding adaptive and maladaptive human behavior as well as variation in psychological characteristics. For example, Nettle (2006) argues that each of the "Big Five" personality traits (i.e., extraversion, neuroticism, openness to experience, conscientiousness, and agreeableness) are adaptations that can maximize fitness in certain contexts. Neuroticism may result in increased costs involving stress and depression, but also conveys advantages in terms of vigilance to danger and increased striving and competitive behavior. In addition, all the different personality types may confer a combined set of advantages that together raise the inclusive fitness of the group further in comparison to groups with only limited variation in personality. Reviewing all this research is obviously impossible here, although interested readers are referred to several excellent volumes (Bargh, 2017; Buss, 2005a; Christakis, 2019; Dunbar, 2016; Dunbar & Barrett, 2007b; Fisher, 2016; Harari, 2011, 2015; Lieberman, 2013; Pinker, 2018; Roberts, 2012; Sapolsky, 2017; Stringer, 2012a; von Hippel, 2018; Vonk & Shackelford, 2012; Wrangham, 2019). The next chapter also outlines the evolutionary origins of human moral reasoning and behavior, another topic that is essential for understanding human nature.

The necessity of evolutionary theory for understanding humankind

The implications of all this research for understanding human nature are tremendous. First of all, we are all Africans in terms of our long-term ancestry. Incredibly, all human beings now alive are actually descended from the same mother, who lived about 200,000 years ago (about 10,000 generations ago), and the same father, who lived about 142,000 years ago (7000 generations ago). This amazing fact literally makes us all members of the same extended human family! Further, the purported differences between the sexes that were used to justify the subjugation of women over the past several thousand years are cultural developments that are not based on biology and were not even part of our hunter and gatherer past. Purported racial differences throughout history are also cultural constructions that have little biological meaning.

These well-established scientific findings are critical for understanding human nature, including human cognition, emotion, behavior, relationships, social life, and culture. They also raise the possibility that the divisiveness and conflict that have caused such tremendous human misery over the millennia could be minimized if more people became aware of our evolutionary history and we learned to treat the whole human community as "family." Humans have always treated family better than nonfamily, but due to deep evolutionary cognitive biases, have almost always had a very myopic view of who was family.

All these areas of research are critical for a comprehensive understanding of human psychology. As the field of evolutionary psychology was getting established just a few decades ago, one of its founders, David Buss (1991), explained, "At some fundamental level of description, evolution by natural selection is the process that creates physiological, anatomical, and psychological mechanisms. Therefore, the crucial question is not *whether* evolution is relevant to the understanding of human behavior but how it is relevant" (p. 461). In addition to being necessary for a scientific understanding of human development and functioning, evolutionary theory provides a unifying perspective that integrates knowledge from across levels of natural organization as well as across scientific disciplines. Due to the reasons discussed in the previous chapter, this type of comprehensive, integrated perspective has been lacking in the applied clinical areas of psychology. Nonetheless, science has now progressed to the point at which this perspective is necessary for the field to move forward in a unified science-based manner.

The foregoing discussion shows how evolution provides a logical starting point for gaining a scientific understanding of the tremendous complexity of human psychology. There are of course many, many additional topics associated with biopsychosocial influences on human development and functioning across the life span. Research continues to uncover the tremendous complexity associated with these influences, and it takes a whole graduate curriculum to begin to grasp this material in a comprehensive manner. One particularly important factor in behavioral health care concerns the nature of behavior change. This topic is tremendously complicated as well, but an overview is presented next from the perspective of one of the most famous questions in all of psychology, the role of nature versus nurture in human development and functioning. This overview also shows how far scientific research in psychology has come in recent decades and demonstrates the necessity of the biopsychosocial developmental perspective for understanding behavior change and clinical intervention.

Behavior change and nature versus nurture in human development

The question of the influence of nature versus nurture on human development and functioning is among the oldest and best known questions in all of psychology. This question has been answered in different ways over the history of the field. The eugenics movement, which started in the 1880s and was very influential in the U.S. through World War II, focused on the importance of genetically inherited traits. It was used as the rationale for the severe neglect and abuse of the mentally ill in the

U.S. and several European countries (including the extermination of 70,000 psychiatric patients at the beginning of the Holocaust; Dowbiggin, 2008; Whitaker, 2010). Many of the theoretical developments in American psychology during that period focused on the influence of the environment. Although Freud noted that biological drives provided the psychic energy behind mental life, he also emphasized environmental factors as important influences that shaped one's personality and the development of psychopathology. Behaviorism emphasized the influence of one's environment even more, as exemplified by Watson's famous statement: "Give me a dozen healthy infants, well-formed, and my own specific world to bring them up in and I'll guarantee to take any one at random and train him to become any type of specialist I might select—a doctor, lawyer, artist, merchant-chief and, yes, even into a beggar-man and thief, regardless of his talents, penchants, tendencies, abilities, vocations and race of his ancestors" (1924, p. 82).[5]

Far more precise answers to the question of the role of nature and nurture in the development of important human characteristics have emerged in recent decades. First, it became clear that evolution helped shape the structure and function of the human brain just as it did for all the other organs in the body. Although psychology, the social sciences, and humanities have often emphasized differences between groups, the universality of human psychosocial characteristics is, in many ways, even more striking (Christakis, 2019). The field of behavioral genetics also showed how genomic variation plays a substantial role in differences in personality characteristics, psychopathology, and intelligence. Comparisons of concordance in specific traits between identical (monozygotic) and fraternal (dizygotic) twins suggested a pervasive genetic influence on a range of psychological characteristics. More recently, the understanding of the interplay between nature and nurture was extended significantly through research in neural plasticity and epigenetics. This research has dramatically changed commonly accepted views regarding the role of nature versus nurture on behavior and has major implications for clinical intervention as well.

Neural plasticity

Knowledge of brain structure and function evolved dramatically over the past century and a half. The popular conception of a one-to-one correspondence between particular brain structures and specific functions dates to 1861, when Pierre Paul Broca identified the brain region responsible for producing speech (i.e., known as Broca's area, toward the back of the left frontal lobe). Over subsequent decades, researchers found that many bodily functions were associated with specific brain areas. The neurosurgeon Wilder Penfield discovered the point-to-point correspondence between body surfaces that were represented in specific areas of the somatosensory cortex. His pictorial

[5] Watson went on in the same passage to elaborate that he was exaggerating the point because he felt that advocates for the importance of heredity (and eugenics) were exaggerating the importance of inherited traits without good empirical evidence. He went on to say that "I am going beyond the facts, and I admit it, but so have the advocates of the contrary and they have been doing it for many thousands of years" (1924, p. 82).

representation of the cortical homunculus, also known as "the body within the brain," indicated very large neural areas devoted to sensation and motor control for the thumb, lips, and tongue, and small areas for the shoulders and back (Penfield & Rasmussen, 1950). Until recently, the relationships between brain structures and psychological and bodily functions were believed to be strongly hardwired.

The view that the structure and function of the brain were largely fixed by adulthood remained dominant until the 1990s, when it was discovered that the brain functioning of rhesus macaques changed dramatically after the nerves leading from their arms were cut (in studies of possible treatments for stroke). These monkeys' brains no longer received input from their arms, and the area formerly responsible for arm sensation was found to be processing sensations from the face instead (Pons et al., 1991). Similar findings were soon discovered in humans. It was discovered that individuals who were blind at birth and became proficient at reading Braille were using their visual cortex for processing tactile signals from their reading fingers (Sadato et al., 1996). It was also found that blind individuals used their visual cortex for hearing, which gives them the ability to locate the source of sounds more effectively than sighted individuals (Roder et al., 1999). When deaf individuals adept at American Sign Language watch someone signing, there is activity in the part of their auditory cortex that is normally activated by speech (Streim-Amit et al., 2012).

Many neuroscientists were skeptical of these findings because of their strong belief that the neural structure of the brain was largely hardwired, but it was soon found that the brain changed in healthy, normal individuals as well as in people with abnormalities. One study found that the somatosensory cortex devoted to the four fingers of the left hand in master violinists who had started playing in childhood was far larger than in nonmusicians, but it was also somewhat larger in individuals who took up the instrument as adults (Elbert, Pantev, Wienbruch, Rockstroh, & Taub, 1995). The brain was also found to change over very short time periods. For example, Pascual-Leone, Amedi, Fregni, and Merabet (2005) asked volunteers to merely imagine practicing a simple musical piece on a piano for just one week, without ever actually touching any keyboard keys, and their motor cortex responsible for moving those fingers had grown. Even greater change was found when Pascual-Leone and Hamilton (2001) blindfolded volunteers with normal vision for five days to detect possible changes in the primary sensory regions, areas believed to be especially hardwired. The volunteers underwent functional magnetic resonance imaging (fMRI) at the beginning of the experiment, then practiced learning Braille and distinguishing small differences in the pitch of sounds for five days, and then underwent fMRI again. It was discovered that the visual cortex in these individuals, which had stopped receiving visual stimulation, had switched over to processing tactile and auditory information in just five days. Neural plasticity has now been discovered at many levels of brain structures. Experience alters the number and strength of synapses; neurons can form new dendritic connections; neurons can increase or decrease the size of their dendritic tree; and transient stress can increase dendritic spines and connectivity, while sustained stress can do the opposite (Sapolsky, 2017).

One of the most remarkable findings in neuroscience is the finding that adult brains grow new neurons. It was long believed that this was not possible, that you have your maximal number of neurons shortly after birth and you continue to lose them in a steadily declining manner across the life span. The discovery of adult neurogenesis was originally made by Altman and Das in 1965, but was doubted for many years. But neurogenesis was rediscovered and is causing great excitement in the neurosciences. Some areas of the brain show remarkable neurogenesis—roughly 3% of the neurons in the hippocampus are replaced each month (Kempermann, Kuhn, & Gage, 1997)—and it happens across the life span. It can be stimulated by exercise, learning, and environmental enrichment; it can be inhibited by stress; it has been found to be necessary for certain types of learning; and whole structures can increase or decrease in size as when trauma enlarges the amygdala and atrophies the hippocampus (Sapolsky, 2017). In a recent review, Sapolsky (2017) noted, "Basically, most anything you can measure in the nervous system can change in response to a sustained stimulus. And importantly, these changes are often reversible in a different environment" (p. 151).

These discoveries demonstrated that the brain can indeed break the bonds of its own genome and is capable of remarkable malleability. These discoveries also led to clinical treatments for problems that previously were believed to be untreatable. For example, building on the research with the macaque monkeys mentioned earlier, researchers found that patients who had become paralyzed in one arm due to a stroke in a particular region of the motor cortex could regain function in the paralyzed arm. By forcing patients to use their paralyzed arms (i.e., by putting their "good" arm in a sling and their "good" hand in an oven mitt), motor control of the paralyzed arm was gradually taken up by brain areas adjacent to the stroke, or sometimes even by the corresponding region in the other hemisphere of the brain, opposite to where the stroke had occurred (Taub et al., 2006). Even those who suffered their stroke years before improved, sometimes regaining the ability to drink from a glass, comb their hair, and brush their teeth.

The effects of psychotherapeutic interventions on brain function have been examined as well. Naturally, if individuals with behavioral health problems change their behavior as the result of psychotherapy, corresponding changes should be observable in the brain. And this has been found repeatedly. Schwartz (Schwartz & Begley, 2002) treated individuals with obsessive–compulsive disorder (OCD) with mindfulness instruction, teaching them to not react emotionally to an OCD symptom and instead view it as a faulty OCD circuit in their brain (specifically, hyperactivity in the orbital frontal cortex and the striatum, also known as the "worry circuit"). Compared with pretreatment, neuroimaging found that activity in the prefrontal cortex fell dramatically (Baxter et al., 1995). Similar effects were observed following cognitive behavior therapy for depression: reduced activity in the frontal cortex and increased activity in the limbic system, and the changes lasted in most cases (Goldapple et al., 2004). (As discussed in Chapter 11, a major benefit of psychotherapy is that treatment gains often last posttreatment, which frequently is not the case with psychopharmacological treatment.) In the first randomized controlled trial of the effects of "mindfulness-based stress reduction" training, Davidson et al. (2003) examined outcomes associated with an 8-week meditation program. They found that anxiety symptoms in the meditation group fell 12%, left-side frontal activation (associated with a sense of well-being and resilience) tripled, and right frontal activity (associated with negative mood) decreased, and blood tests found that their immune systems produced more antibodies to a flu vaccine. Since then, dozens of clinical trials have found that mindfulness training is associated with reduced distress in breast cancer patients, improved coping in pain patients, reduced side effects in organ transplant recipients, and reduced anxiety and depression in patients with social anxiety disorder (Davidson & Begley, 2012). The brain is indeed highly malleable and changes structurally and functionally as the result of mental activity (e.g., psychotherapy, meditation) and behavior (e.g., practicing a skill).

Epigenetics

Epigenetics is another area in which research has overturned conventional thinking about the role of nature versus nurture in human development and is causing excitement in the neurosciences. Epigenetics refers to physical modifications to the genome that result in functional modifications of the DNA but no change in the genetic sequence itself. Individuals inherit genetic instructions for many types of human characteristics, but epigenetics can determine whether those instructions are "turned on" or "turned off," are expressed or silenced. In many cases, these epigenetic effects can be permanent as well (Sapolsky, 2017).

Cells throughout the body generally share exactly the same genes. Although different cells in the body perform very different functions, they generally all share the same DNA. The process that determines which functions the cell develops depends on which regions of its genome are silenced, and the regions that remain active then determine the specialized functions of those cells. It was long thought that genomic silencing occurred very early in development and remained highly stable throughout the life span, and it was believed that the loss of the silencing resulted in organ dysfunction. It is now known, however, that the silencing of specific genomic functions is a dynamic process that extends across the life span, and that this process is heavily determined by environmental experience (Weaver et al., 2004). (The discovery of human embryonic stem cells by James Thomson in 1998 is similarly remarkable because stem cells can become any cell within the body when their development is manipulated in a specific manner, a discovery that has tremendous potential for curing disease.)

A dramatic example of this process involves the rearing of infant rat pups (Meaney, 2001; Weaver et al., 2004). Rat mothers (like human mothers) vary greatly in their approach to caregiving for their infants. Newborn rat pups that receive high levels of licking and grooming by their mothers have been shown to exhibit lower behavioral and endocrine responses to stress than pups who were licked and groomed relatively little by their mothers. And the effect is permanent. Those who received high levels of licking, grooming, and nursing as infants have lower glucocorticoid levels, are less fearful, and are better able to learn, and their brains even age less quickly as they grow old. What is remarkable is that this is true for rat pups raised by their biological mothers as well as those raised by adoptive mothers. The pups' DNA methylation (the process that accounts for the silencing of gene transcription) takes the pattern of their foster mothers, not their genetic mothers, indicating that it is the soothing care, not the genetic inheritance, that causes the epigenetic changes that regulate endocrine and cardiovascular responses in the pup. Remarkably, the same effect can be achieved by a human gently stroking the infant rat pup with a small paint brush (Jutapakdeegul, Casalotti, Govitrapong, & Kotchabhakdi, 2003). An attentive, sensitive foster parent who can cause epigenetic changes with positive results in an animal can even be a member of a different species! (This effect has long been obvious to many pet owners as well.)

It turns out that epigenetic changes can also be passed on across generations. Meaney and colleagues showed that female rat pups raised by more attentive and responsive mothers grew up to be more attentive and responsive mothers as well, thereby passing this trait that was epigenetically acquired through environmental experience to the next generation (Weaver et al., 2004). Male mice that were made diabetic through diet have also been found to pass that trait to their offspring via epigenetic changes in their sperm (Wei et al., 2014).

The random assignment of infant animals to the various caregiving conditions in these experiments obviously cannot be done with humans. But correlational evidence supporting epigenetic effects comes from cadaver studies of the brains of individuals who died by suicide compared with others who died suddenly from auto accidents, heart attacks, and other causes. A remarkable series of studies was make possible using data from the Quebec Suicide Brain Bank; validated psychiatric evaluations and developmental histories are available for all of the individuals whose brains are in the bank. McGowan et al. (2009) found increased DNA methylation (which accounts for the silencing of gene transcription) in a critical region of the hippocampus in only those individuals who committed suicide *and* had a history of child maltreatment. Child maltreatment further predicted the level of DNA methylation independent of the psychiatric status of the individuals. The effects of the Dutch "Hunger Winter" have also been studied extensively. Toward the end of World War II, Germany occupied part of the Netherlands and blocked all food and fuel shipments during the winter of 1944–45. The children of women who were pregnant during the famine were found to be smaller and more susceptible to diabetes, obesity, and heart disease later in life (Painter et al., 2008). Children in the second trimester of their mother's pregnancy during the famine also experienced a higher incidence of schizophrenia (Brown & Susser, 2008).

Nature versus nurture, or simply biopsychosocial development?

Until about the turn of the 21st century, the structure and function of both genes and neurons were commonly believed to be highly fixed and largely unaffected by environmental influence once the human brain had reached early critical stages of development. But that view has now been overturned. Research has found that the environment and experience change the structure and function of neurons and genomes through a variety of mechanisms. And epigenetic modifications that change the operation of the genome may be at levels similar to the high plasticity found in the growth and synaptic operation of neurons (Zhang & Meaney, 2010).

This research also demonstrates how correlation and causation have been seriously confused in past behavioral science research. When neurophysiological effects are correlated with behavior, the neurophysiological effects are sometimes assumed to be causative simply because they operate at a lower level of natural organization (e.g., depression and anxiety were assumed to be caused by chemical imbalances in the brain). It is now apparent that the environment causes many biological effects, and changes seen at the biological level can be mere manifestations of changes in a person's behavior. The effects of genetic inheritance and environmental influence are continually in dynamic interplay across the life span, and the effects of each can be understood only within the context of the other. Many years ago, the famous neuropsychologist Donald Hebb (the originator of the "cells that fire together, wire together" postulate) was asked about whether nature or nurture was more important in explaining individual differences in personality. Hebb (1958) responded that the question was similar to asking what contributes more to the area of a rectangle, the width or the length? His answer nicely captures the inextricably intertwined nature of biopsychosocial development and functioning.

Neural plasticity and epigenetics have become exciting topics in the neuro- and behavioral sciences recently. Some of the research has been overinterpreted (e.g., many epigenetic effects are actually transient) and the quality of studies has been variable (Sapolsky, 2017). But it is also very exciting to finally be uncovering the biological mechanisms underlying the interplay between nature and nurture. This research is also very helpful for convincing people about the negative effects of adverse experiences such as child maltreatment, toxic environments, and trauma—the relationships between experience and outcome are much more convincing once the underlying biology is understood (Harris, 2018). On the other hand, it is also discouraging because we have known these things for a long time—the argument that trauma, toxic environments, and the quality of one's childhood upbringing are critical in people's development was far more revolutionary when Freud and Watson made it. We have long known that abusive and neglectful parents and socially and physically toxic communities can negatively affect children's development and functioning, but we did not understand the underlying biological mechanisms that accounted for these effects. In behavioral health care and in public discourse generally, it is very helpful to be able to explain the underlying mechanisms associated with behavioral and developmental outcomes. We can also hope that this new knowledge will help change public policy as well as strengthening health care assessment and intervention.

A unified scientific perspective for understanding behavioral health care

Biology and psychology are young sciences but have come a very long way since the 19th century. Biology was still largely a descriptive science until Darwin published *On the Origin of Species* in 1859. The discovery of evolution transformed the understanding of plant and animal life on earth, although it took over a century for many of the details to be unraveled. And psychology has only relatively recently become fully integrated with the rest of the natural sciences. Clearly, there is still a great deal to learn about many biological and psychological processes and we are still near the beginning of learning the details involved.[6] But science has been advancing steadily and we now have a comprehensive, integrated perspective for understanding human nature from a scientific perspective.

Human psychology can be understood only by taking a developmental perspective that integrates the inextricably intertwined biological, psychological, and sociocultural influences on development and functioning. This perspective is so important that it is analogous to the three spatial dimensions (up–down, left–right, and forward–backward) plus the dimension of time that are required to conceptualize the physical world. There also is no scientific debate regarding the importance of evolutionary theory for understanding psychological characteristics and mechanisms. The evolutionary perspective is essential because it provides both ultimate explanations regarding the origin and function of psychological characteristics (i.e., why humans and other organisms are designed the way they are) as well as proximate explanations regarding the specific mechanisms and processes involved. As was noted earlier, human anatomy and physiology are essentially unintelligible without evolutionary theory, and the same is true for human cognition, emotion, and behavior, as well as social functioning and culture.

This volume emphasizes a *science-based* biopsychosocial approach because it is critical that this approach be differentiated from the eclecticism and theoretical integration with which the biopsychosocial approach was sometimes associated in the past. The biopsychosocial approach has been criticized as supporting an anarchic eclecticism whereby "anything goes" in terms of theoretical orientations for understanding and treating clinical syndromes (e.g., Ghaemi, 2010). It is true that behavioral health care was often practiced this way: clinicians had great freedom to choose from among biologically, psychologically, and socially oriented theories for understanding psychological processes. A clinical science operates very differently, however. When scientific knowledge accumulates to the point at which it provides a theoretically unified, evidence-based approach to understanding phenomena in an area, personally choosing from an array of competing theoretical orientations is no longer justified (Melchert, 2016). The contrast between the current scientific understanding of human psychology and the explanations provided by the traditional theoretical orientations is striking; there is relatively little overlap between the two. Therefore, there should be no confusion regarding the difference between the *science-based* biopsychosocial approach and the preparadigmatic eclecticism that was formerly sometimes associated with the term *biopsychosocial*.

Behavioral health care and medicine nonetheless remain extremely complicated enterprises. Especially in behavioral health, outcomes are typically multifactorially

[6] Although she was perhaps overly pessimistic about the current state of psychological science, the neuroscientist Patricia Churchland put it this way: "We're pre-Newton. We're pre-Kepler. We're still sussing out that there are moons around Jupiter" (quoted in Ouellette, 2014, p. 256).

determined, the result of many mechanisms and levels of influence interacting over time. As a result, there are often multiple targets that may be appropriate for clinical intervention. This is particularly true regarding chronic problems that have complex causation (e.g., a range of options are available for treating chronic depression and chronic heart disease, treatment is often lengthy and complicated, and prognosis is often uncertain in both cases). In addition, many serious physical and mental illnesses have a deteriorating course and even the most successful treatment may only slow the rate of deterioration. So even as the scientific understanding of health and illness steadily advances, physical and behavioral health care remain very complicated practices.

A science-based approach to learning and practicing behavioral health care is actually much more difficult than learning to practice on the basis of the traditional theoretical orientations because the actual complexity of human beings is much greater than what the traditional orientations described. The traditional theoretical orientations addressed only part of the biopsychosocial whole of human experience, and many of them focused only on particular psychological mechanisms. The scientific understanding of human psychology, on the other hand, is far more complex. Indeed, the human brain, the most complex system in the known universe, is almost unfathomably complex. In just a 3-lb organ, roughly 86 billion neurons, each with an average of thousand synaptic connections, carry our own personal history, our family's history, and even the entire evolutionary history of our species, while also constantly interacting with, being shaped by, and creating one's environment, at cooccurring subconscious and conscious levels. Despite this astounding complexity, much about our bodies, brains, and minds is also closely shared between individuals. All human beings now alive actually descend from the same parents, and our lineage is not very long, and so we are relatively closely related. The scientific study of the human mind and brain has revealed a wonderfully intricate, astonishingly complex, and truly amazing world of human experience.

Ethical foundations of behavioral health care

4

It was argued in Chapter 1 that science and ethics are both foundational to the responsible practice of psychology. There are many reasons why this is the case. First, the subject matter that patients bring to psychotherapy often involves matters that have major ethical implications. These sometimes even involve life and death issues (e.g., suicide) as well as many others that have ethically imbued and life-changing consequences for the person or others (e.g., responding to abusiveness or boredom in one's marriage or career; engaging in behavior that is harming one's partner or family without their knowledge; taking full responsibility for one's mental illness, substance abuse, or personality pathology; parenting children engaged in risky behavior; dealing with conflicts between personal values and religious or family expectations). Some ethical dilemmas that emerge in clinical practice can be excruciatingly difficult (e.g., an unmarried Muslim girl tells you that she acquired a sexually transmitted infection but begs you not to report it because she says she will be subjected to an honor killing if her very conservative family learns she had premarital sexual relations). Assisting people facing such consequential life decisions involves a very heavy ethical responsibility, and clinicians must be knowledgeable, sensitive, and skilled to be truly helpful and minimize the risks and harms that people face.

A solid foundation in professional ethics is also critical for dealing with many practical issues that clinicians deal with daily. For example, professional ethics and legal issues are strongly emphasized during graduate training and on licensure exams, and ethical behavior is a high priority for employers. Routine aspects of daily practice require solid preparation in professional ethics and legal issues as well (e.g., obtaining informed consent; maintaining appropriate confidentiality; handling a second-hand report of child abuse or a subpoena for patient records; responding to information that a colleague has acted in an unprofessional or unethical manner). Engaging in unethical behavior as a student or an employee is generally taken very seriously by faculty, supervisors, and managers and can quickly lead to major disciplinary consequences.

Ethical considerations are necessary for handling all these situations because competent clinical practice requires expertise that goes well beyond scientific knowledge and skill. Science is necessary for understanding many aspects of biopsychosocial development, functioning, and treatment, but behavioral health care requires a consideration of ethical guidelines and principles to determine how to appropriately apply scientific knowledge and tools. The same is true, of course, in other areas of life. Science can often explain what will happen if different courses of action are taken, but it can be thoroughly unhelpful when faced with a decision about how to respond to some of life's challenges and opportunities. It is also very limited in its ability to answer questions about how to address social, economic, and political problems and opportunities. This is because of the central role that values play in life. This is true not

Foundations of Health Service Psychology. https://doi.org/10.1016/B978-0-12-816426-6.00004-9

just in health care but in virtually all aspects of our social life. Many life circumstances involve value and ethical considerations that cannot be answered through appeals to science alone.

Another perspective for appreciating this point is to note that science is necessary for understanding *health*, whereas ethics is necessary for understanding *care*, and so both are necessary for practicing *health care*. Understanding many aspects of health, illness, and dysfunction requires scientific knowledge, but ethical considerations are critical for figuring out how to appropriately care for individuals with behavioral and physical health needs. All forms of caring relationships (e.g., parental caregiving of children, elder care, medical and nursing care, mental health care) are damaged when respect, compassion, trustworthiness, integrity, and other moral virtues are compromised, and moral principles are violated. These virtues and principles are especially important in behavioral health care due to the nature and role of the therapeutic relationship, patients' vulnerability when revealing very personal and distressing issues, and the stigma that behavioral health issues frequently carry in society (the effects of which can even outweigh the impairments due to the mental illness; Hinshaw & Stier, 2008).

An additional critical reason to focus on ethics in behavioral health care involves the nature of human moral reasoning and behavior. Research finds moral reasoning and behavior to be very complicated processes subject to a variety of emotional, intuitive, subconscious, and irrational influences. This research is critical for understanding why people behave in ways that harm themselves or others, why they can be so thoughtlessly self-centered, and why people can disagree so fundamentally over personal behavior and social issues. Individuals' feelings, thoughts, and behaviors that others frequently find so frustrating, confusing, or morally wrong often seem inexplicable without knowledge of this research. This knowledge is also necessary for therapists to avoid shortcomings in their own ethical reasoning (and those of the organizations and institutions with which we work).

All these considerations point to the central importance of professional ethics in behavioral health care. Scientific analysis and evidence clarify many important issues in the field, but supplementing those with solid preparation in professional ethics is necessary for sound clinical decision-making. At all levels, from managing routine responsibilities of daily practice to developing institutional and social policy, ethics play a fundamental role in behavioral health care.

To clarify the role of ethics in behavioral health care, this chapter focuses on ethical theory and its implications for behavioral health care practice. Humans have always been concerned with questions of right and wrong, good and evil, innocence and guilt (indeed, our daily thoughts and feelings repeatedly return to these questions, and it can be very hard to get them out of our heads). For thousands of years, the world's religions, philosophies, and many of its most important written documents have been centrally concerned with these questions. In fact, an ancient philosopher such as Aristotle could probably follow current discussions regarding the nature of human morality and health care ethics even if he could not follow contemporary discussions about medical science and technology. Ethical theory plays a central role in social life and is critical for understanding health care practice, research, and policy. Before discussing the importance of ethical theory in health care, research on the nature of moral reasoning and behavior is reviewed to convey how complicated the questions are that ethical theory attempts to address. Human moral reasoning is much more complicated than what was commonly believed even just a couple decades ago.

A science-based biopsychosocial perspective on moral reasoning and behavior

Substantial progress has been made recently in the scientific understanding of human moral reasoning and behavior. Comprehensively reviewing the literature in this area is not possible here, but highlighting several recent findings points out the complex dynamics involved and the need for careful attention to this topic. Of particular importance are the findings of substantial irrationality in human moral reasoning.

Irrationality in human cognition and moral reasoning

Before recent decades, moral reasoning was generally thought to result from reflective, deliberative, logical reasoning. Kohlberg's (1971) well-known stage model of moral development provided a very popular perspective. He proposed that people progressed from imitative, obedience-based approaches as small children through increasingly complex approaches involving logical analysis and broader principles. But subsequent research found that moral reasoning was far more complex than that. Carol Gilligan (1982) pointed out that girls and women were more likely to include caring and feelings of responsibility to others in their moral judgments than boys and men were. Haidt (2001) then noted that cognitive approaches to morality could not handle four important observations about moral behavior. First, although conscious reasoning, reflection, and deliberation are important in many moral judgments, many judgments are made very rapidly and automatically without conscious reasoning. Second, individuals are often quite defensive about their moral judgments and seek out evidence and arguments to defend their judgments rather than to analyze them in an objective, logical manner aimed at finding the "truth" of the matter. Third, evidence has suggested that moral reasoning often *follows*, rather than precedes, judgments and behaviors and provides post hoc explanations to justify intuitive judgments and moral or immoral actions. Finally, emotion is found to play a larger role than conscious reasoning in many moral judgments and actions. These findings all suggest that major aspects of moral reasoning are not logical or rational (Bargh, 2017; Bloom, 2016; Haidt, 2001, 2012; Mikulincer & Shaver, 2012; Ramachandran, 2011; Sharot, 2017).

The role of irrationality in human cognition has been studied extensively by Daniel Kahneman (in 2002 he became the second psychologist ever to win a Nobel Prize). Kahneman and his colleague Amos Tversky (who died in 1996) began investigating cognitive biases that unconsciously distort our judgments about the world. These biases operate even among highly trained and experienced professionals (e.g., a group of German judges with an average of more than 15 years of experience rolled a pair of dice that were loaded to give either a 3 or a 9, and after rolling the higher number they stated they would give a shoplifter a much longer sentence than was the case after they rolled a 3; Englich, Mussweiler, & Strack, 2006). Kahneman and Tversky's most famous experiment involved telling research participants about an imaginary 31-year-old woman named Linda who was single, outspoken, very bright, and deeply concerned about discrimination and social justice when she was a student. In one of their studies, a group of doctoral students in the decision-making program at the Stanford Graduate School of Business was asked which is more probable: Linda is a bank teller, or Linda is a bank teller and is active in the feminist movement (Tversky & Kahneman, 1983). Despite having completed several courses in statistics, probability, and decision theory, 85% of the students chose "feminist bank teller" as more likely than "bank teller" (which is wrong because every feminist bank teller is a bank teller and adding an additional condition only lowers the probability of its occurrence).

The Linda experiment illustrates what Kahneman (2012) and others refer to as System 1 and 2 thinking. System 1 thinking is fast, automatic, intuitive, and largely unconscious. It produces a "quick and dirty" draft of reality that is often quite accurate and useful when we must respond quickly to threats and opportunities in life. System 2, on the other hand, is slow, deliberate, analytical, and requires conscious effort. Although the deliberate and rational System 2 thinking is beneficial in many cases, this system is lazy and often accepts the easy though frequently unreliable story about the world provided by System 1. In the "Linda" experiment, six out of seven doctoral business students, despite their expertise in probability, chose the easy, automatic answer provided by System 1. Kahneman (2012) notes that "The sophisticated allocation of attention [to rely on System 1 thinking] has been honed by a long evolutionary history. Orienting and responding quickly to the gravest threats or most promising opportunities improved the chance of survival" (p. 35). Our reliance on the less effortful System 1, however, also suggests that "Laziness is built deep into our nature" (p. 35).

Kahneman also found surprising dynamics in people's judgments about their level of happiness. For example, when asked retrospectively how happy they are with various events in their lives (e.g., a vacation or dental visit), people tend to remember their peak level of pain or pleasure, or the way the experiences ended. If they kept an ongoing record of their actual experience, sampled from moment to moment, their average level of "experienced" well-being could be quite different from their retrospectively "remembered" well-being. This was demonstrated in a study of patients undergoing colonoscopies (Redelmeier & Kahneman, 1996). One group received a standard colonoscopy that was quite uncomfortable (this was before anesthetic drugs were widely used with this procedure), and a second group received the standard colonoscopy but also received several extra minutes of mild discomfort added on to the end of the exam (without being told). The second group obviously experienced all of the pain that the first group did and then some, but their procedure ended less painfully. The researchers found that the patients in the second group remembered their pain as substantially lower. The pain level at the end of the procedure had a large effect, whereas the actual duration of the pain had no effect whatsoever on their reports of the total amount of pain they experienced. Kahneman (2012) wrote that "Odd as it may seem, I am my remembering self, and the experiencing self, who does my living, is like a stranger to me" (p. 390).

Research is now clarifying the neural basis for some of these surprising cognitive processes. For example, people often assume that the natural or strongly felt response to a moral situation is the morally correct one, even though it may be based on automatic processing rather than a deliberate approach to carefully arriving at the correct moral decision. In a demonstration of this effect, Greene (2003) asked one group of participants to imagine they encountered a man who was badly injured in a fall and asked to be taken to the nearby hospital. You want to help but if you give him a ride, his blood may stain the upholstery in your car. Is it appropriate to decline taking this man to the hospital in order to keep your upholstery clean? Greene asked the second group of participants to imagine they were opening their mail and read a letter from a reputable international aid organization asking for a small donation to provide much-needed medical care to poor people in another part of the world. Is it morally acceptable to pass on making a donation?

With regard to the first situation, a large majority of people say that it would be horribly selfish to refuse the man's request for help (Greene, 2003). The man badly needs medical attention and you are in a position to provide it without great cost. On the other hand, in the second situation, most people say it is not morally wrong to ignore the request from the aid organization. It would be admirable to help people in faraway places with life-threatening medical needs, but we are not obligated to provide assistance. The costs involved in these two situations might be similar (i.e., the cost of getting one's car upholstery cleaned may be about the same as the donation). Nonetheless, people tend to respond in opposite ways even though only one person in the first situation would be helped while a larger number of people could be helped in the second.

Functional magnetic resonance imaging studies conducted by Greene and others (e.g., Green, Nystrom, Engell, Darley, & Cohen, 2004; Greene, 2003; Hauser, 2006) found that moral dilemmas that are personal in nature, such as the first one above, are associated with greater activity in the emotional and social cognition areas of the brain. In those situations, people typically experience strong, immediate feelings regarding the appropriate moral response. Impersonal situations, such as the second dilemma, are associated with greater activity in areas associated with abstract reasoning and cognitive control, less activity in the emotion and social processing areas, and no automatic feelings about the morality of the situation. This difference likely has an evolutionary basis because over the course of human history, a survival advantage was gained by those who were concerned about the well-being of people they were close to. Indeed, altruism appears to have developed as a characteristic of humans and other social animals because of its importance to the survival of the group as a whole (see the next section). When examined objectively, however, place of residence may not be a relevant consideration for judging the value of human life; perhaps all human lives should be valued equally. Deep, subconscious biases such as these lead to humans' strong tendencies toward tribalism, preferences and tolerance toward members of one's own group, and fear and disapproval of members of other groups (Greene, 2013; Haidt, 2012; Wrangham, 2019).

Even the deeply admired virtue of empathy has serious limitations. Bloom (2016) noted that empathy can be a very poor guide for how to act morally. First, it is typically biased for people in one's circle such as their family, community, or ethnic group. For example, when a person is motivated to give to charity based on empathy, the person usually gives to people who are like themselves while ignoring many others (perhaps millions of others) who may have a greater need for help. Second, empathizing does not account for the number of people involved (it cannot count). Like a spotlight, it focuses attention on the plight of one person (or even a puppy) while billions of people are currently or will be harmed by factors such as pollution and climate change. Third, the weaknesses of empathy can be used to manipulate the public, as when politicians intentionally use people's empathy for an in-group victim to motivate anger toward out-groups or minorities. It can also lead to very bad public policy, as when advocates against particular policies use stories (true or even false) about particular victims while ignoring the far larger and more important issues involved (e.g., a single death due to a reaction to a vaccine while many, many other lives are saved by the same vaccine).

Another fascinating aspect of human morality concerns the nature of dishonesty. Dan Ariely (2012) and his colleagues have found that individuals commonly cheat in a wide variety of laboratory and naturalistic settings so they can personally benefit. For example, when they can easily get away with it, most college students will report solving roughly 15% more problems on a math exercise than they actually did so they will be reimbursed more for their research participation (Ariely, 2012). To explain these findings, Ariely and his colleagues proposed a "fudge factor theory" that involves two opposing motivations: individuals want to view themselves as honest, honorable people, but they also want to gain as much money as possible (Mazar, Amir, & Ariely, 2008). Ariely and others have also found that a variety of social and cognitive factors affect the amount of cheating people engage in. For example, people are more likely to steal things than they are to steal money (e.g., students will take cans of soda from a dormitory refrigerator, but not one-dollar bills sitting on a plate next to the soda; Mazar et al., 2008); they also will cheat more when they are fatigued (Mead, Baumeister, Gino, Schweitzer, & Ariely, 2009), after they see others cheat and get away with it (Gino, Ayal, & Ariely, 2009), and after they are given counterfeit sunglasses to try out versus those who are given authentic designer sunglasses to try out (Gino, Norton, & Ariely, 2010). They found that few people cheat to a maximal degree, but a large proportion cheat in small amounts, and the amount of their cheating can be significantly increased or decreased through a variety of cognitive and social manipulations (Ariely, 2012).

The above research shows that subconscious cognitive factors not only are a major influence on human moral reasoning and behavior but also can be very disruptive and harmful depending on the situation. Much of human behavior is simply unintelligible without knowledge of this research. These factors affect patients' ethical decision-making within their own lives, but therapists' own decision-making is also affected by these factors. Therefore, therapists need to be familiar with this research so they can process ethical issues with their patients in an informed manner, process their own ethical reasoning and behavior properly, and work to help the profession and society deal more effectively with the ethical complexities of human psychology and behavioral health care.

The evolution of cooperative and prosocial behavior

Evolutionary theory is useful for understanding moral behavior because it focuses on *ultimate* explanations regarding the origin and nature of cooperation, altruism, and pro- and antisocial behavior as well as *proximate* explanations regarding the mechanisms involved (such as those discussed previously). The following section briefly reviews the evolutionary origins of cooperative and prosocial behavior to highlight the importance of a science-based biopsychosocial approach to understanding human psychology.

The nature of cooperative, prosocial behavior and altruism among humans has been one of the most challenging questions in evolutionary theory and research. Humans show remarkable proclivities to cooperate in terms of child-rearing and family life, economic exchanges, religious and political practices, and military defense. Indeed, our remarkable ability to cooperate in these ways is a defining characteristic of human beings and has played an essential role in our success as a species (Krebs, 2005; Price, 2011). Humans evolved to pursue not only their own self-interest to maximize their personal chances of survival and reproduction but also their collective actions to promote the common good of the whole community. Human culture universally fosters norms for self-control, honesty, fairness, cooperation, bravery, empathy for others' distress, and subordinating the interests of the individual to those of the group (Gintis, Bowles, Boyd, & Fehr, 2007; Mesoudi & Jensen, 2012). These critically important prosocial human characteristics were not predicted, however, by Darwin's theory of natural selection and the survival of the fittest.

Darwin (1859) was aware that altruism presented a serious challenge to his theory. The primary engine of adaptation by natural selection involves maximizing the fitness of individuals so that they can survive, outcompete rivals, and reproduce. Altruism necessarily benefits others at one's own expense, however, and would promptly be eliminated by natural selection. Darwin noted that "If it could be proved that any part of the structure of any one species had been formed for the exclusive good of another species, it would annihilate my theory, for such could not have been produced through natural selection" (p. 190). Over a century later, E. O. Wilson (1975) regarded altruism as still "the central theoretical problem of sociobiology" (p. 3).

Explaining altruistic cooperation required a switch in focus in evolutionary theory from the reproducing individual to the replicating gene. W. D. Hamilton (1963, 1964) argued that the gene should be the fundamental focus of evolution and that the gene can successfully replicate not only by promoting the reproduction of its carrier but also by promoting the reproduction of any individuals who carry copies of itself. Based on this concept, Richard Dawkins (1976) noted that genes are "replicators" and individual bodies are the "vehicles" they build in order to enable themselves to replicate. So Darwin's theory was primarily a theory about the adaptation of individuals in competition to survive, while Hamilton showed that genes that promote the survival of genetic relatives increase the *inclusive fitness* of the kin group. Trivers (1971) hypothesized that cooperation between individuals can evolve if partners engage in mutually beneficial exchanges of altruistic acts. The return altruism may happen far into the future, but as long as one can trust that the altruism will be reciprocated, engaging in altruistic acts can be highly adaptive. There are many examples of mutually beneficial relationships between individuals and even species in nature (e.g., puppies huddling together to share body heat, and the flora that live in the human digestive tract but also provide their hosts with a range of beneficial services; Guarner & Malagelada, 2003).

Humans are unique as a cooperative species. Indeed, we are the best example of a truly reciprocally altruistic species (Trivers, 1971). Although many species of social mammals display reciprocal altruism, "genuine altruism" is primarily a human attribute (Moll, Oliveira-Souza, & Zahn, 2008). Our ability to cooperate and altruistically reciprocate in very large groups on a wide variety of economic, political, religious, and cultural activities is a remarkable phenomenon that does not occur in the rest of the animal kingdom. In addition, humans have evolved mechanisms for punishing those who violate prosocial cooperative norms (e.g., "cheaters") and those who take advantage of others' altruism but do not reciprocate by giving back ("free riders"; Boyd, Gintis, Bowles, & Richerson, 2003). Groups that have evolved mechanisms for internalizing these kinds of cooperative norms will outcompete groups with socially neutral or antisocial norms (Gintis et al., 2007). This is a prototypical example of *gene-culture coevolution* (Wilson, 1975). Culture affects the evolution of genetically controlled biological characteristics, but biology also affects the evolution of culture. Biology and culture are not independent but rather codependent realms that continually interact (e.g., humans would not exist if we had not evolved family structures that provided care for the extremely long developmental period needed by human infants and children to mature).

Our evolutionary inheritance of cognitive mechanisms for cooperation has led to humans possessing an innate and universal system of moral evaluation (Bloom, 2016; Haidt, 2001). Human babies, for example, respond to morally relevant properties of events. They display empathy and compassion by crying when they hear other babies cry and soothing others in distress. They will altruistically help out others, including strangers. They distinguish between "good guys" and "bad guys" and show clear preferences for prosocial behavior and punishment of bad behavior (Bloom, 2016). Babies are also alert to outsiders, even unfamiliar accents, and become fearful of strangers. These innate responses of *Homo sapiens* have unfortunately led to high levels of tribalism and mistreatment of others but also to remarkable levels of kindness, cooperation, generosity, and fairness. As Wrangham (2019, p. 3) put it, "We are not merely the most intelligent of animals … We can be the nastiest of species and also the nicest."

We have evolved to care about ourselves, others, and the world, and the evolutionary origins of our moral reasoning and behavior are visible in many of our thoughts, feelings, and actions. Among these are our capacities for cooperation, prosocial behavior, and altruism, which are defining characteristics of humans and ultimately responsible for the unique and powerful nature of human experience and the truly remarkable accomplishments of human culture. Cooperative prosocial behavior provided humans with a distinct survival advantage. And as human communities grew over the last 10,000 years since agriculture was discovered, human relationships became more complex and culture more advanced; various internalized norms for appropriate behavior were eventually formalized and became the basis for ethical theory and law. Contemporary systems of ethical theory, law, and professional codes of ethics are the most recent incarnations of these archaic human qualities. The tragically exploitative and selfish ways that humans frequently behave toward each other are also evolved characteristics. Obviously, though, we would not have made it to the present if we had not also evolved prosocial mechanisms that ensure that we raise our very dependent young children in communities of caring families, friends, and neighbors.

The importance of ethical theory

Science and nature have little to say about ethics and deciding what is right and wrong when it comes to human affairs. The universe and "Mother Nature" are basically silent on these issues. If we behave so badly toward each other or the environment that we all die and *Homo sapiens* go extinct, the universe will not care at all. Science increasingly can show how different courses of action are likely to play out, but it cannot inform us as to the right way to organize human affairs. This is true from the smallest to the largest scales, from deciding on how to respond when you catch a patient telling a falsehood to deciding on whether a nation's military action is justified. One could rely on moral intuition, religion, or cultural traditions to decide these things, but it is essentially impossible to do that in our modern, pluralistic, and highly interdependent world. This is especially true in the context of modern health care.

The conceptual foundations advocated for in this volume emphasize that a grounding in the underlying theory of professional ethics is necessary for gaining a deeper, more thorough, and useful understanding of the role of ethics in behavioral health practice, research, and policy. It is of course essential to be knowledgeable about the many specific ethics codes, laws, rules, and policies that govern mental health practice. But having familiarity with only these codes, rules, and policies without understanding the foundational principles from which they are (or should be) derived can result in a perfunctory and flawed analysis of many ethical dilemmas. The underlying principles are also critical for informing health care, social, and economic policy that should be designed to promote health and well-being in the population in general.

Ethical violations can sting very deeply. Further, deciding moral questions can be very complex. For example, some version of the "Golden Rule" is found in many of the world's religions and secular ethical systems, and it provides reliable guidance for many ethical questions. But upon closer examination, it is evident that many ethical questions are far more complex than those that can be handled by the Golden Rule. This is especially true in modern societies where governmental and societal institutions struggle to manage a staggeringly complicated array of human needs; economic, technological, and environmental issues; and foreign and domestic security issues; as well as attempt to enrich culture and society and promote health and human well-being. Managing all these concerns in a fair and effective manner requires carefully developed ethical systems. This is especially important given all the weaknesses of human moral cognition and behavior outlined above.

Many people in modern, wealthy countries go about their daily lives without major risks to their personal security and property, and so we sometimes forget what a remarkable and recent phenomenon this is. But just over a century and a half ago, millions of people in the U.S. were *owned* by others and forced to do slave labor. Just a century ago, women still could not vote. Just three-quarters of a century ago, wars were common, conscription was the norm, and combatant casualties and civilian atrocities were horrific and commonplace. Human immorality and rights abuses are of course still far too widespread, but it staggers the mind to contemplate the scale of past injustices. It is hard to imagine how our ancestors coped as victims or justified their actions as perpetrators of injustice. (And if we go back far enough, our ancestors probably fell on both sides of the equation at different times.)

Why are humans so completely immoral at times? Trying to understand the tremendous amount of immorality that has existed throughout the world over the centuries is confusing in part because it seems that humans have always had a strong moral sense and many antisocial behaviors have been morally prohibited for a very long time. There is not complete agreement among ethicists regarding the universality of ethics across cultures and religions, but authorities generally agree that all individuals who are committed to morality across cultures, time, and place agree on the basic foundations of ethics, and there consequently does exist a universal common morality (e.g., Beauchamp & Childress, 2013; Council for the Parliament of the World's Religions, 1993; Gert, Culver, & Clouser, 2006; Universal Declaration of Human Rights of the United Nations, 1948). Culturally specific aspects of a universal morality often vary greatly across religious groups, institutions, and even professions, but there is significant agreement among ethicists and religious and political leaders that a basic, universal morality does exist. Why then has it not worked better?

The question of moral status

People have been exploited and treated unjustly, often with horrible cruelty, throughout human history. And yet people have also claimed for just as long that such acts are totally morally wrong and therefore absolutely prohibited. The perpetration of immoral behavior is sometimes attributable to psychopathic behavior committed by a small minority of individuals who frequently justify it on the basis of entirely selfish motives. But a more important reason that moral standards have not been applied consistently across individuals and groups involves the problem of moral status—not everyone is given a status that requires that they are treated morally. Across history, enemies, slaves, and animals often had no moral status, and their rights and interests received essentially no moral consideration at all. Women and children often had lower moral status, and their rights and interests often received limited consideration (Beauchamp & Childress, 2013). Before the Enlightenment, "commoners" in general (which included most of our ancestors) often fell into this latter category as well.

Since the Enlightenment of the 18th century, there has been a dramatic increase in the range of people whose rights and interests have received moral consideration. It might appear that societies and institutions began embracing higher moral standards, particularly with regard to slaves, women, children, and minorities, but the bigger difference is that larger numbers of people were extended moral status that previously was given only to certain privileged groups. Singer (1981) noted how Americans' "moral circle" expanded significantly following the Civil War. Before that time, humans' moral treatment of others normally did not extend beyond their immediate group. Before the Civil War, many Americans were unconcerned about the morality of some people owning others as slaves or the rights of women, minorities, children, or nonhuman animals in general. The eugenics movement was widely supported during the first half of the 20th century, and the rights of psychiatric patients, prisoners, and other "degenerates" were severely limited in many localities in the U.S. Before the Civil Rights era of the 1960s, the majority of Americans thought interracial marriage was wrong, and now few do. Views regarding the rights of LGBT individuals to marry and have full legal rights has recently changed in several parts of the world.

Today, those legally judged to be mentally incompetent normally have limited moral status in the sense that guardians are given the legal right and responsibility to make decisions for them. Many fascinating questions remain about whether comatose patients, anencephalic babies, fetuses, embryos, human eggs, and even animals deserve full moral rights (Beauchamp, Walters, Kahn, & Mastroianni, 2008; Jecker, Jonsen, & Pearlman, 2007). The rights of animals used in research have been a particularly contentious issue. In addition, health care professionals often care for children and adults who are ill, impaired, disabled, or otherwise vulnerable, and important decisions often must be made when these individuals are not able to participate fully in decision-making. Behavioral health professionals also sometimes work with people who represent a risk of harm to others. These cases raise complex ethical and legal questions regarding whether these individuals can be detained even when they have not committed a crime, detained after they have served their criminal punishments (e.g., in the case of child molesters in states that have sexual predator laws), or have their rights restricted in other ways (e.g., in terms of gun ownership).

Examining morality from the perspective of who has moral status shows how moral reasoning and behavior have evolved dramatically in recent decades and centuries. It is simply shocking to consider that many ethical principles that we now take for granted were not even considered when it came to many groups of people in the past. This examination also presents a very different picture than that advocated by some of those who yearn for "the good old days." Much of the progress made resulted from philosophical analyses during the Enlightenment that were subsequently implemented in law and policy, and culture changed dramatically as a result. These cultural changes also changed individuals' behaviors, thoughts, and even emotional responses.

Our review of ethical theory will start with the historically most important general ethical theories developed during and after the Enlightenment. These theories have been very influential for providing the conceptual justification for law, social policy, codes of ethics for the professions, and informing health care ethics specifically. The following overview of the most important general ethical theories that inform contemporary biomedical ethics is very brief but helps convey a sense of their strengths, their weaknesses, and how they can be integrated to arrive at a coherent and systematic approach for managing health care practice, research, and policy.

Consequentialist theory

Jeremy Bentham (1748–1832) and John Stuart Mill (1806–1873) developed the most influential consequentialist approach to ethics, often called utilitarianism because of the priority given to the principle of utility. Actions are right or wrong according to their balance of good and bad consequences—i.e., their utility. This approach is often associated with the maxim that "We ought to promote the greatest good for the greatest number" or at least the least disvalue when all options are undesirable. From this perspective, the ends justify the means if the benefits of an action outweigh harms resulting from the action. Mill and Bentham are considered *hedonistic* consequentialists because they emphasized happiness or pleasure as the goals to be maximized. More recent utilitarians argue that values such as knowledge, health, success, and deep personal relationships also contribute to individual well-being (Beauchamp & Childress, 2013; Griffin, 1986).

Utilitarianism is very helpful for formulating public and institutional policy because it takes an objective approach to evaluating outcomes and emphasizes the promotion of well-being. But neither is it a fully adequate theory of ethics (Beauchamp & Childress, 2013; Cohen & Cohen, 1999; Freeman, 2000). For example, some preferences might be considered immoral regardless of any weighing of harms and benefits (e.g., sadism, pedophilia, inflicting pain on animals). It also does not answer the question of whether maximizing value is an obligation that must be observed (e.g., is one obligated to donate one of his or her kidneys to a relative because one can be fully healthy with just one kidney?). Another problem concerns whether the interests of the majority can override the rights of minorities. Should the rights and interests of even the smallest minority be protected independent of the weighing of costs and benefits? Should education, police protection, and health care be provided to all individuals in a society even if it is relatively costly to provide these services to particular groups (e.g., cigarette smokers)?

Deontological or Kantian approaches

Immanuel Kant (1724–1804) emphasized a very different set of obligations than those of the consequentialists. From his perspective, duties (*deon* is Greek for duty), obligations, and rights are the highest authority, and right actions are not determined solely by the consequences of actions. Ends do not justify means if they violate basic obligations and rights, and human beings must always be treated as ends and never as means only (Beauchamp & Childress, 2013; Donagan, 1977). From Kant's perspective, morally acceptable decisions are applicable categorically in all situations that are similar in relevant ways, and people must never be treated merely as a means to our ends.

Kant made the important point, now generally accepted, that moral rules and obligations must be applied categorically and there should be no exceptions for one's self, one's friends or associates, or any favored group. But his approach also has weaknesses (Beauchamp & Childress, 2013; Cohen & Cohen, 1999). Kant strongly emphasized moral obligations but did not provide solutions for dealing with situations when we have multiple moral obligations (e.g., an emergency at work requires our attention even though we promised to leave with our family on vacation or our mother was hospitalized with a serious illness). Kant has also been criticized for emphasizing reason above all other considerations, including emotion, suffering, and pain, and consequently his arguments against suicide and other issues have been viewed as inadequate. Many of the moral obligations we feel are also based on the nature of the relationships we have with family, friends, coworkers, and neighbors—the ethical correctness of our behavior in these situations is significantly affected by the commitments we have to these individuals, not by objective moral obligations to people in general.

Rights theory

Concern about human rights has been growing in importance, and rights theory is now often considered the most important theoretical perspective informing systems of ethics (Beauchamp & Childress, 2013). Philosophers such as Thomas Hobbes (1588–1679) and John Locke (1632–1704) emphasized the importance of human rights and civil liberties, and their rights-based theorizing became strongly integrated into the Anglo-American legal system. Hobbes famously remarked that without strong government that provides basic protection of individual rights, security, and rule of law, life is "nasty, brutish, and short" (1651/2002, p. xiii).

From this perspective, basic human rights to autonomy, privacy, property, free speech, and worship are foundational to the functioning of civil society. But though these rights are very strong, they are not absolute. For example, one's right to life is perhaps the strongest of the rights an individual can hold, and yet it too can be overridden in cases of war and self-defense (whether there is an exception for those found guilty of capital punishment remains controversial). Rights are also considered prima facie binding (i.e., on first face or impression); that is, when first considering an ethical situation, rights need to be observed, although they may be overridden depending on the circumstances (Beauchamp & Childress, 2013; Dworkin, 1977). In health care, patient rights to informed consent, confidentiality, refusal of treatment, and lifesaving emergency care all function in this way. Rights are also correlated with obligations. If someone has a right to something (e.g., education, health care), then others have obligations to provide the resources and services needed to provide that right. Tensions between having a right to something and the corresponding obligations of others to help provide for that right are a perennial source of conflict between those who emphasize liberal individualism (i.e., freedom from government intrusions) and those who emphasize government services and controls to provide for an orderly, secure, and efficient economy and society (e.g., those who emphasize government regulation of industry, quality education for all children, and health care for all citizens).

In recent decades, rights theory has been more influential than any of the other ethical theories for strengthening civil rights in the U.S. and human rights around the world. This perspective offers individuals clear protections against unjust treatment and is critical to the effective and humane functioning of society. But rights theory can also be viewed as providing a limited perspective on morality (Beauchamp & Childress, 2013; Cohen & Cohen, 1999). Prioritizing rights without considering people's motives or integrity results in a very limited perspective on ethics. For example, it is not always moral to do what we have a right to do (e.g., if the free market is allowed to determine prices, can clinicians and hospitals charge exorbitant rates when someone has a medical or psychiatric emergency? If someone is drunk or confused, is it acceptable to take advantage of their compromised state to get them to give you what you want?). Rights theorists also emphasize protecting individual rights from government intrusion but give limited attention to the interests and well-being of the community, including things like public health and security, educated citizens, the protection of vulnerable individuals and animals, and culture in general (the famous Supreme Court Justice Oliver Wendell Holmes once remarked, "I like to pay taxes. With them I buy civilization"; 1939, pp. 42–43).

Virtue theory

Cultivation of moral virtues and character traits was one of the primary goals of morality for Aristotle. This approach to ethics is quite different and largely independent of the theories described above but is commonly viewed as critical for judging ethical behavior. We respect people who are fair, honest, respectful, and caring but condemn people who are dishonest, uncaring, selfish, or dishonorable (Beauchamp & Childress, 2013; Cohen & Cohen, 1999). People's motivations are critical to judging the consequences of actions. Moral principles, rights, and obligations are important; we judge a person who makes a mistake but acts with the right motives and character more positively than a person who makes the same mistake but feels no remorse because they did not really care about the consequences of their actions.

Acting with virtuous motivations is critical when considering the behavior of those with whom we have relationships. It can be a crushing realization when one becomes aware that a friend or partner who responds in a helpful manner did so merely out of obligation rather than truly valuing the relationship. Likewise, virtue theorists are concerned that health care professionals acting out of perfunctory respect for rules, codes, and policies will provide less compassionate and humane care than that provided by professionals acting out of a sense of respect, compassion, and conscientiousness (Hursthouse, 2001).

The long history of virtue theory dating back to Aristotle reflects its importance in human affairs, and virtue theory is especially important when evaluating caregiving of all kinds. But this approach, too, has limitations. Virtuous motivations alone are insufficient for guiding moral behavior—a health care professional with the strongest moral motivations but who provides incompetent care does not engage in ethical behavior. Therefore, the perspectives outlined earlier also need to be considered to construct a comprehensive system of morality. In addition, moral virtue and character are prized in close relationships where trust has been established but can be less relevant when trust and familiarity have not been established. Other considerations are very important when strangers interact, which is often the case in health services. In health care, ethical principles, codes, and rules play essential roles in terms of obtaining informed consent to treatment, decision-making when a patient is impaired, highly upset, or incompetent, and in many other situations (Beauchamp & Childress, 2013).

Principle-based, common morality approach to biomedical ethics

None of the moral theories outlined above adequately resolves all moral conflicts. Consequently, none can by themselves provide a satisfactory foundation for biomedical ethics (Beauchamp & Childress, 2013; Rawls, 1999). Each has strengths and weaknesses, each brings a valuable perspective the others lack, and some serve particular purposes better than others. Utilitarianism is useful for setting public policy, and rights theory plays an important role in establishing legal standards, while deontological and virtue theories are useful for guiding many health care practices. There is even neuroscientific evidence that the human brain relies on multiple types of information processing when faced with different types of moral dilemmas (e.g., personal and subjective vs. impersonal and objective situations), and these different types of processing correspond to the different priorities associated with the different ethical theories (Greene, Nystrom, Engell, Darley, & Cohen, 2004).

Leading ethicists such as Rawls (1999) and Beauchamp and Childress (2013) use a combination of deductive and inductive approaches to resolve the problem of developing a coherent system of biomedical ethics. They recommend combining common sense moral traditions (inductive) with ethical principles derived from the above theories to provide structure and coherence (deductive). Beauchamp and Childress (2013) define the common morality as "the set of norms shared by all persons committed to morality" (p. 417). They argue that the common morality is universal and not relative to cultures, religions, professional organizations, or individuals. A process called "reflective equilibrium" (Rawls, 1999) is then applied wherein common moral beliefs, principles, and theoretical propositions are analyzed and critiqued so that the resulting system becomes increasingly consistent and coherent internally. New scientific, technological, and cultural developments can also be incorporated into the common morality through this process. It should be noted that scientists use a similar combination of inductive approaches (e.g., careful observation and verification to develop hypotheses) and deductive approaches (e.g., tests of theory-derived hypotheses) to make improvements in theoretical explanations of phenomena.

Beauchamp and Childress (seventh ed., 2013; first edition, 1977) applied this procedure in the case of biomedical ethics and derived four basic ethical principles. Their approach, sometimes referred to as the *four-principles approach*, has become the most influential and accepted approach in biomedical ethics in the U.S., Europe, and probably the world (Gert, Culver, & Clouser, 1997; Schone-Seifert, 2006). Most ethics texts in health service psychology as well as the APA (2010) Ethics Code also incorporate these foundational principles. They need to be appreciated so that ethics codes, laws, policies, and rules are not applied in a perfunctory, mechanical manner insensitive to the circumstances of particular cases. The four principles in the Beauchamp and Childress approach (i.e., respect for autonomy, nonmaleficence, beneficence, and justice) are all important; none is most important, and each can take priority over the others depending on the issue and circumstances.

Respect for autonomy

The word *autonomy* is derived from the Greek words *auto* (meaning self) and *nomos* (meaning rule or governance). The concept originally referred to the self-governance of independent city-states but has since been applied to individuals as well. To be fully autonomous (e.g., to be completely free from control by others and be the source of one's own values, beliefs, and life plans) is unrealistic because humans are highly social animals, and modern life in democratic societies requires high levels of accommodation, collaboration, and participation. Even one's self-identity, values, beliefs, and preferences are highly influenced by socialization and relationships. Therefore, the focus is on individuals who act freely according to self-chosen plans and without limitations that prevent meaningful choices (Beauchamp & Childress, 2013).

In order for a person to choose and act freely without unreasonable limitations, other people need to respect the autonomy of that person (Beauchamp & Childress, 2013). For example, if a woman or member of an ethnic minority hopes to be judged on the basis of merit for a job promotion or admission to a university but those making the promotion or admissions decision employ bias or favoritism based on group membership, then the person's merit may not impact the decision. Therefore, this principle emphasizes *respecting others'* rights to autonomy, not just claiming a right to autonomy for one's self. This emphasis also obligates us to work to overcome barriers and obstacles that prevent people from being autonomous. For example, the American Civil Liberties Union (ACLU) has protected the free speech rights of the American Nazi Party and other similar groups even when those groups expressed views and values that the ACLU finds repulsive. (In 1977, the American Nazi Party planned to hold a parade in Skokie, Illinois, where one in six residents was a survivor or directly related to a survivor of the Nazi Holocaust. The ACLU defended their right to assembly and free speech after the city attempted to stop the parade because of the importance of respecting others' rights to autonomy; Strum, 1999). This principle also obligates health care professionals to encourage autonomous decision-making by patients. Because professionals typically possess expertise not held by patients, professionals are obligated to provide information and explanations using understandable language in a manner that fosters responsible and voluntary decision-making by patients (APA, 2010, Ethics Code 3.10).

Many behavioral health care patients, however, are not in a position to act autonomously. Children as a group are not able to understand and protect their own interests and welfare and consequently are given few of the rights afforded adults. Suicidal individuals in crisis or those with cognitive disabilities or impairments may not be able to make decisions in their own best interests. As a result, in certain circumstances therapists may determine the best interests of these individuals and control their behavior in order to protect them from harm.

There have also been some questions about whether the principle of autonomy applies differently across cultures. For example, Blackhall, Murphy, Frank, and colleagues (1995) found that seniors from different ethnic groups varied substantially in their beliefs about whether patients should be informed about terminal illnesses they have or make decisions about using life support interventions at the end of life. African Americans (63%) and European Americans (69%) were much more likely to believe that a patient should be told of a terminal prognosis than were Korean Americans (35%) and Mexican Americans (48%), and were much more likely (60% and 65%, respectively) to believe the patient should make decisions about using life support than were Korean Americans (28%) and Mexican Americans (41%). Instead, the latter groups were much more likely to believe the family should make those decisions. This does not imply that autonomy is less important to members of these groups, but rather that members of these groups may wish to delegate their rights to information and decision-making authority to their family members. The obligation to respect autonomy is no less important because someone delegates family members to act on their behalf.

The principle of respect for autonomy supports many specific ethical rules such as tell the truth, help people make important decisions when asked, respect people's privacy, protect confidential information, and obtain informed consent (Beauchamp & Childress, 2013). Some of these rules may not apply, however, in emergencies (obviously in medical or psychiatric emergencies when patients are unable to respond responsibly or perhaps at all), in many public health and safety interventions (e.g., the enforcement of traffic laws and hospital rules to ensure safety), and in research using anonymous data. Many of these exceptions result from the balancing of respect for autonomy with other ethical principles.

Nonmaleficence

The principle of nonmaleficence is commonly associated with the maxim to "Above all, do no harm." This principle is implied in the Hippocratic oath and is often considered the fundamental principle of the health care professions. The implications of nonmaleficence for intentional harms are generally obvious—intentional harms to patients are often prosecuted under criminal or civil law. The implications involving unintentional harms, however, are typically much more complex and subtle.

An important implication of nonmaleficence for health care professionals concerns incompetence. Harm can be caused by omission as well as commission, often by imposing risks of harm through either ignorance or carelessness (Beauchamp & Childress, 2013; Sharpe & Faden, 1998; Stromberg, Haggarty, Mishkin, Leibeluft, Rubin, McMillian, & Trilling, 1988). In behavioral health care, examples include having insufficient training and supervised experience to complete an adequate suicide risk assessment or treatment plan, competently diagnose particular disorders or provide certain interventions, or appropriately manage countertransference. If patients are harmed as a result, the therapist can be judged negligent, which can then be grounds for malpractice. The critical question at issue in these cases involves whether the professional was practicing up to the *standard of care* for the profession. A professional is not expected to practice at an "expert" level, but he or she can be negligent if his or her practice falls below professional standards for competent practice (Koocher & Keith-Spiegel, 2008; Stromberg et al., 1988). Therefore, it is critical that therapists obtain training and supervised experience adequate to competently conduct the assessments and interventions appropriate for the patient populations they work with. Therapists also need to maintain their competence and keep up with current standards of practice, in part by completing continuing education requirements.

Concern regarding the safety of medical interventions in the U.S. grew dramatically following the publication of the Institute of Medicine report, *To Err is Human*, in 2000. This report famously estimated that 44,000–98,000 Americans die each year as a result of medical errors—"a jumbo jet a day." These preventable deaths were caused by such factors as misdiagnosis, inappropriate medications, infections acquired while receiving health care, wrong-site surgery, and mishandled cases involving suicide.[1] This report stimulated the development of the modern patient safety movement now well underway in American medicine (e.g., the Joint Commission, which accredits more than 21,000 health care organizations, began unannounced hospital surveys; duty hour limits were established for medical residents; and most U.S. states mandated the reporting of serious adverse events; Wachter, 2009).

The safety of psychotherapy has also long been a concern in the field (one of the most famous case studies in the history of psychotherapy involves Freud's concern that he may have caused harm in his unsuccessful treatment of *Dora* in 1900). But the issue received relatively little attention until the 1990s when the subject of repressed memories of child abuse became highly controversial. Arguments about whether people were harmed as the result of therapists using unsafe memory recovery techniques or offering unsupported interpretations of recovered child abuse memories grew into what is sometimes considered the most contentious controversy ever in the field (the "memory wars"; Loftus & Davis, 2006). Other interventions for which there is evidence of potential or actual harm include rebirthing attachment therapy (Chaffin et al., 2006), group interventions for antisocial youth (Weiss, Caron, Ball, Tapp, Johnson, & Weisz et al., 2006), conversion therapy for gay and lesbian patients (American Psychological Association, 2009), critical incident stress debriefing (Mayou, Ehlers, & Hobbs, 2000), and grief therapy (Bonnano & Lilienfeld, 2008; see also; Lilienfeld, Lynn, & Lohr, 2015).

A growing body of research also finds that patient deterioration or lack of improvement is sometimes missed but can be detected through the routine use of outcome measures, and special attention can then be given to attempt to achieve a positive outcome (Fortney et al., 2017; Lambert, 2010). Research also indicates that individual therapists vary significantly in their effectiveness (e.g., Lambert, 2010; Wampold & Imel, 2015). These findings obligate therapists and their supervisors to ensure that patient nonimprovement and deterioration are identified and efforts are made to achieve the highest quality and most effective care possible (these issues are discussed in Chapters 10 and 11 that follow).

Another set of controversies regarding the effectiveness of behavioral health care involves psychotropic medications. Medications are now used more frequently than psychotherapy for treating mental health issues (Olfson & Marcus, 2010), and

[1] Imagine if a large airliner crashed each day in the U.S. due to terrorism or mechanical failure. There would be outrage and immediate action taken to stop the daily plane crashes.

therapists are naturally concerned about the safety and effectiveness of these treatments even though few psychologists have prescription privileges. The number of individuals taking them has risen dramatically (e.g., 11% of Americans age 12 and over took antidepressant medication during 2005–08, and 23% of women 40–59 took antidepressants; Pratt, Brody, & Gu, 2011). Concerns about the safety and effectiveness of psychopharmacology have existed ever since the first psychotropic medication, Thorazine, was introduced in the early 1950s. Many psychotropic medications do not address a known cause of a disorder, have limited effectiveness for reducing symptoms or correcting dysfunction, and introduce major side effects. There is also concern about the possibility that long-term use of psychotropic medications may disrupt normal brain function and could have long-term negative effects (e.g., Frances, 2009; Goldacre, 2012; Healy, 2012; Whitaker & Cosgrove, 2015). Many researchers and clinicians are now questioning the safety and effectiveness of antipsychotic, antidepressant, mood stabilizer, stimulant, insomnia, and antianxiety medications for children or adults who do not have serious disorders. The possibility of harm that might be caused by our interventions raises major ethical questions, so this issue deserves much more research attention than it currently receives.

Beneficence

The overarching purpose of health care, public health, and health research is to provide benefit to individuals and society. Morality requires that health care providers not only respect patients' autonomy and not harm them but also contribute to their well-being. Obligations of beneficence are weaker, however, than those involving nonmaleficence. Although we are morally prohibited from harming anyone, we are not similarly obligated to help everyone, especially if it requires sacrifice (e.g., risking one's life to save a person in a burning building or giving one's organs for transplantation). People generally feel that we are obligated to benefit our family members, friends, and others with whom we have a special relationship but not necessarily people in general. When a person joins a profession, however, they assume duties to provide assistance and benefit to their patients, students, residents in the community they serve, etc. as part of the professional roles they assume.

The obligation of beneficence includes the balancing of the benefits, risks, and costs of treatment in an optimal manner in addition to providing benefits (Beauchamp & Childress, 2013). Potential risks of psychotherapy include experiencing strong, painful feelings and memories, or ruptured relationships or loss of employment if a person becomes more assertive or changes their life goals. But there are also risks associated with not addressing problems. Without treatment, many problems will not get better and often get worse (e.g., emotionally, interpersonally, vocationally, academically, physically, legally). The Tarasoff case presents a well-known example of how benefits and risks need to be balanced in mental health treatment. A student client at a college counseling center expressed an intent to kill his ex-girlfriend. A major potential benefit might have been provided to Tatiana Tarasoff if the confidentiality of the student, her ex-boyfriend, had been broken (i.e., her ex-boyfriend had stated an intention to kill her, but he also had confidentiality regarding those threats because they were stated in counseling). The Supreme Court of California judged that the potential harm caused by breaking the client's confidentiality in order to warn Tarasoff was outweighed by the potential to save her life (Tarasoff v. Board of Regents of the University of California, 1976).

Even though individual autonomy is highly valued in the U.S., Americans commonly accept many limits on their autonomy because it is in the best interests of individuals and the community. For example, traffic laws, air travel security restrictions, and medical restrictions are commonly accepted without serious questioning. There is also general agreement that some strong forms of beneficence, sometimes referred to as paternalism (i.e., governing "as by a father"), are justified in order for society to function in a secure, efficient manner (Beauchamp & Childress, 2013). A strong form of paternalism in behavioral health care involves suicide intervention. This situation is complicated by the stigma associated with suicide due in part to religious prohibitions and also because suicide was a felony crime in many jurisdictions until recent decades. The question is whether clinicians are obligated to control suicidal individuals, even when they do not want such assistance, through involuntary hospitalization in order to prevent them from harming themselves. Suicidal individuals may be very upset and destabilized by personal crises, mental health problems, or substance use. Suicide is also an irreversible act, and unsuccessful attempts can result in serious bodily harm (e.g., damage to organs resulting from drug overdoses, wounds resulting from gunshots). When individuals are unstable and in serious distress, are professionals obligated to at least temporarily restrict their rights and paternalistically control their behavior in order to prevent serious harm from occurring? (Individuals who decide to end their lives after engaging in careful, logical decision-making represent a different situation; Beauchamp et al., 2008.) Another situation involving paternalism occurs when individuals determined to be incompetent due to neurological disease or injury (e.g., Alzheimer's disease, stroke) or serious psychiatric illness (e.g., serious schizophrenia) are appointed surrogate decision-makers (e.g., guardians) who are given responsibility for making decisions for the individual who is unable to act in his or her own best interests.

Justice

The principle of justice focuses on fairness and how to ethically distribute the benefits and responsibilities of society. If there were no limits to resources, this would be a far less difficult question to decide. It would also be much easier if luck played no role in the distribution of abilities and disabilities in life, or what has been called the biological and social "lottery" of life (Rawls, 1999). Given that health status and access to health care are highly variable, however, and that health care is typically very expensive, these decisions can quickly become controversial (e.g., should prisoners get organ transplants when there is a shortage of organs?).

The minimal principle of justice is traditionally attributed to Aristotle, who argued that equals must be treated equally and unequals must be treated unequally (Beauchamp & Childress, 2013). That is, no person should be treated unequally, despite obvious differences between people, until it has been shown that a difference between them is *relevant* to the treatment at stake. For example, people generally agree that all children should be provided a free public education, despite many obvious differences among children, because those differences are not relevant when judging the value of education. The major problem with Aristotle's approach, however, is that the criteria for judging which differences are relevant are not specified (Rescher, 1966). For example, when individuals need behavioral or physical health care but are not facing a life-threatening issue, is their ability to purchase treatment relevant to whether they receive services? Does the decision change if a person engages in unhealthy behavior that helped create their medical problems? If they desire services that are not medically necessary, should insurance cover those services?

Societies typically use a variety of methods for distributing the benefits and responsibilities of community life (Rescher, 1966). In the U.S., everyone is supposed to be given an equal share of some things, such as an elementary and secondary education for all children. The selection of those who can attend college and graduate school, however, should be based on merit, as with jobs and promotions. Some benefits of society are decided on the basis of need (e.g., unemployment compensation, disability benefits, welfare services), while salaries are generally determined on the basis of the free market. Whether health care should be provided to everyone, regardless of ability to pay, has been controversial in the U.S., while the question of whether mental health care and substance abuse treatment should be provided has been even more controversial. The American Medical Association in 1994 took the position that it is the ethical duty of society to provide an adequate level of health care for all citizens, and passage of the Affordable Care Act in 2010 suggests American society is moving in that direction.

Many political disputes center around which approach to deciding the distribution of society's benefits and responsibilities is viewed as fairest. Communitarian approaches tend to emphasize need and commonalities between individuals, while libertarian approaches emphasize liberty and fair procedure. Utilitarian approaches emphasize a mixture of criteria so that the public utility is maximized, and this is the approach usually taken by most governments around the world. Societies (and even regions within the U.S. or within individual states) often differ in the emphasis given to these various approaches but normally use several of them when developing law and policy (Beauchamp & Childress, 2013; Rescher, 1966).

More recent approaches have been developed that also emphasize social justice and well-being. For example, Powers and Faden (2006) view "justice as concerned with human well-being" (p. 6) and list six core dimensions of well-being that society and the global community should aim to satisfy: health, personal security, reasoning, respect, attachment, and self-determination. From this view, the emphasis is on a right to *health*, rather than a right to *health care*, and on reducing the influence of poverty in causing poor health. In its 2003 report, *Unequal Treatment*, the Institute of Medicine found that ethnic and racial minorities tended to receive lower quality health care even when factors such as insurance status and income were controlled for. These "unacceptable" disparities in health care (Smedley, Stith, & Nelson, 2003, p. 6) were also associated with poorer health outcomes.

Moral character—the necessary context

The four-principles approach as formulated by Beauchamp and Childress across the seven editions of their text (1977–2013) provides the mostly widely accepted perspective on biomedical ethics in the world. Their systematic, comprehensive model is very useful for addressing the extremely complicated and often highly controversial issues involved in health care practice, research, and policy. It is a remarkable achievement. But it needs to be supplemented with one additional perspective.

Discussions of ethical theory typically revolve around principles, rules, obligations, and rights as well as the decisions made and actions taken as a result of applying those considerations. But this approach minimizes the importance of the person performing those actions. As Beauchamp and Childress (2013) note, "What often matters most in the moral life is not adherence to moral rules, but having a reliable character, a good moral sense, and an appropriate emotional responsiveness" (p. 30). Technical knowledge and skill are obviously important for therapists, nurses, physicians, and others who care for people struggling with mental and physical health problems, but compassion, sensitivity, and patience sometimes matter even more.

Moral character emphasizes the person and her or his moral character and virtues (Beauchamp & Childress, 2013; Cohen & Cohen, 1999; Freeman, 2000). Moral character and virtues have received increasing attention in biomedical ethics because principles, rules, and rights can be impersonal and insensitive, whereas the moral character and trustworthiness of professionals are critical in systems that care for individuals who are ill, distressed, and vulnerable. Some philosophers have questioned whether moral virtues are important in a systematic approach to ethical theory because of the difficulty in identifying, measuring, and balancing them (e.g., Bentham, 1834). But it would be wrong to understate the importance of moral character when it comes to caregiving for people who are vulnerable and hurting. Concern has also grown about attempts to minimize costs (e.g., excluding people with preexisting conditions) and maximize profits (e.g., providing unnecessary tests or treatments).

There is significant consistency among characterizations of virtuous health care professionals (e.g., Cohen & Cohen, 1999; MacIntyre, 1982). Beauchamp and Childress (2013) focused on the following five virtues.

Compassion. Caring and compassion are fundamental to humane health care and are consequently emphasized across health care professions. Compassion is usually defined as a desire to alleviate a person's suffering, in contrast to empathy which focuses on the ability to understand and share another person's feelings. This does not imply that health care professionals should be overly or passionately involved with their patients. Too much caring can result in a loss of objectivity and sound judgment. Instead, Beauchamp and Childress (2013) suggest that an empathic concern mixed with an objective evaluative perspective serves patients' interests most effectively.

Discernment refers to the ability to make decisions and judgments without undue influence by extraneous considerations, fears, and personal attachments (Beauchamp & Childress, 2013). Aristotle defined "practical wisdom" as understanding how to act with the right intensity of feeling, in the correct manner, at the right time, and with the proper balance of reason and emotion. In the context of psychotherapy, some therapists are adept at saying just the right thing at the right time and knowing when not to say anything at all, knowing when to provide comfort and reassurance to an upset patient versus when to remain silent and allow him or her to access deeper emotions and thoughts.

Trustworthiness refers to the confidence that one will act with the right motives and apply the appropriate moral norms when encountering a particular situation. Trust has probably always played a central role in health care, while distrust became a significant concern more recently as health care in the U.S. became industrialized and the motives of for-profit managed care companies were questioned. There is also concern that physicians may practice "defensively" as a consequence of the increase in malpractice lawsuits in recent decades. Given the highly personal nature of psychotherapy and the vulnerability that patients often feel, therapist trustworthiness is an especially important concern in behavioral health care.

Integrity. Conflicts between one's core moral beliefs and the demands of mental health practice can be wrenching. Some strongly held political or religious beliefs can also impair one's ability to work effectively with certain patients. Patience, humility, and tolerance are all critical in behavioral health care practice, especially in pluralistic, democratic societies where therapists often learn a great deal about individual patients' personal beliefs, values, and behavior. This does not suggest that one must compromise one's values and beliefs—compromising below a certain threshold of integrity means you lose it. Instead, when these types of conflicts arise, therapists can sometimes refer patients to other therapists.

Conscientiousness. Some people are very capable of judging the right course of action in a problematic situation but are not interested in taking the actions needed to correct the situation if it would be inconvenient or difficult. Conscientiousness refers to determining the right response to a situation, intending to carry it out, and exerting the appropriate level of effort to ensure that the actions are carried out effectively (Beauchamp & Childress, 2013).

Some complex situations arise when the moral character and personal beliefs of providers conflict with the health care needed or sought by patients. Physicians, nurses, pharmacists, psychotherapists, and others sometimes have conscientious objections to participating in abortion or sterilization procedures or the withdrawal of life-sustaining medical support such as artificial nutrition and hydration. In behavioral health treatment, some have been unwilling to work with individuals who are LGBT, want to separate or divorce, or have committed particular crimes. These are complicated situations, but agencies, institutions, professional associations, and public policy have ways to attempt to accommodate conscientious refusals to provide certain types of care in ways that do not compromise patients' rights and interests (Beauchamp & Childress, 2013).

Moral virtues fall on a continuum that ranges from ordinary to extraordinary moral standards, from the level of the common morality (that applies to everyone) to the morality of aspiration and excellence (Beauchamp & Childress, 2013). Although we are all bound to the standards of common morality, we are not bound to more excellent, heroic, and saintly ideals even though they are admirable and have great value when individuals strive for them. Albert Schweitzer, Mohandas Gandhi, Mother Theresa, Dorothy Day, Dolores Huerta, and countless others have inspired generations in ways that ennoble and improve society and civilization. Many moral heroes risk their own safety, sometimes their lives, to help others and yet feel it involved no extraordinary moral effort. In 2007, Wesley Autrey jumped on top of a man who had fallen on the subway track in New York and held him down as the train passed over—the train passed so closely that Autrey got grease on his cap. Autrey explained, "I don't feel like I did something spectacular, I just saw someone who needed help. I did what I felt was right" (Buckley, 2007).

Becoming more ethical

Knowledge of both psychological science and ethical theory are essential to safe, effective, and responsible behavioral health care. Psychological science is necessary for understanding human development, functioning, and behavior change, but health care must also be grounded squarely on ethical principles and standards to be practiced in a compassionate, respectful, responsible, and fair manner. In the modern world, one without the other is simply inconceivable.

Philosophy has developed a coherent system of professional ethics that provides a very serviceable framework for health care. Improvements still need to be made, particularly with regard to issues related to justice, and not all clinicians and health care employees perform in an exemplary fashion. But biomedical ethics provide a very useful framework for delivering respectful, compassionate, responsible, and ethically motivated and guided health care.

Scientific and technological advances will continue to present new opportunities and challenges for behavioral health care ethics. Teletherapy, the centralized storage of electronic health care records (in "the cloud"), and the use of social media for public education about mental health and well-being present many exciting new opportunities but also several concerns. Advanced medical technologies raise new ethical challenges as well (e.g., genetic testing of embryos to select children with particular characteristics, maintaining comatose individuals on life-support machines indefinitely). Increasing diversity in society also raises additional questions. Many personal and family issues are very controversial within and across cultures (e.g., divorce, abortion, LGBT orientations, gender roles, arranged marriages, the control and upbringing of children). Harm can result from a lack of familiarity with a patient's culture, the ethical and family values generally observed within that culture, the specific beliefs and values of a patient and his or her family, and the interaction of those factors with mental health (Knapp & VandeCreek, 2007; Sue & Sue, 2012). As with difficult situations faced by individuals in any culture, these cases often involve a balancing of benefits and harms (e.g., the autonomy of young people facing a traditional arranged marriage they do not want vs. the alienation from their family, religion, and culture that can result if the marriage is not accepted). Attending to the science and ethics underlying all these issues is necessary in order to find satisfactory solutions and continue to improve the ethical functioning of health care and other human services professions.

Although science and ethics focus on different issues and typically use different analytic methods, they are highly complementary in the realm of health care. Science and ethics both examine human nature. Both require strict logical analysis to understand phenomena, and dramatic progress has been made in both areas since the Scientific Revolution and the Enlightenment. The goals of science and ethics also converge in behavioral health care. The ethical perspective emphasizes professionals' responsibilities to not harm, including unintentionally, and to provide benefit by removing harms, suffering, and dysfunction as well as preventing them whenever possible. The scientific perspective emphasizes understanding development and functioning and devising safe and effective interventions to use in treatment and prevention. These goals overlap substantially.

Recent scientific research has found that moral reasoning and behavior are very complicated phenomena governed partly by subconscious, automatic reactions that can conflict with reasoning based on deliberative logical analysis. Human cognition evolved to be able to respond quickly to threats and opportunities in a highly efficient manner necessary for survival in the natural world. But these automatic responses can be maladaptive and counterproductive in the large, complex societies that emerged with the rise of civilization. Just as some of our evolved physical characteristics are not optimal for life in the modern world (e.g., the body's conservation of calories for lean times), some evolved psychological characteristics are a poor fit for life in the modern world. Finding solutions to these problems is a major challenge for societies around the world.

The scientific examination of human ethics also highlights the necessity of the biopsychosocial developmental approach to understanding human psychology. We genetically inherited a long history of evolved characteristics and mechanisms that fundamentally shape our moral reasoning and behavior. The basic features of many of these characteristics and mechanisms are extremely old; some are even shared with other primates and older mammalian species from which we evolved. As human cognition evolved, however, we eventually developed language and civilization, and cultural factors then became much stronger influences on evolution than biological factors were (Dunbar, 2016; Harari, 2011; Stringer, 2012a). Sociocultural factors now have the overwhelming influence on human evolution—biological evolution occurs at a very slow pace over generations, while cultural evolution can change human behavior and norms very quickly, sometimes even within a generation (e.g., particularly in terms of expanding moral status and giving consideration and rights to more individuals within society).

It is ironic that the tremendous cultural variation found around the world is caused by the very same cognitive mechanisms that we all universally share. We marvel at the wonderful variation in people's food, clothing and personal adornment, art and architecture, religion, and family and community practices found in cultures around the world. But it is also tragic that the same cognitive mechanisms that we all universally share have led to the warfare, exploitation, slavery, and genocide that have occurred around the world across human history. The same cultural differences that are at times respected and enjoyed can also become the rationale for the unthinkable savagery against other groups that has occurred around the world across the centuries. Our shared moral cognition leads to the wonderfully compassionate and altruistic behavior found in all cultures but also to the barbaric tribalism, violence, and abuse also found in all cultures. Frequently the violence and abuse even occur within families and intimate relationships with loved ones who at other times may be treated sensitively and compassionately. It is baffling that our universally shared moral cognition can lead to wonderful kindness toward others but also to the horrendous mistreatment of people from other "tribes" and even sometimes neighbors and loved ones. Such is the complexity of human nature that has been so elusive to philosophers, theologians, scientists, and others over the ages.

Living together in a cooperative and collaborative manner has always been one of humanity's greatest challenges. Tremendous progress has been made in many areas, including in how health care services are provided. But there seems to be no end to challenges at all levels for individuals, families, communities, societies, and the global community as a whole. These challenges have been top concerns for religious and governmental institutions throughout human history. Increased scientific understanding of the nature of these challenges will provide crucial insights for addressing them if we are willing to apply science in this way.

Part Two

The public we serve and their biopsychosocial circumstances

Psychological functioning

5

The definition of behavioral health care provided in Chapter 1 is "Behavioral health care involves the clinical application of scientific knowledge and professional ethics to address behavioral health needs and promote biopsychosocial functioning." That definition has two especially important implications for education and practice in health service psychology. First, it identifies science and ethics as the conceptual foundations of the field, the starting points for learning the profession. Scientific knowledge regarding human psychology and biomedical ethics together provide the conceptual foundations, rationale, and justification for applying knowledge of human psychology in clinical practice. Both are needed for practicing the profession knowledgeably and responsibly.

The above definition of behavioral health care also implies that professionals in health service psychology need to possess expertise regarding behavioral health and biopsychosocial functioning. Meeting individuals' behavioral health needs and promoting their functioning are the fundamental purposes of behavioral health care, and so clinicians need to be familiar with the research regarding people's health and functioning not only with regard to behavioral health but also across the biopsychosocial domains. The four chapters in this section of the book address these topics.

There are no clear boundaries between the biological, psychological, sociocultural, and developmental dimensions of functioning. Phenomenologically, they usually appear to interact seamlessly in providing a completely unified experience of the world. Indeed, one of the great mysteries remaining to be discovered in science concerns how the experience of human consciousness arises from the biological functioning of the brain as it is also constantly interacting with its environment (both the internal bodily environment and the external physical and social environments). Nonetheless, the three general biopsychosocial levels of natural organization along with the dimension of time/development are discussed in separate chapters below to keep the very large and complex literature on these issues organized.

The science-based biopsychosocial approach to learning the profession advocated in this volume is very different from the traditional approaches commonly used a generation ago in health service psychology education. Though students were required to learn about the biological, psychological, social, and developmental bases of behavior, there normally was also a requirement (or at least an expectation) to learn one or more of the traditional theoretical orientations to conceptualizing cases. Students were generally expected to adopt one or some combination of those orientations to structure and organize their approach to clinical practice, and they learned how those approaches could be used with different individuals and disorders. Some of those orientations included specific hypotheses about the nature and development of psychopathology, personality, and behavior change, while others addressed

Foundations of Health Service Psychology. https://doi.org/10.1016/B978-0-12-816426-6.00005-0

only some of these issues. The empirical support for those hypotheses also varied greatly. But none of the orientations systematically integrated the scientific knowledge about the full range of biopsychosocial influences on development, functioning, and behavior change (see Chapter 2). Because of their inadequacies as scientific theories, the traditional theoretical orientations cannot provide the scientific foundations for behavioral health care. Nonetheless, many of them do have solid empirical support as treatments for a variety of mental health and substance abuse issues. Therefore, the traditional theoretical orientations in psychology are largely reconceptualized as psychotherapies in the biopsychosocial approach.

The biopsychosocial approach advocated in this volume begins by emphasizing the scientific and ethical foundations of the field followed by an examination of the behavioral health needs and biopsychosocial circumstances of individuals. The treatment process is then reviewed after one is grounded in the former topics. Learning interventions and how to implement them before being well-grounded in the scientific understanding of human biopsychosocial development is viewed as putting the cart before the horse. In the past, therapists often learned how to use therapeutic tools before they had a thorough understanding of when, where, how, and why to use them. Often little attention was given to what psychological mechanisms and processes were being targeted and for what purpose. Therapists who conceptualized cases using cognitive therapy, for example, tended to see a need to address irrational thinking, while family therapists tended to see a need to address dysfunctional family dynamics, and psychopharmacologists tended to see needs for medicating symptoms. The rationale for providing these treatments was typically based on the assumptions of one's adopted theoretical orientation more than the particular biopsychosocial needs, circumstances, and developmental history of the patient.

From a science-based health care orientation, one cannot rationally plan how best to intervene before one understands individuals' needs and circumstances in a comprehensive biopsychosocial manner. Treatment plans need to address individuals' needs not just in the short term. They also need to address the underlying causes and risk factors for psychopathology and promote health, resilience, and optimal functioning in order to prevent relapse and be effective over the long term. This requires a comprehensive, science-based approach to understanding clinical cases. This is true in medicine as well as behavioral health care. Treatment that focuses narrowly on treating symptoms or distress without addressing the underlying causes is less likely to be effective over the long term.

To illustrate a comprehensive, science-based approach to understanding behavioral health care, the next four chapters provide an overview of important psychological, sociocultural, physical health, and developmental factors that need to be incorporated in a biopsychosocial conceptualization of behavioral health care. Summaries of important biopsychosocial characteristics and outcomes are provided to highlight the wide range of variables that need to be considered. Reviewing all these factors thoroughly obviously requires extensive study, whereas the present overview is merely intended to demonstrate the framework needed to understand individuals and their behavioral health needs. This first chapter addresses psychological functioning and begins by reviewing epidemiological research on the prevalence of mental disorders. The prevalence of substance abuse is then reviewed followed by a discussion of suicide and psychological health and well-being.

Mental disorders

Many individuals struggle with mental health issues. Surveys consistently find that large proportions of the general population meet the criteria for a mental disorder or did at some point during their lifetimes.[1] In the largest study of comorbidity ever conducted in the U.S., the National Comorbidity Survey found that nearly 50% of respondents reported at least one lifetime mental disorder, and nearly 30% reported at least one 12-month disorder (Kessler et al., 1994). The most common disorders were depression, alcohol dependence, social phobia, and simple phobia. In addition, a subgroup of 14% of respondents accounted for the vast majority of the severe disorders and had three or more comorbid disorders over the course of their lifetimes. The size of this subgroup (one in seven individuals) is particularly concerning given that its members suffer an especially large amount of psychological distress and dysfunction across their lifetimes. This study was replicated a decade later, and the National Comorbidity Survey Replication found that the prevalence of mental disorders had changed little from the original survey (Kessler, Demler, Frank, Olfson, Pineus, Walters et al., 2005; Wang et al., 2005, 2006). Among its findings were the following:

- Fifty percent of all Americans reported symptoms diagnostic of a mental disorder during their lifetimes.
- The development of these disorders starts early; many emerged as early as age 11, half of all lifetime cases started by age 14, and three-quarters started by age 24.
- More than one-quarter of adults reported having symptoms diagnostic of a mental disorder over the previous year, and most of these could be classified as at least moderate in severity.
- Mental illness is the most prevalent chronic health condition experienced by youth.
- Most people wait years or even decades to seek treatment for their depression, anxiety, or bipolar disorder.

[1] Readers may be familiar with the problem of the lack of clear definitions for terms such as "mental health," "mental disorder," and "mental illness." The classification of mental health problems is based on a variety of factors (e.g., genetic disorder as in Down syndrome, symptom presentation as in depression, reactions to taking a drug as in substance use disorders, an etiological factor as in PTSD). The classification of physical health problems is likewise based on multiple factors (e.g., deviation from a physiological norm as in hypertension, etiology as in pneumococcal pneumonia, symptom presentation as in migraine). The term "mental illness" is infrequently used in this volume because it typically implies a pathophysiological process, whereas many mental health problems are normal reactions and adjustments to negative life events and circumstances. Readers are reminded that the term "mental disorders" merely refers to a psychological or behavioral pattern or syndrome associated with distress or impairment and does not imply pathophysiology or causation (see the DSM-5; American Psychiatric Association, 2013). The field will need to wait for research to clarify what the pathophysiology might be for particular mental health problems.

- Fewer than one-third of those with mental disorders receive adequate treatment for their mental health problems.

Every year the U.S. Substance Abuse and Mental Health Administration conducts a survey of more than 60,000 Americans 12 years of age and older in all 50 states and the District of Columbia. The results provide useful estimates regarding the mental health of the American population as a whole. The report on the 2017 survey (*National Survey on Drug Use and Health*; SAMHSA, 2018) noted that

- 18.9% of the U.S. population aged 18 and older (1 in 5) had a mental illness (excluding substance use disorders) in the prior year (compared with 17.9% in 2008),
- 4.5% of adults (1 in 22) had a serious mental illness that resulted in serious functional impairment during the prior year (compared with 3.7% in 2008),
- 7.1% (1 in 14) experienced at least one major depressive episode in the prior year (compared with 6.7% in 2007),
- 4.5% (1 in 22) experienced major depressive episode with severe impairment in the prior year (compared with 4.0% in 2009),
- 3.4% of the population (1 in 30) had a co-occurring substance use disorder and mental illness.

Mental disorders are also common among children and youth. In the 2017 survey, one of eight adolescents aged 12 to 17 (13.3%) had had a major depressive episode, and 9.4% had had a major depressive episode with severe impairment, in the prior year (SAMSHA, 2018). These proportions were significantly higher than they had been a decade earlier. In 2007, 8.2% of adolescents had had major depressive episode in the prior year and 5.5% had had major depressive episode with severe impairment.

A more detailed perspective on the mental health issues faced by the general population in the U.S. is provided by the prevalence data reported in the *Diagnostic and Statistical Manual of Mental Disorders (fifth ed.;* American Psychiatric Association, 2013). Table 5.1 lists all *DSM-5* diagnoses found to have 1% or higher prevalence, with the most prevalent disorders listed at the top. The cutoff of 1% is

Table 5.1 Psychiatric disorders rank ordered by prevalence as reported in the *Diagnostic and Statistical Manual of Mental Disorders (DSM-5).*

Disorder (DO)	Lifetime prevalence unless otherwise noted
Premature ejaculation	20%–30% of males
Female orgasmic DO	10%–42% report symptoms, 10% do not experience orgasm throughout their lifetimes
Male hypoactive sexual desire DO	6% aged 18–24, 41% aged 66–74
Genito-pelvic pain/penetration DO	15% report recurrent pain
Tobacco use DO	13% adults, 12-month
Panic attacks	11.2%, 12-month
Alcohol use DO	8.5% adults, 12-month

Table 5.1 Psychiatric disorders rank ordered by prevalence as reported in the *Diagnostic and Statistical Manual of Mental Disorders (DSM-5)*.—cont'd

Disorder (DO)	Lifetime prevalence unless otherwise noted
Insomnia DO	6%–10% point prevalence, 1/3 of adults report symptoms
Obstructive sleep apnea	2%–15% of middle-aged adults, >20% older adults
Specific phobia	7%–9%, 12-month
Major depressive DO	7%, 12-month
Social phobia	7%, 12-month
Posttraumatic stress DO	8.7% (3.5%, 12-month)
Somatic symptom DO	5%–7%
Illness anxiety DO	1.3%–10%, 12–24 month
Obsessive-compulsive personality DO	2.1%–7.9%
Restless leg syndrome	2%–7.2%
Schizotypal personality disorder	4.6%
Learning disorders	5%–15% among children, 4% of adults
Hoarding DO	2%–6% point prevalence
Borderline personality DO	1.6%–5.9%
Narcissistic personality DO	0%–6.2%
Conduct DO	2%–10% of children and adolescents, 12-month
Attention-deficit/hyperactivity DO	5% of children, 2.5% of adults
Male erectile DO	13%–21% aged 40–80 occasionally, 2% of males younger than 40–50 frequently
Adjustment DO	5%–20% of outpatients, up to 50% of inpatients
Acute stress DO	20%–50% of people exposed to interpersonal traumatic event
Sleepwalking	29.2% of adults, 3.6% past year
Oppositional defiant DO	3.3%
Paranoid personality DO	2.3%–4.4%
Generalized anxiety DO	2.9% adults, 0.9% adolescents, 12-month
Intermittent explosive DO	2.7%, 12-month
Panic disorder	2%–3%, 12-month
Body dysmorphic DO	2.4% point prevalence

Continued

Table 5.1 Psychiatric disorders rank ordered by prevalence as reported in the *Diagnostic and Statistical Manual of Mental Disorders (DSM-5)*.—cont'd

Disorder (DO)	Lifetime prevalence unless otherwise noted
Cannabis use DO	1.5% adults, 3.4% adolescents, 12-month
Avoidant personality DO	2.4%
Separation anxiety DO	4% children, 1.6% adolescents, and 0.9%–1.0% adults, 12-month
Alzheimer's (major dementia)	5%–10% of those in their 70s, at least 25% thereafter
Circadian rhythm sleep–wake DO	5%–10% of nightshift workers
Dementia (neurocognitive DO)	1%–2% at age 65, up to 30% by age 85
Premenstrual dysphoric DO	1.8%–5.8%, 12-month
Depersonalization/Derealization DO	2%
Histrionic personality DO	1.8%
Bipolar DO (I, II, or NOS)	1.8%
Dissociative amnesia	1.8%, 12-month
Antisocial personality DO	0.2%–3.3%, 12-month
Agoraphobia	1.7%, 12-month
Dissociative identity DO	1.5%, 12-month
Chronic major depressive DO	1.5%, 12-month
Trichotillomania	1%–2%, 12-month
Excoriation (skin picking) DO	1.4%
Obsessive-compulsive DO	1.2%, 12-month
Binge eating DO	1.6% females, 0.8% males, 12-month
Bulimia nervosa	1%–1.5% of young females, 12-month
Disruptive mood dysregulation DO	2%–5% of children and adolescents
Intellectual disability	1%
Autism spectrum DO	1%
Enuresis	1% of individuals 15 and older

Note: Some disorders that appear in a limited age group are not included (e.g., developmental coordination disorder). Rank ordering is approximate given variability of the form in which the estimates were provided.

arbitrary but helpful for considering whether a problem might be viewed as relatively common and within the purview of general behavioral health care practice.

These data indicate that the population deals with a wide range of issues including primarily psychologically and biologically based disorders as well as disorders with significant social components. In fact, the prevalence of mental disorders is so high that they are nearly a normative experience for the population in general. The top nine most prevalent concerns in the table involve sexual functioning, addictions, panic attacks, and sleep problems (which, incidentally, tend not to receive extensive attention in many behavioral health care education programs; this issue is revisited later in the chapter).

Personality disorders. In the first nationally representative survey on personality disorders, Grant et al. (2004) found that an estimated 14.8% of the adult U.S. population (1 in 7) met the criteria for at least one personality disorder. The survey did not assess borderline, schizotypal, and narcissistic personality disorders to reduce interviewing time, and the overall rate of any personality disorder would have been significantly higher if those disorders had been included. All of the personality disorders in the survey except for histrionic were associated with considerable emotional disability and impairment in social and occupational functioning. In the survey, the following proportions met the criteria for specific personality disorders:

- 7.9% had obsessive-compulsive personality disorder
- 4.4% had paranoid personality disorder
- 3.6% had antisocial personality disorder
- 3.1% had schizoid personality disorder
- 2.4% had avoidant personality disorder
- 1.8% had histrionic personality disorder
- 0.5% had dependent personality disorder

A note of caution. Before moving on to other topics, a note of caution is warranted. There has been a dramatic rise in the number of Americans diagnosed with mental health disorders and receiving psychosocial and psychopharmacological treatment over the past 50 years. The number of individuals found to be disabled due to mental illness has also mushroomed. Robert Whitaker (2010) pointed out that in 1955, 566,000 people were in state and county mental hospitals in the U.S., or 1 in every 468 Americans. In 1987, 1.25 million people were receiving Social Security Disability Insurance (SSDI) or Supplemental Security Income (SSI) because they were disabled due to mental illness, or 1 in every 184 Americans. In 2007, the number of people receiving SSI or SSDI because they were disabled due to mental illness rose to 3.97 million, or 1 in every 76 Americans. The increases for children were even more dramatic. In 1987, 16,200 children under age 18 were receiving SSI because they were disabled due to mental illness, but that number grew to 561,569 in 2007, a 35-fold increase. These remarkable increases occurred at the same time that new, presumably more effective pharmacological and psychosocial treatments were being developed that were expected to reduce disability due to these conditions. In fact, the number of children on SSI disability for all reasons other than mental illness steadily declined during this same period.

The reasons underlying the dramatic rise in psychiatric disability and pharmacological treatment of tens of millions of Americans for mental health concerns are not yet well understood. One obviously does not want to minimize the suffering so many people experience as the result of mental disorders. The same is true, of course, with regard to medical disorders and socioeconomic and sociocultural problems. But it is very important to understand more about the underlying reasons for these trends (e.g., are they due to health care professionals and the public becoming more aware of mental health issues and not an actual increase in prevalence? an increase in stress? an increase in the pathologizing of normal adjustment challenges? an increase in environmental toxins? symptoms or disability being induced by psychiatric medications themselves?). It is imperative that the behavioral health field examines these issues more carefully (Whitaker & Cosgrove, 2015).

Substance use disorders

The 2017 *National Survey on Drug Use and Health* conducted by the Substance Abuse and Mental Health Services Administration (SAMHSA, 2018) found that 7.6% of Americans 18 years of age and older (1 in 13) had had a substance use disorder in the past year. Most of these individuals (75.2%) struggled with alcohol use, 36.4% struggled with illicit drugs, and 11.5% struggled with illicit drugs and alcohol. Another 3.4% of Americans had both a substance use disorder and a mental illness.

Alcohol use disorder. The 2017 *National Survey on Drug Use and Health* (SAMHSA, 2018) found that 5.7% of American adults struggled with alcohol use disorder in the past year. This represented a major decline from the prevalence of alcohol use disorder over the prior 15 years. The survey found significant decreases in alcohol use disorders had occurred across all age groups since 2002:

- 1.8% of youth aged 12 to 17 had alcohol use disorder in 2017 compared with 3.4% in 2012 and 5.9% in 2002
- 10.0% of young adults aged 18 to 25 had alcohol use disorder in 2017 compared with 14.3% in 2012 and 17.7% in 2002
- 5.0% of adults aged 26 and older had alcohol use disorder in 2017 compared with 5.9% in 2012 and 6.2% in 2002

Despite the major declines, approximately 1 in 50 adolescents, 1 in 10 young adults aged 18 to 25, and 1 in 20 adults aged 26 and older met the DSM-IV criteria for alcohol dependence or abuse in 2017. In addition, the U.S. Centers for Disease Control and Prevention's *National Health Interview Survey* for 2018 (Clarke, Norris, & Schiller, 2019) found that 20.0% of adult women and 31.3% of adult men had reported at least one heavy drinking day (five or more drinks) in the past year.

Marijuana use disorder. Marijuana is the most used illicit drug in the U.S. The number of Americans meeting DSM-IV criteria for marijuana use disorder in the 2017 *National Survey on Drug Use and Health* (SAMHSA, 2018) had declined for adolescents and young adults but not for those aged 26 and older over the prior 15 years:

- 2.2% of youth aged 12–17 had marijuana use disorder in 2017 compared with 3.2% in 2012 and 4.3% in 2002
- 5.2% of young adults aged 18–25 had marijuana use disorder in 2017 compared with 5.5% in 2012 and 6.0% in 2002
- 0.8% of adults aged 26 and older had marijuana use disorder in 2017 compared with 0.8% in 2012 and 0.8% in 2002

Cocaine use disorder. The number of Americans meeting the DSM-IV criteria for cocaine dependence or abuse in 2017 was similar to levels found in 2012, although it was significantly lower than levels found 15 years before (SAMHSA, 2018):

- 0.1% of youth aged 12–17 had cocaine use disorder in 2017 compared with 0.2% in 2012 and 0.4% in 2002
- 0.7% of young adults aged 18–25 had cocaine use disorder in 2017 compared with 0.6% in 2012 and 1.2% in 2002
- 0.3% of adults aged 26 and older had cocaine use disorder in 2017 compared with 0.4% in 2012 and 0.6% in 2002

Heroin use disorder. The number of Americans meeting the DSM-IV criteria for heroin use disorder (DSM-IV dependence or abuse) in 2017 showed a major increase for young adults over the prior 15 years (SAMHSA, 2018):

- 0.0% of youth aged 12–17 had heroin use disorder in 2017 compared with 0.1% in 2012 and 0.1% in 2002
- 0.5% of young adults aged 18–25 had heroin use disorder in 2017 compared with 0.5% in 2012 and 0.2% in 2002
- 0.2% of adults aged 26 and older had heroin use disorder in 2017 compared with 0.1% in 2012 and 0.1% in 2002

In addition to heroin use disorder, many Americans also meet the criteria for pain reliever use disorder. In 2017, 0.4% of adolescents aged 12 to 17, 1.0% of young adults aged 18 to 25, and 0.6% of those aged 26 and older met the DSM-IV criteria for pain reliever dependence or abuse (SAMSHA, 2018).

Tobacco use. The 2017 *National Survey on Drug Use and Health* (SAMHSA, 2018) found an estimated 22.4% of Americans 12 or older used tobacco in the past month, a significant decrease from 30.4% in 2002. Some of the decline may be due to the use of electronic vaporizing devices for delivering nicotine, but the 2017 survey did not ask about e-cigarette use:

- 3.2% of youth aged 12–17 smoked cigarettes in 2017 compared with 6.6% in 2012 and 13.0% in 2002
- 22.3% of young adults aged 18–25 smoked cigarettes in 2017 compared with 31.8% in 2012 and 40.8% in 2002
- 18.9% of adults aged 26 and older smoked cigarettes in 2017 compared with 22.4% in 2012 and 25.2% in 2002

Substance use among pregnant women. The 2017 *National Survey on Drug Use and Health* (SAMHSA; 2018) found that 11.5% of pregnant women (aged 15–44) had used alcohol, 14.7% had used tobacco products, and 8.5% had used illicit drugs during their pregnancies in the past month. The survey also found that 3.1% of pregnant women used marijuana daily.

Drug overdose. Though accidental deaths of all kinds in the U.S. have fallen substantially over the last century, death due to drug overdose has risen dramatically in recent decades and is now the most frequent cause of accidental death, even exceeding deaths due to traffic accidents. Opioids have been the main problem, though previously there was a significant rise in cocaine overdoses during the 1980s. The recent rise in opioid overdoses has been shocking, however. The number of people who died from drug overdoses was six times higher in 2017 than in 1999 (Scholl, Seth, Kariisa, Wilson, & Baldwin, 2018). Relatively few of these deaths involved suicide, and most (two-thirds) involved an opioid. The first wave of opioid overdose deaths began in the 1990s with prescription opioids (natural and semisynthetic opioids). A second wave began in 2010 with a rapid rise in overdose deaths due to heroin. A third wave began in 2013 with synthetic opioids, particularly illicitly manufactured fentanyl (Kolodny et al., 2015).

Suicide

Suicide is a serious public health problem that also affects large numbers of individuals. It is of course a tragedy for the individuals involved, but also for their families, friends, neighbors, colleagues, and communities. The prevalence and seriousness of suicide is not always apparent, however, because the literature on mental and substance use disorders usually refers to suicide infrequently.

Suicide was the 10th-leading cause of death in the U.S. in 2016, the 2nd-leading cause of death among those aged 10 to 34, and the 4th-leading cause among those aged 35 to 54 (Center for Disease Control and Prevention, 2017). Suicide accounted for 45,965 deaths, an average of 126 per day (Xu, Murphy, Kochanek, Bastian, & Arias, 2018). This number is more than double the number of homicides that occurred in 2016 (19,362).

The overall rate of suicide across the U.S. was 15.6 per 100,000 people in 2016 (age-adjusted rate; Stone et al., 2018). The rate of suicide varies substantially across regions of the country. The rate ranged from 6.9 in the District of Columbia to 29.2 in Montana. The number was also more than three times higher for males (34,727) than for females (10,238).

The rate of suicide declined substantially over the past century but has risen over the past 2 decades. The suicide rate was 17.0 per 100,000 in 1929 at the beginning of the Great Depression and rose to 21.3 in 1932 during the worst year of the financial crash (Galbraith, 1955). The suicide rate declined substantially after that point until its low was reached in 1999 at 12.3 per 100,000 (Stone et al., 2018). Since 1999, suicide rates have increased among both sexes, all racial and ethnic groups, in rural and urban areas, and among all age groups younger than 75 years old. From 1999 to 2015, suicide rates increased in 44 states, and 25 states had increases of greater than 30%. In addition, the rate of emergency department visits for nonfatal self-harm increased 42% from 2001 to 2016 (Stone et al., 2018).

Firearms were used in the majority of suicide deaths in 2016 (48.5%), followed by hanging, strangulation, or suffocation (26.9%), and poisoning (10.4%) (Stone et al., 2018). Most of those who died by suicide had been using substances, including antidepressant medication. Of those who received toxicology tests following a suicide, 74.4% tested positive for at least one substance, 40.6% tested positive for alcohol, 30.3% tested positive for benzodiazepines, 26.6% tested positive for opiates, and 22.4% tested positive for marijuana. Among those who were tested for antidepressants, 40.8% tested positive (Stone et al., 2018).

Precipitating circumstances were identified in the survey for over 90% of those who died by suicide (Stone et al., 2018). Overall, 37.5% experienced a depressed mood at the time of their deaths, 28.3% had problematic substance abuse (17.4% had problematic alcohol use), 27.4% were currently receiving mental health or substance abuse treatment at the time of their deaths, and 35.8% had received treatment at some point in their lives. Of those with a diagnosed mental disorder, 75.2% had a diagnosis of depression and/or dysthymia, 16.8% had an anxiety disorder, 15.2% had bipolar disorder, 5.4% had schizophrenia, and 4.5% had PTSD. Large proportions were also experiencing a variety of problems and stressors at the time of their deaths:

- 42.4% had a relationship problem or loss (27.2% an intimate partner problem, 8.9% a family problem, and 8.0% a death of a loved one)
- 22.3% had a physical health problem
- 16.2% had a job or financial problem
- 14.4% had been released from jail or prison or detention facility
- 8.5% had a recent criminal legal problem
- 3.8% had been evicted or lost their home
- 19.9% of the adolescents had a school problem
- 7.6% had been released from an institution within the past month

Large proportions of those who died by suicide were also known to be at risk of suicide or to have had a history of suicide attempts (Stone et al., 2018):

- 34.5% had left a note
- 23.5% had disclosed their suicide intent
- 31.9% had a history of suicidal ideation
- 19.9% had a history of suicide attempts

While the number of suicides is very high, the number of individuals who attempt suicide or have suicidal ideation is far higher. For every suicide death by adults in the years 2008–2011, 31 individuals had attempted suicide (SAMSHA, 2018). In addition, in 2017 4.3% of the population had thought seriously about trying to kill themselves. Young adults 18 to 25 were much more likely to have these thoughts (10.5%) than those 26 to 49 (4.3%) and those 50 or older (2.5%). The percentage of adults in 2017 who made suicide plans was 1.3% of the population, while the percentage who made suicide attempts in that year was 0.6%.

It has been estimated that 10%–12% of U.S. adults report having made at least one suicide attempt (Chiles & Strosahl, 2005) and up to 40% of the U.S. population has had suicidal ideation at some point in their lives (Chiles & Strosahl, 2005; Hirshfeld & Russell, 1997). A large survey of college students found that slightly more than one-half reported ever having had suicidal ideation (Drum, Brownson, Denmark, & Smith, 2009). Among American youth in grades 9 to 12, 15.7% reported having seriously considered attempting suicide in the previous 12 months, 12.8% reported having made a suicide plan during the previous 12 months, 7.8% reported attempting suicide at least once in the previous 12 months, and 2.4% reported making a suicide attempt that resulted in injury, poisoning, or an overdose that required medical attention (Schiller, Lucas, & Peregoy, 2012). A smaller survey also found that 40% of youths who reported attempting suicide said they had made their first attempt already in elementary or middle school (Mazza, Abbott, Catalano, & Haggerty, 2011).

Well-being and flourishing

The biopsychosocial approach requires a comprehensive perspective on human development that includes an examination of the full range of functioning across the biopsychosocial domains. Though individuals' problems, disorders, and vulnerabilities obviously require the attention of health care providers, people's strengths and resources also greatly impact their development and functioning. Indeed, people's strengths often have a greater impact on their overall well-being than their disorders and weaknesses do. Gaining a complete understanding of people's needs consequently requires consideration of their strengths, resources, and well-being in addition to their problems, disorders, and vulnerabilities. This is of course true across all the biopsychosocial domains.

Medicine and behavioral health care have long emphasized problems, disorders, and vulnerabilities. Over the past half century, this emphasis on problems and pathology was frequently criticized as narrow and wrongheaded and was often referred to pejoratively as "the medical model" of mental illness. But it is critical to recognize that an emphasis on problems and pathology was entirely appropriate given the historical context. Strengths, resources, and assets have always been important in people's lives, but disease, injury, and disability were very common over most of human history, caused major amounts of suffering, and were frequently fatal. As a result, people were naturally very concerned about problems, disease, and weakness. The primary causes of illness and death have shifted over the past century, however, from injuries and infectious disease to chronic diseases associated with behavior and lifestyle (see Chapter 7). This has resulted in a gradual shift from the historical focus on treating pathology to the promotion of physical and mental health and well-being.

The epidemiological data reviewed above indicate that many individuals are not enjoying high levels of functioning and well-being. Keyes (2007) defined a positive state of mental health as "flourishing" and found that functioning at any level lower than flourishing is associated with increased functional impairment and increased physical and mental health problems. Based on national survey data, Keyes estimated that roughly only 2 in 10 Americans are flourishing while nearly 2 in 10 are in poor mental health, which he refers to as "languishing." Most of the rest were in between, a level associated with moderate distress, lower social well-being, and a moderate number of chronic physical conditions.

The nature of human well-being is a very complicated subject that has been hotly debated since ancient times. As a result of recent empirical research, however, there has been significant progress in understanding several aspects of the processes involved. One's subjective sense of well-being, life satisfaction, and meaning and purpose in life are affected by many factors. Internal psychological factors are important influences, but physical health and external social and environmental factors also are important influences on well-being. After these various factors are reviewed in the following two chapters, the topic of well-being is revisited in more detail in Chapter 8.

Importance of psychological factors

The topics reviewed above provide an introduction to the psychological functioning of the general population. Each of the factors mentioned can significantly influence individuals' development and functioning and each has an impact on the course of behavioral health treatment as well. As a result, these topics are integrated into commonly accepted approaches to assessment and treatment planning in the mental health field (see Chapter 9). The data reviewed also have important implications with regard to behavioral health care education, policy, and research in addition to clinical practice.

The range of issues and disorders faced by the public is extensive. In addition to mood and anxiety disorders, people experience a wide variety of issues involving sexuality, addictions, sleep problems, maladaptive reactions to major stressors, learning and attention deficit disorders, and personality disorders. Suicidal ideation is common and co-occurring problems are also prevalent. In addition, only a minority of individuals are flourishing or functioning at an optimal level with high positive emotion and social well-being and few health problems and disabilities. This complicated picture of the biopsychosocial health and well-being of the general public will become more evident as social and medical functioning are integrated into the discussion. Clearly, many individuals are dealing with major behavioral health problems negatively affecting multiple areas of their lives.

Education and training in the behavioral health field often have not focused extensively on some of the prevalent behavioral health issues noted above. Individuals commonly face problems related to sexual functioning, addictions, sleep, somatic symptoms, personality disorders, learning disorders, suicidality, and a lack of positive mental health, but many graduate programs in the field give only limited attention to several of these issues. Chronic and comorbid problems are prevalent, and these too often receive limited attention. The significant prevalence and consequences of substance use disorders are generally well known, but graduate training on the topic has often been limited or sometimes even nonexistent (Corbin, Gottdiener, Sirikantraporn, Armstrong, & Probber, 2013; Harwood, Kowalski, & Ameen, 2004). Many experts believe the topic of suicide should receive far more attention in behavioral health care training as well; a 2012 task force report of the American Association of Suicidology concluded that training in the assessment and management of suicidal patients had serious gaps (Schmitz et al., 2012). Several studies found that only about one-half of psychology trainees received training on suicide, and the training provided was often very limited.

A biopsychosocial approach to behavioral health care takes a holistic perspective that gives attention to the full range of issues that individuals face. The above overview of individuals' psychological functioning suggests that behavioral health care professionals should take a comprehensive perspective to addressing behavioral health needs and promoting biopsychosocial functioning. But additional factors need to be considered. Individuals' mental health concerns should not be considered in isolation. People's social circumstances and physical health also need be considered to gain a thorough understanding of their development and functioning. Treatment that effectively addresses individuals' problems and promotes their well-being over the long term requires a comprehensive understanding of their circumstances and functioning across the biopsychosocial domains.

Sociocultural functioning

6

Behavioral health care made major strides in recognizing the importance of sociocultural factors in individuals' development and functioning over the past half century. The civil rights era in the U.S. in the 1960s revolutionized thinking about the ways that race, ethnicity, gender, class, and other sociocultural factors affect psychological development and functioning. A variety of social movements transformed the way people thought about normal and abnormal psychological development, including the Black Power, anti—Vietnam War, women's liberation, American Indian, Chicana, and gay liberation movements. Psychological theory and research also evolved dramatically during this time. Carl Rogers's person-centered theory and other humanistic theoretical orientations became popular within health service psychology and also had major influences on human services and social science fields generally. The methods of psychological research also became more sophisticated as more complex research design, statistical analysis, and theory development were applied to a wider range of psychological phenomena.

The complexity of the interactions among biopsychosocial influences on human development also became apparent over the last half century. Infant attachment provides a prototypical example of the inextricably intertwined nature of biopsychosocial processes. The biologically evolved attachment system helps ensure that human infants receive consistent care from their mothers and other caregivers so they survive their very long period of dependency as they mature into childhood and adolescence. The style of caregiving that babies receive leads them to develop expectations about self and others (i.e., an internal working model) that then influences their personality characteristics, psychopathology, relationships, and even physical health outcomes (see Chapters 7 and 8). These effects are inextricably intertwined across biopsychosocial levels. In rats, for example, the effects of mothers' style of care have been shown to be transmitted through epigenetic changes in the brains of rat pups that regulate endocrine and cardiovascular responses. Rat pups separated from their biological mothers and raised by adoptive mothers end up with their adoptive mothers' attachment style, not the genetically inherited orientation of their biological mothers (Francis, Diorio, Liu, & Meaney, 1999; Meaney, 2001; Weaver et al., 2004). Remarkably, this effect has also been achieved by humans gently stroking the infant rat pup with a small pain brush (Jutapakdeegul, Casalotti, Govitrapong, & Kotchabhakdi, 2003). In addition, these rat pups then pass their acquired attachment style on to their own offspring later on (see Chapter 3).

Race is another example of a highly complex biopsychosocial variable. Historically, many people viewed race as a critically important biological variable that greatly influenced psychological development. But in recent decades race has been found to have limited biological meaning, even though racial appearance is transmitted

Foundations of Health Service Psychology. https://doi.org/10.1016/B978-0-12-816426-6.00006-2

genetically. The importance of race as a cultural variable, however, remains very significant. The cultural impacts of race can significantly affect psychological development and functioning, and these in turn also impact physical health. Therefore, race must be conceptualized in a biopsychosocial manner; portraying it as a biological, psychological, or sociocultural variable alone is completely inadequate.

Despite the inherently interactive nature of human development and functioning, it is useful to separate biopsychosocial categories so they can be learned more easily. Therefore, this chapter reviews variables that are typically viewed as primarily social and/or cultural in nature. Covering all the important sociocultural variables would require extensive review of many subjects, whereas the purpose here is to outline the necessity of the biopsychosocial framework for understanding human psychology and providing behavioral health care. This chapter begins by reviewing demographic characteristics followed by educational attainment along with vocational and financial status; family and relationship functioning; child maltreatment; elder abuse; criminal victimization and legal involvement; and religion and spirituality.

Demographic characteristics

The U.S. is steadily becoming a more diverse society, and basic demographic data highlight the necessity of being able to work with a variety of demographic groups in all areas of health care and human services. Selected estimates for the 2018 U.S. population provided by the U.S. Census Bureau (2019) indicate self-identifications of race and ethnicity (see Table 6.1 below). The definition of "Hispanic" in the U.S. Census refers to people of Cuban, Mexican, Puerto Rican, South or Central American, or other Spanish cultures or origins regardless of race.

Over the past decade, the Asian population in the U.S. has grown the fastest while the White-alone population grew the slowest. As can be seen in Table 6.1, the

Table 6.1 Selected demographic estimates for July 1, 2018 from the U.S. Census.

Total population (327,167,434)	**% of total 100.0%**
White alone	76.6%
Black or African American	13.4%
American Indian and Alaska Native	1.3%
Asian	5.8%
Native Hawaiian and other Pacific	0.2%
Two or more races	2.7%
Hispanic or Latino	18.1%
White alone, not Hispanic or Latino	60.7%

overwhelming majority of the U.S. population reports only one race (U.S. Census Bureau, 2019). But the U.S. population is also changing steadily. The non-Hispanic White-alone population is projected to decrease even while the U.S. population as a whole continues to increase. The population of those reporting two or more races is projected to grow the fastest. By 2020, less than half of children (49.8%) are projected to be non-Hispanic White-alone. By 2044, more than half of all Americans are projected to belong to a minority group, and by 2060 nearly one in five is projected to be foreign born (Colby & Ortman, 2015). The country is also getting older on average. The baby boomers born after World War II (i.e., those born between 1946 and 1964) will all have reached age 65 by 2030, and one of every five residents will be a member of the older population. The U.S. Census Bureau (2018) also projects that by 2035, there will be more people 65 years of age and older than children under the age of 18 for the first time in U.S. history.

Educational and vocational achievement are obviously important to one's development, functioning, and well-being. The U.S. Census data presented in Table 6.2 indicate that nearly 9 of 10 American adults (88.4%) in 2015 reported obtaining at least a high school diploma or equivalency diploma, nearly three in 5 (58.9%) had completed at least some college, and one-third held a bachelor's degree or higher (32.5%; Ryan & Bauman, 2016). This represents more than a threefold increase in high school attainment and more than a fivefold increase in college attainment since 1940 when educational data were first collected by the Census Bureau. Nonetheless, nearly 12% Americans aged 25 and older report not obtaining a high school diploma or its equivalent. It is also estimated that one in seven Americans lacks basic English literacy skills such as those needed to read a map, review a paycheck for accuracy, or understand a warning label on a tool or medicine bottle (National Center for Educational Statistics, 2008). Asian Americans were much more likely to hold a bachelor's degree or higher (53.9%) compared with non-Hispanic Whites (36.2%), Blacks (22.5%), or Hispanics (of any race; 15.5%). Until just recently, men were more likely to hold a bachelor's degree or higher, but college completion has grown significantly for younger generations of women in particular. Before 1986, more men aged 25 to 29 held a bachelor's degree or higher than women of the same age, but women's college completion has risen to at least 5% higher than that of men in the last decade (Ryan & Bauman, 2016).

Table 6.2 Educational attainment for Americans aged 25 years and over in 2015.

Educational attainment for those aged 25 years and over (2015)	
High school diploma or GED (equivalent)	88.4%
Some college or more	58.9%
Associate's degree or more	42.3%
Bachelor's degree or more	32.5%
Advanced degree	12.0%

Financial stability is obviously very important to individuals' functioning, stress, and well-being. The median household income in the U.S. in 2017 was $61,372 (Fontenot, Semega, & Kollar, 2018). Households with a married couple had incomes roughly 50% higher than households headed by a male, but that figure was more than twice that of households headed by a female (see Table 6.3). The poverty rate was 12.3% in 2017 (it has fluctuated between 12% and 15% most years since the 1970s, and was above 15% before 1965; Fontenot et al., 2018). The data reported in Table 6.3 indicate that many families with children live in poverty, and the number of children in families with a single female head of household and living in poverty is shocking. Roughly two-fifths of all children living in a female-headed household in 2017 lived in poverty compared with less than one in 10 children living in families with married-couple parents. Young children under 6 years of age living in a female-headed household were even more likely to be living in poverty (48.5%).

Table 6.3 Income and poverty in the U.S. in 2017.

Median Income	
All households	$61,372
Type of household	
Family households	$77,713
Married-couple	$90,386
Female head, no husband present	$41,703
Male head, no wife present	$60,843
Nonfamily households	$36,650
Female householder	$30,748
Male householder	$44,250
Race and Hispanic origin of householder	
Asian	$81,331
White, not Hispanic	$68,145
Hispanic (any race)	$40,258
Black	$50,486
Living in poverty	
Total population	12.3%
Males	11.0%
Females	13.6%
White, not Hispanic	8.7%
Black	21.2%
Asian	10.0%

Table 6.3 Income and poverty in the U.S. in 2017.—cont'd

Hispanic (any race)	18.3%
No high school or GED (aged 25 or older)	24.5%
High school, no college (aged 25 or older)	12.7%
Some college (aged 25 or older)	8.8%
Bachelor's degree or higher (aged 25 or older)	4.8%
Total families	9.3%
Married couple families	4.9%
Female headed family, no husband present	25.7%
Male-headed family, no wife present	12.4%
Children < 18 in married-couple families	8.4%
Children < 18 in female-headed household	40.8%
Children < 6 in married-couple families	9.5%
Children < 6 in female-headed household	48.4%

Income inequality has grown to be a major concern in the U.S. and other countries. In the U.S., households in the lowest quintile had incomes in 2017 of $24,638 or less, households in the middle quintile had incomes between $47,111 and $77,552, and households in the highest quintile had incomes of $126,856 or higher. Households in the top 5% of income were at $237,035 or higher (Fontenot et al., 2018). Men have also earned more than women in general. In 2017, women working full-time, year-round, of all ages earned 80.5% of what men earned from working full-time, year-round, at all ages.

Stress due to financial status is very common. Surveys find that financial difficulties and stress are the leading causes of marital problems in the U.S. (Vyse, 2008). The APA's 2018 Stress in America survey found that the most frequently cited sources of stress among adults are money (64%) and work (64%) (APA, 2018). Extremely serious problems with financial insecurity are prevalent as well. The causes of homelessness are complicated, but lack of finances is a leading cause. The prevalence of homelessness in the U.S. is high; lifetime prevalence of homelessness is estimated to be 4.2%, and past-year homelessness is 1.5% (Tsai, 2018).

The Gallup poll has included a question regarding sexual orientation in its national Daily tracking survey in recent years. In response to the question, "Do you, personally, identify as lesbian, gay, bisexual, or transgender?" 4.5% responded "Yes" in 2017, a rise over the 3.5% who responded "Yes" in 2012 (Newport, 2018). Millennials (born between 1980 and 1999) were the most likely to respond affirmatively (8.2%), while "Traditionalists" (born between 1913 and 1945) were the least likely to respond "Yes" (1.4%). Females were more likely to respond affirmatively (5.1%) than males (3.9%), and non-Hispanic Whites were the least likely to respond affirmatively (4.0%), while Hispanics were the most likely (6.1%).

Families, relationships, and living arrangements

Families have always been a critical source of support for individuals at the same time that they have been a source of negative effects on development and functioning. For evolutionary reasons, families are a requirement for the survival of *Homo sapien* babies, children, and communities and have always been a main feature of human communities. Nonetheless, living arrangements for many Americans have changed significantly in recent decades.

The median age at first marriage in the U.S. has been rising. It grew to 27.8 years for females and 29.8 years for males in 2018 compared with 25.3 and 27.1, respectively, in 2003 (U.S., Census Bureau, 2018b). The proportion of young adults who are married has also decreased by half over the last 4 decades. In 2018%, 29% of Americans aged 18 to 34 were married compared with 59% in 1978. In 2018, 32% of all Americans aged 15 and over had never been married, compared with 23% in 1950.

The living arrangements of younger Americans have also changed significantly compared with those of earlier generations. The number of young adults living with an unmarried partner had increased to 15% for those aged 25 to 34 by 2018. Of younger adults aged 18 to 24, more are now living together (9%) than living with a spouse (7%). In 2018, single-person households comprised 28% of the total number of households in the U.S. compared with only 13% in 1960 (U.S., Census Bureau, 2018b). Over half (54%) of young adults aged 18 to 24 and 16% of young adults aged 25 to 34 lived in their parents' home in 2018.

Unfortunately, relationship and family dysfunction are common, and intimate partner violence, sexual violence, and stalking are all major public health problems. In the U.S., the Centers for Disease Control and Prevention conducts a national survey on sexual violence (Smith et al., 2018). The 2015 survey included the following findings:

- Over two-fifths of women (43.6%) had experienced some form of contact sexual violence during their lifetimes, with 4.7% experiencing this form of violence in the past year.
- Approximately one in five women (21.3%) reported completed or attempted rape at some time in their lives (13.5% forced penetration, 6.3% attempted forced penetration, and 11.0% alcohol/drug-facilitated penetration)
  - 1.2% of women reported completed or attempted rape in the past year.
- More than one-third of women (37.0%) reported unwanted sexual contact (e.g., groping) in their lifetime.
- 16% of women experienced sexual coercion (e.g., being worn down by repeated requests for sex, sexual pressure by someone using their influence or authority) in their lifetime.

These forms of sexual violence were common, though less frequent, among men as well:

- Nearly one-quarter of men (24.8%) experienced some form of contact sexual violence during their lifetimes, with 3.5% experiencing contact sexual violence in the past year.
- 7% of men (approximately one in 14) were made to penetrate someone else (attempted or completed) in their lives, with 0.7% being made to penetrate in the past year.
- 2.6% of men experienced being victims of completed or attempted rape during their lifetimes.
- 9.6% of men experienced sexual coercion (e.g., being worn down by repeated requests for sex, or sexual pressure by someone using their influence or authority) during their lifetimes.

- 17.9% of men reported unwanted sexual contact (e.g., groping) during their lifetimes.

Many individuals are also victimized through stalking, a pattern of harassing or threatening tactics that causes a person to be fearful or to believe they or someone close to them may be harmed or killed. Nearly one in six women (16.0%) have been victims of stalking in their lifetimes (3.7% in the past year), and about one in 17 men (5.8%) have been victims of stalking during their lifetimes (1.9% in the past year) (Smith et al., 2018).

The U.S. Centers for Disease Control and Prevention defines intimate partner violence as including sexual violence, stalking, physical violence, and psychological aggression (Smith et al., 2018). In 2015

- Over one-third of women (36.4%) had experienced contact sexual violence, physical violence, and/or stalking by an intimate partner during their lifetimes (18.3% contact sexual violence, 30.6% physical violence, and 10.4% stalking)
  - 5.5% had experienced these forms of intimate partner violence in the past year
- Over one-third of women (36.4%) had experienced psychological aggression by an intimate partner during their lifetimes
- Approximately one-third of men (33.6%) had experienced contact sexual violence, physical violence, and/or stalking by an intimate partner during their lifetimes (8.2% contact sexual violence, 31.0% physical violence, and 2.2% stalking)
  - 5.2% had experienced these forms of intimate partner violence in the past year
- Over one-third of men (34.2%) had experienced psychological aggression by an intimate partner during their lifetime

Divorce and relationship dissolution are common as well, and often involve children. Both marriage and divorce rates have been declining in recent years. The marriage rate declined from 8.2 per 1000 of the total U.S. population in 2000 to 6.9 in 2016, while the divorce rate fell from 4.0 per 1000 in the total U.S. population in 2000 to 3.2 in 2016 (CDC, 2018). Divorce affects roughly half of the ever-married population. Of couples in their first marriage, approximately 33% divorce or separate within 10 years, and the rate of divorce is higher for subsequent marriages (Blaisure & Geasler, 2006). Over half of divorces occur in families with minor children, affecting over one million children each year. Cohabitating couple relationships are even more likely to dissolve than marriages, and 46% of these include minor children.

Child maltreatment

Before the 1960s, parents' approach to raising their children was generally considered a private, family matter, and parents were typically considered the best judges of how to raise their own children. The landmark paper by the pediatrician C. Henry Kempe on *The Battered Child Syndrome* in 1962 is regarded as the most important event that exposed the reality of child abuse to human services professionals and the public in general. Researchers began examining the prevalence of different forms of child maltreatment, and evidence quickly accumulated showing that large numbers of children and adolescents were being abused and neglected in various ways.

The U.S. Department of Health and Human Services has been collecting data submitted from all 50 states regarding the reports made to child protective services (CPS) agencies across the country involving suspected child abuse and neglect. There are of course many more children being abused and neglected than those reported to CPS agencies, but these reports are informative nonetheless. The *Child Maltreatment 2016* report (U.S. Department of Health and Human Services, 2018) found that 3.5 million children were the subjects of at least one report to a CPS agency alleging maltreatment. The large majority of these, 82.8%, were determined not to be maltreated, resulting in a victim rate of 9.1 victims per 1000 children. There were also 1700 children reported as being killed as a result of maltreatment.

Population surveys are also used to obtain information about the prevalence and nature of child maltreatment. An important advantage of these surveys is that they include many instances of maltreatment that do not come to the attention of professionals and child welfare agencies. Indeed, these surveys do find much higher rates of child abuse and neglect than those reported in the annual DHHS *Child Maltreatment* reports. One of the most reliable national surveys conducted to date was published by Finkelhor, Vanderminden, Turner, Hamby, and Shattuck in 2014. For children and youth aged 0 to 17, these researchers found the following:

- 8.9% of children were reported to have a lifetime history of physical abuse by caregivers; 4.0% had a history of physical abuse within the past year
- 10.3% were reported as having been emotionally abused by caregivers; 5.6% in the past year
- 0.7% were reported as having a history of sexual abuse by caregivers; 0.1% in the past year (this included all children in the sample, from age 0 to 17)
- 2.2% were reported as having a history of sexual abuse by caregivers and noncaregivers (this included all children, from age 0 to 17)
- The rate of sexual abuse was much higher for older children and adolescents; the lifetime rate of sexual abuse by caregivers and noncaregivers for 14- to 17-year-olds was 10.6%, and the rate for females was higher still (17.4%)
- 11.6% were reported as having experienced neglect; 4.7% in the past year
- 4.7% were reported as experiencing custodial interference (e.g., a parent attempted to hide the child to keep them away from the other parent); 1.2% in the past year
- ***Overall***, 12.1% of the children in the survey experienced at least one of these forms of maltreatment in the past year
- 23% of these maltreated children experienced two or more forms of maltreatment
- 34% of the maltreatment reported as occurring within the past year was known to some authority (which increases the likelihood of intervention and appropriate assistance)

Extensive research finds that child maltreatment has major effects on psychological development and functioning, and rates of child maltreatment are routinely found to be much higher in clinical samples than they are in the general population (Finkelhor, 2008; Myers, 2011). Although mental health practitioners are generally well aware of the significance of child maltreatment in clients' lives, graduate education in behavioral health care often has not covered this topic extensively.

Significantly increased attention has been given to the prevalence and impact of adverse childhood experiences in the U.S. recently. A 1998 study by Felitti, Anda, and colleagues found that 67% of a very large sample of Kaiser Permanente patients in San Diego, CA, had experienced at least 1 of 10 categories of child abuse or serious family dysfunction, and 12.6% had experienced four or more categories. This study stimulated a large amount of subsequent research that found that adverse childhood experiences greatly influence psychological and physical health and can even significantly shorten one's life span. A section of Chapter 8 is devoted to reviewing this research in more detail.

Elder abuse

The topic of elder abuse is sometimes not included in basic conceptualizations of behavioral health care, not because it is unimportant in any way but rather because it occurs in a particular segment of the population. Child abuse and a history of child maltreatment are relevant when working with all child and adult populations, whereas elder abuse only exists in the older adult population. But all clinicians are concerned about the abuse and neglect of vulnerable adults because the effects can be as damaging as those suffered by any other segment of the population. The topic can also arise in all types of clinical practice because even child therapists, through their work with children and parents, may become aware of grandparents or other older adults who are being abused, exploited, or neglected. Therefore, the issue is highlighted here to ensure that it is not overlooked when conceptualizing practice in the field.

In the first comprehensive U.S. survey of mistreatment among older adults, Acierno et al. (2010) found that more than 1 in 10 respondents (11.4%) aged 60 and older reported experiencing at least one form of mistreatment in the past year. Financial exploitation was the most common form of victimization and was reported by 5.2% of the respondents as occurring in the past year. In addition, 4.6% reported emotional abuse in the past year, 1.6% reported physical mistreatment in the past year, and 0.6% reported sexual mistreatment in the past year. Potential neglect, or reporting that a need that was not being met, was also indicated by 5.9% of the respondents as having occurred in the past year.

In a review of worldwide research on the prevalence of elder abuse, Yon, Mikton, Gassoumis, and Wilber (2017) estimated that the prevalence of any type of abuse of adults aged 60 years and over in the past year was 15.7% (nearly one in six). The estimated past-year prevalence for psychological abuse was 11.6%, financial abuse was 6.8%, neglect was 4.2%, physical abuse was 2.6%, and sexual abuse was 0.9%. The survey found no significant gender difference in overall abuse rates.

Cooper, Selwood, and Livingston (2008) further estimated that one-third of family caregivers caring for dependent older adults reported perpetrating abuse, 16% of professional caregivers report committing psychological abuse, and 1 in 10 professional caregivers reports perpetrating physical abuse. Over 80% of nursing home staff also reported observing abuse by others, though very little of this abuse (2%) was reported to management. Given the few reports of elder abuse made to adult protective services agencies in the U.S., it is apparent that only a small number of elder abuse cases are known to the officials responsible for protecting this population.

Criminal victimization and legal involvement

Criminal victimization is frequently traumatic, and adjustment and acute stress disorders can result from experiencing these types of stressors and trauma. For example, the *DSM-5* (American Psychiatric Association, 2013) reports that one-third to more than one-half of survivors of rape (and military combat) develop PTSD, and 20%–50% of those experiencing assault or rape or witnessing a mass shooting develop acute stress disorder.

Many individuals are victims of crime, though fortunately the numbers have fallen significantly in recent decades in the U.S. The Department of Justice National Crime Victimization Survey (U.S. Bureau of Justice Statistics, 2012b) found that 2.3% of individuals age 12 and over reported experiencing a violent crime in 2011 (which was a dramatic drop from the 1970s when rates were routinely greater than 4.5%). The proportion who experienced serious violent crimes (which included rape or sexual assault, robbery, and aggravated assault) was 0.7%, also a dramatic drop from decades past. An estimated 13.9% of households also reported a property crime in 2005 (which was a dramatic drop from the 1970s when rates were consistently above 50%). These included household burglary (2.9%), motor vehicle theft (0.5%), and other type of theft (10.4%).

Other types of legal involvement occur frequently as well. The total number of newly filed, reopened, and reactivated cases of all different types in the nation's state courts in 2006 was 102.4 million incoming cases (U.S. Bureau of Justice Statistics, 2012b; most [54%] of these fell under the category of traffic violations, however, which are typically much less complicated and stressful). Being victimized by crime or otherwise being involved in legal cases occurs frequently and can be extremely stressful. Sometimes the effects pass relatively quickly, but there obviously can be permanent effects as well.

Religion and spirituality

Surveys consistently find high levels of religiosity in the U.S. compared with other industrialized countries. Gallup's 2017 poll (Newport, 2017) found that about three-quarters of Americans identify with a Christian faith. Protestant was the largest religious group (48.5%), Catholic was the next-largest group (22.7%), and Mormons accounted for 1.8% of the population. Another 6% of the population identified with a non-Christian faith including Judaism (2.1%) and Islam (0.8%). Over 1 in 5 (21.3%) reported no religious identity. The 2017 Gallup poll found that 37% reported being highly religious, 30% reported being moderately religious, and 33% reported being not religious at all.

In an extensive study of religiosity in the U.S., Cox and Jones (2017) noted that the religious landscape in America has undergone a dramatic shift in recent decades. White Christians now account for only 43% of Americans, whereas 81% of Americans identified as White and Christian in 1976. White evangelical Protestants, White mainline Protestants, and White Catholics are all in decline and growing older. In contrast, non-Christian groups (e.g., Jewish Americans, Muslims, Buddhists, Hindus) are relatively young and are growing, although they still represent a small proportion (6%) of the American public. There are now 20 states where the religiously unaffiliated outnumber all other religious groups (e.g., 41% of Vermonters, 36% of Oregonians, 35% of Washingtonians, and 34% of Hawaiians identify as religiously unaffiliated).

Importance of sociocultural factors

Sociocultural factors play a critical role in individuals' development and functioning. They frequently also play a significant role in treatment outcomes because sociocultural support, stressors, and other factors commonly have significant facilitative or debilitative effects on the course of treatment. As a result, these factors are routinely included in most approaches to behavioral health care assessment and treatment planning.

All of the topics discussed above have important influences on people's lives and so they all need to be integrated into therapists' conceptualizations of clinical practice. It is not possible to work clinically with patients without dealing with these topics, because patients routinely bring these issues with them into treatment. For example, the U.S. population is becoming increasingly demographically diverse, and knowledge and skills for dealing with the cultural influences and challenges faced by individuals who are not members of the mainstream culture need to be incorporated into the competencies required for clinical practice. Failing to do so will result in the profession becoming less relevant to increasing numbers of individuals who do not fall within the traditional target groups for many psychotherapeutic treatments (Sue & Sue, 2012). All of the other factors previously discussed here are likewise relevant to clinical practice. Financial difficulties and employment stress are common. Relationship and family dysfunction, violence, and abuse are all too common, and large numbers of individuals experience child abuse and neglect. Religion and spirituality are important factors in people's lives as well, often as important sources of support, though sometimes as sources of stress.

Some of the above topics receive significant attention in behavioral health care education, although others receive only limited coverage in many programs. Coverage of these topics is frequently not systematic, and developing familiarity with them consequently often occurs in a haphazard manner, sometimes outside formal coursework and clinical training. Multiculturalism is one of the few topics reviewed above that normally receives significant attention in graduate curricula. Even child maltreatment, a topic widely viewed as very important in individuals' development, is often not reviewed in a comprehensive manner in many graduate programs.

Although the variables covered in this chapter are all highly influential in people's development and functioning, it is important not to overstate their influence as well. For example, in American psychology, racial and ethnic minority individuals are more likely to be viewed as members of groups that are strongly shaped by cultural processes and less by psychological processes, whereas White European Americans are frequently viewed as individuals whose behavior and characteristics are shaped by psychological processes and less by cultural influences (Causadias, Vitriol, & Atkin, 2018). This bias can result in viewing White members of society as having unique characteristics while stereotyping minority individuals as homogeneous. As a result, more attention may be given to the psychological processes involved in the development of personality and psychopathology for White individuals, while more attention is placed on cultural influences on the development of personality and psychopathology among minority individuals. There appears to be no cumulative scientific evidence to support these biases.

Taking a biopsychosocial approach can help avoid such biases by reminding us to balance psychological, sociocultural, and biological perspectives when attempting to understand all individuals. Viewing people through lenses determined by group membership can lessen one's ability to see their individuality and humanity, their unique personal qualities, and their universal human characteristics. Placing disproportionate emphasis on group membership—whether based on race, ethnicity, gender, religion, or other variables—can lead to the process of dehumanization that has caused so much violence and suffering throughout history in the first place. This of course does not imply that we have any less responsibility to fight racism, sexism, homophobia, ageism, ableism, religious intolerance, and other forms of prejudice and discrimination. Behavioral health professionals' responsibilities to promote health, well-being, and social justice are in no way lessened just because humans are complicated and have unique personal as well as group and universal characteristics.

The biopsychosocial approach to behavioral health care is complex. Individuals' development and functioning as well as the behavioral change process cannot be thoroughly understood without taking an integrative, holistic perspective that incorporates all these factors. Sociocultural factors can be facilitative or debilitative on individuals' development, their current functioning, and the behavioral change process. In addition, building resilience and promoting optimal functioning over the long term typically involves building strengths in these areas. When the focus of health care is broadened beyond the treatment of psychopathology to the prevention of maladjustment and the promotion of health and well-being, then the importance of these factors becomes even clearer. Sociocultural factors also have significant influences on individuals' physical health, the topic considered next.

Physical health and functioning

7

Physical health and functioning obviously have major impacts on behavioral health, and behavioral health has major impacts on physical health as well. Therefore, standard approaches to behavioral health care assessment and treatment all note the importance of patients' physical health and its interactions with psychological functioning. Behavioral health clinicians, of course, are not responsible for assessing and treating medical conditions, but they are responsible for understanding the interaction of physical health and psychological functioning as well as knowing when referrals for medical evaluations may be needed.

The biopsychosocial approach highlights the interactions between physical, psychological, and social functioning, and research is showing in increasing detail how these domains are inextricably intertwined. The importance of behavior and lifestyle to physical health and functioning is also now widely accepted. The Institute of Medicine in 2004 concluded that roughly 50% of morbidity and mortality in the U.S. is caused by behavior and lifestyle factors. They also concluded that medical schools need to increase their coverage of behavioral influences on physical health if physicians are going to increase their effectiveness at treating medical conditions. Integrated care approaches in which behavioral health professionals work collaboratively with medical professionals are also growing more common as the medical world increasingly takes an integrated, holistic approach to health care (see Chapter 13). The growing interest in health and wellness normally focuses on physical health along with psychosocial well-being as well. These changes have resulted in health care professionals giving more attention to the interactions between physical and psychosocial health and functioning.

To provide an overview of the physical health status of the patients cared for in health service psychology, this chapter begins by summarizing the data on life expectancy and the leading causes of death. This is followed by an overview of the prevalence of medical conditions in general. The physical health of individuals with serious mental illness is also discussed because physical disease and premature death are particularly prevalent in this population. The basic evolutionary underpinnings of the chronic medical conditions that have become common in the U.S. and increasingly around the world are also briefly discussed.

Life expectancy, causes of death, and medical conditions

Among the important indicators of the physical health of a population are life expectancy, the leading causes of death, and the prevalence of medical conditions. Life expectancy has generally continued to increase in the U.S. over the past century. In 1900, life expectancy at birth in the U.S. was only 47.3 years. By 2014, it had

Foundations of Health Service Psychology. https://doi.org/10.1016/B978-0-12-816426-6.00007-4

grown to its highest level ever, 78.9 years (National Center for Health Statistics, 2018). Two years later, in 2016, life expectancy had reduced slightly to 78.6 years. This drop was caused largely by deaths from drug overdose and suicide (Redfield, 2018). Life expectancy for males has always been lower than for females: in 2016, life expectancy was 76.1 years for males and 81.1 years for females. The Hispanic population has the highest life expectancy (81.8 years in 2016), followed by the non-Hispanic White population (78.5 years) and the African American population (74.8 years).

Identifying the causes of disease and death can be complicated because diseases and injuries often have multiple causes, and several factors contribute to death in many cases. Nonetheless, the Centers for Disease Control and Prevention summarize data from throughout the U.S. regarding the specific causes of death for the American population. They found that the 12 leading causes of death in 2016 comprised those listed in Table 7.1 (National Center for Health Statistics, 2018).

Many of the leading causes of death actually share a small number of underlying causes. At the most general level, the Institute of Medicine (2004) concluded that roughly 50% of morbidity and mortality in the U.S. is caused by behavior and lifestyle factors. Smoking is the leading cause of preventable morbidity and mortality and has been found to account for nearly one in five deaths (U.S. Department of Health and Human Services, 2014). It accounts for about 90% of all lung cancer deaths and for about 80% of all deaths from chronic obstructive pulmonary disease. Obesity has become the second leading cause of preventable morbidity and mortality in the U.S. and accounted for 16.6% of deaths (Mokdad, Marks, Stroup, & Gerberding, 2004). Alcohol consumption is the

Table 7.1 Leading causes of death in the U.S., 2016.

Cause	Rate (deaths per 100,000)
1. Heart disease	165.5
2. Cancer	155.8
3. Chronic lower respiratory diseases	40.6
4. Unintentional injuries (accidents)	47.4
5. Stroke (cerebrovascular diseases)	37.3
6. Alzheimer's disease	30.3
7. Diabetes	21.0
8. Influenza and pneumonia	13.5
9. Suicide	13.5
10. Nephritis, nephrotic syndrome, and nephrosis (kidney disease)	13.1
11. Chronic liver disease and cirrhosis	10.7
12. Homicide	6.2

The category of unintentional injuries includes primarily drug overdoses and vehicle deaths.

next most important factor (3.5% of deaths). The World Health Organization (2008c) arrived at very similar conclusions for the world as a whole. They estimate that up to 80% of heart disease, stroke, and type 2 diabetes and more than one-third of cancers worldwide could be prevented by eliminating the shared risk factors of tobacco use, unhealthy diet, physical inactivity, and excessive alcohol use. These four factors have become critical for reducing disease and death globally as well as in the U.S.

The U.S. Centers for Disease Control and Prevention have been monitoring the health status of the nation since 1957 using the National Health Interview Survey. Table 7.2 indicates the percentage of Americans in the latest survey who reported that they had various diseases or risk factors for disease (National Center on Health Statistics, 2018).

The percentage of adults in the 2011 National Health Interview Survey who reported they were told by a doctor or other health care professional that they had a particular medical condition is indicated in Table 7.3 (Schiller, Lucas, & Peregoy, 2012). Conditions are listed in order of decreasing prevalence and for those experienced by more than 1% of adults. Age was correlated with the prevalence of many of these conditions, although prevalence was elevated across age groups for many other conditions.

The data in Tables 7.1–7.3 indicate that large proportions of the population deal with significant discomfort, suffering, disease, and activity limitations. Many of the conditions listed cause pain and limitations in one's ability to carry out basic social roles and responsibilities. All of them have major psychological components in terms

Table 7.2 Risk factors for morbidity and mortality in the U.S., 2016.

Risk factor	Percentage
Heart disease, age 18 and over	11.6
Heart disease, 65 and over	28.9
Cancer, 18 and over	6.9
Cancer, 65 and over	19.2
Diabetes, 20 and over	12.6
High cholesterol, 20 and over	29.4
Obesity, 20 and over	38.9
Obesity, BMI 95th percentile or higher, 2–5 years	11.6
Obesity, BMI 95th percentile or higher, 6–11 years	17.9
Obesity, BMI 95th percentile or higher, 12–19 years	20.6
Cigarette smoking, 18 and over	15.5
Less than recommended physical activity, 18 and over[a]	88.1

BMI, body mass index.
[a]Less than the recommended guideline of at least 150 min of moderate-intensity and 75 min of vigorous-intensity aerobic physical activity per week.

Table 7.3 Medical conditions in U.S. adults rank ordered by prevalence as reported in the CDC 2011 National Health Interview Survey.

Disorder	Prevalence (%)
Overweight	34
Lower back pain	29 (in the past 3 months)
Chronic joint symptoms	29
Obesity	28
Hypertension	24
Arthritis, rheumatoid arthritis, gout, lupus, or fibromyalgia	22
Restlessness	19
Nervousness	17
Migraine/severe headaches	17 (in the past 3 months)
Hearing difficulty without hearing aid	16
Limitations in physical functioning	16
Neck pain	15 (in the past 3 months)
Felt everything was an effort	15
Sinusitis	13
Asthma	13 (8% still have it)
Sadness	12
Heart disease	11
Vision trouble (even with correction)	9
Diabetes	9
Absence of all natural teeth	8
Cancer	8
Hay fever	7
Ulcer	7
Hopelessness	7
Coronary heart disease	6
Worthlessness	5
Face/jaw pain	5 (in the past 3 months)
Chronic bronchitis	4
Stroke	3

Table 7.3 Medical conditions in U.S. adults rank ordered by prevalence as reported in the CDC 2011 National Health Interview Survey.—continued

Disorder	Prevalence (%)
Emphysema	2
Kidney disease	2 (in past 12 months)
Underweight	2
Liver disease	1 (in past 12 months)

of etiology, treatment, and/or consequences. In addition, somatic symptoms are the leading reason for outpatient medical visits in the U.S., accounting for more than 50% of all visits, and at least 33% of these are medically unexplained (Kroenke, 2003). In addition, somatic symptoms are the predominant reason patients with depression, anxiety, or other common mental disorders present in primary care (i.e., 70%–90%). The implications of these symptoms and conditions become clearer when chronic disease prevalence is taken into account.

Increase in chronic disease

The causes of death and disease changed dramatically in the U.S. and other parts of the industrialized world over the past century. Up until the end of the 1800s, illness and death were caused primarily by acute and infectious diseases. Very little was known about the nature of infectious viral and bacterial diseases; they could not be controlled and basically just had to be endured. But science began to understand the causes of these diseases, and vaccines, clean water systems, sewer systems, other public health measures, and antibiotics began to control infectious diseases. Chronic diseases associated with lifestyle and behavior then began to cause most illness and death. This shift has been called the *epidemiological transition* (Gribble & Preston, 1993). The death rate from infectious disease was approximately 800 per 100,000 individuals in 1900 and fell to roughly 50 per 100,000 by 1950, where it has stayed since (Centers for Disease Control, 1999). Most infectious disease deaths now involve influenza in elderly individuals, while other infectious diseases have been nearly or completely eliminated. Public health measures became so effective over the course of the 20th century that the majority of Americans now suffer and die from chronic rather than acute infectious diseases.

Over one-half of the American population now deals with a chronic medical condition (Buttorff, Ruder, & Bauman, 2017). For the population as a whole:

- 6 in 10 (60%) American adults had at least one chronic condition in 2014;
- 4 in 10 (42%) American adults had two or more chronic conditions;
- 12% of American adults had five or more chronic conditions;

- high blood pressure (27% of adults) and high cholesterol (22%) are the most common chronic conditions, followed by mood disorders (12%), diabetes (10%), anxiety disorders (10%), upper respiratory disorders (7%), inflammatory joint disorders (7%) and arthritis (7%), and asthma (6%)
- the prevalence of chronic conditions is highest among older adults, and women report more chronic conditions than men.

These chronic conditions are also common causes of death. The leading causes of death found in Table 7.1 are frequently associated with these chronic health conditions.

People with chronic medical conditions are much more likely to use health care services. For example, those with five or more conditions use twice as many medications per year than people with three or four conditions (Buttorff et al., 2017). People with five or more conditions also average 20 doctor visits per year compared with 12 visits for those with three or four conditions. The patterns for emergency department visits and inpatient stays are similar. Overall, Americans with five or more chronic conditions comprised 12% of the population but accounted for 41% of the total health care spending in 2014. Those with more chronic conditions are also much more likely to have difficulties with activities of daily living and have a variety of social and cognitive limitations (Buttorff et al., 2017).

Co-occurring mental illness and physical disease

Individuals with mental illness are at especially high risk for physical health problems. These individuals have significantly higher rates of disease and their life span is actually 9 years shorter than those without a mental health disorder (Druss et al., 2011). The most common causes of death for individuals with a mental health disorder are chronic medical conditions such as cardiovascular disease and cancer (69%), whereas suicide, accidents, and homicide were relatively infrequent causes of death in this population (together accounting for 5% of deaths).

As mentioned in Chapter 5, an estimated 18.9% of the U.S. population had any mental illness in the past year and 4.5% had a serious mental illness (SAMHSA, 2018). These individuals are at higher risk for some of the most prevalent health conditions and are more likely to use an emergency room or be hospitalized within the past year (see Table 7.4).

Individuals with serious mental illness and who rely on the U.S. public mental health care system suffer much higher rates of chronic disease and early death. The average life span of Americans in the public health system with serious mental illness is only 53 years, a remarkable 25 years shorter than the general population (National Association of State Mental Health Program Directors, 2006). In the state of Oregon, individuals with a dual diagnosis of mental illness and substance abuse in the public health system were found to have an average life span of only 45 years, 32 fewer than the general population (Oregon Department of Human Services, 2008).

Most of the premature death among individuals with serious mental illness is the result of preventable conditions. Of individuals with serious mental illness in the U.S. public mental health system, an estimated 60% of premature deaths are due to preventable

Table 7.4 Chronic health conditions, emergency room use, and hospitalization in the past year for adults with or without mental illness (SAMHSA, 2012).

	Any mental illness (%)		Serious mental illness (%)	
	Yes	No	Yes	No
High blood pressure	21.9	18.8	21.6	17.7
Asthma	15.7	10.6	19.1	12.1
Diabetes	7.9	6.6	7.7	6.6
Heart disease	5.9	4.2	5.2	4.2
Stroke	2.3	0.9	2.6	1.1
Emergency room use	38.8	27.1	47.6	30.5
Hospitalization	15.1	10.1	20.4	11.6

chronic conditions such as cardiovascular and pulmonary diseases and another 30%−40% is due to suicide and injury (National Association of State Mental Health Program Directors, 2006). Nearly half of all cigarette consumption is by individuals with mental illness or substance use disorders (Lasser et al., 2000), and nearly 75% of people with serious mental illness are tobacco dependent, compared with 22% of the general population (Grant et al., 2004). Taken together, these findings suggest a major public health crisis for this segment of the population. These individuals and their families endure major amounts of stress, worry, and suffering, much of it preventable.

Quality of life and well-being

The evaluation of individuals' health status and well-being extends beyond traditional indicators of disease, disability, and premature death. As the World Health Organization noted as early as 1948, the absence of disease does not imply health (see Chapter 7). Likewise, the presence of disease or disability does not imply poor quality of life. Many individuals with vision loss, difficulty with mobility, intellectual disability, or chronic diseases live long, productive lives with high levels of quality of life and well-being. On the other hand, many individuals with no disease or disability lead lives with low quality of life and well-being.

A major effort to promote the health and well-being of the U.S. population involves the Healthy People project, which is coordinated by the U.S. Department of Health and Human Services. The first version of the Healthy People project was initiated by the surgeon general's 1979 report on the health of the nation as a whole. Each decade since then, a new set of national objectives was developed to improve the health and well-being of the general public. The latest version of this effort, called Healthy People 2020, was initiated in 2010 and includes the following four overarching goals:

- Attain high-quality, longer lives free of preventable disease, disability, injury, and premature death.

- Achieve health equity, eliminate disparities, and improve the health of all groups.
- Create social and physical environments that promote good health for all.
- Promote quality of life, healthy development, and healthy behaviors across all life stages (U.S. Department of Health and Human Services, 2013).

In the progress update on the project conducted in March, 2014, there was improvement on just over half of the health indicators compared with 2010 and little or no change for nearly a third of the indicators. Areas in which noteworthy progress was achieved included decreases in cigarette smoking, children exposed to secondhand smoke, and adolescents using alcohol or illicit drugs. There was also progress in the number of people engaged in aerobic physical activity. The three indicators that indicated worsening, however, included the number of people who died by suicide, number of adolescents with major depressive episodes, and number of people who visited the dentist (U.S. Department of Health and Human Services, 2019). (See also Chapters 8 and 13 for more discussion of quality of life and well-being.)

Underlying causes of chronic disease

As noted earlier in this chapter, the world's population began a fundamental transition in terms of its experience with disease and death at the end of the 19th century. People in industrialized countries began undergoing the *epidemiological transition* whereby the primary causes of disease and death, for the first time in human history, shifted from acute and infectious diseases to chronic diseases associated with behavior and lifestyle (Gribble & Preston, 1993). The top five leading causes of death in the U.S. are now heart disease, cancer, chronic lower respiratory diseases, accidents, and stroke (National Center for Health Statistics, 2018). Many of these conditions share a small number of underlying causes that are directly related to people's behavior and lifestyle. Smoking, obesity, and alcohol consumption are the leading causes of these conditions. These trends that started in the U.S. and other industrialized countries are now affecting societies around the world. The World Health Organization (WHO, 2008b) estimated that up to 80% of heart disease, stroke, and type 2 diabetes and more than one-third of cancers worldwide could be prevented by eliminating the shared risk factors of tobacco use, unhealthy diet, physical inactivity, and excessive alcohol use.

The underlying reasons for the dramatic changes in human morbidity and mortality since the turn of the 20th century are becoming clear. Research from biological, social science, and medical disciplines has demonstrated that the long evolution of hominins over the past 6 million years has resulted in capacities and vulnerabilities that are poorly suited to modern diets, physical activities, and lifestyles (Lieberman, 2013). Before the discovery of agriculture 10,000 years ago, hunter—gatherers ate primarily nuts, fruits, tubers (e.g., sweet potatoes, cassava), and some meat. Most of their food contained large amounts of fiber, and chewing these foods actually required large amounts of time and energy; a typical meal might require thousands of chews (Lieberman, 2011). Before the hybridization of domesticated plants, the fruits that our hunter–gatherer ancestors ate contained far less sugar than modern fruits (e.g., wild crab apples are similar to carrots in sweetness), and the only really sweet food that could be consumed was honey. The meat our ancestors ate came from wild animals and contained only a fraction of the fat found in modern farm-raised meat, fish, and poultry. Salt was generally consumed only in the miniscule amounts that are naturally found in plants and animals. Hunting and gathering (and even chewing) required large amounts of physical activity compared with the activity levels of most individuals in modern societies. People consequently were very lean (Lieberman, 2013).

Homo sapiens evolved to crave sweets and fats so that any excess calorie intake was quickly and easily converted into fat and people could survive periods of insufficient food intake. Human diets changed dramatically, however, after the agricultural revolution 10,000 years ago, when people began eating large amounts of grains. Diets changed radically again with the rise of industrialized agriculture in the 20th century. Since the end of World War II, people in wealthy countries have eaten large amounts of refined grains that contain little fiber, large amounts of sugar, and large amounts of fatty meats (Cordain et al., 2005). Humans' bodies evolved over millions of years to consume foods very different from what modern people eat and to be far more active than most people in wealthy countries today. This has caused widespread problems related to high cholesterol, high blood pressure, and obesity, along with conditions that are caused by inactivity and disuse such as back pain, osteoporosis, and dental problems, all of which are rare in hunter–gatherers (Lieberman, 2013). This lack of fit between evolved traits that were once advantageous but became maladaptive due to changes in the environment is commonly referred to as *evolutionary mismatch*.

The Scientific and Industrial Revolutions and the Enlightenment improved the human condition in many very important ways. Our lives are now far safer, easier, and much more comfortable. But those benefits came at a cost. Although we die far less from infectious disease and injury than our ancestors, we now suffer large amounts of chronic disease and disability associated with modern lifestyles. Over recent decades, research has shown that much of this disease is caused by our own behavior and lifestyles and is, in a sense, self-imposed. Nonetheless, behavior change can be very difficult. Addressing this is a major challenge for human service professionals, researchers, and public health professionals.

Importance of physical health

The *epidemiological transition* that started in the late 19th century has had a dramatic effect not just on physical health but also on human psychology, society, and culture. As acute and infectious disease were brought under control over the next half-century, human beings began enjoying levels of health and security never before known. Diseases that we did not understand and could not control were greatly reduced and even, in some cases, eradicated (although some have begun to return recently due to skepticism by some about the safety of vaccines). Getting one's basic needs met in an environment of relative safely, predictability, and comfort is now possible for large proportions of the population. This never happened before in human history. Even people living at the poverty level often have fresh food, safe water, appliances, indoor plumbing, heat, and even air conditioning that was unavailable to royalty just a century and a half ago.

But the tremendous benefits associated with the epidemiological transition and with scientific and technological advances over the past century also came with costs. One cost is that the leading causes of morbidity and mortality are now chronic diseases associated with behavior and lifestyle. (Another even more serious and threatening cost involves climate change.) Fortunately, we now understand these problems well. The biological mechanisms and processes that account for the rise in chronic diseases are now well understood, and we have a much better understanding of the basic evolutionary reasons for why we are so vulnerable to these diseases in the modern world.

Sadly, individuals with mental illness are particularly likely to suffer chronic disease and early death. Indeed, the data regarding this issue are alarming. Individuals with mental illness die nearly 9 years earlier than those without a mental disorder, and individuals in the public health care system with serious mental illness die on average 25 years earlier than the general population. There is an epidemic of serious chronic illness and shortened life span among those with serious mental illness. This takes a huge toll on the lives of these individuals and their loved ones and represents a public health crisis that receives far less attention than it deserves.

Health care professions are increasingly recognizing the critical importance of behavior and lifestyle to physical health and the importance of physical health to mental health. Physical illness, disability, and poor health frequently prevent individuals from participating fully in life and carrying out important responsibilities. Virtually all of the most prevalent physical health conditions experienced by the American public have major psychological components in terms of etiology, treatment, and/or consequences. The specialization of health psychology has long focused on these issues, but they are increasingly being addressed by health care professionals in general.

Graduate education in behavioral health care often gave limited attention to these issues in the past. Medical education also gave insufficient attention to the role of behavior and lifestyle to physical health. Even the serious physical health problems of those dealing with serious mental illness were (and still are) typically addressed in only a limited manner, if at all. Despite the past neglect of these issues in health care education, all health care professionals need to integrate knowledge and skills regarding these topics into their clinical competencies.

Development: biopsychosocial factors interacting over time

8

The foundational framework for understanding human development and functioning that is taken in this volume is depicted in Fig. 1.2. That figure included a cube intersected by an arrow. The three dimensions of the cube represent the biological, psychological, and sociocultural levels of natural organization, while the arrow depicts the dimension of time. The interaction of these four dimensions of the natural world together create the human experience. The three biopsychosocial levels of natural organization provide the structures, mechanisms, and processes, and it is through the fourth dimension of time that these biopsychosocial factors interact and processes play out. The interaction of the biopsychosocial factors across time results in the wondrously varied experience of human development and consciousness.

The interaction of the four developmental biopsychosocial processes is astoundingly complex. Each of the biological, psychological, and sociocultural levels is tremendously complex on its own, plus they interact in countless ways over time. There is a great deal of regularity and pattern in this process, but chance factors and luck also play important roles, although only within the constraints allowed by each of the four developmental biopsychosocial dimensions.

This chapter highlights essential aspects of the time dimension, which provides the developmental perspective on human psychology. Development and change continue across the whole life span, of course, but most of the discussion here focuses on childhood because of its importance in establishing the foundation for the interplay of vulnerabilities, dysfunction, strengths, and resources across the life span. Readers are reminded that this subject is very complex and requires extensive study to fully appreciate. The purpose of this chapter is merely to outline the basic features of the developmental framework that are necessary for appreciating the science-based biopsychosocial approach to understanding human psychology. The discussion begins with an overview of key features of a developmental framework and then describes the process of infant attachment as a prototypical example. This is followed by a discussion of the importance of risk and protective factors in development before going on to a discussion of health, well-being, and flourishing.

Key features of a developmental framework

The development of maladjustment and psychopathology, as well as strengths and health, all needs to be considered in terms of the individual and contextual factors that shape peoples' lives over the life span. There is substantial agreement regarding key features of the developmental perspective that can bring together those factors into a single integrative framework (Cicchetti & Toth, 1992; Kellam & Rebok,

Foundations of Health Service Psychology. https://doi.org/10.1016/B978-0-12-816426-6.00008-6

1992; Masten, Faden, Zucker, & Spear, 2008; National Research Council and Institute of Medicine, 2009). Those features include the following:

1. age-related changes in abilities
2. multiple contexts within which development occurs
3. interactions among biological, psychological, and social factors
4. developmental tasks and competence

Age-related changes in abilities

Appreciating age-related changes in cognitive, emotional, and behavioral abilities is essential for understanding human development. These changes are fundamental to the development of health and competence as well as maladjustment and disorder. Biological, cognitive, emotional, behavioral, interpersonal, and social changes take place throughout life. The earliest period, however, from conception to about age 5, receives special attention because the opportunity to establish a solid foundation for future development is greater during this stage than at any other time in a person's life (National Research Council and Institute of Medicine, 2000, 2009). Competencies and resilience developed in these early years form the foundation for the development of future competencies throughout later childhood, adolescence, and adulthood. Likewise, the development of vulnerabilities and dysfunction at this stage can lead to repeated challenges across the biopsychosocial domains and across the life span.

Multiple contexts within which development occurs

Urie Bronfenbrenner's (1979) ecological perspective on human development is a widely used approach for conceptualizing the many levels of environmental influence on human development. This model posits that human development occurs within an ecological system comprising five subsystems that include the *microsystem* (the immediate environment, e.g., family, school, neighborhood, friends), *mesosystem* (relations between microsystems, e.g., relations between one's family members and school personnel), *exosystem* (relations with settings in which one does not have an active role, e.g., a spouse's work requirements affect child care and home life), *macrosystem* (one's culture, e.g., socioeconomic class, ethnicity, religion), and *chronosystem* (the historical context, in terms of both how personal events such as a divorce play out over time and the sociohistorical context in which one lives). Bronfenbrenner (2001) later added a sixth level that recognizes the importance of one's *biology*, and he termed this newer version of the model *bioecological theory*. Developmental processes play out within the context of these nested subsystems, as do behavioral health care interventions and prevention programs.

Interactions among biological, psychological, and social factors

The biopsychosocial perspective is essential to the developmental framework for understanding human psychology. As emphasized throughout this volume, human development and functioning cannot be understood without recognizing the interactions among genetic and other biological processes, psychological processes, and the multiple levels of sociocultural and environmental influences, from the family to culture and the sociohistorical context. The interplay of these factors is obviously tremendously complex, although research continues to uncover how their interaction produces vulnerabilities and dysfunction as well as competence and strengths (see below and the discussion of epigenetics and neural plasticity in Chapter 3).

Developmental tasks and competence

A fourth key feature of the developmental perspective for understanding human psychology involves the behavioral expectations that individuals encounter across social contexts over their lifetimes. These situations, often referred to as developmental tasks, change as one grows older and differ according to culture, gender, and historical period (Kellam & Rebok, 1992; Masten, Burt, & Coatsworth, 2006). Success or difficulty with one developmental task can have major consequences for success in other tasks and for the later development of problems and psychopathology.

Successfully accomplishing developmentally appropriate tasks leads to a positive sense of mastery, self-esteem, social inclusion, well-being, and resilience, whereas failure with these tasks can contribute to maladjustment and psychopathology. The National Research Council and Institute of Medicine (2000) found that accomplishing the developmental tasks of secure attachment, emotional regulation, executive functioning, and appropriate conduct during infancy and early childhood was associated with healthy development and the prevention of behavioral health problems over the long term. Masten et al. (2006) refer to the accomplishment of these tasks as *developmental competence*. In a longitudinal study called Project Competence, they examined the development of three dimensions of competence during childhood (academic, social, and conduct) and five dimensions of competence in late adolescence (academic, social, conduct, job, and romantic).

There are many age-related change processes and developmental tasks that take place from conception through the end of life, far too many to review here. One of the most important of these processes, however, is attachment. It embodies all of the key features of a developmental framework and has major effects on individuals' personality, psychopathology, and adjustment across the life span. These effects are also the focus of a significant amount of psychotherapeutic intervention. Therefore, the importance of attachment is highlighted next as a prototypical example of a developmental task.

Attachment as a prototypical example

Infant attachment provided a solution to one of the most daunting problems faced by our early hominin ancestors. Human infants have very large brains and take many years to mature into relatively independent organisms who can fend for themselves. Given the small size of the human birth canal, they are born very early in their development, essentially highly premature, and then require years of consistent, attentive care while their brains and bodies grow to become more self-sufficient creatures. Infant attachment provides the mechanism that ensures that mothers and other caregivers provide the care that infants need to survive the long years of extreme vulnerability resulting from our very long maturation period (Simpson & Belsky, 2008).

John Bowlby provided the most thorough explanation of this process. As a result, Bowlby could be considered the first modern evolutionary psychologist (Belsky, 2007). He drew heavily from Darwin when formulating attachment theory (and Darwin himself [1859] predicted that psychology would develop an evolutionary basis). His theory was described in his famous *Attachment and Loss* trilogy of books (Bowlby, 1969, 1973, 1980) and has developed into the dominant approach to understanding early socioemotional development.

Mary Ainsworth and her colleagues developed the classic "Strange Situation" laboratory procedure for assessing attachment security when infants are 12 months of age (Ainsworth, Blehar, Waters, & Wall, 1978). This procedure involves a series of eight 3-minute episodes involving separations and reunions between the child, the mother, and a female stranger in an experimental room. The child never leaves the room, although the mother and female stranger leave on two occasions. Based primarily on patterns of infant behavior toward their mothers during the second reunion, the infants are placed into the specific classifications of A1 (high avoidance), A2 (low avoidance), B1 (secure with some avoidance), B2 and B3 (secure), B4 (secure with some anxiety), C1 (anxious, angry, and ambivalent), C2 (anxious, passive, and ambivalent), or D (disorganized, highly ambivalent, unpredictable behavior that includes avoidance of the mother).

Infant attachment has been shown to be an important predictor of socioemotional adjustment across the life span. Infant attachment initiates developmental trajectories that probabilistically lead to differences in important areas of personal and interpersonal functioning. Infant attachment classifications predict behavior problems and psychopathology during childhood and adolescence (e.g., DeKlyen & Greenberg, 2008) as well as the quality of individuals' personal and interpersonal functioning in adulthood (e.g., Berlin, Cassidy, & Appleyard, 2008; Mikulincer & Shaver, 2007). Infant attachment is clearly not deterministic—subsequent developmental experiences such as a change in family circumstances, intimate relationships, or psychotherapy can push developmental trajectories in either positive or negative directions (e.g., Salvatore, Kuo, Steele, Simpson, & Collins, 2011; Sroufe, Egeland, Carlson, & Collins, 2005). The landmark studies by the Meaney research team (2004) showed that the DNA methylation of infant rat pups' brains takes on the pattern of their foster mothers, not their genetic mothers. If a rat pup born to a soothing, high-licking mother is adopted by a low-licking mother, the pup grows up to be an anxious adult with high levels of stress hormones. If the pup is female, she also becomes a low-licking mother herself later on when she has her own pups. It is the early care provided by the adoptive mothers that causes the epigenetic changes that regulate endocrine and cardiovascular stress responses in the rat pups (see Chapter 3).

Children's relationships with their early caregivers provide critical experiences that can set important developmental trajectories in motion. Sroufe and Siegel (2011) concluded that "the emotional quality of our earliest attachment experience is perhaps the single most important influence on human development" (p. 34). Research finds that one's attachment style is associated with a wide range of outcomes across the psychological, interpersonal, and social realms, including emotional regulation, behavioral self-regulation, psychopathology, interpersonal and relationship functioning, sexual functioning, behavioral functioning in work settings, and engagement in psychotherapy (Cassidy & Shaver, 2008; Mikulincer & Shaver, 2007). More serious problems with attachment (e.g., disorganized style) that are associated with more adverse early experiences (e.g., severe child maltreatment) are also more likely to lead to more serious developmental outcomes (e.g., borderline personality disorder). One's own attachment has a strong effect on one's approach to parenting as well. Parents' perceptions of their own childhood attachments have been found to predict the attachment classification of their children 75% of the time (Main, Kaplan, & Cassidy, 1985; Steele, Steele, & Fonagy, 1996).

Research finds that attachment style is also relatively enduring. The continuity of attachment from infancy to adulthood is moderately stable and the continuity of attachment across early to middle adulthood is quite stable (approximately 70% of adults receive the same attachment classification across time periods up to 25 years; Mikulincer & Shaver, 2007). The stability of attachment into older age may moderate somewhat (the longest longitudinal study of attachment has now extended from age 13 to 72; Chopik, Edelstein, & Grimm, 2019). Given the importance of attachment style to individuals' development, it is unfortunate that only about 65% of infants in the general population are found to be securely attached, while the remaining 35% are distributed among the three insecure categories (i.e., avoidant, anxious–ambivalent, and disorganized).

Risk and protective factors

Risk and protective factors play critical roles in the development of dysfunction, disorder, developmental competence, and resilience. Risk factors are "characteristics, variables, or hazards that, if present for a given individual, make it more likely that this individual, rather than someone selected from the general population, will develop a disorder" (Institute of Medicine, 1994, p. 6). Some risk factors such as genetic inheritance or gender are generally not malleable to change. Causal risk factors, on the other hand, are factors that can be changed, such as a lack of social support, low reading ability, or being victimized by bullying (Durlak & Wells, 1997; Kraemer, Kazdin, & Offord, 1997).

Protective factors are internal or external influences that improve an individual's response to a risk factor (Rutter, 1979). Supportive parents or other adults in the community, for example, are important external protective factors against developing a wide range of maladaptive outcomes in children (National Research Council and Institute of Medicine, 2009). Resilience is an important internal protective factor affecting an individual's response to stressors or traumatic events across the life span (Garmezy & Rutter, 1983). Protective and risk factors sometimes fall on the same bipolar continuum in which the positive end represents protective factors (e.g., effective parenting, high academic achievement) and the negative end represents risk factors (e.g., poor parenting, low academic achievement; Luthar, 2003). Attachment insecurity may be the most important risk factor of all in terms of socioemotional outcomes and operates in a bipolar manner: attachment insecurity is a major risk factor, while attachment security is protective. Child maltreatment is an important risk factor that is unipolar, ranging from none to severe (the absence of maltreatment, although a good thing, does not imply effective parenting). Risk and protective factors also tend to be inversely correlated. In a sample of 6th to 12th graders, students in the highest quintile on cumulative risk factors were likely to also be in the lowest quintile on protective factors (Pollard, Hawkins, & Arthur, 1999).

Adverse childhood experiences

The study of risk and protective factors was reenergized in 1998, when Felitti et al. (1998) published the article titled "Relationships of Childhood Abuse and Household Dysfunction to Many of the Leading Causes of Death in Adults: The Adverse Childhood Experiences (ACE) Study." These physicians obtained data from 17,421 patients who were receiving routine medical evaluations at Kaiser Permanente in San Diego. In addition to demographic information, previous diagnoses, family history, and current conditions and diseases, the patients were asked if they had experienced any of 10 adverse childhood experiences (ACEs) before age 18. These included the following:

1. emotional abuse (recurrent)
2. physical abuse (recurrent)
3. sexual abuse (contact)
4. physical neglect
5. emotional neglect
6. substance abuse in the household (e.g., living with an alcoholic or a person with a substance-abuse problem)
7. mental illness in the household (e.g., living with someone who suffered from depression or mental illness or who had attempted suicide)
8. mother treated violently
9. divorce or parental separation
10. criminal behavior in household (e.g., a household member going to prison)

The findings of Felitti et al. (1998) were consistent with a great deal of previous research but became highly influential because of the very large sample size, the socioeconomic characteristics of the sample (e.g., all receiving quality health care, 70% were college educated, 70% were Caucasian), and the comprehensive medical information available due to the nature of the data collection. Their first major finding was that ACEs were shockingly common: 67% of the sample had at least one category of ACEs and 12.6% had four or more categories of ACEs. Most U.S. states have collected ACE data since the Felitti et al. study was published. Overall, it appears that approximately 61.5% of the population has experienced at least one category of ACEs and 15.8% have an ACE score of 4 or more (Bethell, Newacheck, Hawes, & Halfon, 2014; Gilbert et al., 2015; Merrick, Ford, Ports, & Guinn, 2018).

The second major finding of the Felitti et al. (1998) study was even more startling. They found a strong cumulative effect (referred to as a dose–response relationship in medicine) between ACEs and poor health outcomes. For example, patients in their sample with four or more ACEs were twice as likely to develop heart disease and cancer and 3.5 times more likely to develop chronic obstructive pulmonary disease compared with patients with no ACEs. Brown et al. (2009) also found that individuals with an ACE score of 6 or more had a life expectancy 20 years shorter than those with no ACEs. In the first systematic review and meta-analysis of the outcomes associated with ACEs (based on a total of 253,719 participants that did not include high-risk or clinical samples), Hughes et al. (2017) found that individuals reporting having at least four ACEs compared with those reporting none were far more likely to have several negative health and behavioral outcomes (see Table 8.1). The odds of having made a suicide attempt were 30.1 times greater, were far higher for being a perpetrator or a victim of violence, were strong for a variety of psychological problems, and were weak for overweight and diabetes.

The cumulative effect of childhood risk factors had been observed before. Rutter (1979) first proposed the cumulative risk model to show that as the number of risks that children face increases, the developmental status of the child decreases. Children with difficult temperaments and low intelligence; who live in families with serious parental conflict, violence, or substance abuse; and live in a distressed community with inadequate schools face an accumulation of risk factors that are associated with a variety of negative outcomes. A dramatic example of this was found in a nationally representative sample of 5501 children who were investigated for child maltreatment before the age of 3 (Barth et al., 2008). These children as a whole experienced a large number of risk factors, including the following:

Child maltreatment (100%)	Caregiver mental health problem (30%)
Minority status (58%)	Low caregiver education (29%)
Single caregiver (48%)	Biomedical risk condition (22%)
Poverty (46%)	Teen-aged caregiver (19%)
Domestic violence (40%)	Four or more children in home (14%)
Caregiver substance abuse (39%)	

Large numbers of the children in this study also had measurable developmental delays in their cognitive, language, or emotional functioning that would prevent many of them from being ready to enter kindergarten or first grade (Barth et al., 2008).

Table 8.1 Odds of outcomes associated with adverse childhood experience (ACE) score of 4 or more compared with 0 (Hughes et al., 2017).

Outcome	Odds ratio
Suicide attempt	30.1
Problematic drug use	10.2
Violence perpetration	8.1
Violence victimization	7.5
Sexually transmitted infection	5.9
Problematic alcohol use	5.8
Depression	4.4
Low life satisfaction	4.4
Teenage pregnancy	4.2
Anxiety	3.7
Respiratory disease	3.1
Smoking	2.8
Liver or digestive disease	2.8
Cancer	2.3
Poor self-rated health	2.2
Cardiovascular disease	2.1
Diabetes	1.5
Overweight or obesity	1.4

The especially remarkable finding, however, was the very strong relationship between the number of risk factors the children faced and the chance of having a developmental delay. Having just one or two of the aforementioned risk factors (i.e., maltreatment alone or maltreatment plus one other risk factor) was associated with only a 5% rate of developmental delay. But the risk of delay went up very quickly as the number of risk factors increased, and virtually all the children (99%) having seven risk factors had measured developmental delays (see Fig. 8.1).

One of the important consequences of the Felitti et al. (1998) study was that it helped stimulate research into the biological mechanisms that account for the relationship between ACEs and negative health outcomes. The negative psychosocial outcomes noted above are alarming (e.g., the 30-fold increase in attempted suicide by those who scored 4 or more on the ACEs test), but one can imagine connections between ACEs and psychosocial outcomes more readily than the connections between ACEs and medical conditions and disease. Since 2000, research also has been uncovering the neurophysiological connections between ACEs and a range

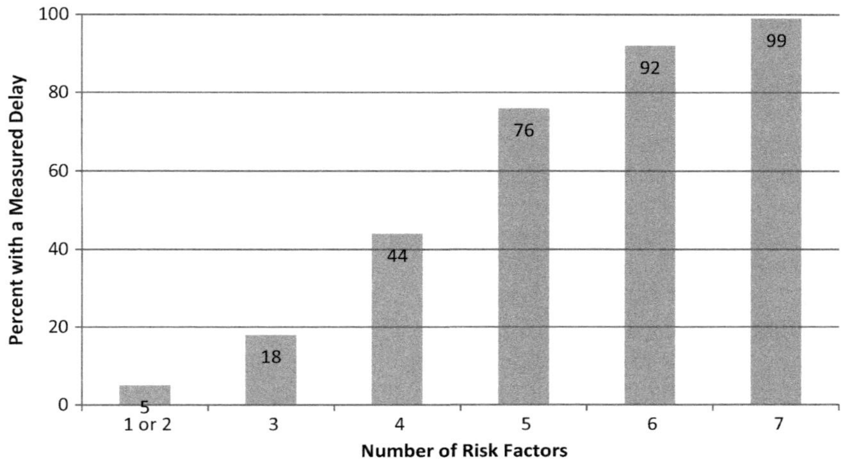

Figure 8.1 Percentage of maltreated children with a measured developmental delay by number of risk factors present in the National Survey of Child and Adolescent Well-Being (Barth et al., 2008).

of disease outcomes (Harris, 2018). The research on the epigenetic changes in infant rat pups caused by the amount of soothing licking by mother rats (genetic or adoptive mothers) by the Meaney research team (2004) was very influential in this regard.

An example of an important area of research that helps explain the connections between ACEs and disease involves telomeres, the sequences at the ends of chromosomes that protect DNA from damage. Telomeres are noncoding sequences at the ends of DNA strands that ensure that replicas of cells are exact copies of the originals (Harris, 2018). Telomeres, however, are also very sensitive to the environment. Biochemical insults (including stress) damage telomeres first before the cell's DNA is damaged. When telomeres are damaged, the rest of the cell can age or die, which can lead to dysfunction (e.g., when the pancreas stops making enough insulin and causes diabetes) or the cells can become precancerous or cancerous (i.e., the ability of the cell to replicate correctly is compromised). In the U.S. Health and Retirement Study (4598 participants), Puterman et al. (2016) found that cumulative childhood adversity predicted telomere shortening. They found that each category of childhood adversity a participant experienced was associated with an 11% increase in the chance of having short telomeres. Interpersonal and traumatic stressors such as having a parent with problematic alcohol or drug abuse or experiencing abuse were more predictive of telomere shortening than household financial stress. O'Donovan et al. (2011) also found that patients with posttraumatic stress disorder tended to have shorter telomeres if they had early childhood adversity, while those without childhood adversity did not tend to have shorter telomeres.

Health, well-being, and flourishing

Much of the foregoing discussion focused on risk factors for negative developmental outcomes. As noted in the previous chapter, medicine historically emphasized pathology because of the overwhelming impact of disease, injury, and disability on people's survival in the challenging environments that characterized most of human history. Since the late 19th century, however, scientific advances have led to dramatic improvements in understanding and controlling disease, far more children surviving to adulthood, mothers surviving childbirth, and much longer life spans. After remaining fairly constant for most of human history, life span began rising a couple centuries ago and has roughly doubled since then. In the U.S., life span rose from 47 in 1900 to 77 a century later (Arias, 2004). For the first time in human history, the primary causes of illness and death shifted from acute and infectious disease to chronic diseases associated with modifiable lifestyle causes, a shift known as the *epidemiological transition* (Gribble & Preston, 1993).

The dramatic extension of life expectancy over the past couple centuries never occurred before in human history. As a result, humans' psychological experience of life also underwent a fundamental shift. Focus has shifted from meeting primarily lower level biological needs to also meeting psychological and social ones. The famous economist John Maynard Keynes (1930/1972) expressed the challenge as how "to live wisely and agreeably and well" (p. 328) once desperation and deprivation are no longer the driving forces of human existence. Abraham Maslow (1943) conceptualized individuals' needs in terms of a hierarchy in which one's basic material and security needs had to be met before the needs for feeling loved, a sense of belonging, and self-esteem could be met. And after these needs were met, one could also then focus on self-actualization and the pursuit of meaning and fulfillment in life. The leaders who met to organize the United Nations following the devastation and horror of World War II had similar aspirations. The World Health Organization was created in 1948 and adopted a very broad, positive, and modern definition of health that reads, "Health is a state of complete physical, mental and social well-being and not merely the absence of disease or infirmity." For the first time in history, large numbers of people began to look beyond meeting just their basic needs for survival to a more complete state of health that included psychosocial well-being.

Although wellness and related concepts have now become well established in psychology and in culture generally, there remain major disagreements about the exact nature of happiness, health, well-being, and meaning and purpose in life. There have probably been debates about these issues ever since *Homo sapiens* developed language, and every culture has addressed these issues differently at different times. In ancient Greece, the debate often focused on the importance of pleasure as the goal of life (hedonia, primarily associated with Epicurus) versus the pursuit of a virtuous and excellent life in which one is able to achieve one's full potential (eudaimonia, typically associated with Aristotle). With the rise of Christianity in the West, questions about the nature of happiness, fulfillment, and purpose in life were often answered through scripture and religious teachings. Following the Scientific Revolution and

Enlightenment, infectious disease gradually became to be understood in scientific terms, and positive, humanistic attitudes emphasized the use of science and reason to solve problems and improve the human condition. Major progress in realizing these hopes was made in the 20th century as science-based public health measures and medical technology ushered in the epidemiological transition, and material conditions improved dramatically in many places around the world. Especially during the Civil Rights Era, large numbers of people became interested in the nature of well-being, happiness, and fulfillment in life in addition to questioning the limitations and injustices imposed on marginalized groups in society.

The positive psychology movement in the U.S. gained traction in the 1990s as dissatisfaction grew with the mental health focus on pathology and "what is wrong" rather than "what is right." In 2000, Seligman and Csikszentmihalyi defined positive psychology as "the scientific study of positive human functioning and flourishing on multiple levels that include the biological, personal, relational, institutional, cultural, and global dimensions of life." Although several of the issues involved continue to be vigorously debated, empirical research has clarified several questions. At the most basic level, there is consensus that the most useful perspective for conceptualizing and measuring wellness involves a biopsychosocial approach. There are times when one's physical health and functioning are the top priorities, but at other times one's psychological, family, or vocational functioning, or even the economic or political functioning of the community become top considerations. Therefore, for people in general, the measurement of wellness is best approached through a comprehensive biopsychosocial perspective (Melchert, in press).

A second critical consideration in defining well-being concerns the importance of both objective and subjective perspectives. For example, it might seem that objective measures of strong physical health and high income would tend to be related to high life satisfaction and well-being, but that frequently is not the case (e.g., elite athletes, individuals with quadriplegia or terminal illness, or those living with little or great wealth fall at many different points with regard to well-being, life satisfaction, meaning, and fulfillment). Correlations between many objective and subjective aspects of well-being are also actually surprisingly low. For example, objective measures of income are typically considered important to understanding well-being given the importance of getting basic needs met, and low and moderate levels of income do have fairly strong positive correlations with emotional well-being and happiness. But the correlation weakens considerably as income rises above the point at which people's basic needs are met (Kahneman & Deaton, 2012). In fact, the correlation between income and emotional well-being is essentially zero at levels above approximately $75,000 in the U.S. (the amount varies depending on the cost of living across countries).

Research regarding the relationship between loneliness and mortality also highlights the importance of considering both objective and subjective perspectives on well-being. Meta-analyses have found that loneliness substantially increases the risk of death by approximately the same amount as being obese, smoking 15 cigarettes a day, or drinking more than six drinks of alcohol per day (Holt-Lundstad, Smith, Baker,

Harris, & Stephenson, 2015). The increase in mortality associated with loneliness was also found to be essentially the same if social isolation was measured objectively (in terms of having infrequent social contact and living alone) or subjectively (in terms of *feeling* lonely, even if one has frequent social contact). Surveys also suggest that loneliness is widespread: a large national 2018 survey found that 47% of Americans felt alone and 13% reported there were zero people who knew them well (Cigna, 2018).

Another important area of recent research on well-being focuses on meaning in life. Meaning and purpose in life (eudaimonia) have long been considered important to well-being but were often thought to be too elusive and idiosyncratic to be researched empirically. But Heintzelman and King (2014) asked why meaning in life is widely believed to be a necessity that makes one's life livable and worthwhile, but is also viewed as extremely difficult to attain and chronically lacking. They argued that "Nothing that human beings require to survive can be next to impossible to obtain" (p. 561). Their review of the research resulted in three conclusions: (1) lonely, socially isolated individuals consistently report lower meaning in life and "Social relationships are a foundational source of meaning in life" (p. 562); (2) experiencing positive emotion is consistently related to meaning in life; and (3) viewing life as making sense and having coherence and regularity is associated with life feeling more meaningful. They further noted that surveys typically find that most people report that their lives are meaningful (e.g., 91% responded affirmatively in a 2007 Gallop Global Poll of 137,678 individuals from 132 nations). Many people are attracted to the mystique of the idea of finding meaning in life, but Heintzelman and King (2014) noted that these findings call into question whether meaning in life is something that individuals must search for and create. Instead, perhaps people do need meaning in life to survive, and that is why it is commonplace (Baumeister & Landau, 2018; Heintzelman & King, 2014). And even though people commonly may feel that they have meaning in their lives, they may also seek to find more meaning and purpose in their lives—people may pursue more meaning even though they already feel meaning in life.

Although large numbers of people report feeling meaning and purpose in their lives, clearly many are not in a strong state of physical and mental health. The data reviewed in the previous three chapters found large numbers of people suffering from a range of physical, mental, social, and economic problems. Keyes applied an integrative biopsychosocial perspective to this issue and found that anything less than a state of positive mental health (which he refers to as "flourishing") is associated with increased functional impairment and increased physical and mental health problems. Using nationally representative survey data, Keyes (2007) estimated that roughly only 2 in 10 Americans are flourishing, while nearly 2 in 10 are in poor mental health, which he referred to as "languishing." He found that most of the rest were in between, a level that is associated with moderate distress, lower social well-being, and a moderate number of chronic physical conditions. By his measure, nearly 8 in 10 Americans are not experiencing positive mental health and are instead experiencing moderate to serious distress and dysfunction. This represents a serious public health issue that is not getting sufficient attention from the profession nor the public.

Integrating the biopsychosocial dimensions

The developmental perspective on human psychology provides the time dimension that integrates the many biopsychosocial influences on development and functioning into a unified conceptual framework. It highlights the connections between the biopsychosocial domains in terms of age-related changes and developmental tasks and helps explain the development of personality, strengths, competencies, vulnerabilities, weaknesses, and psychopathology across the life span. It also highlights the multiple environmental contexts within which development occurs. It integrates influences from the point of conception to early caregiving and family experiences, to the building of social, conduct, academic, romantic, and vocational competencies in late adolescence, and through all the important milestones that occur across adulthood and to the end of life.

Human development and functioning have been investigated from the perspective of numerous psychology subfields, multiple biological specializations, medicine and public health, and several social science disciplines. These fields sometimes use terminology differently, rely on different research methodologies, and focus on different variables and processes. The research literature on human development and functioning is consequently fragmented. The developmental biopsychosocial perspective reminds us of the importance of integrating the various bodies of scientific knowledge and considering all levels of natural organization so that behavioral health care is grounded on the firmest scientific foundations.

The ability of science to explain the interactions among the biopsychosocial mechanisms and processes of life has advanced rapidly in recent decades. Although the complexity of the subject matter is daunting, predicting developmental outcomes based on biopsychosocial processes is improving steadily. Nonetheless, predicting outcomes for any particular individual can still be highly imprecise. The number of variables involved and the role of chance factors are simply too great to reliably predict outcomes in many individual cases. This is true of medical outcomes just as it is with psychological and social outcomes. Many different developmental pathways can result in the same outcome (*equifinality*), while one particular developmental starting point can lead to many different outcomes (*multifinality*; Cicchetti & Rogosch, 1996). Research continues to progress, however, and the ability to predict physical, psychological, and social outcomes for the general population continues to improve.

As behavioral science explanations for human development strengthen, social policy and public health measures to reduce risk factors and increase protective factors can likewise be strengthened. Doing so will improve the health and well-being of individuals and society. For example, Bigland, Flay, Embry, and Sandler (2012) proposed an integrative perspective to translate developmental research knowledge into a practical framework that can lead to more effective preventive interventions. They concluded that the available evidence supports the following basic principle: "If we want to prevent multiple problems and increase the prevalence of young people who develop successfully, we must increase the prevalence of nurturing environments" (p. 258). They argued that nurturing environments can be fostered by focusing on four key features: (1) biologically and socially toxic conditions (e.g., unhealthy diets, child abuse, poverty) need to be minimized because they interfere with healthy development; (2) opportunities for young people to engage in problem behavior need to be limited through improved monitoring and appropriate enforcement of behavioral expectations and rules; (3) prosociality (i.e., the motivation and skills needed to play prosocial roles in society) needs to be taught, promoted, and reinforced because it increases mental, emotional, and behavioral well-being; and (4) psychological flexibility (e.g., mindfulness) need to be promoted.

The data reviewed in the previous four chapters indicate that many people are dealing with serious problems across the biopsychosocial domains. The scientific understanding of how this happens has advanced dramatically in recent decades. Although we are still early in explaining the immense complexity of human development and functioning, we are steadily learning more about how these problems develop and how they can be prevented. Finding the political will to do so is a very difficult problem, although learning more about how to improve people's well-being may help in building the motivation to tackle these problems. The four chapters that follow discuss how current scientific knowledge can be applied in clinical practice to treat behavioral health problems and promote biopsychosocial functioning. The treatment process begins with assessment, so that is the topic of the next chapter.

Part Three

Conceptualizing the behavioral health care treatment process

Assessment

9

The overarching purpose of behavioral health care is the application of science and ethics to meet individuals' behavioral health needs and promote their biopsychosocial functioning. Assessment plays the essential role in the initial stages of the treatment process for meeting this purpose. Assessment also occurs continuously throughout treatment; at each patient contact, therapists engage in some type of assessment of the patient's functioning and the progress of treatment. Therapists also assess the effectiveness of treatment at termination and often afterward in terms of follow-up, and the ongoing monitoring of patient functioning is now standard in integrated primary care and other settings. Assessment is therefore essential throughout the treatment process. It is especially important at the outset, however, because the initial assessment of a patient's concerns and circumstances has a significant impact on how the patient and treatment providers involved evaluate the issues. Decisions about how to proceed are based on that initial evaluation, including even the basic question of whether any further intervention or contact is needed.

A wide variety of conceptual frameworks have been applied to understanding the psychological assessment process over the history of behavioral health care. A dominant approach in the U.S. over the past four decades has involved the *Diagnostic and Statistical Manual of Mental Disorders* published by the American Psychiatric Association. Although this system has been very valuable in several respects, many issues important in the development and continuation of individuals' mental health problems are beyond psychiatric diagnosis. As a result, clinicians historically have employed a variety of frameworks for understanding individuals' problems and concerns in need of clinical attention.

Before the biological revolution in American psychiatry in the 1970s, psychiatric assessment and treatment planning were typically based on a psychoanalytic approach to understanding personality, psychopathology, and the treatment process. The field changed dramatically at that point, however, and now most psychiatrists primarily prescribe psychotropic medicines based on a biological formulation of assessment and treatment (Mojtabai & Olfson, 2008). Humanistic therapists, meanwhile, took a dramatically different approach to case conceptualization. Carl Rogers (1951) argued that "psychological diagnosis is unnecessary for psychotherapy, and may actually be detrimental to the therapeutic process" (p. 220). Instead of assessment and treatment planning, Rogers argued that providing empathy, genuineness, and unconditional positive regard within the therapy relationship were "necessary and sufficient" for a successful therapy outcome and constructive personality change. Behavior therapists also tended to neglect formal psychological assessment and instead focused on symptoms (Hayes & Follette, 1992). Behaviorists often viewed symptoms *as* the problem and conducted a functional analysis of behavior to identify the environmental

Foundations of Health Service Psychology. https://doi.org/10.1016/B978-0-12-816426-6.00009-8

contingencies that reinforced behaviors and would then be used to guide treatment. Cognitive therapists traditionally relied on general formulations about the causes, precipitants, and maintaining influences of depression (Beck, Freeman, Davis, & Associates, 2004), anxiety (Beck, Emery, & Greenberg, 1985), personality disorders (Freeman et al., 1990), and other disorders. These general formulations revolved around the rationality of thinking and tended to be applied to everyone within a diagnostic category, though more individualized CBT case formulations are now advocated (Persons & Tompkins, 2007). Like humanistic therapists, postmodern constructivist therapists also generally deemphasized assessment and case conceptualization. Solution-oriented therapists were largely uninterested in the nature or causes of a person's problems (de Shazer, 1985), while narrative therapists might argue that objective knowledge is not even possible and so the client and therapist together need to co-construct an understanding of the client's life and situation (White & Epston, 1990).

These varied approaches to assessment and case conceptualization presented a very complicated picture emblematic of the preparadigmatic era of the behavioral health field. Therapists could select from an eclectic array of theoretical orientations to guide their clinical work, and the orientation they chose frequently influenced the type of assessment information they collected, their interpretation of that information, and the type of treatment they would then recommend and provide. Extensive psychosocial history information often had to be collected because it was required for hospitals and clinics be get accredited by the Joint Commission (which accredits over 21,000 health care organizations in the U.S.). In many cases, however, some of that information went unused. When practicing on the basis of a traditional theoretical orientation, one's adopted orientation could determine the focus of the assessment one conducted and treatment one provided. Gathering comprehensive psychosocial history information and understanding the patient in a more holistic manner was not always considered important.

Practicing behavioral health care in an evidence-based biopsychosocial manner is quite different from these traditional approaches in important respects. Instead of choosing from one of the traditional theoretical orientations, one relies on the best available research evidence for understanding development, functioning, and behavioral change. This approach incorporates the numerous evidence-based therapies shown to be effective for addressing behavioral health needs (see Chapter 11). Evidence-based practice also requires that patient values, preferences, culture, and other characteristics be assessed so that these considerations are integrated into treatment planning. The understanding of which treatment approach should be considered in particular cases is based on a comprehensive biopsychosocial assessment and treatment plan, not on one's preferred theoretical orientation. This approach to assessment and case conceptualization can be quite complex, particularly in comparison with some traditional approaches that focus on a limited set of issues highlighted by a particular theoretical orientation. This chapter clarifies that complexity by discussing the important components and processes involved and placing them into a logical sequence.

The importance of assessment in behavioral health care has been growing over the past two decades. Systematically measuring treatment progress using standardized assessments was not a standard part of traditional psychotherapy or psychopharmacology practice. This stands in stark contrast to the treatment of many medical problems that require regular monitoring of treatment progress, often at every patient contact (e.g., high blood pressure) or sometimes even daily by the patients themselves (e.g., measuring glucose levels with diabetes). The benefits and importance of measuring the progress of behavioral health care treatment are quickly becoming recognized (see Chapter 12). This typically requires that patient symptoms and functioning are assessed using standardized measures at intake as well as regularly throughout the treatment process and at the termination of treatment. What is often called *measurement-based care* helps engage patients in the treatment process, alerts therapists to the need to modify treatment or find alternative treatments when patients do not improve, supports quality improvement efforts, and informs insurers and other stakeholders about the value of mental health services. Data regarding treatment progress and outcome are increasingly also expected by a variety of stakeholders (e.g., the Joint Commission began requiring it in 2018; the Centers for Medicare and Medicaid Services and numerous insurers strongly encourage it).

Before examining the assessment process in more detail, it is important to recall the critical importance of multicultural and ethical issues in behavioral health care. Evidence-based practice requires that patient demographic and cultural characteristics, values, and preferences be incorporated into case conceptualization. Failing to do so has repercussions for developing therapeutic rapport and patient engagement in the treatment process. All of this is also required to meet ethical obligations involving respect for autonomy, nonmaleficence, beneficence, and justice. Sensitively and respectfully responding to the patient as an individual with a unique developmental history, current life circumstances, and hopes and plans for her or his future is necessary not only for treatment effectiveness but also from the perspective of health care ethics.

This chapter outlines the general conceptual framework for an evidence-based biopsychosocial approach to behavioral health care assessment. The following chapters then show how to use that information to plan and carry out treatment, monitor its progress, and assess its effectiveness as treatment progresses, at termination, and at follow-up. The frameworks discussed in this chapter encompass behavioral health care in general. They can be applied across all types of general and specialized practice and behavioral health care settings. The discussion includes the following topics:

- conceptual foundations underlying behavioral health care assessment
- basic purposes of assessment
- areas to include in behavioral health care assessment
- reliability, validity, sources, and thoroughness of assessment information
- assessing severity of patient problems and strength of their resources
- overall evaluation and integration of assessment information

Conceptual foundations of behavioral health care assessment

The purpose of behavioral health care is to provide health services to meet individuals' behavioral health needs and improve their biopsychosocial functioning. The conceptual foundations for pursuing that purpose rest on professional ethics and on scientific knowledge regarding human development, functioning, and behavior change. Translating those conceptual foundations into clinical practice is done using the principles of evidence-based practice.

The importance of evidence-based practice

First, it is important to differentiate the evidence-based biopsychosocial approach advocated here from approaches based on the traditional theoretical orientations. In a traditional approach, one's theoretical orientation often dominated the assessment findings such that a clinician's orientation frequently determined how a patient's concerns and disorders were diagnosed, conceptualized, and treated (Garb, 1998). The results of an assessment and treatment plan were often quite predictable depending on whether one consulted a clinician with a cognitive, systemic, EMDR, psychopharmacological, or other orientation. This approach developed for clear historical reasons (see Chapters 2 and 3), but its assumptions and conceptual foundations are different from those of a biopsychosocial approach.

The evidence-based biopsychosocial approach to behavioral health care assessment is instead based on the principles of evidence-based practice, the "three-legged stool" that integrates the best available research evidence, clinical expertise, and information regarding patients' characteristics, culture, and preferences (APA Presidential Task Force, 2006; Institute of Medicine, 2001). This approach guides the knowledge, skills, and dispositions that therapists bring to their clinical work. It utilizes just one integrated scientific framework for understanding human development, functioning, and behavior change, though therapists might employ a variety of empirically supported interventions to treat problems and disorders depending on the specific factors involved in individual cases. The scientific understanding of human psychology is obviously extraordinarily complex and much remains to be discovered, but the field has evolved to the point where human development and functioning, as well as the practice of behavioral health care, can all be understood from a single integrated scientific perspective that includes a range of empirically supported interventions.

The importance of reliability and validity

The reliability and validity of behavioral health assessment findings are important from the perspective of both the scientific and the ethical foundations of behavioral health care. The scientific underpinnings of the field emphasize reliable and valid measurement of human characteristics. Measurement reliability and validity are fundamental in psychology and all of science—science simply does not progress without precise measurement. Reliable research into human development, the effects of life events such as trauma on developmental outcomes, the epidemiology and etiology of psychopathology, the effectiveness of treatment for different conditions, and a host of other important psychological questions cannot be addressed without reliable and valid assessment data. Behavioral health care likewise loses its scientific and professional credibility without reliable, valid assessment and diagnosis.

The ethical foundations of behavioral health care also require reliable and valid assessment. The principle of nonmaleficence obligates health care providers to not harm people, and beneficence obligates providers to prevent harms and remove them if they have already occurred. Unreliable and inaccurate assessments carry major risks of not helping patients and actually causing harm. Among the clearest examples of this are unreliable suicide or homicide risk assessments. Failing to detect problems a person is having can result in negative consequences that can even be fatal in some cases.

Unreliable and inaccurate behavioral health assessments can be unhelpful or harmful in more subtle ways as well. Assessment findings often have major impacts on how problems, dysfunction, strengths, and resources are understood by the patient, therapist, and other stakeholders, and on the services provided. If relevant issues are not pursued or insufficient rapport with patients results in important information not being elicited, problems can easily be missed or misidentified. For example, a child's academic failures in school might be misattributed to a lack of motivation and effort rather than to a learning disability; discrimination the child is facing due to gender, race, culture, or sexual orientation; or abuse or neglect the child is experiencing at home. When this happens, the child's problems may go unresolved, and this can have negative consequences in the child's life over the short and long term. In addition, children may internalize negative self-concepts that might remain with them over their lifetimes, potentially affecting important developmental outcomes across their life span. Therapists' ethical obligations to not cause harm, to prevent harms, and provide benefit can be violated when assessments are unreliable or invalid.

The necessity of a comprehensive perspective

A main feature of the biopsychosocial perspective is its comprehensive approach to understanding development and functioning. Developmental outcomes are multifactorially determined from the interaction of biological, psychological, and sociocultural influences, and individuals clearly have strengths as well as weaknesses across all these domains. A person's strengths and what they do well can also have a larger impact than what they do poorly or what they lack. For example, a person who has had highly conflictual relationships with her parents and siblings and little success with intimate relationships may nonetheless have very fulfilling friendships and be a highly competent and valued employee as well as enjoy excellent physical health as a result of careful attention to diet and exercise. Another individual may suffer from a severe and persistent mental illness but is reliable, caring, loyal, and a valuable source of support to his family and friends. Focusing only on the problems and deficits these individuals have would result in seriously incomplete assessments that could easily communicate negative messages that may be not only unhelpful but even hurtful and unfair. These negative effects obviously have an impact on not only the patient but also other people important in her or his life. Health care ethics obligate us to practice in ways that minimize these possibilities. Conducting comprehensive, reliable, and valid assessments is important for ensuring that these obligations are met.

Basic purposes of behavioral health care assessment

Although a wide variety of theoretical orientations were applied to behavioral health care assessment historically, a review of the literature suggests significant consensus regarding its primary purposes. The basic purposes of assessment help inform the processes and procedures needed to meet those purposes.

At the most basic level, the treatment process does not proceed without the identification of behavioral health problems that warrant clinical attention. But assessment serves several important additional purposes. For example, Maruish (2004a) noted that psychological assessment is important for treatment planning, providing baseline data for monitoring the progress of treatment, and as a therapeutic intervention in itself as feedback is provided to the patient and then discussed with the patient and therapist arriving at mutually-agreed-upon treatment goals.

An examination of major guidelines and resources for conducting behavioral health care assessment finds significant convergence around its primary purposes (Melchert, 2011). While their emphases differ, these guidelines have significant overlap regarding several basic purposes for behavioral health care assessment (e.g., see American Psychiatric Association, 2006; Groth-Marnat & Wright, 2016; Lezak, Howieson, Bigler, & Tranel, 2012; Maruish, 2004b; Turner, DeMers, Fox, & Reed, 2001; Wiggins, 2003). A synthesis of these guidelines results in the following basic purposes of psychological assessment:

1. Identify behavioral health problems and concerns that need clinical attention.
2. Gather information regarding a patient's behavioral health and biopsychosocial functioning in order to develop a comprehensive case conceptualization and treatment plan.
3. Engage the patient in the treatment process through a collaborative approach that includes patient self-assessment and a discussion of objective feedback provided to the patient.
4. Provide ongoing assessment during the course of treatment in order to monitor progress, refine the treatment plan, and refocus interventions as needed.
5. Provide baseline data for an outcomes evaluation and assessment of the effectiveness of treatment.

These overarching purposes of behavioral health assessment apply even though the specific purposes of assessment in particular cases vary substantially. Assessment procedures can vary greatly depending on the specific setting and purpose (e.g., outpatient psychotherapy clinic, integrated primary care, inpatient psychiatry, neuropsychological consultation, substance abuse treatment, medical, educational, forensic, industrial, organizational, sports, and correctional). Initial intake assessments with new patients are also very different from the reevaluation for the ongoing care of long-term issues with patients the therapist knows well. Assessments conducted for consultation to others for purposes of evaluating learning problems, job performance issues, or forensic or neuropsychological questions often do not lead to subsequent treatment or outcomes assessment at all. For behavioral health care assessment in general, however, there is substantial agreement regarding the above basic purposes.

The sections that follow discuss the issues that need to be addressed to achieve the overall purposes of behavioral health assessment. The focus here is on a general conceptualization of behavioral health assessment that can be adapted and applied across clinical practice settings. The discussion begins with a consideration of which areas of patients' lives need to be considered in developing comprehensive case conceptualizations to meet their behavioral health and biopsychosocial needs.

Areas to include in behavioral health care assessment

Behavioral health assessment has become much more biopsychosocial in orientation over the last half century. This is also reflected in the evolution of the *Diagnostic and Statistical Manual of Mental Disorders* (*DSM*), by far the most important system for identifying mental health problems that need clinical attention. The first two editions, published in 1952 and 1968, relied heavily on psychoanalytic theory. Symptoms for specific disorders were not specified in detail, and many were seen as reflections of broad underlying conflicts or reactions to life problems that could be categorized generally as either neurosis or psychosis. But concern grew regarding the low diagnostic reliability of this approach at the same time that alternative theoretical orientations for understanding human psychology were growing in popularity (e.g., humanistic, cognitive, feminist, biological, and multicultural approaches).

To address the weaknesses of the *DSM-II*, the third edition of the *DSM*, published in 1980, presented a thoroughly revised approach to conceptualizing psychiatric diagnosis. This edition employed an atheoretical descriptive approach that did not specify or imply etiology for most of the disorders and also introduced the multiaxial assessment system that, with modifications, was used for over three decades until the publication of latest edition, the *DSM-5*, in 2013. The multiaxial system incorporated what is essentially a biopsychosocial approach to assessment by including clinical disorders and conditions on Axis I, personality disorders and pervasive developmental disorders on Axis II, medical issues on Axis III, environmental stressors on Axis IV, and general, overall level of functioning on Axis V. In the *DSM-5*, Axes I, II, and III are now combined, and separate notations are made for important psychosocial and environmental factors (formerly Axis IV) and disability (formerly Axis V). The same biopsychosocial information is to be documented as before but in a less differentiated manner.

The five-axial system of the *DSM-III* (American Psychiatric Association, 1980) greatly expanded the scope of assessment for mental health and biopsychosocial functioning, but it provided little guidance regarding the breadth and specificity of the information that should be evaluated when conducting an assessment. Because *DSMs*

III, IV, and *5* are descriptive systems with little emphasis on etiology, they also provide little guidance on how to understand the causes and development of patients' problems, the roles of risk, protective, and sociocultural factors, or the integration of all these factors into a holistic formulation that captures the individual's unique development and current functioning. Clinical intervention generally requires much more comprehensive assessment information to identify treatment goals that will resolve people's problems over the long term (e.g., American Psychiatric Association, 2006; Beutler, Malik, Talebi, Fleming, & Moleiro, 2004; Goodheart & Carter, 2008).

The controversy surrounding the publication of the *DSM-5* also suggests additional problems. Many improvements were incorporated into the *DSM-5* (American Psychiatric Association, 2013), but it too relies on the same general approach as earlier editions, including the use of voting by committees to make decisions about the inclusion of disorders. Well-known problems with this approach are excessive comorbidity, the proliferation of hundreds of putatively different pathological entities, and the lack of knowledge regarding the biology underlying the pathological syndromes (Cuthbert & Kozak, 2013; Frances, 2009). The science of psychopathology, however, has not yet advanced far enough to indicate an alternative approach. The National Institute of Mental Health was well aware of these problems when it launched the Research Domain Criteria project in 2008 to research relationships between dysfunctional behavior and neurobiological systems. Because that research has not yet progressed sufficiently, the *DSM-5* is widely regarded as the best available classification of mental disorders despite weaknesses in its scientific foundations (Insel & Lieberman, 2013).

Psychiatric diagnosis is necessary in behavioral health assessment to identify what psychological issues are causing distress or impairment and need to be treated. But a great deal more needs to be known to address the etiology of problems, resolve problems effectively over the long term, and help people achieve optimal health and well-being. Fortunately, there is significant consensus about the types of additional information needed to reach these goals.

Virtually all contemporary behavioral health assessment systems indicate the importance of addressing all three biopsychosocial domains when conducting behavioral health assessment. Most also further note specific areas within these domains to include. These assessments are often referred to as the *psychosocial history*. Melchert (2011) found substantial overlap when the specific areas included in six influential behavioral health assessment systems were compared. All 26 specific components listed in Table 9.1 were included in at least 2 of the 6 systems, and 18 of the components were included in at least 4 of the systems. The overlap in these assessment systems suggests that all 26 component areas are important at least some of the time. To evaluate the content-related validity of this set of assessment areas, Meyer and Melchert (2011) examined the content of 163 individual outpatient therapy files from three different clinics and found that these 26 components captured 100% of the intake information found in the patient files. There was no intake information in any of the patient files that could not be categorized into these component areas, and each of them was necessary to capture all of the information.

Table 9.1 Biopsychosocial component areas of behavioral health care assessment.

Domains (in bold) and components	**Issues commonly included**
Biological	
General medical history	Current medical functioning, recent and past medical history, chronic medical conditions, physical disability, nondiagnosed health complaints, previous hospitalizations, surgery history, seizure history, physical trauma history
Childhood health history	Birth history, childhood illnesses, childhood psychiatric history
Medications	Dosage, efficacy, side effects, duration of treatment, medication adherence
Health habits and behaviors	Diet and nutrition, activity, exercise
Psychological	
History of present problem	Reason for seeking treatment at the present time, recent symptoms, exacerbations or remissions of current illness or presenting problem, duration of current complaint, previous attempts to solve the problem, treatment readiness (motivation to change, ability to cooperate with treatment)
Level of psychological functioning	Overall mood and affect, level of distress, impairment in functioning
Individual psychological history	Current psychiatric problems, previous diagnoses, treatment history (format, frequency, duration, response to treatment, satisfaction with treatment)
Substance use and addictions	Types of substances used (alcohol, tobacco, caffeine, prescribed, over-the-counter, illicit), quantity and frequency of use, previous treatments, other addictive behaviors (gambling, overeating, viewing pornography)
Suicidal ideation and risk assessment	Intent, plan, previous attempts, other self- and other-destructive behaviors (e.g., injury to self, neglect of self-care, homicidal risk, neglect of children or other dependents)
Individual developmental history	Infancy, early and middle childhood, adolescence, early and middle adulthood, late adulthood
Childhood abuse and neglect history	Physical, sexual, emotional, psychological abuse or neglect
Other psychological traumas	Traumas and stressful life events, exposure to acts of war, political repression, criminal victimization

Continued

Table 9.1 Biopsychosocial component areas of behavioral health care assessment.—continued

Domains (in bold) and components	Issues commonly included
Mental status examination	Orientation, attention, memory, thought process, thought content, speech, perception, insight, judgment, appearance, affect, mood, motor activity
Personality style and characteristics	Coping abilities, defense mechanisms, problem-solving abilities, self-concept, interpersonal characteristics, intrapersonal characteristics
Sociocultural	
Relationships and support system	Immediate and extended family members, friends, supervisors, coworkers/other students, previous treatment providers, current parent-child relationship, involvements in social groups and organizations, marital/relationship status and history, recurrent difficulties in relationships, presence of past and current supportive relationships, sexual and reproductive history
Current living situation	Current living arrangements, satisfaction with those arrangements
Family history	Family constellation, circumstances, and atmosphere; recent problems with family; family medical illnesses, psychiatric history, and diagnoses; history of suicide in first- and second-degree relatives, family problems with alcohol or drugs
Educational history	Highest level completed, professional or trade skills
Employment	Current employment, vocational history, reasons for job changes
Financial resources	Finances and income, financial stress
Legal issues/crime	Current legal issues and legal history, criminal victimization
Military history	Positions, periods of service, termination
Activities of interest/ hobbies	Leisure interests and activities, hobbies
Religion	Organized religious practices and activities, active in faith
Spirituality	Personal beliefs, meaning, and sense of purpose (which may or may not include a "higher power" or organized religious practices)
Multicultural issues	Race/ethnicity, ethnic heritage, country of origin, immigration status, sexual orientation, gender identity, gender expression, socioeconomic class

Each of these areas of patients' lives can be important in their development and/or current functioning, so all of them need to be considered when learning to conduct comprehensive biopsychosocial assessment. The depth and detail that one pursues in particular assessments depends greatly on one's specialization, the setting where one practices, and the specific purpose of the assessment. For example, just a small number of these areas might be included when using screens and other brief assessments of students' needs in university counseling centers or patients' needs in primary health care clinics. As a general framework for conceptualizing behavioral health care assessment, however, the above categorization is important for delineating areas of patients' lives that can have a significant impact on their current functioning as well as growth and development over their life spans.

Reliability, validity, sources, and thoroughness of assessment information

Reliability and validity of assessment information is a major priority in behavioral health care from the perspectives of both science and ethics. The legitimacy and credibility of the field as a science-based health care profession is weakened if scientific principles requiring accurate measurement are ignored. Unreliable, incomplete, or inaccurate assessments can also have ethical implications, because they not only may be unhelpful but also may have the potential to result in negative consequences (i.e., they can be harmful) to patients, their families, and others.

What makes this situation more complicated, however, is that a highly thorough assessment is not needed in numerous behavioral health assessment situations. The level of reliability, validity, and thoroughness of assessment information needed varies significantly depending on the purpose of the assessment. Within the clinical context, assessment needs vary greatly depending on whether they are conducted for emergency purposes when patients are suicidal or homicidal; to comprehensively evaluate the needs of patients in inpatient treatment for serious, complex, chronic conditions; for consulting purposes to assist other professionals regarding specific legal, psychological, or employment issues; or to screen patients for an initial assessment to determine whether more assessment or treatment is needed (as frequently happens in integrated primary care, school counseling departments, university counseling centers, employee assistance programs, and social service agencies). One's approach to an assessment therefore depends heavily on the specific purpose of that particular assessment.

The referral question also plays an important role in deciding how to approach an assessment. Many psychotherapy cases involve individuals who self-refer for mild or moderate problems regarding their emotional functioning, and they personally can often provide most or all of the information needed for the assessment. When the therapist plans to provide ongoing treatment in these cases, establishing an effective therapeutic relationship becomes a priority and may take precedence over the timely gathering of comprehensive assessment information. One's assessment approach can be much different in cases where parents, spouses, partners, physicians, or educators initiate the referral. The information provided by third parties in these cases can be critical to the reliability and validity of the assessment. Third-party information is often critical for addressing legal or administrative questions such as child custody, disability status, readiness to return to employment, or the insanity defense. Some of these cases involve complicated questions with potentially major implications for people's health, family, employment, or even their freedom in terms of criminal issues. Of course, the reliability and validity of these assessments are critical issues.

Although the accuracy of assessments is always a priority, limited time and resources prevent highly thorough assessments from being conducted in many cases. An overwhelming amount of information from across the biopsychosocial domains can be collected, and extensive record review and interviews with significant others and relevant professionals are very time-consuming and costly. Many behavioral health care settings cannot provide such costly assessments. Crisis hotlines, employee assistance programs, university counseling centers, and school counseling departments limit the services they provide given the large number of people served by a small number of personnel. As a result, screening and other brief assessment procedures are commonly used to identify cases to refer for more thorough assessment. On the other hand, inpatient psychiatric care routinely requires that medical and psychosocial evaluations be completed in order to thoroughly evaluate the severity and complexity of the issues involved. Questions involving intellectual or neuropsychological functioning often require psychological and educational testing. Cases that enter the legal arena sometimes focus extensively on the reliability and validity of the assessment information gathered.

The issues addressed in the assessment also play a role in deciding the best sources from which to collect information. Patient self-report can efficiently provide reliable information regarding some issues, while other issues are most reliably assessed through the use of questionnaires or psychological tests. For example, one's levels of distress, mood, and other subjective states are typically assessed through self-report—self-report is often the only reliable source of information regarding one's internal subjective state. Variables such as personality characteristics, educational achievement, and intellectual or neuropsychological functioning are often most reliably, validly, and efficiently assessed through the use of test instruments. When an assessment is needed of an individual's performance of responsibilities at work or at home, work supervisors and family members often provide more reliable and complete information than what patients themselves may be aware of or willing to report. Children and cognitively disabled adults are often unable to provide reliable reports regarding several aspects of their lives. Some legal, medical, substance abuse, educational, and child protective services issues also may not be reliably reported by individuals themselves. Although patient self-report information is often the most time-efficient data to collect, it carries the risk of being incomplete or inaccurate (sometimes completely inaccurate) for many purposes.

The need for reliable assessment information is evident when one considers how often an individual's perception of their behavior or performance varies from that of family members, employers, educators, or various public officials (Miller & Berman, 1983). For example, a husband entering treatment might ask for help with getting along with a "nagging" wife, while the wife might report that the husband's violence and alcohol abuse are about to result in a divorce and child custody battle. A person might report that his or her work supervisor is angry, unfair, and prejudiced, but the supervisor might report that the employee is argumentative, makes sexually inappropriate comments, has substandard work productivity, and has not responded positively to supervision. Children referred for treatment frequently report circumstances and behaviors that conflict with reports from others, as do the reports of those who have been caught lying or engaging in criminal behavior. Minimization or exaggeration of problems is frequently subconscious or unintentional, although of course not always. When distortion occurs, it is often important to know whether it was intentional or conscious. Relying only on patient self-report in these cases obviously can result in seriously inaccurate assessments that might be unhelpful and potentially hurtful for the patient or others.

A useful model for conceptualizing the reliability of different sources of assessment information was proposed by Strupp and Hadley (1977). First, they noted that the patient is typically the best judge of his or her own distress and discomfort. Second, the patient's family and particular community members often have the best perspective for judging a patient's functioning in important life roles within the family, at work, or in the community. Third, therapists are normally the best judges of patients' psychological functioning and psychopathology. Speer (1998) expanded on this model by specifying the sources who are likely to provide the most reliable and useful information regarding these different perspectives. The capitalized bold letters in Table 9.2 below indicate the individuals who are likely to provide more reliable information regarding different aspects of a patient's health and functioning. In this model, significant others could include employers, neighbors, and friends in

Table 9.2 Reliable sources of behavioral health assessment information.

Source	Distress	Symptoms, disorder, diagnosis	Functioning, role performance
Patient	**A**	**B**	c
Significant others	d	e	**F**
Public gatekeepers	g	h	**I**
Independent observers	j	**K**	l
Therapist/provider	m	**N**	o

Bold capital letters indicate sources more likely to provide reliable information.
From Speer, D. C. (1998). *Mental health outcome evaluation*. San Diego, CA: Academic Press.

addition to family members. Public gatekeepers are those who have professional responsibilities involving the patient but not a social relationship such as law enforcement officials, emergency room staff, court officials, and child or adult protective services staff. Independent observers are professionals or specialists who can perform medical, psychiatric, or other evaluations of the patient.

The use of standard intake questionnaires and interview protocol forms can help ensure that the collection of assessment information is thorough. Standardized screening instruments are also widely recommended because they can provide psychometrically reliable and valid data, and a patient's scores can be compared with normative data that are usually available. These instruments can also be readministered during and after treatment, providing an important mechanism for monitoring treatment progress and evaluating outcomes (see Chapters 11 and 12).

At a basic level, the adequacy and thoroughness of the assessment information collected for a given case can vary from completely inadequate (e.g., almost nothing is known about important issues) to fully adequate for the purpose. Meyer and Melchert (2011) developed a five-point rubric to rate the general thoroughness of assessment data with regard to each of the biopsychosocial component areas listed in Table 9.1. The descriptors for the five points on the rating scale are noted in Table 9.3 below. To illustrate the application of this approach, Table 9.4 provides examples of intake assessment notes for each of the five levels on the scale. Missing important details is typically problematic with potentially serious consequences. Comprehensive, detailed information, on the other hand, minimizes those risks while increasing the likelihood of effective treatment over both the short and long term.

Table 9.3 Detail and comprehensiveness scale for assessing biopsychosocial components.

Score	Rating description
0	Information regarding component area is not present at all.
1	Only a few details or basic data are mentioned, or a checkbox for this component is marked but no further information is provided.
2	Most or nearly all basic details or data are present; strengths and/or weaknesses may be mentioned minimally but not clearly assessed as a strength or a deficit.
3	Most or nearly all details or data are present, plus one of the following two is also met: (1) strengths associated with this component are described or (2) deficits associated with this component are described.
4	All of the following criteria are met: (1) most or nearly all details or data are present; (2) strengths associated with this component are described; and (3) deficits associated with this component are described.

Adapted from Appendix F in Meyer, L. (2008). *The use of a comprehensive biopsychosocial framework for intake assessment in mental health practice* (Doctoral dissertation). Milwaukee, WI: Marquette University.

Table 9.4 Examples of intake assessment notes documenting particular assessment issues.

Score	Substance use example	Medication example	Religion example
0	[Information regarding this component area is missing]	[Information regarding this component area is missing]	[Information regarding this component area is missing]
1	"Patient states she drinks alcohol."	"Patient takes Paxil."	"Patient is Roman Catholic."
2	"Patient reports drinking alcohol socially, approximately twice per month. She reports not smoking and does not consume caffeine or any illicit drugs."	"Patient currently takes Paxil, 20 mg, once daily for depression."	"Patient is Roman Catholic, is active in her faith, attends church regularly, and was raised Catholic."
3	"Patient reports drinking alcohol socially, approximately twice per month. She reports not smoking and not consuming caffeine or any illicit drugs. Patient reports drinking has a negative impact because when she goes out and drinks with friends, she usually drinks too much and does not want to get out of bed the next day."	"Patient currently takes Paxil, 20 mg, once daily for depression. He states that the medication is helpful because he no longer feels depressed and is more active socially."	"The patient reports that she is Roman Catholic, is active in her faith, goes to church regularly, and was raised Catholic. She states that her religion has helped her by providing a positive support group during her recent difficulties."
4	"Patient reports drinking alcohol socially, approximately twice per month. She reports not smoking and not consuming caffeine or any illicit drugs. Drinking on a social basis has been helpful, according to the patient, because she gets to go out with friends and feels more comfortable socializing and meeting new people. Patient reports that drinking also has a negative effect because when she goes out and drinks with friends, she usually drinks too much and does not want to get out of bed the next day."	"Patient currently takes Paxil, 20 mg, once daily for depression. He states that the medication is helpful because he no longer feels depressed and is more active socially. He reports the medication has a downside as well—he strongly dislikes the side effects of dry mouth, insomnia, sexual dysfunction, and weight gain, and is afraid he will have to take the medication 'forever.'"	"The patient reports that she is Roman Catholic, is active in her faith, goes to church regularly, and was raised Catholic. She states that her religion has helped her by providing a positive support group during her recent difficulties. She also states that her religion has had a detrimental effect because she does not always agree with church doctrine and feels a great deal of internal conflict and guilt as a result."

Adapted from Tables 3.3, 3.4, and 3.5 in Meyer, L. (2008). *The use of a comprehensive biopsychosocial framework for intake assessment in mental health practice* (Doctoral dissertation). Marquette University, Milwaukee, WI.

Assessing severity of patient problems and strength of resources

The information gathered through the methods discussed above needs to be evaluated at multiple levels to gain a thorough understanding of an individual's development and functioning and develop treatment plans most likely to be effective over the short and long term. The first of these levels concerns the severity of patients' problems that have been identified.

The severity of patient problems and needs obviously varies widely and has direct implications for treatment planning. Many individuals face a serious problem in just one area of their lives, while others face major problems in several areas. Need severity consequently must be assessed with regard to particular issues. The most severe and urgent problems typically involve emergency issues that must be attended to immediately. Emergency behavioral health problems often involve suicidality or homicidality, though individuals may face family, medical, legal, financial, and other crises that also require immediate attention. Other problems may be quite serious and require intensive intervention but not on an emergency basis. At the other end of the continuum are minor problems and needs that can be addressed through psychoeducation or a referral to external sources of information or support. Many models for assessing the severity of patient problems range from "none" to "severe" (e.g., the *DSM* system has used "mild," "moderate," and "severe" to indicate the level of severity of mental disorders since the third edition was published in 1980).

In addition to noting the severity of individuals' problems, needs, and disorders, the biopsychosocial perspective also emphasizes positive functioning and personal resources. Behavioral and medical health assessment in the past tended to emphasize deficits and pathology because of the major impact that disease and disability had on people's lives. A contemporary biopsychosocial perspective to health care, on the other hand, emphasizes the whole person and the full continuum of functioning across the biopsychosocial domains. Gaining a holistic assessment of individuals' needs and functioning consequently requires an assessment of strengths and resources as well as problems and vulnerabilities. Strengths and resources include both internal resources (e.g., coping skills) and external resources (e.g., social support). These serve critically important roles in people's lives and can be especially important sources of support when individuals face serious mental health problems. For example, the U.S. Substance Abuse and Mental Health Services Administration (SAMHSA, 2011) initiated a program to focus more attention on developing strengths and resources among individuals with mental illness and substance use disorders. They identified eight dimensions of wellness and recovery: physical, emotional, social, occupational, intellectual, financial, environmental, and spiritual well-being.

The full spectrum of functioning within particular areas of people's lives is illustrated in Table 9.5. Rather than using a unipolar scale ranging from no problem to severe problem, a bipolar scale is used to assess positive functioning as well. This conceptualization, ranging from severe problem at the low end to major strength at the high end, does not apply neatly to all areas of individuals' lives. For example, if

Table 9.5 Assessing severity of problems and strength of resources within biopsychosocial areas.

+3	**Major strength**—a major strength or resource that is an important contributor to the health and well-being of the individual
+2	**Moderate strength**—a moderate strength or resource that adds significantly to the individual's health and functioning; could be developed or amplified further
+1	**Mild strength**—a mild strength or resource for the individual; could be developed and amplified further
0	**No problem or need**—no evidence of problem or need in this area, though not an area of strength; could be developed into an area of strength
−1	**Mild problem**—individual is experiencing mild psychological distress and/or impairment in functioning or faces minor risks for a decline in functioning
−2	**Moderate problem**—individual is functioning significantly less than optimally and/ or is facing risks for a significant deterioration in level of functioning
−3	**Severe problem**—individual is functioning far below an optimal level and/or risks a major deterioration in their level of functioning with dangerous or disabling consequences possible

one experienced no child maltreatment, it is unclear whether that is best viewed as a strength or simply as having no needs in that area. If a person with a history of serious child abuse worked through the consequences of those experiences and conscientiously developed healthy relationships and strong resiliency as a result, these outcomes would be viewed as strengths and not vulnerabilities. Positive responses to stress, adversity, and trauma are exceedingly important in many people's lives (for a review of "benefit finding" and "posttraumatic growth," see Lechner, Tennen, & Affleck, 2009). These issues would need careful analysis if this scale were used as a measurement model. But as a conceptual model, a bipolar conceptualization of problem severity is very useful as a reminder of the importance of assessing both problems and strengths across biopsychosocial areas.

Table 9.6 illustrates the use of a bipolar conceptualization of patient needs and strengths. The dots in the table summarize the assessment of needs and strengths across the biopsychosocial areas for the case of a mildly depressed business executive who is effective at work and manages a large number of important responsibilities with positive appraisals by the chief executive. Many of her subordinates view her as arrogant and difficult, although she is widely regarded as efficient in managing her department. This individual has distant and perfunctory relationships with her husband and children as well as distant and conflictual relationships with her parents. Her husband told her that he expects to leave their marriage once their two children graduate from high school. She consumes significant amounts of alcohol and neglects her physical health. She also privately worries that her life will not be meaningful after retirement because the only thing she finds interesting is her work. The checks in the table refer to the assessment of a homeless man diagnosed with bipolar affective disorder and substance

Table 9.6 Example of biopsychosocial assessment for two cases: a business executive and a homeless person (dots and checks, respectively).

Biopsychosocial domains and components	*−3 Severe problem*	*−2 Moderate problem*	*−1 Mild problem*	*0 No problem or need*	*+1 Mild strength*	*+2 Moderate strength*	*+3 Major strength*
Biological							
General physical health		✓		●			
Childhood health history		✓		●			
Medications		✓	●				
Health habits and behaviors	✓		●				
Psychological							
Level of psychological functioning		✓ ●					
History of present problem	✓		●				
Suicidal ideation and risk assessment		✓	●				
Substance use and abuse	✓	●					
Mental status examination			✓			●	
Individual psychological history	✓		●				
Childhood abuse and neglect	✓		●				
Other psychological traumas		✓		●			
Effects of developmental history		✓	●				
Personality style and characteristics		●				✓	

Sociocultural							
Relationships and social support		✓●					
Current living situation	✓				●		
Family history	✓	●					
Educational history			✓				●
Employment	✓						●
Financial resources	✓						●
Legal issues/crime	✓				●		
Military history				✓●			
Activities of interest/hobbies		✓●					
Religion				✓●			
Spirituality			✓●				
Multicultural issues			✓	●			

dependence. He has a pleasant and engaging personality, is funny and widely liked, but has significant needs and problems in many areas of his life. He was severely physically and emotionally abused during childhood and has had difficulty trusting others ever since. His substance abuse makes him vulnerable to criminal victimization, but he is determined to "make it on my own" and has a long history of rebounding after experiencing thefts and assaults. Note that even though these two individuals' lives differ dramatically, they were both rated as having a moderately serious problem in terms of their level of psychological functioning.

Comprehensively assessing patients' problems and strengths is critical for gaining a thorough understanding of these two individuals. To develop treatment plans with a maximum likelihood of being effective over the long term, it is important to identify problems, needs, and vulnerabilities but also to identify strengths and resources that can be relied on for support or perhaps developed even further. Focusing on strengths along with problems also helps individuals gain a more accurate self-identity and communicates that their therapists are interested in them as whole persons and not just their problems. This in turn helps develop rapport and the stronger therapeutic relationship that is important to positive treatment outcomes (see Chapter 11).

Overall evaluation and integration of assessment information

The assessment information collected and evaluated using the above guidelines needs to be evaluated at two additional levels to develop adequately informed treatment plans. The problems and needs that are identified have to be prioritized, and their overall severity and complexity need to be evaluated as well.

Prioritizing problems and needs

Patients with emergency needs provide the clearest example of the importance of prioritizing problems and needs. The most common emergencies in behavioral health care involve danger to self or others, though many individuals also face crises involving family, medical, legal, financial, criminal, or other problems that may require intensive, urgent intervention. In all these cases, failing to address emergency needs as the first priority can of course have serious consequences. For example, consider a college student who becomes seriously destabilized and suicidal after his romantic relationship is terminated by his partner in a public and embarrassing manner. This student's suicidality needs to be addressed before his lack of educational and career goals is addressed. Addressing the career and educational decisions before the suicidality could increase stress, uncertainty, and the chances of a suicide attempt.

Maslow (1943) presented the best-known approach to conceptualizing the prioritization of human needs. His *Hierarchy of Needs* model (depicted in Fig. 9.1) considered the four lowest levels of needs (physiological, safety, love/belonging, and esteem) to be "deficiency" needs that, when met, allow one to move up the

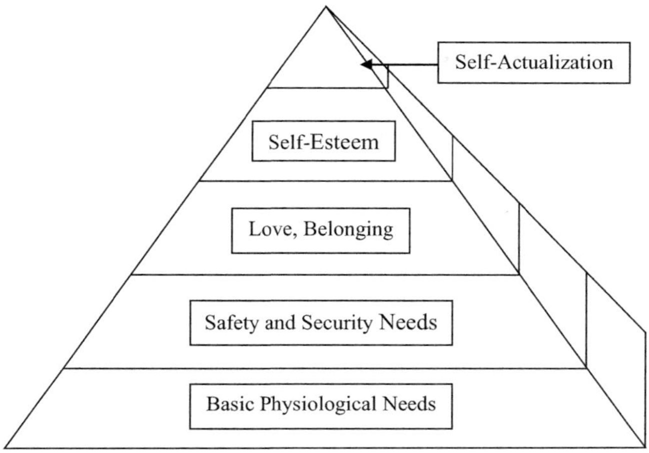

Figure 9.1 Maslow's hierarchy of needs model.

hierarchy and establish new priorities for personal growth. Research has shown that need fulfillment is more fluid than that suggested by a stepped hierarchical model (Wahba & Bridgewell, 1976), but Maslow's model is nonetheless widely used for categorizing different types of needs and arranging their priority. For example, the suicidal college student must address his basic safety and security needs (i.e., as a result of being a danger to himself) before he can address issues related to self-esteem, self-identify, meaning, and purpose. Likewise, a homeless person who is worried about basic needs for food, clothing, shelter, and physical safety may find it impossible to focus on higher-level needs until some level of basic physical stability is achieved. Focusing on self-esteem and existential issues regarding meaning and fulfillment in life can be very difficult and potentially counterproductive if one's lower-level needs are not met first.

Overall complexity of problems and needs

Assessing the severity of individuals' problems and the strength of their resources along with a prioritization of their needs allows for another level of evaluation that is also critical for planning treatment. This evaluation involves the complexity of patients' problems and needs in the context of their biopsychosocial circumstances as a whole. Very complex problems obviously can be very challenging to resolve both for patients and their treatment providers. Significant comorbidity within the psychological domain is common, and coexisting problems across the biopsychosocial domains occurs frequently as well. For example, a significant number of people deal with cooccurring substance dependence, personality disorders, or other clinical syndromes as well as serious family, medical, and/or financial problems that can greatly complicate treatment. The complexity of a patient's situation needs to be assessed before a rational treatment plan can be devised that has a good likelihood of resolving problems and needs over the short or long term.

Table 9.7 Overall complexity of patient problems and needs.

Level of complexity	General guideline
No or very little	Minimal or no clinically significant mental health problems or concerns; significant strengths prevent issues from developing into clinically significant problems
Mild	A small number of problems, usually of lesser severity; presence of strengths helps mitigate their effects
Moderate	Intermediate number of problems usually of intermediate severity, and intermediate level of strengths
Major	Multiple problems of moderate or higher levels of severity and/or risk; strengths insufficient to counterbalance problems

The complexity of biopsychosocial problems and needs can be conceptualized as falling on a continuum. Patients without clinically significant mental health problems would be assessed as having problems of essentially no complexity, while those with one or a small number of problems of lesser severity would be viewed as having problems of little or mild complexity. Patients with problems of major complexity include those with multiple problems at moderate or severe levels of need and/or risk along with strengths that are insufficient to counterbalance the problems (see Table 9.7). Cases of major complexity often involve severe and persistent mental illness or substance dependence; significant comorbidity; a developmental history that includes serious abuse, neglect, or other trauma; or serious personality pathology. Some individuals have a serious problem in just one area, and although the complexity of their problems may be low, the severity of the problem may nonetheless be quite serious. For example, a young adult who enjoys strengths and resources in many areas may nonetheless experience serious destabilization surrounding a humiliating relationship breakup.

More complex and serious behavioral health and biopsychosocial needs often require more comprehensive and detailed evaluation. Patients with serious problems across the biopsychosocial domains may need medical and neuropsychological evaluations, the findings of which are combined with input from family members, employers, teachers, parole officers, or others. For example, these types of thorough and detailed assessments are more frequent in inpatient psychiatric and substance abuse treatment programs where patients often experience more complex problems. The interaction of problems and resources across the many areas of people's lives can result in a very complex array of combinations. Therefore, evaluating the interaction of developmental, etiological, risk, protective, sociocultural, and medical factors in patients' lives in complex cases can require significant clinical experience. Case consultation with more experienced and expert clinicians typically also increases as the severity and complexity of problems increases, at least until clinicians gain extensive experience with these types of cases themselves.

Putting it all together

Conducting behavioral health assessment using the foregoing guidelines is complicated. It requires extensive data collection across many areas of biopsychosocial functioning and the evaluation of that information at several levels. Clinical interviewing and relationship-building skills are necessary to develop good rapport with patients so they will share personal and sensitive information and so their concerns are understood within the context of their values, culture, preferences, and circumstances. Strong communication and collaboration skills are needed to work effectively with all the parties involved in particular cases. Large bodies of knowledge regarding development, personality, psychopathology, biopsychosocial influences on behavior, and psychometric measurement need to be learned and applied in order to properly analyze and evaluate the information collected. This is especially important when assessing more complicated issues involving learning, neuropsychological functioning, personality psychopathology, and forensic questions. Professional ethics and legal issues need to be handled appropriately in all cases. Significant amounts of clinical experience and expertise are also needed to assess the reliability and validity of the information collected and properly evaluate and integrate the data (see Fig. 9.2 for a summary of the processes involved).

This approach to assessment also meets the requirements of evidence-based practice. One needs to have strong interpersonal skills to obtain thorough, reliable information. Through the process of obtaining information about patients' lives across

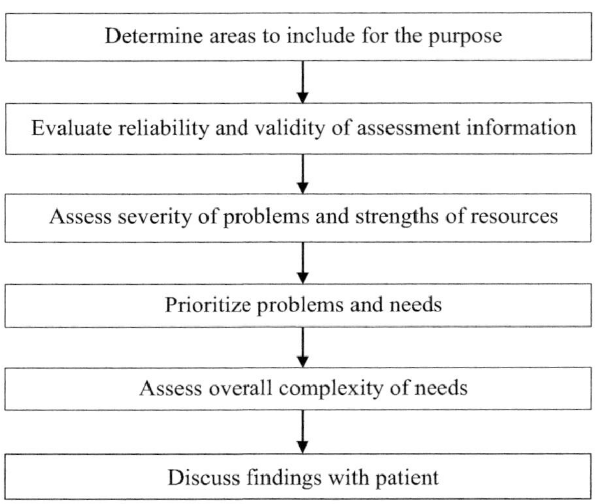

Figure 9.2 Steps of the behavioral health care assessment process.

the biopsychosocial domains, one also learns about their values, preferences, and culture. Learning which factors are relevant and salient in individuals' development and functioning is often a challenge, but it becomes easier with coursework and clinical experience. Integrating all that information with findings from the best available research in a manner that engages and motivates patients represents solid clinical experience, expertise, and mastery of the therapeutic process.

As discussed above, behavioral health assessments in many settings do not require detailed, thorough information in order to proceed with clinical decision-making. It is not practical to conduct thorough assessments in all cases, and screens and other brief assessment procedures are sufficient for many purposes. Learning a thorough conceptualization of the assessment process is critical, however, for putting clinical cases into proper context and appropriately evaluating the information obtained. It is difficult to judge the seriousness and complexity of people's problems if one does not understand the full spectrum of problem severity, the interaction of strengths and vulnerabilities across the biopsychosocial domains, and the significance of etiological and developmental factors. A broad perspective on assessment is also needed to judge the reliability of the information provided by the patient, significant others in their lives, and professionals who may be involved. Applying a comprehensive approach to assessment allows one to properly analyze, evaluate, and integrate assessment information so one can make judgments about whether further intervention is needed, whether a referral is appropriate, or what type of treatment plan is needed to address particular issues and maximize the likelihood of successful outcomes in both the short and the long term. These issues are discussed more thoroughly in the next chapter.

This comprehensive assessment approach is more complex than descriptive approaches that merely focus on gathering information without thoroughly evaluating it or other approaches based on one of the traditional theoretical orientations that focus primarily on just one area of functioning. Unfortunately, some evidence indicates that comprehensive, well-integrated assessments are not common. McClain, O'Sullivan, and Clardy (2004) investigated the adequacy of the case formulations completed by 79 psychiatry residents according to an integrative biopsychosocial framework. They found that, on average, none of the groups of residents (first through fourth year from four different institutions) wrote biopsychosocial case formulations that reached what was identified as the basic level of competency. The reports typically included information regarding a wide range of biopsychosocial factors, but the information was not well integrated and was judged to have the potential to lead to problems in treatment.

A study by Meyer and Melchert (2011) found similar results. They examined the treatment records for 163 psychotherapy outpatients to evaluate the comprehensiveness of the written assessment documentation and the extent to which that information was integrated and formulated in a manner that would maximize treatment effectiveness. Table 9.8 provides the rubric used to rate the level of comprehensiveness and integration of assessment information in that study.

Table 9.8 Levels of comprehensiveness and integration of behavioral health care assessments.

Score	Rating description
0	Assessment is missing critical biological, psychological, and sociocultural information in the context of the particular case.
1	The clinician obtained information regarding a variety of components across the biological, psychological, and sociocultural domains, but a lack of focus and attention to important concerns could lead to less effective treatment.
2	Basic competency. The clinician obtained comprehensive biological, psychological, and sociocultural information, and there is some evidence of integration of this information to address the patient's most important concerns.
3	The clinician obtained comprehensive biological, psychological, and sociocultural information and obtained information about some of the strengths and weaknesses the patient possesses; the integration of this information helps to prioritize the patient's concerns and problems.
4	The clinician addressed the patient's strengths and weaknesses comprehensively across the biopsychosocial domains with attention given to individual and sociocultural differences. This information is integrated so that strengths will be reinforced and amplified, and weaknesses and problems will be addressed. Issues are prioritized to reflect the patient's needs, circumstances, and preferences and to maximize treatment effectiveness.

Adapted from Meyer, L., & Melchert, T. P. (2011). Examining the content of mental health intake assessments from a biopsychosocial perspective. *Journal of Psychotherapy Integration, 21*, 70–89.

The mean rating of the files in the Meyer and Melchert (2011) study was only 1.17 ($SD = 0.45$), and only 14.1% of the files were rated as 2 or higher, the midpoint indicating "basic competency." The findings from this and the McClain et al. (2004) study suggest that assessment information is often reported descriptively, with too little depth and detail, and without an analysis and integration that explains a patient's current problems in the context of strengths, resources, weaknesses, vulnerabilities, and developmental history. To illustrate comprehensive, integrative assessments, Table 9.9 provides examples for each of the five levels of thoroughness in the Meyer and Melchert study for three different types of patient cases.

Table 9.9 Examples of comprehensive and integrated behavioral health care assessments.

Score	Anxiety example	Depression example	Adjustment example
0	Patient presents with symptoms related to an anxiety disorder and indicates she has been under the treatment of a physician for these concerns for 3 months. She states he prescribed anxiolytics for these symptoms but she does not like taking the medication. Her symptoms have recently gotten worse. In the intake assessment, the therapist does not obtain information related to medication, including what the patient is taking, side effects, efficacy, or medication adherence.	Patient presents with symptoms of depression, but the therapist does not obtain information related to suicidal ideation.	Patient presents with adjustment concerns related to her pending divorce, but the therapist does not obtain sociocultural information regarding the quality of her social support network.
1	Patient presents with symptoms related to an anxiety disorder and indicates she has been under the treatment of a physician for these concerns for 3 months. She states he prescribed anxiolytics for these symptoms but she does not like taking the medication. Her symptoms have recently gotten worse. The therapist notes the medication and dosage the patient has been taking, but does not assess side effects and medication adherence.	Patient presents with symptoms of depression and therapist obtains some information regarding psychiatric history, but does not assess previous diagnoses of mood disorders, previous treatments and their outcome, and past psychological traumas.	Patient presents with adjustment concerns related to her pending divorce, and therapist obtains some information the quality of her social support network, but does not assess the quality of her current relationship with her soon-to-be ex-husband.

2	Patient presents with symptoms related to an anxiety disorder and indicates she has been under the treatment of a physician for these concerns for 3 months. She states he prescribed anxiolytics for these symptoms but she does not like taking the medication. Her symptoms have recently gotten worse. The therapist notes the medication and dosage the patient has been taking including important components such as side effects and medication adherence. The therapist notes that these issues may be related to current problems.	Patient presents with symptoms of depression and therapist obtains information related to psychiatric and personal history and past traumas. Therapist shows link between current symptoms and this history.	Patient presents with adjustment concerns related to her pending divorce, and the therapist obtains information regarding the quality of her social support network, and notes how these relationships are stressful and beneficial to her.
3	Patient presents with symptoms related to an anxiety disorder and indicates she has been under the treatment of a physician for these concerns for 3 months. She states he prescribed anxiolytics for these symptoms but she does not like taking the medication. Her symptoms have recently gotten worse. The therapist notes the medication and dosage the patient has been taking, including important components such as side effects and medication adherence. The therapist notes that the medication has helped reduce anxiety symptoms in recent months, but they have also had undesirable side effects such as weight gain and tiredness.	Patient presents with symptoms of depression and therapist obtains information related to personal history. Therapist shows link between current symptoms and history. Therapist discusses with the patient detrimental and beneficial patterns of responses to the life events.	Patient presents with adjustment concerns related to her pending divorce, and the therapist obtains information regarding the quality of her social support network. Therapist also obtains information regarding how marriage and divorce have been detrimental to her functioning and have had positive impacts as well.

Continued

Table 9.9 Examples of comprehensive and integrated behavioral health care assessments.—continued

Score	Anxiety example	Depression example	Adjustment example
4	Patient presents with symptoms related to an anxiety disorder and indicates she has been under the treatment of a physician for these concerns for 3 months. She states he prescribed anxiolytics for these symptoms but she does not like taking the medication. Her symptoms have recently gotten worse. The therapist notes the medication and dosage the patient has been taking including important components such as side effects, medication adherence, and how the medication has helped ameliorate her anxiety symptoms in recent months, but also unpleasant side effects such as weight gain and tiredness. The therapist notes the concern that treatment of the anxiety with medication only has not actually helped manage the effects of her anxiety, but merely managed the symptoms. The therapist also notes that the patient believes her anxiety is related to her family of origin issues and developmental history.	Patient presents with symptoms of depression and therapist obtains information related to personal history. Therapist shows link between current symptoms and history. Therapist discusses with the patient detrimental and beneficial patterns of responses to the life events. Therapist makes links between patient's personal history and current functioning, highlighting recurrent patterns that also appeared in the patient's parents' relationship.	Patient presents with adjustment concerns related to her pending divorce and the therapist obtains information regarding the quality of her social support network. Therapist obtains information regarding how marriage and divorce have been detrimental to her functioning and have positive impacts as well. Therapist prioritizes the patient's problems in the context of her current resources and takes patient's religious beliefs and preferences into account in order to maximize treatment effectiveness.

Adapted from Table 3.6 in Meyer, L. (2008). The use of a comprehensive biopsychosocial framework for intake assessment in mental health practice (Doctoral dissertation). Marquette University, Milwaukee, WI.

Case example: assessment with a mildly depressed patient

Jessica is a 41-year-old married African American female presenting with concerns about depressed mood. Jessica writes on the clinic intake questionnaire that "My husband wants me to see a therapist for mild depression." The patient indicates no concerns about her physical health, marriage, work, or finances. She notes that she has two daughters, 12 and 14 years old. She denies any suicidal ideation or disturbing thoughts or feelings, and reports drinking alcohol "socially." She lists her occupation as nurse practitioner. She also completes the two intake questionnaires the clinic uses to screen for depression and anxiety.

The psychologist introduces himself to Jessica, reviews her questionnaires, and quickly scores the scales. He notes that Jessica scored in the mild-to-moderate range of depression on the intake questionnaire, and he asks her about her depressed mood. She reports that she is "a little depressed. It's not really a problem, but my husband is concerned about it."

The psychologist asks her to describe her family life, and Jessica explains that she has been married for 16 years to a firefighter who works for the city. She reports that she and her husband have a good marriage and family life. She says she was "head over heels, totally in love on my wedding day. It was the happiest day of my life! He's interesting, really nice, smart, and has a good career. He's funny and positive. He's incredibly fit and attractive." She says, "My girlfriends love him; they're jealous of me."

The psychologist asks her what her marriage is like now, and she reports that she and her husband became very busy after their children were born and gradually stopped going out on dates. Jessica explains that her mother will babysit for them but also criticizes their parenting, so they stopped asking her to babysit. "My mother wants me to live closer to home and interact more with the family. She thinks I work too much. She likes my husband and adores our girls. But she criticizes me too much." She also notes that her parents are very disappointed that she and her husband do not belong to a church and the kids are not being raised in a religion. When asked about the quality of her intimate relationship, she reports that she and her husband used to have an active and satisfying sexual relationship, but that dropped off. The psychologist asks what her two children are like, and she reports that they are in sixth and eighth grade and are both doing well. "They like school, they are doing above average in their classes, and they have nice friends. They're normally well behaved at home."

The psychologist asks about her physical health and she reports that she has good health. She doesn't offer more, so the psychologist asks about her level of physical exercise and activity, and she reports that she used to exercise regularly, nearly as much as her husband, but she gradually stopped after the children were born. She reports that she eats healthy: "I have to—my husband is a fitness fanatic and he makes most of the meals. And I don't snack between meals. I suppose you might not believe that because I'm a little heavy now. I look a lot different than what I used to." When asked how she gained weight if she eats

Continued

Case example: assessment with a mildly depressed patient—cont'd

well, she said it was due to alcohol—"I drink a glass of wine in the evening to unwind."

The psychologist asks about her hobbies and interests, and she reports that she used to enjoy reading, music, movies, and seeing friends, but that now she mostly watches TV and reads the news. She says that her husband goes out with his friends and is active socially, but she hasn't seen her friends much recently. She says that she'd like to be involved in the parent–teacher organization at school but hasn't found the time. When asked about her relationship with her own family, she reports that she has been avoiding her parents mostly because she doesn't like the criticism from her mother, and she doesn't see her siblings or other relatives often.

The psychologist explains to Jessica that couples often make a lot of lifestyle changes after they have children. The psychologist shares his opinion that she and her husband appear to have been very successful with their careers and children but have neglected their relationship. He also notes that she sounds quite disappointed about neglecting her exercise and physical health. He asks whether she would like to explore possibilities for improving her relationship with her mother and the rest of the family.

The psychologist explains that there are several ways to address her issues, but before they decide on the best approach, he would like to hear her husband's perspective on these issues. He asks if she would ask him to come in for their next appointment. At the end of the session, the psychologist completes the table below with the patient to help summarize the patient's situation. Jessica notes that the summary ratings give a picture of her life that she never thought about before, and that helps her realize that things could be a lot better.

Table 9.10 Summary of the biopsychosocial assessment for the case example.

Biopsychosocial Domains and Components	***-3*** ***Severe need***	***-2*** ***Moderate need***	***-1*** ***Mild need***	***0*** ***No need***	***+1*** ***Mild strength***	***+2*** ***Moderate strength***	***+3*** ***Major strength***
Biological							
General physical health			✓				
Childhood health history				✓			
Medications				✓			
Health habits and behaviors		✓					
Psychological							
Level of psychological functioning		✓					
History of present problem			✓				
Individual psychological history			✓				
Substance use and abuse			✓				
Suicidal ideation and risk assessment				✓			
Effects of developmental history			✓				
Childhood abuse and neglect				✓			
Other psychological traumas				✓			
Mental status examination							✓
Personality style and characteristics				✓			

Continued

Table 9.10 Summary of the biopsychosocial assessment for the case example.—continued

Sociocultural							
Current relationships and social support		✓					
Current living situation					✓		
Family history			✓				
Educational history							✓
Employment						✓	
Financial resources						✓	
Legal issues/crime				✓			
Military history				✓			
Activities of interest/hobbies		✓					
Religion				✓			
Spirituality				✓			
Multicultural issues			✓				

The importance and usefulness of comprehensive and thoroughly evaluated assessment information is evident when considering treatment planning, the next general phase of the treatment process. Well-designed treatment plans that effectively resolve problems and address needs while also building resources and resilience over the long and short term require comprehensive and reliable assessment information that is appropriately evaluated and integrated. Before discussing that subject, the following case example is provided to illustrate how behavioral health care assessment can be approached using the evidence-based biopsychosocial approach (see also Table 9.10).

Treatment planning

10

People whose lives have been filled with distress, confusion, and psychological pain are sometimes greatly relieved when they receive a psychological diagnosis and assessment that explains their difficult life experience. The explanation alone sometimes provides major relief, even though absorbing the significance of the explanation might entail feelings of loss and regret for the suffering one endured, the difficulty one had pursuing life goals or meaningful relationships, and perhaps the suffering that one caused to others. But at least what had been so confusing and frustrating is now understandable, and this can lead to optimism that things can improve and the feeling that a great weight has been lifted off one's shoulders. Medical diagnoses can provide the same type of relief when a person finally gets a diagnosis that explains symptoms or pain for which no cause had ever been identified.

But most patients want more than just a diagnosis. Most people also want solutions to their problems. This is the point at which the assessment phase of health care transitions into the treatment planning phase. This is when the patient and therapist work together on a plan to address the problems identified in the assessment.

The evidence-based biopsychosocial approach to treatment planning relies on a holistic understanding of patients' needs that recognizes the full range of interacting biopsychosocial influences on development, functioning, and behavior change. Treatment plans from this perspective address patients' needs within the context of their unique developmental history and current circumstances. The goal is to relieve psychological distress and reduce symptomatology while also strengthening health and functioning across the important areas of a person's life. Evidence-based therapies and other interventions are used to resolve problems and build strengths and resources, taking advantage of the synergy that is possible when strengths are bolstered at the same time that problems are lessened across the biopsychosocial domains. The overarching goal is to develop treatment plans that maximize treatment effectiveness and lead to optimal functioning over the short term as well as the long term.

This approach can be very different from many traditional approaches to treatment planning. In traditional approaches, therapists often formulated a conceptualization of the patient's personality and psychopathology from the perspective of a particular theoretical orientation and then implemented the treatment that was consistent with that orientation. Cognitive therapists conceptualizing cases involving major depression, for example, were likely to identify irrational or depressogenic thoughts and beliefs, and then develop a therapy plan to replace those thoughts with rational ones. A biologically oriented psychiatrist to whom those same patients were referred was likely to include antidepressant medication in the treatment plan, while a solution-oriented therapist might ask the patients about how they will know that their problems have been resolved and then focus on creating those conditions. All of these therapies

Foundations of Health Service Psychology. https://doi.org/10.1016/B978-0-12-816426-6.00010-4

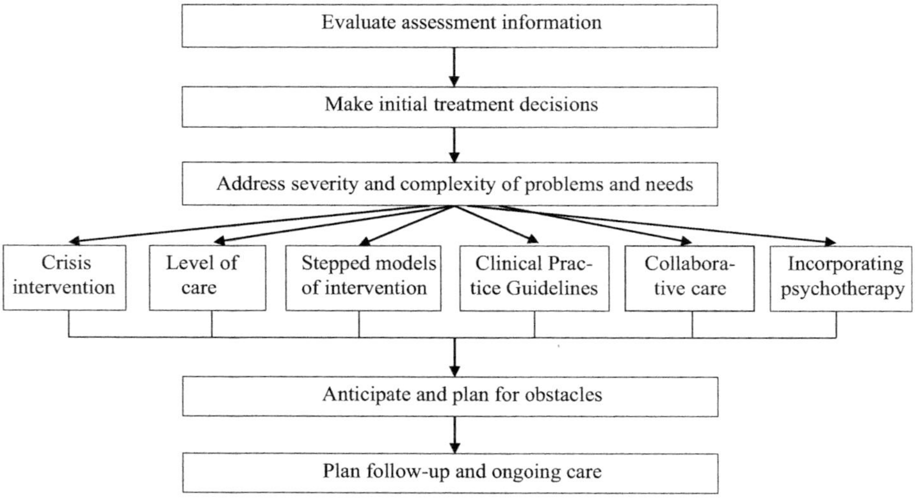

Figure 10.1 Overall process of behavioral health care treatment planning.

can be very useful and effective and completely appropriate depending on the case. But these therapists' preferred approaches will not provide the best solutions for all patients. There is tremendous variation in patients' needs and biopsychosocial circumstances, and this variation needs to be incorporated into the treatment planning process.

This chapter examines the basic processes involved in approaching behavioral health treatment planning from an evidence-based biopsychosocial perspective. It covers the treatment planning process from beginning to end, emphasizing the important decisions that need to be made and the important patient variables and contextual issues that need to be considered to help ensure treatment effectiveness. The general process involved is depicted in Fig. 10.1. Each of the components included in the figure are discussed in the following sections. Also included at the end of the chapter is a listing of examples of alternative interventions that might be considered when planning behavioral health care from a comprehensive biopsychosocial perspective.

Treatment planning from an evidence-based biopsychosocial perspective

The evidence-based biopsychosocial approach to behavioral health care treatment planning includes several essential characteristics. First, its conceptual foundations rest squarely on science and ethics. Like all the rest of the treatment process, treatment planning is based on the scientific understanding of human development, functioning, and behavior change, and its overarching purpose is to apply science and ethics to meet the needs of patients and promote their biopsychosocial functioning. These basic conceptual foundations and purposes guide the whole treatment process, including the specific activities involved in treatment planning.

A second essential characteristic that follows from this approach is the priority given to the safety and effectiveness of treatment. Across all of health care, professionals need to ensure the safety and effectiveness of their interventions by relying on the best available research, sound clinical experience and expertise, and careful ethical procedures and practices. As discussed in Chapter 4, the ethical obligations of nonmaleficence and beneficence require that health care professionals provide care that benefits individuals and does not introduce disproportionate risks of side effects or harm. Patients need to be able to trust that the treatment they receive is safe and effective.

A third essential characteristic of this approach is its reliance on evidence-based practice. This entails three important considerations. The first leg of the "three-legged evidence-based practice stool" involves consideration of the best available research evidence regarding the patient's diagnoses and circumstances and the effectiveness of interventions for treating her or his problems and disorders. The third leg of the evidence-based practice stool requires consideration of the patient's characteristics, preferences, values, and culture. The second leg of the evidence-based practice stool involves the integration of one's clinical experience and expertise with the best available research evidence regarding the case in the context of the patient's characteristics, preferences, values, and culture. The integration of all this information is complex, but following the guidelines discussed in the chapters in this part of the book keeps it manageable.

A fourth characteristic of the biopsychosocial approach to behavioral health care is its comprehensive perspective on human development and functioning. Treatment planning builds directly from the findings of the psychological assessment, addressing patients' unique problems, needs, and circumstances within the context of their particular developmental history, vulnerabilities, strengths, and resources. A comprehensive, long-term perspective is applied to address problems and promote biopsychosocial functioning across the important areas of individuals' lives. Treatment plans are designed to not only relieve distress and symptoms in the short term, but also help patients make changes that will be effective over the long term. They use a developmental perspective that addresses the causes of individuals' problems, disorders, and vulnerabilities to the extent possible based on existing scientific knowledge. They also focus on bolstering strengths and resources to build resilience and competence for facing challenges and taking advantage of opportunities in the future.

Initial decisions

Behavioral health care practice encompasses a wide range of interventions and is conducted in many different settings with individuals at many levels of functioning. In some cases, individuals have severe problems in multiple biopsychosocial areas of their lives and few resources. Other cases involve critical needs that require immediate attention (e.g., suicidality, the safety of the children of an unstable parent). At the other end of the spectrum are individuals who have minor developmentally appropriate questions within the context of substantial strengths and resources. For example, a person may need only to be reassured that her response to a relationship partner or a career decision is responsible and appropriate and she does not need treatment at all. Other cases involve long-term therapy, in which individuals face an absence of meaning in life, work through a very dysfunctional family of origin history, or learn to replace deep dysfunctional personality characteristics with more adaptive ones. Sometimes therapy is delayed for a period because certain issues need to be addressed (e.g., substance abuse or employment problems) or resources need to be strengthened (e.g., personal coping resources or external social support) before it is appropriate to examine difficult personal or family issues.

Based on people's particular problems, vulnerabilities, strengths, and developmental history, interventions can take many different forms. But the first treatment planning decision that needs to be made is often at a very basic level. Given the findings of the assessment that was conducted, is there a clinically significant problem or concern that needs professional attention? Is intervention warranted at this time? It is not appropriate to assume that treatment is indicated whenever someone raises a concern or presents a problem; clinicians instead need to evaluate whether intervention is the best way to address the concern or problem and, if so, the approach that will best address the issues. This evaluation revolves around the severity and complexity of the issues that were identified in the psychological assessment and the third leg of the evidence-based practice stool (i.e., patient characteristics, preferences, values, and culture). At this first, most basic, level of evaluation, normally just four options are considered: not intervening, postponing the decision to intervene, intervening, or referring to another professional (see Table 10.1).

Many people have questions or concerns that do not rise to the level that requires clinical attention because the questions or concerns have no significant implications for their development or functioning. For example, they may wonder whether a particular emotional, cognitive, behavioral, or sexual response they experience is healthy. After learning that their experience is normal and no sign of a mental health problem, many people will be reassured that no further assessment or intervention is needed.

Table 10.1 Initial decision-making options regarding proceeding with intervention.

1.	**Do not intervene** because the problem or concern does not warrant clinical intervention or the patient (or surrogate decision maker) declines treatment in non-emergency or non-mandated situations
2.	**Postpone a decision about intervening** because it is unclear whether a clinically significant problem currently exists, or the patient (or surrogate decision maker) is ambivalent about treatment at this time; if appropriate, observe and monitor the patient in the meantime (i.e., "watchful waiting")
3.	**Intervene** with clinically significant problems (i.e., provide treatment oneself or in collaboration with other providers)
4.	**Refer** to another professional for more assessment or to provide the needed intervention

Of course, these individuals should always feel free to return if these or other issues become concerning at a later point.

Some individuals have clinically significant issues that cause distress or impairment but they are unwilling to receive treatment for those problems. Sometimes others are affected significantly by these issues as well (e.g., in cases of substance abuse, agoraphobia, sexual preoccupations). But if there is no clear issue involving safety or danger to self or others, there may be little that can be done when these individuals reject treatment. These situations are sometimes very difficult for family members, partners, friends, and neighbors, and occasionally these third parties can collaborate on an intervention designed to motivate a person to accept treatment. In any case, the needs of these third parties may need to be addressed separately. If there are concerns about risks to self or others (including dependent children or disabled adults), clinicians need to evaluate those risks and take appropriate action. Students and clinicians without sufficient clinical experience and expertise to handle these situations need to consult with more experienced professionals.

Some individuals have questions or concerns that do not indicate a clinically significant problem, although the issue will become problematic if it worsens. Others have questions or concerns that are likely to resolve on their own after receiving minimal guidance or informational resources, although intervention will be needed if the issues do not resolve. These sorts of situations sometimes arise when individuals enter a developmental stage that is new and unfamiliar (e.g., when first dating, entering a committed relationship, having children, having children leave the home, approaching retirement). In cases like these, there is a middle option between providing and not providing treatment that can be very useful. Rather than proceed with treatment, therapists may judge that it is appropriate to postpone formal intervention and instead monitor the patient's progress with the issues. "Watchful waiting" is common in medicine because many developing conditions are still approaching the boundary of clinical significance and/or there is a reasonable likelihood they will resolve on their own without intervention. It is very important in both physical and behavioral health care to intervene early to prevent problems from developing or increasing in severity. But it is also important not to waste resources, identify normal questions or minor issues as mental health disorders that require professional intervention, or risk other undesirable side effects if there is a reasonable likelihood an issue will resolve on its own.

When patients have clinically significant problems and therapists are competent to treat those problems within the context of the patients' background and cultural characteristics, then therapists often provide the needed services themselves. Sometimes therapists are fully competent to provide the needed services but are unable to because of factors largely unrelated to the patient (e.g., a dual relationship through a third party, having too many suicidal patients in one's caseload to responsibly take another one). In these situations, referring to other qualified therapists is the usual practice.

Referring clients to other professionals is the normal practice when therapists have not had sufficient education and clinical experience to safely and effectively provide the needed interventions, or their department or agency does not provide the types of treatment or level of care that a patient needs (e.g., employee assistance programs, college counseling centers). It is also not uncommon for therapists to possess the experience and expertise to diagnose a problem (e.g., substance abuse, parent–child conflicts, posttraumatic stress disorder [PTSD]) but not to have the expertise to provide the treatment that is needed.

Addressing severity and complexity of problems and needs

The severity and complexity of a patient's problems and needs are critical factors in identifying the appropriate type, level, and intensity of intervention in treatment planning. Once clinically significant problems have been identified in the psychological assessment, decisions about how to proceed are based on the severity and complexity of those problems, the best available research evidence, and the patient's characteristics, preferences, values, and culture. The complexity of patients' problems taken together as a whole must be considered along with the severity of their individual problems, any additional vulnerabilities, and their strengths and resources as well.

A basic principle of behavioral health care treatment planning is that the particular problems and needs of an individual patient should be addressed at the appropriate level and intensity of intervention. The ethical and legal principle involved refers to providing treatment using the least restrictive means possible and is discussed later in the section "Levels of care." In general, problem severity and complexity are correlated with intervention intensity. Less serious problems require less intensive interventions, while complex, serious problems will require intensive interventions. Interventions should be sufficient to achieve a positive outcome, but they also should not interrupt people's lives or restrict their autonomy unnecessarily, waste resources, or introduce undesirable side effects that are not justified by the benefits of intervention.

General treatment planning guidelines for identifying the type, level, and intensity of intervention with regard to individual biopsychosocial areas of functioning are found in Table 10.2. (The levels of problem severity listed were identified in Table 9.5.) As the number of co-occurring problems across biopsychosocial areas increases and the strength of resources decreases, the clinical picture becomes more complex, and treatment planning becomes more complex as well. Within individual areas of functioning, however, the following basic guidelines apply.

Therapists need to be mindful that the treatment planning process is frequently dynamic as a result of the evolution of the therapy relationship or challenging events and obstacles that arise in patients' lives. External events may occur and new issues may emerge during the course of treatment as therapeutic rapport and trust develop and patients are willing to reveal more sensitive aspects of their lives. Patients frequently assess whether their therapist is trustworthy in terms of handling sensitive subjects before they will reveal them (e.g., compulsive behaviors, sexual orientation, heavy substance use). Some patients realize connections between past experiences and current issues only after they gain insight into how past events affected their personality development and psychopathology. In all cases, therapists need to continually monitor

Table 10.2 Basic treatment planning options associated with level of problem severity for individual areas of biopsychosocial functioning.

Severity of problem or strength of resource	Basic treatment planning options
+1 to +3: mild, moderate, or major area of strength or resource	• Reinforce strengths, amplify assets, and build resources (internal as well as environmental) to build resilience over the long term
0: no evidence of problem	• Do not intervene • Build this area into a source of strength or a resource for the patient • Refer patient back to referral source with opinion that no significant problem exists and provide suggestions for future monitoring or prevention
−1: mild problem	• Provide support, psychoeducation, and/or brief treatment for making changes • Postpone interventions until other higher priority needs are addressed • Observe and monitor the problem or concern; postpone decision about intervening to a later point
−2: Moderate problem	• Provide intervention oneself • Refer to other professional(s) to provide intervention • Collaborate with other professional(s) on providing intervention(s) • Postpone intervention until other higher priority needs are addressed • Provide aftercare and follow-up as needed
−3: Severe problem	• Immediate and/or intensive interventions are generally needed; monitor with extra care • Provide intervention oneself • Refer to other professional(s) to provide intervention • Collaborate with other professional(s) on providing intervention(s) • Plan ongoing care, aftercare, and follow-up as needed

the progress of treatment and modify treatment plans appropriately when it becomes evident that the nature, severity, and complexity of the patients' problems have changed.

Treatment planning can be particularly dynamic in cases of greater severity and complexity. For example, intensive and immediate interventions are often needed when severe biopsychosocial problems are present and when significant risks of harm to self or others exist. When immediate, intensive care is needed, the target for achieving the most urgent treatment goals may be just hours or days (e.g., to achieve stabilization following a suicidal crisis). The target for achieving less urgent medium-term goals may be several weeks, while other goals may become part of a long-term plan. In the case of serious alcoholism, for example, immediate treatment for detoxification and medical stabilization might be needed acutely. This might be followed by relatively intensive substance abuse treatment that is followed by family therapy and vocational counseling to address medium-term goals. Involvement in Alcoholics Anonymous may become a permanent part of a plan to maintain long-term sobriety and higher levels of biopsychosocial functioning.

Extensive coursework and supervised clinical experience are required to gain the knowledge and skills needed to develop treatment plans for addressing a full range of behavioral health issues. Treatment planning can be particularly complicated in cases with high problem complexity and severity. Many different types of interventions are available for use in these cases. A listing of alternative interventions is provided at the end of this chapter to illustrate some of the options that are available to address cases at all levels of severity and complexity. But several additional issues need to be considered before one can develop safe and effective treatment plans for addressing a full range of behavioral health problems.

Crisis intervention

The most common emergency situation in behavioral health care involves suicidality. Millions of people have thoughts about killing themselves each year. As noted in Chapter 5, the number of Americans who died by suicide in 2016 was 45,965, more than twice the number who died by homicide (19,362; Xu et al., 2018). It is also estimated that for every death by suicide from 2008 to 11, there were 31 individuals who attempted suicide (SAMSHA, 2018). In 2016, an estimated 4.3% of the population had seriously thought about killing themselves, and young adults ages 18 to 25 were much more likely to have those thoughts. In addition, 1.3% of the population had made suicide plans and 0.6% had made a suicide attempt (SAMSHA, 2018; see Chapter 5 for more information on suicide). The behavioral health field is the primary profession with expertise for dealing with this issue, and clinicians consequently need to be competent in this area.

There are also other types of emergency situations that arise less frequently in behavioral health care practice. Occasionally individuals who arrive at our offices require emergency medical attention if they are experiencing an alcohol or drug overdose, delirium due to an infection or disease process, or some other medical problem. Other issues that may rise to the level of a crisis situation involve serious substance abuse, psychotic decompensation, seriously disordered eating, self-harming behaviors such as cutting, severe panic episodes, major sleep disturbance, and the abuse or neglect of children, vulnerable adults, or dependent elders. Accidents and criminal victimization can also be life threatening, and individuals may face other serious family, medical, financial, or legal problems that may require immediate attention to prevent a crisis from developing. Therapists also need to remain alert to the possibility that third parties are affected by a patient's crisis, such as when an unstable parent is responsible for the care of dependent children, disabled adult children, and/or elderly, dependent parents.

When severe problems or risks of harm are identified, immediate interventions are often needed to prevent harm from happening or to treat harm that already occurred. When these situations occur, crisis intervention becomes the first priority, and addressing other issues is usually postponed altogether until the emergency needs are addressed. These are frequently complicated situations that require significant knowledge and experience to manage effectively, and so students and less experienced clinicians tend to rely on more experienced supervisors and colleagues to assist when these cases arise. Suicidality occurs relatively frequently and in all types of general and specialized practice, and so all practitioners need to be proficient with risk assessment and intervention for this issue. Graduate training on this topic has frequently been insufficient (e.g., a task force of the American Association of Suicidology found serious gaps in training on suicide risk assessment and management; Schmitz et al., 2012). Therefore, students and practicing clinicians may need to make special efforts to ensure adequate preparation in this area.

Level of care

If there are no emergencies or other crises that need to be evaluated and managed, the next consideration in treatment planning typically involves the level of care that is needed to effectively and efficiently meet the patient's needs. As always, the goal is to address individuals' problems and needs while also developing strengths, resources, and resilience to optimize biopsychosocial functioning, all within the context of the patients' characteristics, preferences, values, and culture. Individuals' problems and circumstances vary greatly and so treatment planning needs to be individualized. At one end of the continuum are patients with limited problems and significant strengths and resources who may need limited psychoeducation, referral to a support group, or a small number of therapy sessions to resolve their concerns. At the other end are patients with serious mental illnesses and cooccurring problems in multiple biopsychosocial areas who need comprehensive interdisciplinary treatment to achieve stabilization and rehabilitation. These cases can require the collaboration of psychologists, psychiatrists, medical providers, rehabilitation counselors, occupational therapists, social workers, and legal professionals, as well as the patient's family members and others who together provide the care and support needed to assist a patient in achieving the highest levels of functioning and quality of life possible.

The need to identify appropriate levels of care to effectively meet patients' needs grew quickly in the 1960s following the deinstitutionalization of individuals with chronic mental illnesses in the U.S. A major principle underlying that movement was the legal requirement to provide patients with treatment that restricts their liberty the least while still remaining efficient and effective (Project Release v. Prevost, 1983). This resulted in attempts to increase the involvement of patients and their families in managing the treatment so that care could be provided in the least restrictive manner possible while still being effective (Durbin, Goering, Cochrane, Macfarlane, & Sheldon, 2004).

Several models for evaluating the level of care needed by behavioral health care patients have been developed. The American Association of Community Psychiatrists developed one of the most widely used systems, called the Level of Care Utilization System for Psychiatric and Addiction Services (LOCUS) (American Association of Community Psychiatrists, 2016; Sowers, George, & Thompson, 1999). This system matches patients' behavioral health needs with the appropriate intensity of service and level of care needed to address and manage those needs. The level of care recommendation is based on scores from six assessment scales that measure (1) level of risk of harm to self or others; (2) level of general functioning (e.g., ability for self-care, appropriate interaction with others); (3) medical, addictive, and psychiatric comorbidity; (4) level of stress and level of support in the patient's environment; (5) the patients'' treatment and recovery history; and (6) the patient's level of acceptance of responsibility for maintaining his or her health and his or her engagement with helping resources. A modified version of the LOCUS was also developed for use with children and adolescents (i.e., the CALOCUS; Sowers, Pumariega, Huffine, & Fallon, 2003). It follows the same format as the LOCUS but incorporates additional considerations that are relevant for children (e.g., the sixth assessment scale focuses on the primary caretaker's acceptance and engagement as well as the child's).

The LOCUS and CALOCUS include six levels of care that represent increasingly intensive services. These levels include:

1. recovery maintenance and health management personally managed by the patient;
2. low-intensity community-based (outpatient) services;
3. high-intensity community-based services;
4. medically monitored nonresidential services (e.g., partial hospital programs);
5. medically monitored residential services (e.g., residential programs in the community, nursing homes);
6. medically managed residential services (e.g., psychiatric hospitals).

The substance abuse treatment field also relies on level of care models. The most widely known approach was developed by the American Society of Addiction Medicine (Mee-Lee, 2013). Based on an assessment of a patient's risks, needs, strengths, skills, and resources, one of five levels of care is identified that matches intensity of treatment services to the identified patient needs. These levels include:

1. early intervention;
2. outpatient services;
3. intensive outpatient/partial hospitalization services;
4. residential/inpatient services;
5. medically managed intensive inpatient services.

Identifying the optimal level of care to ensure the maximal functioning of psychiatric patients in the least restrictive manner possible became an important clinical responsibility following the deinstitutionalization movement that began more than a half-century ago. It is now a standard component of treatment planning.

Stepped models of intervention

Graduated, stepped models of intervention are based on the same underlying concept as level of care models, that more severe and complex problems need to be addressed through more intensive approaches to care. Several stepped models of care have been developed to address specific behavioral health issues. The best known of these involves treatment planning for suicidality. Other stepped models of intervention that will be noted in this section address substance abuse, depression, anxiety, and concerns about sexuality (see Forand, DeRubreis, & Amsterdam, 2013, for applications in schizophrenia, bipolar, and other disorders). These models are extremely useful for developing treatment plans that address patients' problems and concerns at all levels of severity and complexity.

Suicidality. Given the prevalence and significance of suicidality, conducting assessments and developing treatment plans for suicidal ideation and behavior are critical competencies for behavioral health care professionals. Understanding and implementing graduated, stepped level of care approaches are necessary components of these competencies. These approaches revolve around the principle that more immediate and intensive interventions for managing and treating suicidality are indicated as the risk for suicide increases. For example, the Columbia-Suicide Severity Rating Scale (Columbia Lighthouse Project, 2019) recommends possible interventions based on an individual's responses on the screening instrument. For those at the lowest levels of risk, clinicians are advised to make a referral to a behavioral health professional; at the next level, consult with a behavioral health professional and consider taking patient safety precautions; and at the highest level, consult with a behavioral health professional and take patient safety precautions. The Suicide Assessment Five-Step Evaluation and Triage model provided by the U.S. Substance Abuse and Mental Health Services Administration (SAMHSA, 2019b) identifies three general levels of risk. Possible interventions at the low-risk level include outpatient referral, symptom reduction, and providing emergency and crisis call numbers. For the moderate-risk level, it notes that hospital admission may be necessary depending on risk factors and recommends developing a crisis plan and giving emergency and crisis call numbers. At the high-risk level, the recommendations for possible interventions are hospital admission and other suicide precautions.

Substance abuse. Substance abuse is also a common problem that can be associated with major medical, mental, social, and economic consequences. To more effectively address the problem, SAMHSA initiated the SBIRT program in the 1990s to expand treatment capacity and early intervention for substance abuse. This program is widely used in inpatient and outpatient medical settings to provide early intervention for those who are not dependent on substances but may be engaging in problematic substance use or abuse (SAMHSA, 2019a). The SBIRT (Screen, Brief Intervention, Brief Treatment, and Referral to Treatment) screening program begins with questions for assessing substance use and abuse that are designed to be incorporated into routine medical practice and other health services. If the screening questions indicate a moderate risk for substance abuse, brief interventions are recommended to try to increase awareness of substance use patterns and consequences and motivate behavior change to reduce harmful drinking and substance misuse. If moderate to high risks are identified, then more comprehensive brief treatment is recommended. If severe risk or dependence is indicated, a referral for specialty treatment is then recommended.

Depression and anxiety. In 1999, the United Kingdom undertook a pioneering country-wide effort to develop treatment recommendations for a full range of medical problems. The program, now referred to as the National Institute for Health and Care Excellence (NICE), started by examining the effectiveness of an antiviral medicine for flu and the removal of healthy wisdom teeth before developing treatment guidelines for schizophrenia in 2002. To decrease depression and anxiety disorders on a national basis, two pilot programs were initiated in 2007 to improve the availability of evidence-based psychological treatments (Clark et al., 2009). Given the effectiveness of the pilot programs, a full national implementation was undertaken the following year. This program provides systematic assessment and ongoing measurement of depressive and anxiety symptoms to inform the level of intervention and care that are needed. At lower levels of depressive symptoms, self-help activities with guidance from a *psychological well-being practitioner* are provided along with computer-assisted cognitive behavior therapy, psychoeducational groups, and structured physical activities. Also available are behavior therapy, couples therapy, and short-term psychodynamic therapy. Higher intensity services are available for moderate to severe depression and may include cognitive behavior therapy, interpersonal therapy, and medication (Clark, 2011). The program has accumulated substantial evidence regarding its effectiveness (Fonagy & Clark, 2015).

Sexuality concerns. One of the early stepped treatment planning approaches was developed to assist with concerns involving sexuality (Annon, 1976). The PLISSIT model (Permission, Limited Information, Specific Suggestions, and Intensive Treatment) recommends providing individuals with assurance ("permission") or limited answers for common, less complicated questions and concerns about one's sexuality. More specific guidance and finally intensive treatment are recommended for more complicated issues and problems.

These models illustrate the basic treatment planning principle that the severity and complexity of individuals' problems drive the intensity, type, and level of interventions that are considered to address those problems. Stepped models of care and intervention are very useful and efficient tools for implementing this principle and ensuring that patients' problems and needs are addressed efficiently and appropriately.

Clinical practice guidelines

A recent initiative in health service psychology is the development of clinical practice guidelines that provide treatment recommendations for specific clinical disorders. The American Psychological Association (APA) has assembled panels of experts who review the available research and develop recommendations for treating particular conditions or diagnoses. The guideline recommendations are based on the strength of the evidence found in systematic reviews of the outcome research for particular conditions (as opposed to recommendations developed by the American Psychiatric Association that are based entirely on consensus by panels of psychiatrists).

Based on the strength of the evidence, the guidelines recommend for or against the use of particular interventions, either strongly or conditionally, for treating the condition.

The first set of APA clinical practice guidelines was published in 2017 for the treatment of PTSD (American Psychological Association, 2019). Since then, guidelines have been completed for the treatment of obesity and overweight in children and the treatment of depression across the life span, and plans are in place to develop guidelines for a full range of behavioral health issues. As of this writing, it remains unknown how influential these guidelines will become. The guideline development initiative undertaken in the United Kingdom by the National Institute for Health and Care Excellence (NICE) is significantly increased access to behavioral health care for large numbers of people in that country. But the health care system in the United Kingdom is quite different from the American system, so the impact of the APA clinical practice guidelines is more difficult to predict.

Collaborative care

The scientific knowledge base for understanding health and disease grew dramatically over the 20th century. As a result, medicine and health care became far more specialized. Two generations ago there were still many generalists in medicine and behavioral health care who cared for the "whole person," including the full range of concerns and problems a person might encounter across his or her life span. Now there are a vast array of specialists who treat only particular organ systems or disorders, and leave the care of the rest of the patient to others. Sometimes the various health professionals involved in caring for a particular patient communicate and collaborate well, but frequently this does not happen. Miscommunication and lack of collaboration can lead to errors, omissions, and patient dissatisfaction with services.

As a result of the fragmentation of health care, there has been growing interest in the benefits of and need for interprofessional treatment teams for assessing and evaluating cases, planning and implementing treatment, and monitoring patients' health status. In the 1970s, the Institute of Medicine (1972) and the World Health Organization (1978) began emphasizing the importance of teamwork and collaborative care, and more recently the Institute of Medicine (2000, 2001) and the World Health Organization (2008a, 2008c, 2010) have recommended collaborative care to improve the quality and effectiveness of health care.

The 2010 Affordable Care Act, which represents the most significant change in health care delivery in the U.S. in decades, strongly encourages the development of new interprofessional team-based delivery systems such as accountable care organizations and patient-centered medical homes (Nordal, 2012). These new health care delivery models take a biopsychosocial approach to meeting the behavioral as well as the physical health needs of patients. These models involve health professionals from multiple disciplines working in collaborative teams to address the full range of patients' health care needs in a much more integrated and holistic manner. These approaches are currently being implemented in many health care systems, and the topic is discussed more extensively in Chapter 13.

Incorporating psychotherapy and counseling in the treatment plan

Psychotherapy is often part of the treatment plan in behavioral health care, and many behavioral health care professionals have practices that are composed entirely of providing psychotherapy. But many psychologists, psychiatrists, and other therapists provide very little formal psychotherapy; for example, psychotherapy is uncommon in many neuropsychology and medical, school, forensic, and correctional psychology settings. Instead, limited symptom reduction and behavior change interventions, problem solving, and supportive counseling are commonly used in these settings. Psychotherapy is a very effective intervention (for a review, see the next chapter), but other forms of psychosocial intervention are also very effective and useful for addressing many concerns. Therefore, behavioral health care professionals need to know the basic indications for when psychotherapy and other psychosocial interventions should be considered in treatment plans.

Much of the history of the behavioral health care field centered around the traditional theoretical orientations for understanding human development and conducting psychotherapy, and these orientations were frequently viewed as the starting point for case conceptualization and treatment planning. On the other hand, the evidence-based biopsychosocial approach is based on very different conceptual foundations. From this perspective, the traditional theoretical orientations do not comprise the foundations for case conceptualization. Instead, assessment and treatment planning are based on the full body of scientific knowledge regarding human development, functioning, and behavior change. But the traditional theoretical orientations remain critical in their capacity to inform empirically supported treatments. Many of the traditional psychotherapies are very effective for treating particular issues, and formal psychotherapy is the appropriate intervention in many cases. But other psychosocial, psychopharmacological, and/or other interventions are often indicated depending on the case, setting, and purpose of intervention.

From an evidence-based perspective, treatment planning recommendations are highly individualized. In some cases, patients might reject any form of treatment or prefer medications over psychotherapy. In other cases, treatment plans might involve short-term symptom relief or problem-solving to improve functioning or adjustment regarding circumscribed issues. Problem solving and supportive counseling are often very appropriate in these cases. In other cases, the goal of treatment is to find comprehensive, long-term solutions to maladaptive patterns of emotional, cognitive, or behavioral functioning and to improve adjustment and functioning generally in a persons' life. In these cases, individual or group psychotherapy is often the treatment of choice. Psychotherapists frequently attempt to identify the underlying causes and sources of distress and dysfunction so that problems and psychopathology are resolved on a more permanent basis. The goal in these cases is often to make fundamental changes in maladaptive personality characteristics, emotional and behavioral responses, or cognitive distortions and/or to work through trauma or a difficult family history so that patients can function more effectively in their important life roles and lead more meaningful lives. Therefore, psychotherapy is often the treatment of choice when thorough solutions to problems are desired.

Recognizing and anticipating obstacles

Carefully constructed treatment plans also anticipate challenges and obstacles that patients are likely to face during the treatment process. In the ideal case, treatment plans are developed with complete information and no major challenges or obstacles arise that interfere with treatment progress. But, of course, cases often do not proceed in the ideal manner. Some challenges that arise during treatment are the result of events outside a person's control and are impossible to anticipate (e.g., loss of employment, major medical illnesses, family crises, criminal victimization, major auto accidents). Events such as these often take priority and need to be dealt with after they arise.

Some issues that complicate the treatment process are more predictable and should be incorporated into the treatment plan. For example, one common, predictable difficulty involves the termination process for individuals with abandonment histories or dependency issues. But challenges and obstacles take many forms and can occur in any of the biopsychosocial areas of functioning. Table 10.3 notes several common contextual factors that can complicate treatment. Anticipating and effectively managing these types of factors often require substantial clinical experience, and the success of treatment may depend on working through and around these issues. In addition, it is important to recognize and incorporate facilitative factors into treatment. Utilizing

Table 10.3 Common contextual factors affecting treatment.

Limited insight into one's own problems or lack of responsibility for one's own problems and recovery	Patient's level of stressors (from family, work, neighborhood)
Changes in family, peer, and other support	Patient's coping style and related personality characteristics (e.g., resilience, impulsivity)
Changes in employment	Loss of insurance or insurance restrictions
Seriousness and nature of psychopathology	Changes in financial status or security
Co-occurring medical, psychiatric, and substance use disorders	Cultural factors
Patient's level of suicidality	Disagreement among stakeholders in a patient's treatment
Strength of the therapeutic alliance	Patient's decision-making capacity is questionable
Accidents, injuries, criminal victimization	Patient's treatment history and previous attempts to solve problems

individuals' strengths and resources and incorporating newly developed strengths into treatment can result in more meaningful and enduring improvements (e.g., a reestablished relationship with a parent, sibling, or friend that had been ruptured; a job promotion resulting from improved work performance; stronger physical health resulting from improved diet, exercise, and substance use). These are all reasons that treatment planning must remain dynamic and accommodate changes that occur during the treatment process.

Follow-up and ongoing care

Many patients are unable to maintain their treatment gains without ongoing monitoring, support, and care. This is the normal case when severe need and chronic conditions are present and particularly when illnesses are following a progressively deteriorating course (e.g., serious schizophrenia or neuropsychiatric diseases such as Alzheimer's or Parkinson's). The need for ongoing care and follow-up interventions is a critical consideration in cases involving suicide risk (e.g., Joiner, 2005; Rudd, 2006), and parts of the substance abuse treatment field have shifted from an acute to an ongoing care model as well (Hazelton, 2008).

Providing follow-up and ongoing care is a fully embedded feature of integrated primary care models of health care. In patient-centered medical homes and other integrated care models, treatment teams work collaboratively to ensure that patients' needs are addressed from a holistic perspective and patients are followed over the long term. When these models are appropriately implemented, behavioral health issues and needs are addressed alongside physical health issues in complementary ways that increase chances of improvements in both areas. This approach is often critically important in the treatment of chronic medical and behavioral health conditions, but can be extremely useful across the spectrum of severity and complexity of health issues. Given its importance, this topic is discussed more extensively in Chapter 13.

Range of alternative interventions

Significant coursework and clinical training are needed to address the evaluation and selection of therapies and other interventions that are most likely to be effective for individuals with particular behavioral health needs and biopsychosocial circumstances. Many different psychologically oriented, socially oriented, and biologically oriented behavioral health interventions have been developed since the early 20th century, and the safety and effectiveness of many of these have been thoroughly tested (see the next chapter). The range of alternative treatments available is also growing. For example, a variety of complementary and alternative medicine procedures are gaining increasing acceptance in behavioral health care and throughout medicine (Barnett & Shale, 2012; Micozzi, 2018). One national survey found that 38% of adults and 12% of children in the U.S. reported using a form of complementary and alternative medicine practices and products in the preceding year (Barnes, Bloom, & Nahin,

2008). The most frequently used were dietary supplements, meditation, chiropractic, aromatherapy, massage therapy, and yoga. Mindfulness techniques have become especially popular and have been judged to be beneficial across a broad range of outcome variables (Emotional Well-Being Roundtable, 2018, p. 14m). Virtual reality interventions are being evaluated for far more than just PTSD and hold promise as an effective treatment for a variety of behavioral health problems (Freeman et al., 2017).

The number of mental health applications that can be conveniently used on cell phones has recently grown quickly as well. The U.S. Food and Drug Administration has approved hundreds of "mHealth" apps (FDA, 2018). There are also many new social media sites that focus on a wide variety of health issues that can be of great benefit to people dealing with the full range of biopsychosocial challenges. For example, a closely watched experiment to facilitate treatment and promote health among patients with Crohn's, colitis, and other inflammatory bowel conditions is Crohnology.com. This social media site provides tools for tracking symptoms; sharing information on nutrition, diet, and remedies; and providing support and encouragement to others dealing with the same conditions. Peer-to-peer "e-client" social networking sites like this could potentially change the delivery and even the economics of health care.

To illustrate the wide variety of options that might be incorporated into treatment planning, Table 10.4 provides examples of interventions that could be used to address issues within particular areas of biopsychosocial functioning. This listing is provided only to illustrate the wide range of interventions that are available for addressing problems and disorders at varying levels of intensity. It is not exhaustive nor does it address the empirical evidence regarding the effectiveness of the interventions. Other resources will need to be consulted for that information. This is also an area in which keeping current with the research literature is important.

The importance of treatment planning

Mastering treatment planning for the wide variety of clinical issues encountered and the wide range of life circumstances faced by patients requires extensive study and clinical experience. The biopsychosocial approach can be much more complex than many traditional approaches to case conceptualization that involved implementing the psychotherapy dictated by one's adopted theoretical orientation. Many clinical cases are straightforward and relatively simple, but others involve a daunting amount of complex and challenging circumstances.

The guidelines and principles discussed in this chapter are necessary for understanding the complexity of the behavioral health treatment planning process. A basic principle of this process involves addressing the severity and complexity of need with the appropriate type, intensity, and level of intervention. Some questions and concerns require watchful waiting or no treatment at all, while emergency needs require immediate attention. Level of care and stepped care models can be used to address many issues that fall between these extremes. Carefully crafted treatment plans also anticipate barriers and obstacles to treatment and the need for follow-up and

Table 10.4 Examples of possible interventions across the biopsychosocial domains and levels of severity or need.

Domains and components	Strengths (mild, moderate, or severe, +1 to +3)	No problem (0)	Mild problem severity (−1)	Moderate problem severity (−2)	Severe problem (−3)
Biological					
General medical history	• Reinforce healthy eating, exercise, and lifestyle	• Reinforce healthy eating, exercise, and lifestyle	• Persuade client to engage in healthier lifestyle • Online resources and apps	• Refer for a physical exam • Help monitor compliance with prescribed treatments • Online resources and apps	• Refer for immediate physical evaluation or emergency care • Help monitor compliance with prescribed treatments • Online resources and apps
Childhood health history	• Reinforce healthy coping, adjustment, and treatment adherence if problems were overcome	• Same	• Same	• Same	• Same
Medications	• Reinforce healthy habits and healthy use of medicines and substances	• Reinforce healthy habits and healthy use of medicines and substances	• Refer for medical evaluation • Help monitor effectiveness and side effects of medications	• Refer for psychiatric or medical evaluation • Help monitor effectiveness and side effects of medications • Coordinate family members to supervise patient medicine use	• Refer for immediate psychiatric or medical evaluation or hospitalization • Coordinate family members to supervise client medicine use

Psychological					
History of present illness/problem	• Reinforce positive mental health and role functioning • Amplify resources and strengths where helpful	• Reinforce positive mental health and role functioning • Recommend helpful psychoeducational interventions and online resources	• Individual therapy • Group therapy • Support group • Bibliotherapy • Further develop strengths and resources • Mindfulness, yoga • Online resources and apps	• Individual therapy • Group therapy • Develop compensating strengths and resources • Mindfulness, yoga • Online resources and apps	• Evaluate need for hospitalization • Refer for evaluation for psychotropic medicine • Develop compensating strengths and resources • Mindfulness, yoga
Individual psychological history	• Reinforce positive mental health and role functioning • Amplify resources and strengths where helpful	• Reinforce positive mental health and role functioning • Recommend helpful psychoeducational interventions • Further develop strengths and resources	• Conduct neuropsychological screening • Individual therapy • Group therapy • Support group • Bibliotherapy • Further develop strengths and resources • Mindfulness, yoga • Online resources and apps	• Refer for neuropsychological evaluation • Consider intensive long-term therapy (e.g., psychodynamic, ACT, DBT • Develop compensating strengths and resources • Mindfulness, yoga • Online resources and apps	• Refer for neuropsychological evaluation • Consider residential or intensive outpatient treatment • Refer client for vocational rehabilitation, social services, etc., as needed • Refer family members for support group

Continued

Table 10.4 Examples of possible interventions across the biopsychosocial domains and levels of severity or need.—continued

Domains and components	Strengths (mild, moderate, or severe, +1 to +3)	No problem (0)	Mild problem severity (−1)	Moderate problem severity (−2)	Severe problem (−3)
Substance abuse history	• Reinforce positive mental health and role functioning • Amplify resources and strengths where helpful	• Reinforce positive mental health and role functioning • Recommend helpful psychoeducational interventions	• Discuss substance use and its consequences • Work on reducing substance misuse • Online resources and apps	• Refer for brief substance abuse treatment • Support group • Online resources and apps	• Consider detox hospitalization • Refer for intensive substance abuse treatment
Suicidal ideation	• Reinforce positive mental health and role functioning	• Reinforce positive mental health and role functioning	• Outpatient therapy • Ongoing monitoring of suicidality	• More intensive outpatient therapy • Ongoing monitoring of suicidality	• Evaluate need for hospitalization • Refer to specialist • Ongoing monitoring of suicidality
Individual developmental history	• Reinforce positive mental health and role functioning • Amplify resources and strengths where helpful	• Reinforce positive mental health and role functioning • Recommend helpful psychoeducational interventions	• Reinforce positive mental health and role functioning • Reinforce and further develop strengths and resources • Online resources and apps	• Reinforce positive mental health and role functioning • Reinforce and further develop strengths and resources • Refer to mutual support group • Online resources and apps	• Reinforce positive mental health and role functioning • Reinforce and further develop strengths and resources • Refer to mutual support group

Childhood abuse history	• Reinforce positive mental health and role functioning • Amplify resources and strengths where helpful	• Reinforce positive mental health and role functioning • Recommend helpful psychoeducational interventions	• Individual therapy • Bibliotherapy • Mindfulness, yoga • Online resources and apps	• Individual therapy • Group therapy • Family therapy if appropriate • Mindfulness, yoga • Online resources and apps	• Consider intensive long-term therapy (e.g., psychodynamic, ACT, DBT) • Meditation, yoga
Other psychological traumas	• Reinforce positive mental health and role functioning • Amplify resources and strengths where helpful	• Reinforce positive mental health and role functioning • Recommend helpful psychoeducational interventions	• Individual therapy • Bibliotherapy • Further develop strengths and resources • Mindfulness, yoga • Online resources and apps	• Consider exposure and related therapies • Mindfulness, yoga • Online resources and apps	• Consider exposure and intensive long-term therapies (e.g., psychodynamic, ACT, DBT) • Mindfulness, yoga
Personality style(s) and characteristics	• Reinforce positive mental health and role functioning • Amplify resources and strengths where helpful	• Reinforce positive mental health and role functioning • Recommend helpful psychoeducational interventions	• Social skills training groups • Bibliotherapy • Recommend helpful psychoeducational interventions and online resources	• Individual therapy • Group therapy • Online resources and apps	• Consider intensive long-term therapy (e.g., psychodynamic, ACT, DBT)
Mental status examination	• Reinforce positive mental health and role functioning • Amplify resources and strengths where helpful	• Reinforce positive mental health and role functioning • Recommend psychoeducational interventions if it would be helpful	• Conduct neuropsychological screening	• Conduct psychological testing • Refer for neuropsychological exam	• Refer for psychiatric or neuropsychological exam

Continued

Table 10.4 Examples of possible interventions across the biopsychosocial domains and levels of severity or need.—continued

Domains and components	Strengths (mild, moderate, or severe, +1 to +3)	No problem (0)	Mild problem severity (−1)	Moderate problem severity (−2)	Severe problem (−3)
Sociocultural					
Relationships and social support	• Reinforce healthy relationships	• Further develop strengths and resources	• Couple session to assess nature and severity of relationship issues	• Individual therapy • Couple therapy • Communication skills training • Develop safety plan if relevant • Support group	• Individual therapy • Couple therapy • Develop safety plan if relevant • Support group
Family history	• Maintain positive family relationships	• Further develop strengths and resources	• Family session to assess nature of family issues • Bibliotherapy	• Family therapy • Support group	• Family therapy
Current living situation	• Reinforce positive living situation	• Further develop strengths and resources	• Invite in roommates to conduct assessment session	• Facilitate temporary move to family member or friend	• Refer for evaluation of need for shelter and social services
Employment	• Maintain positive work history and vocational development	• Maintain positive work history and vocational development	• Assist client with planning job search • Refer for career counseling • Reinforce strengths and resources	• Refer for career counseling • Develop strengths and resources	• Psychological testing to determine reasons for employment problems • Refer for vocational rehabilitation

Educational history	• Anticipate future educational and training needs	• Anticipate future educational and training needs	• Refer for GED program, vocational training, job retraining, career counseling • Recommend online resources	• Complete psychological testing to determine nature and extent of cognitive deficits • Recommend online resources	• Refer for neuropsychology evaluation of cognitive deficits
Financial resources	• Reinforce responsible financial planning	• Reinforce responsible financial planning	• Review client's budget • Bibliotherapy • Online resources	• Refer for financial counseling • Family sessions to assess nature of problems • Online resources	• Coordinate application for welfare, SSDI • Refer for financial counseling • Pursue guardianship for finances
Legal issues	• Reinforce responsible approach to legal and safety issues	• Reinforce responsible approach to legal and safety issues	• Individual therapy • Obtain copies of legal proceedings or reports	• Monitor attendance and performance at school or work • Monitor client's appointments with court officials	• Enlist legal aid • Invite probation officials to periodic meetings • Refer client to ex-offender programs
Military history	• NA	• NA	• Individual therapy	• Refer to VA	• Refer to VA • Refer to veterans support group
Activities of interest/hobbies	• Maintain activities and interests • Maintain healthy balance of work and leisure	• Encourage engagement in past interests • Explore new interests and hobbies	• Facilitate involvement in community activities • Explore new interests and hobbies • Online resources and apps	• Individual therapy regarding enjoyment and meaning in life • Online resources and apps	• Refer for occupational therapy • Meet with family or friends to coordinate activities • Online resources and apps

Continued

Table 10.4 Examples of possible interventions across the biopsychosocial domains and levels of severity or need.—continued

Domains and components	Strengths (mild, moderate, or severe, +1 to +3)	No problem (0)	Mild problem severity (−1)	Moderate problem severity (−2)	Severe problem (−3)
Religion	• Maintain meaningful religious involvements	• If interested, encourage engagement in past interests • If interested, explore new religious involvement	• Bibliotherapy • If interested, explore new religious involvement	• Consult with religious leader	• Refer to specialist
Spirituality	• Maintain meaningful spiritual involvements	• If interested, encourage engagement in past interests	• Bibliotherapy • If interested, explore new spiritual involvement • Mindfulness, yoga	• Refer to spiritual leader or community • Online resources and apps	• Refer to specialist
Multicultural issues	• Maintain meaningful cultural involvements	• If interested, encourage engagement in past interests • If interested, explore new cultural involvements	• Bibliotherapy • Refer to community organizations	• Refer to community organizations • Refer to specialist	• Refer to specialist

ACT, acceptance and commitment therapy; *DBT*, dialectical behavior therapy; *GED*, general education diploma; *NA*. not applicable; *SSDI*, Social Security Disability Insurance; *VA*, Veterans Administration.

ongoing care. This comprehensive approach to treatment planning allows behavioral health care professionals, frequently working collaboratively with other professionals, to address the full range of issues that individuals bring with them into the health care setting.

Case example: Treatment planning with a mildly depressed patient

The case example involving Jessica, the 41-year-old married African American female who was discussed in the last chapter, is discussed here again in terms of treatment planning from a biopsychosocial approach. In her first session with the psychologist, Jessica reported that she had disengaged from multiple activities that used to be important to her. She reported that she used to exercise regularly and had been in good physical condition before her children were born, and that drinking wine in the evenings contributed to her moderate weight gain. She also reported that she and her husband had gradually stopped going out on dates together after their two children were born. The psychologist asked Jessica to bring her husband to the second session so he could get a clearer picture of their relationship and family situation. After their meeting together, the psychologist talked with Jessica about her goals for therapy. She agreed to begin exercising again, decrease her alcohol consumption, and begin having weekly dates with her husband. The psychologist also noted that Jessica's work situation appeared to be going very well and that this was an area of major strength in her life, and they both agreed that no changes were needed or desired in that area at this time.

After noting how much Jessica cared about her two children and that she was very interested in their education, the psychologist suggested that getting more involved with her children's schooling would help her feel good about her parental guidance around their education and that it would also be helpful to know more of the other parents in the school. Jessica agreed to attend a parent–teacher organization meeting and consider the possibility of getting involved in her daughters' school. Jessica had reported that she had disengaged from her own family of origin because she disliked her mother's criticism. Although she was uncomfortable with this situation, more contact with her mother was not worth the criticism that came with it. Nonetheless, she agreed to explore possibilities for improving her relationship with her mother.

After discussing the above topics, Jessica and the psychologist decided on six goals for her therapy. The initial treatment plan focused on making changes in physical health and her involvement with her husband and children, the most important people in her life at present. Getting more involved with her children's school would increase her knowledge about her daughters' education, increase her social engagement, and potentially make her and her husband more comfortable about their children's friends. It was less clear how to address the issues related to her family of origin at this initial stage of treatment, although they

Continued

Case example: Treatment planning with a mildly depressed patient—cont'd

agreed that it would be helpful to address the other issues first before exploring how she might improve her relationship with her own mother:

1. Monitor level of depression.
2. Stop drinking during weekdays for the next 2 months.
3. Schedule dates out with her husband at least once per week.
4. Begin a regular exercise routine.
5. Go to parent–teacher organization meetings at the children's school.
6. Explore the possibility of improving the relationship with her mother.

Treatment

11

In the past, the behavioral health care field relied heavily on an eclectic set of diverse theoretical orientations for conceptualizing the treatment process. Although allegiance to these orientations has declined in recent years, they still often play a significant role in case conceptualization and treatment. But the field has been transitioning to a science-based biopsychosocial approach that takes a very different perspective on behavioral health care. This new approach is oriented around being a clinical science that is founded on a unified scientific understanding of human psychology. The primary purpose of health service psychology as a clinical science is to apply the scientific and ethical foundations of the field to meet the behavioral health and biopsychosocial needs of the public.

The previous two chapters outlined how patients' behavioral health needs and functioning can be assessed and treatment plans developed to address their needs in the context of their biopsychosocial circumstances. This chapter discusses the conceptualization of behavioral health treatment from the clinical science, biopsychosocial perspective on health service psychology. Behavioral health treatment is a vastly complex topic that has been examined in thousands of studies. Many of these investigated the methods and processes associated with the different theoretical orientations, topics that are not the focus here. Readers will need to consult other resources for presentations of those topics. Instead, this chapter begins by discussing the overarching framework for approaching behavioral health treatment from the biopsychosocial approach. It then focuses on several issues related to the safety and effectiveness of psychotherapy. The topics addressed include the following:

- Conceptualizing biopsychosocial behavioral health care treatment:
  - broad perspective on treatment
  - priority on the safety and effectiveness of treatment
  - systematic monitoring of the progress and effectiveness of treatment
  - communication and collaboration with other professionals and third parties
- The safety and effectiveness of psychotherapy:
  - effectiveness of psychotherapy in general
  - returning to level of normal functioning
  - duration of therapy gains
  - comparison of psychotherapy with psychotropic medication
  - deterioration in psychotherapy
  - factors accounting for therapy effectiveness
  - importance of therapist skills
  - reducing treatment failures

Foundations of Health Service Psychology. https://doi.org/10.1016/B978-0-12-816426-6.00011-6

Conceptualizing behavioral health care treatment

This volume argues that education and training in behavioral health care should be approached from the perspective of a clinical science. From this perspective, behavioral health care education revolves around the current body of scientific knowledge regarding human psychology and the ethical foundations of the field. Building on this foundational knowledge, evidence-based practice and the treatment process for addressing behavioral health needs is then learned. Competence in carrying out the whole treatment process is acquired, from assessment to outcomes evaluation and follow-up, and competence in a range of interventions is also acquired so that therapists are able to address the variety of behavioral health concerns that they will encounter in clinical practice.

This approach to behavioral health care emphasizes the understanding of individuals as whole persons in the context of their biopsychosocial life circumstances. Chapters 5 through 8 noted the range of biopsychosocial issues that are common in the general population. For example, the most common psychiatric disorders included in the *Diagnostic and Statistical Manual of Mental Disorders*, 5th edition (DSM-5), are sexuality concerns, addictions, panic attacks, and sleep problems (see Table 5.1). A substantial proportion of the population (approximately 15%–20%) meets the criteria for a personality disorder as well. In the domain of physical health, large proportions of Americans are dealing with overweight and obesity, lower back pain and chronic joint symptoms, high blood pressure, arthritis, other pain conditions, and restlessness and nervousness (see Table 7.1). These medical conditions frequently cause substantial distress and impairment, and psychological factors are involved in the etiology, consequences, and/or treatment of all of them. In the sociocultural domain, large proportions of the population deal with relationship problems and family dysfunction or intimate partner and sexual violence, and many children experience maltreatment. Many people also experience loneliness, financial stress, vocational instability, and criminal victimization. In addition, all aspects of biopsychosocial functioning occur within the context of cultural, ethnic, and socioeconomic diversity that greatly influences development and functioning as well. The co-occurrence of problems within and across these domains is common as well.

Understanding individuals in the context of the totality of their lives requires a recognition that psychological outcomes are multifactorially determined based on the interaction of many biological, psychological, and sociocultural processes. This recognition is necessary for understanding personality functioning, psychopathology, intellectual and social functioning, physical health, the nature and causes of acute and chronic problems, risk factors, strengths and resources, and virtually all the issues one encounters in behavioral health care practice. From career decision-making to the treatment of serious mental illness, this type of comprehensive, integrative perspective is necessary for understanding problems in context and providing interventions that maximize the likelihood of treatment effectiveness over the short term and the long term.

The biopsychosocial approach also incorporates a health and wellness perspective aimed at optimizing functioning across the biopsychosocial domains. Even when patients have no significant problems in particular areas of their lives, converting these to areas of strength can help develop greater resilience and promote optimal functioning. Stronger physical health, psychological resilience, and social resources and support are very beneficial for individuals at all levels of functioning. They can also be especially valuable for vulnerable individuals such as children or seniors dealing with serious biopsychosocial problems or individuals with serious, persistent mental illness. Minimizing vulnerabilities and risk factors while strengthening internal and external resources is often critical for maximizing treatment effectiveness and optimal functioning for these populations. A broad perspective on behavioral health care is needed for conceptualizing cases from this type of comprehensive, holistic approach.

Broad perspective on treatment

Knowledge of human psychology has advanced dramatically in recent decades, and findings continue to accumulate that demonstrate the complex multifactorial biopsychosocial nature of human development and functioning. Understanding the biopsychosocial nature of human psychology is necessary for understanding behavioral health treatment as well. One's approach to treatment will vary greatly depending on one's specialization and the setting where one practices. General practitioners need to be able to address a broad range of common behavioral health issues, while specialists possess extensive knowledge regarding a narrower range of issues. Whether one is a general practitioner treating depression, anxiety, relationship, and other common issues, or a specialist in treating severe complex posttraumatic stress disorder (PTSD), clinicians are expected to conceptualize cases from an integrated biopsychosocial perspective.

Several trends currently underway reflect this broad biopsychosocial perspective on behavioral health care. The passage of the Affordable Care Act in 2010 was controversial, and its future remains uncertain at this writing, but the law has been the largest driver of change in the health care delivery system since the 1960s in the U.S. Particularly important to the health care experience, for both patients and providers, is its strong encouragement of new delivery systems such as accountable care organizations and patient-centered medical homes (Nordal, 2012). These systems aim to integrate behavioral and physical health care in a single setting through interprofessional team-based care. The goal of these approaches is to address patients' needs in a holistic manner and thereby improve the quality of care and reduce costs (see Chapter 13). Therapists working in these settings need to be able to efficiently assess and treat a wide range of behavioral health issues in a collaborative manner with other health care professionals. This requires familiarity with a range of treatment options and solid grounding in the biopsychosocial approach (e.g., APA Presidential Task Force on the Future of Psychology Practice, 2009). It can be very difficult to apply an approach that revolves around one of the traditional theoretical orientations in primary health care settings.

Another trend that is well underway is the emphasis on health and wellness. The positive psychology movement is well established within psychology, and wellness is becoming more firmly established within the medical community as well (e.g., IsHak, in press). The medical community has recognized the importance of behavior and lifestyle in the development and treatment of disease (Institute of Medicine, 2004) and is increasingly focusing on these factors to promote health and prevent illness and disease. These movements will continue to focus attention on promoting health and wellness across the biopsychosocial domains and bring these issues into the mainstream of health care.

Another trend that has been underway for decades involves the increasing number of treatments that psychologists themselves provide. Psychologists' endorsement of eclectic and integrative approaches to practice has grown in recent decades (Prochaska & Norcross, 2018), and some have even begun offering pharmacological treatment in addition to psychotherapeutic intervention (in Illinois, Idaho, Iowa, Louisiana, New Mexico, and Guam, and within the U.S. Department of Defense as of this writing). Psychologists have also been practicing in an increasing diversity of settings. Many psychologists work in a variety of medical, educational, industrial and organizational, military, rehabilitation, sport, and correctional settings (APA Center for Workforce Studies, 2011). Providing traditional psychotherapy may not be a high priority in many of these settings, whereas assisting individuals to function effectively and meet the goals and needs of the institution or organization they are a part of is a top priority. Being able to offer a range of interventions beyond traditional psychotherapy is typically necessary in these settings. The increased use of stepped models of treatment is another reflection of this trend. These models are very practical and efficient for increasing the number of issues one can address in primary care, general practice, and specialty health care settings. As noted in the previous chapter, stepped models of care often include brief screens and a range of minimal to intensive intervention options that match the severity of patients' needs (e.g., Screen, Brief Intervention, Brief Treatment, and Referral to Treatment [SBIRT] and Permission, Limited Information, Specific Suggestions, and Intensive Treatment [PLISSIT]). Increasing numbers of therapists are using these stepped approaches, delivering the less intensive interventions themselves and then referring individuals with more serious needs to specialists, because it allows them to address a larger number of issues with their patients, thereby providing more holistic care as well (Nordal, 2012).

Priority on the safety and effectiveness of treatment

The clinical science approach advocated in this volume is grounded in science and ethics. As discussed in Chapter 4, health care ethics are very clear with regard to the obligations to provide safe and effective treatment. The implications of the ethical obligation of nonmaleficence ("do no harm") are obvious when a health care professional intentionally harms others. But the obligation to do no harm unintentionally is perhaps even more important because these harms can happen outside of one's awareness, particularly when professionals are not diligent with regard to developing and maintaining their clinical competencies. Harm can be caused by omission as well as commission, by imposing risks through either ignorance or carelessness such as when a therapist has insufficient training and supervised experience to accurately diagnose common mental disorders or complete adequate suicide risk assessments and treatment plans, or fails to appropriately manage countertransference. If patients are harmed as a result, therapists can be judged negligent and potentially guilty of malpractice. In addition, the ethical principle of beneficence obligates health care professionals to provide benefits and promote patients' welfare. It obligates us to meet patients' behavioral health needs, prevent harms from occurring when possible, remove them once they occur, and balance benefits and harms in an optimal manner.

The principles of evidence-based practice are entirely consistent with the emphasis on the safety and effectiveness of treatment. In their landmark 2000 report, *To Err Is Human*, the Institute of Medicine famously estimated that 44,000–98,000 Americans, "a jumbo jet a day," die each year due to preventable medical errors. The next year in their 2001 report, *Crossing the Quality Chasm: A New Health System for the 21st Century*, the Institute of Medicine identified safety and effectiveness as core needs in health care. They further concluded that clinical decision-making should be based on evidence as well as being customized according to patient needs, values, and preferences. The American Psychological Association Presidential Task Force on Evidence-Based Practice (2006) soon after adopted a policy of evidence-based practice in psychology that endorsed the same principles.

Therapists have always been concerned about the safety and effectiveness of their interventions, but the safety of psychotherapy received relatively little empirical research attention until recently. Bergin (1966) was among the first to investigate patient deterioration that appeared to be caused by psychotherapy, but little further attention was given to the issue until the 1990s when recovered memories of child abuse became very controversial. Other therapies for which there is evidence of potential or actual harm include rebirthing attachment therapy, group interventions for antisocial youth, conversion therapy for gay and lesbian patients, critical incident stress debriefing, and grief therapy (see Chapter 4).

Research has also found that individual therapists vary significantly in their effectiveness (e.g., Lambert, 2010; Wampold & Imel, 2015). In addition, therapists frequently miss that their patients have deteriorated or failed to improve. Cases in which patients did not improve or have deteriorated are often detected through the routine use of outcome measures, and special attention can then be given in an attempt to achieve a positive outcome (Fortney et al., 2017; Lambert, 2010). These findings obligate therapists and their supervisors to ensure that patient nonimprovement and deterioration are identified and efforts are made to achieve the highest quality and most effective care possible.

Systematic monitoring of the progress and effectiveness of treatment

Emphasizing the safety and effectiveness of treatment focuses attention on the systematic monitoring of treatment outcomes. The importance of outcomes measurement is highlighted by both the ethical emphasis on providing care that is safe and effective and the scientific emphasis on measuring outcomes in a reliable and valid manner to determine the outcomes of one's interventions. The research that finds that patient deterioration and lack of improvement are sometimes missed without the routine use of outcome measures reinforces the need to integrate progress monitoring into one's clinical practice. The recognition that current levels of health care spending in the U.S. are not sustainable also focuses more attention on the importance of progress monitoring to ensure the effectiveness and efficiency of health care services.

As a result of both ethical and scientific priorities, the clinical science perspective on behavioral health care emphasizes progress monitoring and outcomes assessment. Monitoring the progress of treatment is important for detecting cases of no improvement or deterioration so appropriate adjustments can be made. Outcomes assessment at termination and afterward at follow-up is necessary to properly evaluate the effectiveness of treatment. Given how important these issues are in the treatment process, they receive more attention later in this chapter as well as in the following chapter.

Communication and collaboration with other professionals and third parties

Multiple health care professionals are frequently involved in the assessment and treatment of patients in modern health care systems. Problems with communication and collaboration between these professionals can easily result in errors and omissions. Awareness of these problems has grown substantially since 2000. As noted earlier, the 2000 report by the Institute of Medicine, *To Err Is Human*, alarmed policy makers and the public about widespread problems with the safety of American health care ("a jumbo jet a day" of Americans die due to preventable medical errors). Problems with communication and collaboration were cited as basic causes of these problems. In their call for a fundamental redesign of the American health care system to improve quality, the 2001 Institute of Medicine report *Crossing the Quality Chasm* found that active collaboration and communication among clinicians and institutions was imperative for improving the safety and effectiveness of American health care. Their 2003 report, *Health Professions Education: A Bridge to Quality*, further concluded that interdisciplinary teamwork was one of five core competencies for all health professionals. The Interprofessional Education Collaborative (2011) also included interprofessional communication and teamwork in its *Core Competencies for Interprofessional Collaborative Practice*.

In addition to working with other health care professionals, therapists frequently communicate and collaborate with family members, educators, employers, criminal justice and social service professionals, and others who can assist with assessment or treatment. Chapter 9 emphasized the importance of collateral contacts for obtaining reliable and valid assessment information in many cases, and collaborating with these individuals on treatment can be critical for treatment effectiveness as well. Collaborative treatment approaches are seen as necessary for effectively intervening with the large number of behavioral health needs found among infants, children, and adolescents (Egger & Emde, 2011; Kazak et al., 2010). Collaborative approaches are typically also necessary when problem severity and complexity are high (e.g., serious substance abuse, psychiatric disorders, medical conditions, relationship and family dysfunction) and when patients are more vulnerable and dependent (e.g., children, adults with disabilities, frail seniors).

The need for behavioral health professionals to collaborate with other professionals is also growing as they increasingly work in more diverse clinical settings. Interprofessional collaborative primary care teamwork is necessary for integrating behavioral health, disease management, and preventive interventions into primary care (see Chapter 13). Behavioral health professionals working in hospital, educational, military, industrial and organizational, rehabilitation, sport, and correctional settings also need to communicate and collaborate effectively with other professionals to meet institutional and agency goals as well as patients' individual needs and goals.

The safety and effectiveness of individual psychotherapy

The safety and effectiveness of treatment are of central concern in behavioral health care and so these issues will now receive closer examination. In addition to addressing whether treatment is effective, a more thorough and detailed examination of treatment effectiveness will be conducted. A science-based and health care-oriented approach to behavioral health care tends to increase the specificity of the questions asked because practitioners need to know much more than just whether a treatment has been found to be effective.

The following discussion of treatment effectiveness will focus on individual adult psychotherapy. Several of the findings discussed also apply with regard to family, child, adolescent, and group therapy, but readers will need to consult other resources for discussions of those treatment formats. As illustrated in the previous chapter, a variety of additional interventions are useful in behavioral health care, such as computer-assisted and online interventions, bibliotherapy, self-help groups, supportive counseling, combined medication and psychotherapy, mindfulness, biofeedback, and diet and physical exercise. Readers will also need to consult other resources for evaluations of those interventions. The questions addressed in this section include the following:

- Is psychotherapy effective?
- Is the effectiveness of psychotherapy clinically significant? How often do patients return to normal functioning following treatment?
- Do the benefits of psychotherapy last?
- How does the effectiveness of psychotherapy compare with the effectiveness of psychotropic medications?
- Does psychotherapy work better for some individuals than for others? Do some patients get worse following therapy?
- What factors account for the effectiveness of psychotherapy?
- How important are the skills of the individual therapist to psychotherapy effectiveness?
- If not all psychotherapy patients improve, can the number of treatment failures be reduced?

Is psychotherapy effective?

In 1952, Hans Eysenck presented a fundamental challenge to the psychotherapy field when he concluded that the available research failed to support the effectiveness of psychotherapy. He specifically argued that psychotherapy did not result in more improvement beyond what occurred with natural spontaneous remission. It took a quarter-century of therapy outcome research before the evidence convincingly reversed his conclusion. By the 1980s, the accumulated data showed that psychotherapy is generally effective for a broad range of mental health disorders and across a wide range of therapy approaches. Smith and Glass (1977) conducted the first meta-analysis of the therapy outcomes research and found an overall effect size of 0.85 (Smith, Glass, & Miller, 1980). Many meta-analyses followed, in fact enough to conduct meta-analyses of metaanalyses. Lipsey and Wilson (1993) reviewed all the metaanalyses they could locate and determined that the mean effect size was 0.81. Lambert and Bergin (1994) conducted a similar analysis and found an average effect size of 0.82, while Grissom (1996) found an aggregate effect size of 0.75. Wampold (2001) evaluated the results from these and other meta-analyses and concluded that "A reasonable and defensible point estimate for the efficacy of psychotherapy would be .80 ... This effect would be classified as a large effect in the social sciences, which means that the average patient receiving therapy would be better off than 79% of untreated patients, that psychotherapy accounts for about 14% of the variance in outcomes, and the success rate would change from 31% for the control group to 69% for the treatment group. Simply stated, *psychotherapy is remarkably efficacious*" (italics in the original; pp. 70–71). Wampold and Imel's 2015 updated review of the evidence regarding this question resulted in the same point estimate of 0.80 (see also Munder et al., 2019).

The effectiveness of psychotherapy is substantial compared with many medical, psychopharmacological, educational, correctional, and other human service interventions (Barlow, 2004; Leucht, Helfer, Gartlehner, & Davis, 2015; Meyer et al., 2001; Reed & Eisman, 2006). In fact, the effect size for psychotherapy of $d = 0.80$ (which translates to $r = 0.37$) exceeds that of many common medical treatments. For example, Meyer et al. (2001) found that the correlation between coronary artery bypass surgery for stable heart disease and survival at 5 years is 0.08, between antibiotic treatment for acute middle ear pain in children and improvement at 2–7 days is 0.07, and between taking aspirin and reduced risk of death by heart attack is 0.02. These would be categorized as small or exceedingly small effect sizes ($r = +0.10$ is considered a small effect following Cohen's (1988) guidelines).

A popular and easily interpreted metric for measuring the effectiveness of treatment is the number needed to treat (NNT). It refers to the number of patients who need to be treated (e.g., with a medicine) for one patient to benefit compared with the patients in a control group not receiving the treatment (e.g., receiving a placebo instead of a medicine; Laupacis, Sackett, & Roberts, 1988). A perfect medicine would have an NNT of 1.0, meaning that only one patient needs to receive the drug for one patient to benefit. But there may be no perfect treatments and placebo controls often have some positive effects as well. Therefore, very effective treatments are usually in the range of 2–4 and clinicians are often pleased with NNT values of less than 10 for brief treatments of active disease (Kramer, 2008; Moore, 2009). Antibiotics can be an exception because they are highly effective in many cases. One of the most effective treatments in all of medicine is antibiotics to treat *Helicobacter pylori* bacteria that cause peptic stomach ulcers; they have an NNT of 1.1, which means that if 11 people receive the medicine, the bacteria will be eradicated in 10 of them.

Many medical treatments unfortunately have very large NNT values. For example, the very small correlation between taking aspirin to prevent death by heart attack ($r = 0.02$) translates into an NNT of 127 (Wampold, 2007). The statin medicine atorvastatin (Lipitor) for lowering cholesterol, the best selling drug in pharmaceutical history, was found to have an NNT of 99.7 after 3.3 years—100 patients would need to take the medicine for 3.3 years to prevent one heart attack (Bandolier, 2008; Carey, 2008). This does not mean that treatments with very high NNT values are not indicated in many cases. As long as the risks of taking a medicine are minimal (e.g., the incidence of internal bleeding is low for those taking aspirin) and the costs are reasonable (e.g., aspirin is cheap), the benefit of preventing even a very small number of devastating events (e.g., death by heart attack) may result in a positive balancing of risks, costs, and benefits. The sometimes limited benefit of many heavily marketed medications in comparison to their risks and costs, however, is a very controversial topic (e.g., Goldacre, 2012; Healy, 2012; Whitaker & Cosgrove, 2015).

In contrast to the very large NNT values of many medicines, the NNT for psychotherapy based on an effect size of $d = 0.80$ is 2.7, a very low value indicating very effective treatment. This means that 2.7 psychotherapy patients would need to be treated before one of them can be expected to benefit from the treatment (i.e., compared with those in the control group). Although not all psychotherapy patients improve, this is in the range of treatments considered very effective. Therapists, patients, insurance companies, and the general public can all be assured that psychotherapy has been found to be a very effective treatment that compares favorably with many other health care interventions.

Although the present discussion focuses on individual psychotherapy the effectiveness of group versus individual psychotherapy will be briefly noted, because a recent meta-analysis was conducted that helps clarify the effectiveness of each of them. Historically, there have been mixed findings regarding the superiority of individual versus group psychotherapy as a treatment format. But a 2016 meta-analysis compared the effectiveness of the two formats using within-study comparisons, an important improvement over previous between-study comparisons (Burlingame et al., 2016). This meta-analysis found no differences in outcome between individual and group treatment formats. The aggregated effect size for the two treatment formats was large (Hedges $g = 0.72$), and there were no differences between the formats in rates of treatment acceptance, dropout, remission, or improvement. Most of the studies in this meta-analysis focused on treating depression and anxiety, although several studies examined medical, eating, childhood, and substance use issues. Because the number of studies examining these additional issues was smaller, further research is warranted. Nonetheless, this meta-analysis helps support treatment recommendations for group over individual treatment for patients who prefer that format. In addition, given the increased cost effectiveness of group treatment, these findings offer important evidence for the efficiency and effectiveness of group therapy as a treatment option.

Is the effectiveness of psychotherapy clinically significant? How often do patients return to normal functioning?

Psychotherapy is a very effective treatment that works well compared with many other treatments used in medicine. But the amount of improvement patients make is very important too. Ideally, one wants to return to normal functioning, not just a small though statistically significant level of improvement.

Fortunately, psychotherapy has been found to result in clinically meaningful improvement for most patients. In fact, most patients return to normal functioning following treatment (APA, 2012). Research that examines this question typically uses standardized measures of therapy outcome, and posttreatment scores falling to within 1 standard deviation of the normative mean are generally accepted as a return to normal functioning. Three meta-analyses have found that patients' average post-treatment scores on outcome measures moved into the range reflecting normal functioning (Abramowitz, 1996; Nietzel, Russell, Hemmings, & Gretter, 1987; Trull, Nietzel, & Main, 1988). After reviewing these and other studies, Lambert and Archer (2006) concluded that approximately three-quarters of patients who undergo treatment show positive benefits, and 40%–60% return to a state of normal functioning.

Do the benefits of psychotherapy last?

The effectiveness of a treatment over the long term is critical to judging how successful it is. Treatments that alleviate symptoms in the short term but do not address the underlying causes and improve functioning over the long term are generally much less valuable. Many individuals with chronic medical or psychiatric conditions need treatment on a long-term or permanent basis (e.g., type 2 diabetes, chronic schizophrenia). But this is not the desirable outcome, especially when treatments are costly, are inconvenient, and/or have negative side effects. The long-term effectiveness of treatment is consequently a major priority.

In the case of therapy, research finds that treatment gains are frequently maintained over the long term. This question is difficult to research because many patients drop out of follow-up studies or obtain other forms of therapeutic intervention during the follow-up period. Nonetheless, numerous studies have tracked patients up to 5 or more years following the end of treatment and consistently found that therapy improvements tend to endure (Lambert, 2013). There tends to be some decay in improvements over time for most psychotherapies, although the decay is far less than for psychotropic medications (see the next section). There is also some evidence that therapy benefits sometimes increase over time. In five independent meta-analyses, effect sizes for psychodynamic therapy at long-term follow-up (ranging from 0.75 to 3.2 years) were actually higher than they were at posttreatment—the effect sizes at follow-up ranged from 0.94 to 1.57, which are very large effect sizes (Shedler, 2010).

Long-term positive treatment effects have even been found with disorders considered among the most difficult to treat. For example, Bateman and Fonagy (2008) were able to follow 100% of the patients who completed treatment for borderline personality disorder 5 years after they finished a randomized, controlled trial comparing the effectiveness of psychodynamic therapy and treatment-as-usual. The psychodynamic group was found to have much lower rates of suicidality, further outpatient treatment, and use of medication. They also had much improved vocational functioning and higher DSM-IV-TR Global Assessment of Functioning scores. Only 13% of the patients in the psychodynamic group still met the diagnostic criteria for borderline personality disorder at the 5-year follow-up compared with 87% in the treatment-as-usual group. In another study with an even longer follow-up period, Resick, Williams, Suvak, Monson, and Gradus (2012) were able to follow three-quarters of a sample of female patients 5–10 years after they completed cognitive behavioral and exposure treatment for PTSD that resulted from being rape victims. They found that only 18%–22% still met the criteria for PTSD. Another study found that less than 10% of borderline personality disorder patients still met the criteria for the disorder at a 6-year follow-up (Antonsen et al., 2017).

How does the effectiveness of psychotherapy compare with psychotropic medications?

The use of psychotropic medications to address behavioral health concerns has grown dramatically in the U.S. over recent decades. Antidepressants have become the most frequently used medication by Americans ages 18–44 years, an increase of nearly 400% since 1988–94. In 2005–08, 11% of Americans 12 and over took antidepressant medication, and 23% of women ages 40–59 took antidepressants (Pratt, Brody, & Gu, 2011). The use of any psychotropic medication by adolescents 12–17 years of age in the U.S. has increased to 6.6% of the population, an increase of approximately 500% from a decade and a half earlier (Jonas, Albertorio-Diaz, & Gu, 2012). The use of psychotherapy only, on the other hand, decreased from 16% of those who received outpatient mental health care in 1998 to 11% in 2007, while the use of medications alone increased from 44% to 57% of those who received outpatient mental health care (Olfson & Marcus, 2010).

Despite the rapid growth in the use of medications over psychotherapy for many behavioral health concerns, psychotherapy has been shown to be quite effective compared with pharmacological intervention. Although medications have often been considered the first line of treatment for mental disorders in the medical community, psychotherapy has generally been shown to be equal to or greater in effectiveness than medicines for a range of psychological disorders, except for the most severe conditions, such as schizophrenia and bipolar affective disorder (APA, 2012; Barlow, 2004; Fournier, DeRubeis, & Amsterdam, 2013; Meyer et al., 2001; Thase & Jindal, 2004).

The most comprehensive systematic review and meta-analysis of the effectiveness of antidepressant medications was recently undertaken, and it showed mostly modest effects compared with a placebo pill (Cipriani et al., 2018). This review included 522 trials comprising a total of 116,477 participants and examined 21 different antidepressants. All of the antidepressants were found to be more effective than placebo. There were few differences found between the antidepressants, with odds ratios ranging from 1.37 for reboxetine to 2.13 for amitriptyline. (Chen, Cohen, and Chen (2010) note that an odds ratio of 1.68 is equivalent to a Cohen's *d* of 0.2, which is considered a small effect size. A commonly reported effect size for psychotherapy is a Cohen's *d* of 0.80, which is considered a large effect size; Wampold & Imel, 2015.)

Methodological differences between medication and psychotherapy trials are significant and make it difficult to directly compare the effect sizes found for these two types of treatment. But the effect sizes found for antidepressants have not been large. When the effects of antidepressants are compared with those of placebo, a meta-analysis found that antidepressants were no more effective than placebo for mild, moderate, and severe depression (Fournier et al., 2010). Both placebo and antidepressant medication were associated with clinically significant improvements in depressive symptomatology, but the effect of the antidepressant was found to be superior to placebo only for those with very severe depression, which is a relatively small proportion of the total population with depression.

Psychological interventions have some important advantages over pharmacological approaches. Medicines frequently have significant unwelcome side effects (e.g., for antidepressants, these include sedation, insomnia, headache, fatigue, dry mouth, constipation, gastrointestinal distress, and sexual disturbance; metabolic side effects for second-generation antipsychotics include major weight gain, high cholesterol, and onset of diabetes; Virani, Bezchlibnyk-Butler, & Jeffries, 2009). Surveys consistently find that the public prefers psychological to pharmacological interventions, when they are given a choice, by a wide margin. A meta-analysis found that 75% of patients preferred psychological treatment over medication for psychiatric disorders (McHugh, Whitton, Peckham, Welge, & Otto, 2013).

Concern regarding the safety and effectiveness of psychotropic medication has also grown significantly in recent years. Even though few psychologists prescribe psychotropic medications, the safety of these medicines is naturally of significant concern to all psychotherapists as well as to patients and the public generally. The underlying neurophysiology of most mental disorders is still unknown at this point, these medications do not address a known cause of a disorder, their effectiveness for reducing symptoms or correcting dysfunction is limited, and they introduce major side effects, which can be very unhealthy in some cases (e.g., obesity and diabetes). Many clinicians and researchers are additionally concerned about the possibility that they disrupt brain function in deleterious ways, particularly with long-term use and use in children and adolescents (e.g., Frances, 2009; Goldacre, 2012; Healy, 2012; Whitaker & Cosgrove, 2015). These are important concerns that deserve much more research attention than they receive because the possible side effects of these drugs are so great.

An advantage of psychotherapy over pharmacological interventions that is rarely disputed involves the enduring benefits of psychotherapy. In the case of major depression, for example, medicines, placebo, and psychotherapy are all typically helpful in reducing symptoms. Depressive episodes also tend to eventually remit on their own without treatment. The critical problem, however, is that depressive episodes usually recur (Judd, 1997). Consequently, treatments need to prevent recurrence to be truly effective. Studies consistently find that psychological treatments provide durable benefits that last long after therapy is discontinued, while depressive symptoms are more likely to return once antidepressants are no longer taken (e.g., Barlow, 2004; Cuijpers, Hollon, van Straten, Bockting, Berking, & Andersson, 2013; de Maat et al., 2006; Hollon & Beck, 2004). A meta-analysis of treatments for depression found that cognitive-behavioral therapy and antidepressants were equivalently effective at the end of treatment, but the odds ratio for having a depressive relapse by the 1-year follow-up was 2.61 for those receiving antidepressants (i.e., the average patient receiving antidepressants was 2.61 times more likely to have had a relapse compared with those receiving cognitive-behavior therapy; Cuijpers et al., 2013). Similar results have been found for anxiety disorders (Gould, Otto, & Pollack, 1995; Gould, Otto, Pollack, & Yap, 1997; Otto, Smits, & Reese, 2005). An important exception to this trend involves more biologically based disorders such as bipolar disorder and schizophrenia, for which psychotherapeutic interventions are typically viewed as second in effectiveness to pharmacologic ones (although Fournier, DeRubeis, & Amsterdan, 2013, and Seikkula et al., 2006, presented data that draw this conclusion into question). Aside from these conditions, however, psychotherapy can be considered the treatment of choice for many of the most common forms of psychological distress and disorder.

Does psychotherapy work better for some individuals than for others? Do some patients get worse?

Although psychotherapy is quite effective overall, there is large variability in the rate of improvement across patients. On one end of the continuum, there is a significant proportion of patients who improve dramatically in just short periods of time. Numerous studies have found that a large minority of patients make dramatic improvements after the first few sessions of treatment and that this improvement is maintained up to 2 years posttreatment. Across these studies, between 17% and 50% of patients were early responders, and the median session at which the largest improvement was made was commonly the fifth (Lambert, 2013). Lambert (2007) estimated that perhaps 25% of patients are early responders who may need only brief treatment. Not surprisingly, low severity of psychopathology is an important predictor of patients who respond quickly to treatment (Haas, Hill, Lambert, & Morrell, 2002).

At the other end of the continuum, there also are a significant number of patients who do not benefit from psychotherapy. This is not unexpected given the severity and complexity of many patients' problems. Some individuals experience major losses or crises or have mental illness or substance dependence that includes a steadily declining trajectory of functioning. Even the most effective therapists may not be able to help in reversing these cases. This same pattern, of course, happens in medicine as well. A significant proportion of patients have serious persistent mental illness, chronic substance dependence, or serious personality disorder, and have a poor prognosis and may be on a deteriorating course of illness. In such cases, however, even slowing the rate of deterioration can be a highly beneficial outcome of treatment. Based on the available research, Lambert (2013) estimates that 5%–10% of patients deteriorate during treatment. There are a variety of reasons for this deterioration. It appears that these cases can be attributed to both client variables (e.g., more severe problems at intake, greater interpersonal problems, low motivation) and therapist variables (e.g., lack of empathy, negative countertransference, poor interpersonal skills).

The possibility of deterioration as a direct result of the therapy techniques being used grew into a major concern during the controversy in the 1990s regarding therapy involving repressed memories of child abuse (Barlow, 2010; Lilienfeld, 2007). In addition, treatments such as rebirthing attachment therapy, conversion therapy for gay and lesbian individuals, critical incident stress debriefing, and grief therapy have also been found to be potentially harmful (Lilienfeld, Lynn, & Lohr, 2015). None of these would necessarily be considered to be psychotherapy, even though they are psychosocial interventions aimed at reducing or preventing symptoms. There is generally much less concern about the potential harm of psychotherapy that is based on experimental research and focused on particular psychological mechanisms that have been well researched.

There clearly is a substantial number of patients who do not benefit from behavioral health care treatment, and more research needs to be conducted regarding the causes of deterioration and lack of improvement and what can be done to reduce the number of these cases. Lambert and Archer (2006) estimated that about 5%–10% of patients actually deteriorate during treatment and an additional 15%–25% do not measurably improve. Because it appears that there are both patient and therapist variables that explain these cases, it is important that treatment progress is monitored so that patient deterioration and nonimprovement are identified, appropriate adjustments are made, and as many treatment failures as possible are prevented. This issue is discussed more extensively in the next sections.

What factors account for the effectiveness of psychotherapy?

The factors that account for the effectiveness of psychotherapy have been debated throughout the history of the field. Right from the beginning, this issue became very controversial in Freud's inner circle and famously resulted in the removal of Alfred Adler, who disagreed about the role of sexual instincts in personality functioning and the best approach to treat neuroses (Gay, 1988). Heated disagreements regarding the effective elements and processes of psychotherapy continued and are still being debated. Gradually, however, better controlled research has been providing data for addressing some of these issues.

Psychotherapy clinicians and researchers have long hypothesized that several specific factors contribute to the effectiveness of psychotherapy. It appeared obvious that the skill and competence of the therapist was a significant factor. It was also believed that specific methods and techniques are more effective for certain disorders or personality characteristics than for others. Many researchers also argued that there are factors common across therapies, such as the therapist's empathy, warmth, acceptance, and encouragement, that account for the effectiveness of therapy. It also appeared obvious that a major part of the reason that some patients improved while others did not was not related to the quality of the therapist or the treatment being offered, but rather depended on characteristics of the patient (especially the severity of the psychopathology) or the patient's environment (e.g., positive and negative aspects of the patient's family, support system, and community; Garfield, 1994).

After reviewing the available research, Lambert (1992) identified four general factors that he believed accounted for the effectiveness of treatment. He estimated that the following proportions of the total variance in therapy outcome could be attributed to (see Fig. 11.1):

1. specific techniques (15%)—the effectiveness of particular treatments or techniques for treating particular disorders;
2. expectancy (15%)—expectations that one will improve as the result of being in treatment; this has also been referred to as the placebo effect;
3. common factors (30%)—factors found across therapies, such as empathy, warmth, acceptance, and encouragement to take risks;
4. patient variables (40%)—factors associated with the patient (e.g., severity of psychopathology) or the patient's environment (e.g., availability of social support).

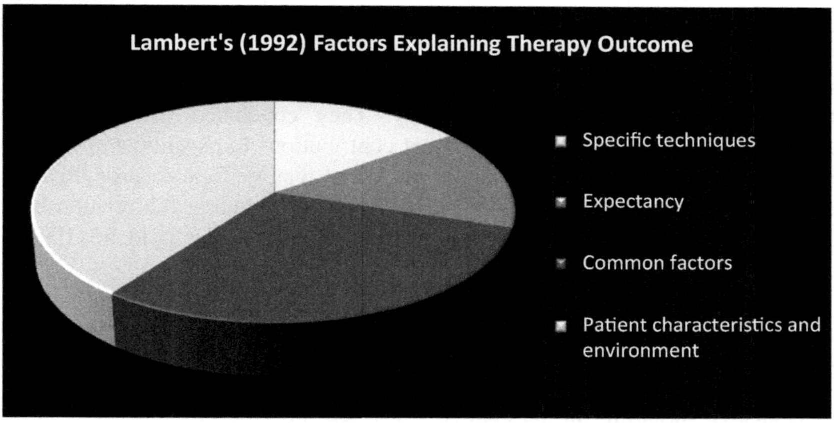

Figure 11.1 Lambert's (1992) estimates regarding the factors explaining the effectiveness of psychotherapy.

It is very difficult to empirically measure and parcel out the total variance in therapy outcome attributable to these various factors. In the first major attempt, Wampold (2001) analyzed the findings from several therapy outcome studies and obtained estimates that varied from Lambert's approximations. He concluded that very little of the variance in outcome was attributable to the specific type of therapy used but that the competence of the individual therapist had a major effect on therapy outcome. Wampold estimated that only between 0% and 8% of the total variance in therapy outcome is accounted for by the specific type of treatment provided, whereas the competence of the therapist accounted for up to 70% of therapy outcomes. The remainder of the outcome variance was not explained by either of these two factors and much of it probably consisted of patient factors such as severity of psychopathology. Wampold and Imel (2015) revisited these questions and found the same general pattern of results using all the data that had accumulated since the first review.

A meta-analysis of therapy outcomes for depression obtained results that were close to Lambert's original 1992 estimates. Cuijpers et al. (2012) found that 49% of the variance in depressive symptom improvement was accounted for by common factors, 33% was accounted for by patient characteristics (i.e., the patient and her or his environment), and 17% was attributable to the specific therapy used. But when the original researchers' allegiances to the therapy under investigation were controlled for, the portion of variance associated with the specific therapy factors fell by nearly one-half. If common factors are attributable in large part to the competence of the therapist, then these results are also not far from Wampold's (2001) estimates.

More precise estimates of the proportions of therapy outcome that are attributable to particular factors need to await further research. The severity of patient psychopathology, the quality of their social support, and other patient variables certainly account for a substantial portion of the variance in treatment outcome. The portion attributable to the type of therapy provided, on the other hand, appears to be small. The portion attributable to the therapy relationship and the competence of the therapist, also known as common factors, is substantial. Experts are virtually unanimous in their conclusion that the quality of the therapist–patient relationship is critical to positive therapy outcomes. This conclusion was also reached by an expert panel assembled by the APA Divisions of Clinical Psychology and Psychotherapy. They concluded that "The therapy relationship makes substantial and consistent contributions to psychotherapy outcome independent of the specific type of treatment," and that "Efforts to promulgate best practices or evidenced-based practices (EBPs) without including the relationship are seriously incomplete and potentially misleading" (Norcross & Wampold, 2011, p. 423).

How important are the skills of the individual therapist to psychotherapy effectiveness?

There is clearly variability in the quality of services provided by individual psychotherapists. This pattern holds not just in behavioral health care, of course, but is found throughout health care and human services, as well as in most all areas of life. Research consistently finds that therapist's qualities and skills are important determinants of therapy outcome (for reviews, see Baldwin & Imel, 2013; Lambert, 2013; Norcross, 2011; Wampold & Imel, 2015).

The importance of therapist effects on treatment outcome was demonstrated in two large overlapping studies that compared patient outcomes across 71 therapists who each treated a minimum of 30 patients (Okiishi et al., 2006; Okiiski, Lambert, Nielsen, & Ogles, 2003). The therapists were categorized according to the improvement seen in their patients' treatment outcomes. Therapists who were in the middle 50% of the distribution tended to be largely indistinguishable from one another. At the extremes, however, there were distinct differences. The top 10% of the therapists who were associated with the best outcomes saw their patients for an average of 7.9 sessions and had an improved or recovered rate of 44% and a deterioration rate of 5%. The bottom 10% of therapists, on the other hand, saw their patients for an average of 10.6 sessions, and had an improved or recovered rate of 28% and a deterioration rate of 11%. One particularly effective therapist who saw more than 300 patients had a deterioration rate of less than 1%, while a less effective therapist who saw more than 160 patients had a deterioration rate of 19%. Another large study conducted in the United Kingdom resulted in similar findings (Saxon & Barkham, 2012). Roughly two-thirds of therapists had largely similar patient outcomes in the middle of the distribution. But the 17.7% of therapists with the best outcomes had a mean patient recovery rate of 75.6%, while the 16.0% of therapists with the worst outcomes had a mean recovery rate of 43.3%.

Evidence finds that a critical element accounting for therapy outcome is the therapist's ability to create therapeutic alliances and relationships. Even in pharmacotherapy, in which the medication would be expected to be responsible for symptom improvement, the therapeutic alliance has an important effect on patient outcome. In an analysis of the NIMH Collaborative Depression Study, Krupnick et al. (1996) found that the quality of the therapeutic alliance was the most important factor explaining improvement in patients' depression in both the psychotherapy and the pharmacotherapy conditions. An expert panel sponsored by the APA Divisions of Clinical Psychology and Psychotherapy concluded that "Adapting or tailoring the therapy relationship to specific patient characteristics (in addition to diagnosis) enhances the effectiveness of treatment" (Norcross & Wampold, 2011, p. 423). Therapists' sensitivity, flexibility, and nondefensiveness are critical to establishing therapeutic relationships and alliances, and these make important contributions to therapy outcomes.

If not all psychotherapy patients improve, can the number of treatment failures be reduced?

The evidence reviewed above suggests that large numbers of psychotherapy cases involving deterioration are due to patient variables such as severe psychopathology or a lack of social support, while others are due to therapist characteristics or a failure to tailor the therapy relationship to the personality, needs, and sociocultural context of the patient. Regardless of the cause, there are practices that can identify patients who are not improving or are deteriorating so that adjustments in treatment can be made and outcomes improved.

An uncomplicated and inexpensive approach to accomplishing this goal is beginning to be widely implemented. Lambert and his colleagues (see Lambert, 2007, 2010) have investigated the effect of providing therapists, and sometimes their patients, with patient outcome feedback regarding the ongoing progress of treatment. The benefits of these procedures were found to be substantial. Using a standardized outcome measure to track patient symptomatology and level of functioning, patients were assigned (in four of the five studies, at random) to either the treatment-as-usual control condition or the condition in which their therapist received feedback regarding the patient's level of functioning. In the group of patients who began deteriorating during the course of treatment, the patients of therapists who did not receive feedback had posttest scores that were slightly worse, on average, than when they entered treatment. All of the groups in which feedback was provided to the therapists, however, improved significantly by posttest. The effect size between those who received feedback versus the treatment-as-usual groups was substantial, approximately 0.40, and the deterioration rate fell substantially in the groups that received the feedback (Lambert, 2010).

Although high-quality behavioral health care interventions are remarkably effective and their effectiveness may be increased even somewhat further through the use of systematic outcomes assessment, unfortunately, treatment will never be 100% effective. Many patients have very serious behavioral health problems characterized by a progressively deteriorating course of functioning. Many have very unhealthy family and social environments and others have deeply entrenched personality dysfunction. Therapists have only a limited amount of influence in people's lives and cannot be expected to reverse all psychopathology. The best that can be hoped for in many cases is to slow the rate of deterioration—the same is, of course, true in medicine as well. In a study in which outcome data were provided to therapists so that lack of improvement could be identified, therapists were also provided clinical problem-solving feedback to help them make decisions about conducting additional assessment and modifying the treatment plan for patients who were not improving (e.g., assessing motivation to change, reevaluating the diagnosis, referring for evaluation for medication; Slade, Lambert, Harmon, Smart, & Bailey, 2008). The researchers found that the deterioration rate under these conditions reduced to 4.6%, a rate that they considered to be perhaps the lower limit of what can be achieved. Approaching such a low level of deterioration is a remarkable accomplishment, but it is also a reminder about the nature of behavioral health. In addition, inpatient and other programs in which serious psychopathology is the usual referral would not be expected to achieve such a low deterioration rate.

There has long been reluctance among therapists to routinely monitor patients' progress during the ongoing course of treatment or at termination. A reluctance to being evaluated is natural, but it should be noted that therapists have always monitored patient progress in nonstandardized ways. Therapy progress is routinely monitored by simply asking patients how they are doing, and the overall effectiveness of treatment is normally a significant topic of discussion at termination. In addition, behavioral interventions typically incorporate systematic measurement of treatment progress and sometimes in a very detailed manner. Wolpe's (1958) systematic desensitization, for example, monitors the progress of treatment by having patients indicate the success of the counterconditioning on a moment-by-moment basis by raising their finger or verbally indicating their level of distress during the reciprocal inhibition sessions. Sobell and Sobell (2000) noted that an inherent feature of the graduated nature of most substance abuse treatment, whereby more intensive treatment is provided as the severity of the problem increases, is that it is self-correcting. Patients' progress is monitored in an ongoing manner (and urinalyses are frequently used to supplement the unreliability of patient self-report), and treatment strategies are adjusted to match deterioration or improvement in patients' progress.

Demands for accountability throughout health care continue to grow, and the safety, effectiveness, and efficiency of behavioral health treatment will undoubtedly grow as priorities as a result. Techniques that can reliably identify nonimprovement or deterioration will probably become more widely adopted in behavioral health care, and therapists and their supervisors will naturally want to focus special attention on cases where they know that the patients are not improving or are worsening. This practice has such great promise that the expert panel assembled by the APA Divisions of Clinical Psychology and Psychotherapy concluded that "Practitioners should routinely monitor patients' responses to the therapy relationship and ongoing treatment. Such monitoring leads to increased opportunities to reestablish collaboration, improve the relationship, modify technical strategies, and avoid premature termination" (Norcross & Wampold, 2011, p. 424). The APA Presidential Task Force on Evidence-Based Practice (2006) also noted that: "Clinical expertise also entails the monitoring of patient progress ... that may suggest the need to adjust the treatment" (pp. 276–277). These conclusions have begun taking hold in behavioral health care and are also addressed more extensively in the next chapter.

Effective behavioral health care treatment

Behavioral health care treatment has evolved significantly in recent years. The role of the traditional theoretical orientations has declined substantially as the biopsychosocial approach increasingly takes their place. The traditional theoretical orientations are certainly still critical for informing psychotherapy techniques and methods, but their role in conceptualizing cases is being replaced by the comprehensive science-based biopsychosocial perspective. This perspective also focuses attention on strengths, resilience, and well-being in addition to the traditional emphasis on problems, vulnerabilities, and disorders. The focus on health and well-being also focuses more attention on long-term treatment effectiveness. Symptom relief and improved functioning in the short term are certainly important, but improvements need to be maintained over the long term for treatments to be considered maximally effective and useful.

The general effectiveness of psychotherapy for treating behavioral health issues is well established. The effect size of psychotherapy indicates that it is a very effective treatment that compares favorably with many medical interventions. The effectiveness of psychotherapy is also very meaningful clinically, enabling large numbers of individuals to return to normal functioning. The effects tend to be enduring and continue well beyond the end of treatment, unlike the benefits of many psychotropic medications. There is also evidence that even complex, serious disorders can be treated effectively with psychotherapy.

Research on the effectiveness of different psychotherapies finds that the type of psychotherapy provided appears to account for a small amount of the total variance in outcome. On the other hand, the severity of patients' psychopathology, the quality of their social support, and other patient variables account for a substantial portion of the variance in outcome. Some individuals have serious psychopathology and a poor prognosis. Although psychotherapy may not resolve their issues, slowing the rate of deterioration in health and functioning can be a very important treatment outcome in these cases. The portion of outcome variance attributable to the quality of the therapy relationship and alliance is also large. Research clearly finds that the therapist's skill in creating therapeutic relationships and alliances is important to the overall effectiveness of psychotherapy.

Demands for accountability in health care will surely continue to grow, which means that the safety and effectiveness of behavioral health treatment will continue to grow in importance as well. Research related to improving therapy effectiveness is steadily advancing. This is also reflected in the movement within the APA to develop clinical practice guidelines for the treatment of particular problems and disorders based on the accumulated treatment outcome research. The first set of guidelines was published in 2017 and addresses the treatment of PTSD in adults (APA, 2017). Another active research area involves treatment progress monitoring and procedures for identifying cases of nonimprovement and deterioration. Given the importance of these procedures, the next chapter examines them in more detail.

Case example: treatment with a mildly depressed patient

The case example that was discussed in the previous two chapters is presented again to illustrate the biopsychosocial approach to behavioral health care treatment. The treatment plan discussed in the previous chapter was implemented with Jessica, the 41-year-old married female with mild depression. That plan included six components: (1) monitor her depressed mood, (2) stop drinking alcohol during weekdays for the next 2 months, (3) schedule dates out with her husband a minimum of once per week, (4) begin a regular exercise routine, (5) go to parent–teacher organization meetings at the children's school, and (6) explore the possibility of improving the relationship with her mother.

Jessica had been completing the clinic's standard outcomes questionnaire every other week when she came in for her appointments. The psychologist noted that her scores indicated steady improvement with her depressed feelings and in other areas as well. At the sixth session, the psychologist asked if Jessica would ask her husband to join her once again the following week to reassess how things were going. The couple had a very productive conversation when he came to her second session, although they did not appear to have a close relationship. They interacted respectfully and comfortably but with little affection and limited awareness of each other's feelings or thoughts; there were multiple times when they expressed mild surprise after hearing the other's thoughts and feelings. The husband did not realize how much his wife was drinking and was surprised to hear how hurt she was by her own mother's criticisms. But it was clear that they cared about each other and they enjoyed recalling several very happy times together.

The wife and husband interacted more warmly when they came in for her seventh session. They sat closer to each other and their words and gestures suggested more comfort and warmth between them. He was quite impressed with how she had started exercising again. They reported going out on dates

Case example: treatment with a mildly depressed patient—cont'd

once per week, as Jessica had agreed to, and that their sex life had returned in a way they hadn't experienced in years. They said their younger child even asked "Mom and Dad, why are you so happy?" Jessica noted that "This actually made me sad. I told John that they probably couldn't remember me being happy like this because I sort of retreated a little into my shell after they were born. I didn't even realize it was happening, it was so gradual. I'm just really sorry I let it happen." Jessica said she enjoyed going to a parent–teacher organization meeting at her children's school and was planning to attend the next meeting. She also said that she was ready to work on improving her relationship with her own mother. Jessica and her husband decided to attend Jessica's parents' church the following Sunday before going to the big family gathering that followed the service.

After church the next Sunday, the extended family gathered at Jessica's parents' home for a meal and socializing. People were very happy to see Jessica and she received many compliments about their children and how fit she looked. At the next session, Jessica and her psychologist discussed how Jessica could broach questions she had for her mother. The next weekend, Jessica visited her mother so they could talk without the children along. Her mother said she didn't like it that Jessica worked so much and they weren't going to church, but she also noted that Jessica had the best husband and kids among the relatives. She said that she was beginning to realize that seeing her daughter be so successful actually made her jealous and that was the reason she sometimes criticized Jessica. She said she still wanted them to raise their children in the church, but she was trying to accept that that wasn't her decision to make.

At the ninth session, Jessica said that she was very happy with how things were going. There was a large drop in her scores on the clinic's outcome assessment questionnaire into the nonclinical range. She said she felt like a huge weight was lifted from her shoulders in terms of the conversation she had with her mother. After attending just two parent–teacher organization meetings at school, she said she was very happy to have been invited to join the parent advisory committee for her children's school. She said that she was committed to exercising and staying fit because it felt so good. She noted that she now only occasionally feels a desire to drink more than a couple of glasses of wine at special dinners or parties and that she feels better physically as a result. Jessica and the psychologist talked about her mother's criticism, and Jessica said her mother seemed honestly remorseful how she let her own jealous feelings affect her daughter when actually she thought her daughter's life had turned out really well. After acknowledging major progress with her issues, she agreed to come back in a month to discuss progress, challenges, and future goals.

Outcomes assessment

12

Psychotherapists often have mixed feelings about outcomes assessment. Many therapists are concerned about how patient outcome data might be used. Psychopathology and psychotherapy involve very complicated issues, and simple outcome measures may not meaningfully capture the complexity of a patient's life or the complicated process of therapy. In addition, how can therapists be assured that outcome data will not be used in ways that are detrimental to patients? Are safeguards sufficient to prevent these data from affecting patients' future insurability, their employability, or their reputations in general? Patients are also sometimes irritated by having to complete questionnaires. Therapists are also concerned about how the data might be used to evaluate them. How might one's job security, salary, or workload be affected by these data? A reluctance to being evaluated is understandable—student course evaluations are common in colleges, and customer satisfaction surveys are now common in medical settings, but they have not been normal practice in many sectors of behavioral health care. Therapists already routinely discuss the effectiveness of treatment with their patients during and at the termination of therapy, so why does this need to be supplemented with outcomes assessment data?

Despite all these concerns, outcomes assessment has grown significantly in behavioral health care. It has been essential in many areas of medicine for decades, as those with high blood pressure, cholesterol, or blood sugar know; patients with these conditions normally have their symptoms checked at every encounter with their health care provider. Behavioral health providers also normally ask how their patients are doing at every clinical encounter. The difference now is that these discussions are increasingly supplemented with more objective and psychometrically sound outcome measures.

Patients, therapists, supervisors, managers, payors, and researchers all have an interest in objective data that help evaluate the effectiveness of intervention. This chapter outlines the conceptual framework for approaching behavioral health care outcomes assessment from the clinical science perspective advocated in this volume. It begins by reviewing the rationale for incorporating outcomes assessment into routine behavioral health care practice and then reviews the major decisions that have to be made to conduct outcomes assessment. It covers the following topics:

- The rationale for outcomes assessment in behavioral health care
- Outcomes assessment in health care generally
  - global outcome measures
  - condition-specific measures
  - patient satisfaction
  - cost-effectiveness
- Outcomes assessment in behavioral health care
  - content and focus of outcome measures
  - sources of outcome data

Foundations of Health Service Psychology. https://doi.org/10.1016/B978-0-12-816426-6.00012-8

- schedule for collecting data
- follow-up

Rationale for outcomes assessment in behavioral health care

The clinical science approach to behavioral health care advocated in this volume has its foundations in science and professional ethics. This has critical implications for the assessment of outcomes as well. First, the science-based orientation of the approach emphasizes, among other things, the necessity of accurate measurement of important variables in order to understand phenomena. If one needs to understand the safety and effectiveness of behavioral health interventions, then accurate measurement of treatment outcomes is essential. When the primary purpose of behavioral health care is meeting individuals' needs and promoting their functioning, the attainment of that purpose cannot be evaluated without reliable measurements of the outcomes of intervention. Discussions between therapists and patients about the effectiveness of treatment are of course important, but it is not reliable or responsible to rely on those discussions alone without also collecting objective measurements regarding how patients are doing. People receiving care for hypertension, high cholesterol, or diabetes normally expect that there will be objective symptom measurement conducted in addition to conversations about how they are doing as part of their contacts with their providers. A clinical science approach to health care requires that important variables are measured using instruments with demonstrated reliability, validity, and clinical utility.

Second, the ethical foundations of the approach taken in this volume include obligations of nonmaleficence, beneficence, and justice that prioritize the safety and effectiveness of treatment as well as an obligation to use resources efficiently and fairly. If the field is conceptualized as primarily a service industry where individuals are responsible for choosing how to get their needs met, then accountability is managed primarily by the market. But behavioral health care is generally considered a health services profession where professionals have ethical obligations to provide services that are safe and effective. If certain individuals or groups are not receiving optimal care due to poverty, discrimination, or other issues, objective outcomes assessment can also clarify the extent of the problem and the success of efforts to correct it. Systematic, objective outcomes assessments help ensure that therapists are meeting these obligations.[1]

[1] Several of the ethics codes of the behavioral healthcare professions specifically refer to the importance of these issues. The Code of Ethics of the National Association of Social Workers states that "Social workers should monitor and evaluate … practice interventions" (Standard 5.02(a), National Association of Social Workers, 2017) and the American Counseling Association Ethics Code (2014) states that "Counselors continually monitor their effectiveness as professionals" (Code C.2.d). The APA Ethics Code is less specific about this issue though it does include the requirement that psychologists terminate therapy when it becomes reasonably clear that the patient no longer needs the service, is not benefitting, or is being harmed (see Standard 10.10, APA, 2010). These issues can be identified through the use of outcomes assessment.

Third, the biopsychosocial approach to behavioral health care identifies its primary purpose as meeting individuals' behavioral health needs and promoting their biopsychosocial functioning. Emphasis needs to be placed on whether treatment is effective in the individual case, not just whether a treatment has been demonstrated to work in general, in controlled research for treatment group participants on average compared with control group participants on average. Historically, the psychotherapy field did not emphasize that treatments work in individual cases. From the time of Freud through the 1960s, major effort was devoted to defining and perfecting theoretical systems of psychotherapy. This was followed by extensive efforts to establish whether therapies worked on average in a treatment group compared with a control group. These efforts were crucial of course, but the field is now moving to the point where it is focusing on ensuring that treatment is effective in the individual case and not just for groups on average. Routine outcomes assessment is necessary for realizing this objective.

Routinely using outcomes assessment to monitor the effectiveness of treatment and identify when improvements are needed can also enhance the therapeutic relationship and increase engagement by patients in their treatment (Fortney et al., 2017). Patients who regularly complete outcomes assessments are likely to be more knowledgeable about their symptoms and aware of influences on their symptoms and functioning. This may help them feel validated for how they are feeling, which can lessen the self-blame many patients feel. Completing outcomes assessments can also help patients notice even small improvements early in the course of treatment that may increase hopefulness and engagement in the therapy. All of these factors can help improve communication and collaboration between patients and therapists, potentially resulting in more thorough and rapid improvement and fewer treatment failures (Valenstein et al., 2009).

Existing research also points to the benefits of monitoring treatment progress. Monitoring outcomes is important not only for identifying treatment successes, but in some ways, it is more important for identifying treatment failures, so that adjustments can be made to potentially reverse the deterioration. In was noted in the previous chapter that Lambert and Archer (2006) estimated that perhaps 15%−25% of patients do not measurably improve during treatment and 5%−10% of patients actually deteriorate. Certainly not all patients could be expected to improve; many have very serious problems, a poor prognosis, and unhealthy support systems and social environments, and therapists only have limited influence in patients' lives. Nonetheless, therapists may lack reliable information about what is happening in these cases. For example, Hannan et al. (2005) asked 40 therapists whether each of their patients was worse off than when they entered treatment and whether they thought the patients would leave treatment in a worse condition. Their judgments were then compared with weekly Outcome Questionnaire-45 (OQ-45) data provided by the patients ($N = 550$). The therapists were also told that past research would suggest that 8% of their patients were likely to deteriorate (i.e., their OQ-45 score would increase by 14 or more points). The actual deterioration rate found in the sample was 7.3% ($n = 40$), very close to what the therapists were told. Out of these 40 deteriorated cases, the therapists judged that nearly 40% of them had improved. In addition, the therapists predicted that only three of the 550 patients (0.55%) would leave treatment worse off than when they began, and only one of those three patients actually deteriorated.

Another study showing that therapists can be unreliable judges of patients' improvement found a deterioration rate of 9% (386 out of 4253 cases) in a clinic that used the OQ-45 to track patient progress (Hatfield, McCullough, Plucinski, & Krieger, 2009). The patient files for 70 of the deteriorated cases were inspected (an increase of 14 or more points on the OQ-45 indicated deterioration) and it was found that therapists had noted deterioration for only 21% of these cases, no mention of progress in 59% of these cases, and 3% were noted as improved. There were also 41 patients whose OQ-45 scores increased by at least 30 points, indicating severe deterioration, and only 32% of these files included a note indicating deterioration. Therapists may have a positive self-evaluation bias that helps explain these findings. Walfish, McAlister, O'Donnell, and Lambert (2012) asked 129 private practice therapists to compare their overall skills with others in the profession and estimate what percentage of their patients improved, stayed the same, or deteriorated. Twenty-five percent of these therapists viewed their skill level at the 90th percentile or higher, 92% viewed their skill level at the 75th percentile or higher, and none viewed their skill level as below the 50th percentile. Nearly half (48%) of the therapists estimated that none of their patients had deteriorated. (This same type of positive self-evaluation bias is found among professionals in other fields as well.)

For all these reasons, systematically monitoring treatment outcomes is considered integral to evidence-based practice in health care. The APA's *Report of the Presidential Task Force on Evidence-Based Practice* included the following definition in its 2006 edition: "*Evidence-based practice in psychology* (EBPP) is the integration of the best available research with clinical expertise in the context of patient characteristics, culture, and preferences" (p. 273, emphasis added). The task force also specifically noted that monitoring of treatment outcomes was an essential component of clinical expertise:

> *Clinical expertise also entails the monitoring of patient progress (and of changes in the patient's circumstances—e.g., job loss, major illness) that may suggest the need to adjust the treatment (Lambert, Bergin, & Garfield, 2004a). If progress is not proceeding adequately, the psychologist alters or addresses problematic aspects of the treatment (e.g., problems in the therapeutic relationship or in the implementation of the goals of the treatment) as appropriate. (pp. 276–277)*

In 2015, the Centers for Medicare & Medicaid Services, Anthem Blue Cross Blue Shield, and UnitedHealthcare announced that they would create incentives for programs that utilized outcomes assessment to improve services. In 2018, the Joint Commission (which accredits over 21,000 health care organizations in the U.S.) began requiring *measurement-based care*, the term now often used for routinely gathering and using outcomes assessment results to inform treatment. The integration of outcomes assessment into routine behavioral health care obviously is now well underway.

Another reason that outcomes assessment is growing in importance involves accountability and cost-effectiveness. Health care in the U.S. is very expensive, and by several measures, outcomes are poor. Society increasingly demands accountability in general, and health care organizations are under growing pressure to ensure that services are effective and efficient. More money is spent on health care in the U.S. per capita and as a proportion of gross domestic product than in any other nation in the world, while at the same time morbidity and mortality rates are relatively high (see Chapter 13). As discussed in the previous chapter, there is evidence that the effectiveness of psychosocial treatment can be improved when therapists are provided with outcomes assessment data. Many cases where patients have deteriorated or not improved can be turned around, resulting in significantly improved overall effectiveness for behavioral health treatment.

As economic pressures and the expectations for evidence-based practice grow, emphasis on the safety, effectiveness, and efficiency of behavioral health care will also grow. Tools are now available that can demonstrate the effectiveness of behavioral health care intervention, and the data can be aggregated to show accreditors, payors, and the general public that behavioral health services are effective and cost-efficient. As acceptance of these practices grows, monitoring treatment outcomes may become as well integrated in behavioral health care as lab tests are in medicine (Lambert, 2010). In the treatment of diabetes, high cholesterol, or high blood pressure, most people would be very surprised if there was not ongoing monitoring of treatment progress—patients expect that glucose levels, lipids, or blood pressure will be routinely tested, often at every patient contact. Many behavioral health care professionals now view outcomes assessment in their work in a similar manner.

Outcomes assessment in health care generally

There are many different approaches to assessing health care outcomes. The focus of outcomes assessment in medicine is generally on what is most meaningful to patients and other stakeholders. Naturally, what is most meaningful depends heavily on patients' particular conditions and situations. Outcome measures in health care typically focus on (1) improvement in symptomatology specific to the condition a patient has; (2) improvements in global functioning and quality of life; (3) satisfaction with services delivered; and (4) cost-effectiveness.

Condition-specific outcome measures

Condition-specific measures of health care outcomes assess specific aspects of functioning closely related to a patient's disease or condition. Condition-specific measures are designed to be highly sensitive so that they can detect even small treatment effects. These measures are basically of two types: clinical measures focus on the signs, symptoms, or test results associated with a particular disease or condition, and experiential measures focus on the impact of the disease or condition on the patient (Atherly, 2006). Clinical measures such as blood tests and blood pressure checks are routinely used to screen for and monitor treatment outcomes for high cholesterol, diabetes, and hypertension, because experiential health outcome measures can easily miss clinically important signs of problems with those conditions. A successful treatment for hypertension, for example, is often imperceptible to patients because changes in blood pressure are difficult to detect. Even when patients cannot detect the effect, a successful or failed treatment for hypertension obviously can profoundly affect the long-term health of the patient (Atherly, 2006). Both clinical and experiential measures are therefore critical for monitoring the effectiveness of treatments in many areas of medicine.

Global outcome measures

Global measures of health are designed to assess a full range of important physical, psychological, and social aspects of health. These approaches also focus on the *quality* of health in addition to its *quantity* in terms of life span and other easily quantified indicators. Measures emphasizing quantity of health generally focus on morbidity, mortality, and life expectancy, whereas measures emphasizing quality of health focus on overall health and functioning. These measures tend to focus on individuals' perceptions of their physical, psychological, and social functioning as well as overall quality of life, factors that people frequently view as more relevant than condition-specific outcomes (Maciejewski, 2006).

Quality of life is generally considered critical to measures of life satisfaction and the overall outcome of health care, but it can be difficult to measure because individuals place very different priority on different aspects of their lives. Therefore, measures of quality of life are typically multidimensional, and eight dimensions have often been included in comprehensive assessments of the quality of general life functioning: physical functioning, social functioning, emotional functioning, sexual functioning, cognitive functioning, pain/discomfort, vitality, and overall well-being (Maciejewski, 2006; Patrick & Deyo, 1989). The 36-item Short-Form Health Survey (also known as the SF-36; Ware & Sherbourne, 1992) measures all eight of these dimensions and has become the most widely used generic measure of functioning in medical research.

Patient satisfaction

Patients' satisfaction with health care services began getting research attention in the 1950s when it was noticed that increased patient satisfaction was associated with improved appointment keeping, medication use, and adherence to treatment recommendations (Williams, 1994). It was also found to be associated with a decreased likelihood of being sued for malpractice (Hickson et al., 1994). Patient satisfaction with services has grown in importance in the U.S. as the result of the increased marketing of health care services and is also receiving more attention as an indicator of quality of services. A variety of approaches to measuring patient satisfaction include services that can be easily integrated into clinic practice (Smith, Schussler-Fiorenza, & Rockwood, 2006).

Cost effectiveness

Concern surrounding the cost-effectiveness of health care in the U.S. has been growing given the relatively poor health outcomes achieved despite spending by far the largest per-capita amount of money on health care of any country in the world (World Health Organization, 2019). The cost-effectiveness of medical treatments can be relatively easily examined in terms of number of lives saved or years of life gained as a result of providing particular treatments. Emphasis has shifted from these simple measures of treatment outcome to measures of quality of life, because simply lengthening life if quality is not also achieved is not always preferable (Beauchamp & Childress, 2013). For example, disability-adjusted life-years have become widely used to provide a more adequate measure of treatment outcome for use in cost-effectiveness analyses (see the next chapter).

Outcomes assessment in behavioral health care

Evaluating behavioral health care often requires a similar combination of condition-specific and global measures of treatment outcome for the same reasons that medicine does. Individuals' lives and functioning are complex, particularly when viewed from a biopsychosocial perspective, and the outcomes of treatment need to be evaluated in a multifaceted manner to begin to capture that complexity. Focusing on single dimensions of functioning (e.g., decreasing the symptoms of a disorder) can simplify an assessment so much that its meaningfulness becomes limited. People dealing with mental problems and disorders also should not be defined by their symptoms. This is true for intake as well as outcomes assessments. Maruish (2004b) noted that "outcomes" is commonly used in its plural form to emphasize the importance of taking a multifaceted approach to outcomes assessment that covers multiple domains of functioning.

It is important to note that outcomes assessment is not limited to measuring outcomes only at the termination of treatment; the same measures can be used throughout treatment to monitor progress. Readministering outcome measures throughout treatment may be the only way to reliably detect lack of improvement or deterioration (just as in the case of many medical treatments), which then gives therapists the chance to try alternative interventions that may reverse the lack of progress. For this reason, outcomes assessment is often now referred to as *progress monitoring* or *measurement-based care*, which emphasizes the systematic use of symptom measures for informing treatment (Fortney et al., 2017). It is also important to note that many psychologists work in settings that do not provide significant amounts of psychotherapy or other psychosocial treatments. Although the general principles discussed here apply, specific procedures for outcomes assessment for many medical, school, correctional, and forensic psychologists, as well as neuropsychologists, will deviate from the recommendations presented here. In addition, the large majority of outcome measures used in published research have focused on psychological symptoms and intrapersonal factors. Psychologists working in settings that provide little or no psychotherapy may instead focus more on interpersonal, behavioral, social role, and physical functioning. Outcomes assessment needs to be designed around the particular purposes of the services provided and the needs of the individuals served.

Content and focus of outcome measures

Global measures. Global measures that provide information about patients' general level of distress and overall functioning are often the most practical outcome measure for many therapists and agencies. These measures can be used routinely with all patients receiving services except for those needing immediate attention for suicidality or another type of crisis. There are several brief, well-established, and widely used instruments that provide useful measures of overall functioning including the: (1) Brief Symptom Inventory (BSI; Derogatis & Melisaratos, 1983); (2) OQ-45 (Lambert et al., 1996); and (3) SF-36 (Ware & Sherbourne, 1992). The four-item Outcome Rating Scale is a very brief alternative that is very easy to use in clinical practice (Bringhurst, Watson, Miller, & Duncan, 2006). A widely used instrument for children and youth is the Child Behavior Checklist (CBC; Achenbach & Edelbrock, 1983). The BSI focuses primarily on psychological symptoms, while the SF-36 and CBC include scales measuring variables from across the biopsychosocial domains. Of course, there are many alternatives to these instruments (see Ogles, 2013; The Kennedy Forum, 2016).

Condition-specific measures. When patients are receiving treatment for a specific problem or disorder, condition-specific measures may be needed to adequately assess the effectiveness of that treatment. These measures are often used in conjunction with global measures to evaluate changes regarding particular symptoms as well as overall functioning. Condition-specific measures are also often needed as part of intake assessment to obtain information necessary for completing the assessment, making proper diagnoses, and obtaining baseline data to evaluate the progress and effectiveness of treatment. The specific signs and symptoms of particular disorders or problems (e.g., substance abuse, obsessive-compulsive disorder, enuresis, psychotic disorders, eating disorders) are often missed entirely by global outcome measures.

Many standardized instruments with strong psychometric properties are available for assessing specific disorders and problems. Examples widely used in general practice for monitoring specific symptoms include the Beck Depression Inventory (Beck, Steer, & Brown, 1996), the State-Trait Anxiety Inventory (Speilberger, Gorsuch, & Lushene, 1970), the Fear Questionnaire (Marks & Matthews, 1978), and the Dyadic Adjustment Scale (for measuring relationship satisfaction in couples; Spanier, 1976). Therapists working in specialized areas are usually familiar with the instruments commonly used in their respective areas.

The United Kingdom is currently implementing a nationwide screening and intervention program aimed at depression and anxiety (also noted in Chapter 9 in the section on stepped-care treatment approaches). To monitor treatment progress, patients are asked at each patient contact to complete very brief outcome measures such as the 9-item Patient Health Questionnaire Depression Scale (Kroenke, Spitzer, & Williams, 2001) or the 7-item Patient Health Questionnaire Anxiety Disorder Scale (Spitzer, Kroenke, Williams, & Lowe, 2006).

Individualized measures. In addition to standardized instruments, it is sometimes important to use individually tailored measures designed to assess a person's particular symptoms or behaviors (Clement, 1999; Ogles, 2013). A patient's unique experiences, problems, and biopsychosocial circumstances are of course evaluated during intake assessment. When particular aspects of an individual's life become a focus of treatment, it can be important to develop individualized measures that can capture change in those aspects. One individual with substance dependence, depression, agoraphobia, or sexual dysfunction may share few similarities with another person with the same problem, and it is important to incorporate that individuality into the treatment process.

Several approaches to conducting individualized assessment have been developed. One well-known approach involves the use of target complaints, a system that was included in the National Institute of Behavioral Health Core Battery initiative (Waskow & Parloff, 1975; this important initiative attempted to establish a standardized approach to outcome measurement but was never widely adopted). In this system, the patient, the therapist, or the patient and therapist together identify targets for treatment and then rate the level of problem severity for each target complaint (e.g., missed workdays, shoplifting incidents, arguments with one's mother). This unique list of complaints can then be tracked periodically starting from intake. Goal Attainment Scaling (Kiresuk & Sherman, 1968) uses essentially the same approach, where treatment goals are established collaboratively by the patient and therapist and progress toward meeting those goals is assessed across treatment. Behavior therapy that includes a functional analysis and target behaviors is also a highly useful approach to intervention and outcomes assessment (e.g., Hersen & Rosqvist, 2008).

Individualized assessment is essential for monitoring treatment progress in areas where the consequences of behaviors have important implications for patient well-being. For example, the monitoring of an individual's suicidal behaviors, thoughts, or feelings is typically critical when assessing and treating suicidality and other forms of danger to self or others (Joiner, 2005; Rudd, 2006). Monitoring high-risk thoughts, feelings, and behavior is generally important whenever self- or other-harming behavior is involved such as with disordered eating, high-risk sexual behavior, self-mutilation, severe substance abuse, and the neglect or abuse of children, vulnerable adults, or dependent seniors. Condition-specific or global measures are often inadequate for monitoring treatment progress and potential deterioration when these issues are a focus of treatment. These measures also are often repeated at follow-up after treatment has ended to help assess whether treatment was effective over the longer term.

Sources of outcome data

The reliability and validity of assessment data are critical considerations when conducting outcomes assessment and evaluating the effectiveness of treatment. As discussed in Chapter 9, in order to obtain reliable and valid behavioral health information, it is frequently important to rely on a variety of sources, particularly when treatment goals involve the patient's functioning in social roles such as at work, home, or school as well as in the community. When treatment focuses on intrapersonal issues (e.g., depression or anxiety), patients themselves are typically the most reliable reporters regarding their internal state. When treatment focuses on externalizing disorders or patients' functioning in social roles, however, individuals' perceptions of their behavior or performance can vary significantly from those of family members, employers, educators, or public officials (Miller & Berman, 1983). The minimization or exaggeration of problems sometimes is not conscious or intentional, though of course sometimes it is. In either case, individuals' perceptions and reports often need to be supplemented because people (especially children) are not always objective and reliable reporters of this information.

Engaging significant individuals in a patient's life as collateral reporters on the patient's progress can also be very helpful for building social support for the patient and reinforcing changes he or she has made. This is often essential in the treatment of children, adults with substance use disorders or criminal involvement, many people with disabilities, and seniors in declining health. This can be crucial after formal treatment has ended because patients' ability to maintain treatment gains can depend on the level of social support and reinforcement they receive from significant others who are invested in their well-being. Although clinicians often minimize the involvement of significant others in their treatment of patients because of time pressures, they also need to make the effort necessary to help ensure positive patient outcomes over the long term. This is true not just for patients in health service psychology but also for students, employees, and others who are served by school, consulting, correctional, forensic, and other types of psychologists.

Schedule for collecting data

Therapists also need to decide on when to gather outcome data. At a minimum, patients should be assessed at intake and again at termination or discharge (Maruish, 2004b). It is very difficult to quantitatively demonstrate the effectiveness of treatment without baseline data, so administering outcome measures at the initiation and termination of treatment is critical to conducting meaningful outcomes assessment.

On the other end of the continuum are cases where patients are experiencing crises, and assessing and monitoring their functioning are done on a continual basis. When individuals are having severe problems with suicidality, substance abuse, or other issues that involve significant risks of harm to self or others, they may require continual observation and monitoring. The monitoring might be done by staff in an inpatient psychiatric unit or outpatient treatment facility or by family and friends, but continual monitoring and assessment may be needed to ensure the safety and security of the patient until the crisis resolves.

Readministering outcomes assessment measures regularly across treatment is now recommended for behavioral health care practice (Fortney et al., 2017; Lambert, 2010; Ogles, 2013). This approach has major benefits. Monitoring treatment progress by regularly administering outcome measures helps patients become more familiar with their symptoms and recognize influences on their symptoms and functioning. It can aid in communication between the patient and therapist and increase collaboration. It can help identify the significant number of patients who do not improve or who actually deteriorate during treatment, something that therapists do not reliably identify themselves without this addition information. Treatment intensity in these cases might be increased, consultations or referrals might be made, or other changes can be implemented that may prevent a significant number of treatment failures. When patients are not improving in an expected manner given their diagnoses and circumstances, it is critical to also reevaluate one's assessment of the case. Many factors might account for the lack of treatment progress (e.g., physical disease that is causing psychological symptoms or a history of child abuse or current substance abuse the patient has not revealed).

An initiative of the National Institute for Health and Care Excellence (NICE) in the United Kingdom began providing screening and treatment for depression and anxiety on a national basis in 2008. Attempts are made to screen all patients in the National Health Service for anxiety and depression, and patients referred for treatment for these issues are then given brief instruments that are readministered at each patient contact. In one of the pilot sites for the program, pre- and posttreatment scores were available for 99% of patients who completed at least two sessions in the program, while the second pilot site had these scores for 88% of patients (Clark, 2011). This approach to outcomes assessment is very useful for evaluating the effectiveness of treatment in individual cases as well as the national effort as a whole. Aggregated outcomes data from these two sites showed very large treatment effect sizes ranging from 0.98 to 1.26 (see also Fonagy & Clark, 2015 for more comprehensive data).

Follow-up

Posttermination follow-up is essential to appropriate care in many behavioral health care cases. This is particularly true for patients who have dealt with more serious problems and problems characterized by high relapse rates. For example, follow-up, ongoing monitoring of functioning, and repeated evaluations of the need for recurrent treatment can all be critical to appropriate care for individuals who experience chronic suicidality (e.g., individuals who have attempted suicide more than once; Joiner, 2005; Linehan & Dexter-Mazza, 2008; Rudd, 2006) or substance dependence (Hazelton, 2008).

In all behavioral health care cases, maintaining treatment gains for months and years after treatment has ended is generally much more meaningful in patients' lives than making treatment gains that do not last long after termination or discharge. Therefore, follow-up assessment of treatment outcomes can provide the most important and meaningful measurement of the outcomes of therapy (Maruish, 2004b). Mailing or emailing patients at, for example, three or 6 months posttreatment can provide very useful follow-up data, though this request for information will likely result in a low response rate by itself. A mailing can be followed up with a phone call to the initial nonresponders to increase the response rate. Even when patients choose not to respond, it can be important that they know that their therapist is concerned about their well-being and is available to offer support and treatment if needed. It is very easy to provide follow-up assessments in integrated primary care settings. Indeed, long-term follow-up and monitoring of past treatment progress are inherent features of patient-centered medical home models of care (see the next chapter).

Benefits of outcome measurement

The biopsychosocial approach to behavioral health care revolves around meeting the behavioral health and biopsychosocial needs of patients. Its scientific basis emphasizes reliable and valid measurement while its ethical basis emphasizes high quality, safe, and effective treatment. Therapists should be sensitive about not reducing the complexity of people's lives to scores on simple outcome measures. But they also need to be sensitive about scientific requirements involving accurate measurement of important variables, the evidence that therapists may be poor judges of whether patients are not improving or are deteriorating, the evidence that significant numbers of these cases turn around once they are identified, and reasonable expectations for accountability from all the stakeholders involved. The effectiveness of services is particularly important to patients, their therapists, and therapist supervisors. Treatment effectiveness affects people very directly and meaningfully in the "real world" where distress, functioning, and well-being make a huge difference in people's lives. For all these reasons and more, therapists need to consider the benefits of integrating systematic outcomes assessments into their routine clinical practice.

Some of the research findings noted in this chapter challenge standard clinical thinking. It is clear that significant numbers of patients do not improve as a result of treatment, and that therapists may not be good judges of which patients do not improve or those that deteriorate. Therapists clearly also vary in their effectiveness, and this can be assessed through the outcomes data provided by their patients. Research also suggests that informally discussing the effectiveness of treatment with patients, as has long been normal practice with many types of psychological and psychopharmacological treatment, is inadequate for evaluating its effectiveness. If research continues to support these findings, failing to incorporate outcomes monitoring into standard treatment may eventually be viewed as substandard practice (Lambert, 2010). All clinicians should be committed to ensuring quality care, improving clinical practice, strengthening clinical science, and maintaining the profession's ethical commitment to quality services. Therapists therefore also need to keep abreast of the research in this area.

The benefits of routine progress monitoring and measurement-based care are becoming clearer as research accumulates. At this point, the current literature recommends a number of means for performing outcomes assessment in routine behavioral health care practice. A list of best practices in this area would likely include the following:

1. *Select global, condition-specific, and individualized outcome measures that provide information relevant for the individual case.* Global functioning is often a priority, whereas target symptoms and behaviors are more likely to be measured with condition-specific and individualized measures.
2. *Collect baseline data to aid in interpreting results.* Outcomes cannot be fully interpreted without baseline data.
3. *Use standardized, normed, and psychometrically sound global and condition-specific instruments* so that data obtained are more interpretable and normative comparisons are possible.
4. *Brief instruments that are quickly administered and scored are generally preferred.* Time, cost demands, and clinical utility are important in virtually all types of clinical practice.
5. *Gaining information from multiple sources is often critical for obtaining reliable data,* particularly when treatment focuses on externalizing issues or the patient's functioning in social roles (e.g., at home, work, or school as well as in the community).
6. *Readministering measurements over the course of treatment is very useful for monitoring progress and making adjustments as needed.* For example, the weekly readministration of outcome measures often will identify cases showing no improvement or deterioration, and a significant number of these cases can be turned around and positive outcomes achieved.
7. *Follow-up is generally important but is especially important when patients have dealt with issues involving high rates of relapse or risks of harm to self or others.*
8. *Outcome data should be aggregated for quality improvement purposes.* It is difficult to reliably identify strengths or areas for improvement without aggregated data. Therapists should aggregate data from their individual practices, and programs should aggregate at the program level. Researchers should aggregate across systems both for quality improvement purposes and to be able to inform health care professionals, payors, accreditors, and the public generally about the effectiveness of behavioral health care.

Making full use of treatment outcome data has the potential to significantly improve the effectiveness of behavioral health care. Routine outcome measurement has already shown promise for preventing treatment failures. Greater use of these data may also improve the training and supervision of therapists. These data can also be aggregated on large scales across practice networks and provider systems to allow researchers to examine the characteristics of effective psychological treatment for different types of patients with different disorders, circumstances, vulnerabilities, and strengths. Measurement improvements will likely also result from the use of new psychometric methods such as item response theory and Rasch modeling, and possibly neuroimaging and stress hormone measurement (Ogles, 2013). These research programs will almost certainly lead to a more thorough and detailed understanding of behavior change processes, more effective treatment, greater patient satisfaction with services, improved cost-effectiveness, and more effective training and supervision. The behavioral health care field can move beyond the point where it focuses primarily on demonstrating the effectiveness of its interventions in general. The field is now ready to also focus on systematically ensuring the effectiveness of treatment in individual cases.

Case Example: Monitoring treatment outcomes with a mildly depressed patient

The case of Jessica, the 41-year-old mildly depressed female patient, was discussed in the last three chapters. This was a particularly successful case where the patient made significant improvement in several areas over the 3 months of treatment. In her last session, Jessica noted that she was very glad that she gotten back into better physical shape. She now exercises regularly and has lost 20 pounds. Her alcohol consumption has dropped significantly and she has more energy. She said she hadn't realized how the weight gain and being out of shape had affected her self-esteem. She said she also now feels more physically attractive to her husband and has become involved athletically with her children in the way that she had originally imagined before she had children. She also reports that her depressive feelings have left almost completely. She reports enjoying being on the parent advisory committee at her children's school and has met many interesting people in that group. Knowing them has made her feel significantly more connected to the community as well.

Jessica reports that she is beginning to have a completely different relationship with her mother. She said that she and her mother have had very honest conversations about Jessica's orientation to her career and approach to parenting. She said that her father even acknowledged knowing about her mother's own torn feelings toward her own education and career and that he also thought she was too critical of Jessica.

Jessica reported that she has been interested in the possibility of pursuing management positions in her hospital because she thinks there are several improvements that should be made. She and her psychologist discussed when she might explore those interests and they agreed that it could be unwise to pursue them at least until her children finished middle school.

After reflecting on the changes that had occurred since her first visit, the psychologist refers back to the original biopsychosocial assessment summary that he and Jessica completed during their first session and to her scores across sessions on the clinic outcomes questionnaires. The scores indicate steady improvement into the nonclinical range in both depression and anxiety where she has remained over the last month. The psychologist asks Jessica what she would consider to be her current level of functioning in each of the biopsychosocial areas and he enters dots into the table to indicate the level of functioning posttreatment as compared with pretreatment (indicated by checks in Table 12.1). Following this discussion, Jessica and the psychologist decide to terminate treatment, though Jessica says she will contact him if her progress reverses or questions arise. The psychologist asks if it is okay if he calls her in 1 month to follow up on how she is progressing.

Table 12.1 Pre- and posttreatment assessment of biopsychosocial functioning for the case example (checks represent pretreatment and dots represent posttreatment).

Biopsychosocial Domains and Components	***-3 Severe need***	***-2 Moderate need***	***-1 Mild need***	***0 No need***	***+1 Mild strength***	***+2 Moderate strength***	***+3 Major strength***
Biological							
General physical health			✓			●	
Childhood health history				✓ ●			
Medications				✓ ●			
Health habits and behaviors		✓					●
Psychological							
Level of psychological functioning		✓				●	
History of present problem			✓		●		
Individual psychological history			✓ ●				
Substance use and abuse			✓	●			
Suicidal ideation and risk assessment				✓ ●			
Effects of developmental history			✓	●			
Childhood abuse and neglect				✓ ●			
Other psychological traumas				✓ ●			
Mental status examination							✓ ●
Personality styles and characteristics				✓		●	

Continued

Table 12.1 Pre- and posttreatment assessment of biopsychosocial functioning for the case example (checks represent pretreatment and dots represent posttreatment).—cont'd

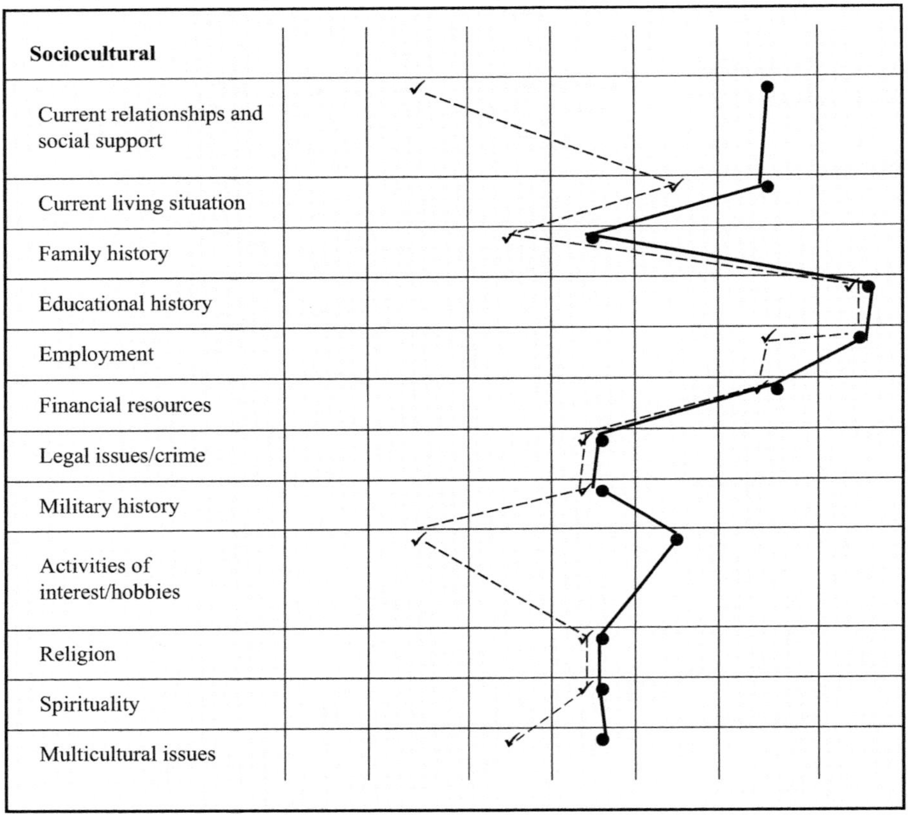

Part Four

Additional implications for health service psychology

Public health and integrated primary care

13

This chapter addresses the broader perspectives on behavioral health care that are becoming higher priorities within public health, health care systems, and health service psychology specifically. These perspectives aim to improve the health of the population as a whole in terms of both preventing health problems from developing in the first place and assessing and treating them more universally within primary care after they do occur.

A century ago, disease, disability, and death were still major fears and preoccupations for much of the world's population, in wealthy countries as well as poor ones and for the wealthiest and most privileged as well as everyone else. Just one century ago, the "Spanish" flu of 1918–19 is estimated to have infected one-third of the world's population and killed between 50 and 100 million people worldwide (Taubenberger & Morens, 2006). This brought back fears of the even deadlier Black Death (or Great Plague), one of the worst pandemics in human history that is estimated to have killed between 30% and 60% of Europe's population in the middle of the 14th century (Alchon, 2003). Public health measures have been so extraordinarily successful that people in most parts of the world today have forgotten how fundamentally and dramatically the human experience of life and death have been transformed over the last century and a half.

The public health field has a long history that spans many disciplines. Early on, it focused primarily on infectious disease. But issues involving behavior and mental health have grown to be top priorities in recent decades. Its broad perspective on improving the health of the whole population is also being incorporated more fully into health care systems in recent years. The difficulty and cost of reversing health problems after they develop is now clear. Public health measures and integrated primary care can prevent dysfunction and illness from developing as well as promote biopsychosocial health and resilience. As a consequence, these approaches can greatly reduce the enormous burden that behavioral and physical health problems pose for individuals, their families, and society generally.

This chapter outlines the basic principles of public health and provides an overview of integrated primary care. The term "population health" is often used to refer to many of the same topics covered by public health. Population health typically focuses on the health outcomes of a community or a nation, including the distribution of those outcomes within the group and disparities between subgroups (Kindig & Stoddart, 2003). Public health likewise focuses on the health outcomes of a community or nation, but the term is often used to also refer to the activities of public health professionals such as epidemiological research and the development of prevention measures and policy recommendations. The historical disagreements about these issues among

Foundations of Health Service Psychology. https://doi.org/10.1016/B978-0-12-816426-6.00013-X

experts in population and public health are not important for the purposes of the present chapter. Instead, both terms are used to refer to the health of the general public.

This chapter will focus on the basic principles involved in public health before outlining integrated primary care approaches. The following topics will be included:

- Public health
  - the remarkable history and effectiveness of public health
  - key features of public health
  - measuring public health
  - prevention
  - effectiveness of prevention
- Integrated primary care
  - primary care as the de facto behavioral health care system
  - integrated health care models

The remarkable history and effectiveness of public health

For most of human history, disease was essentially synonymous with epidemic (Turnock, 2015). Epidemics of plague, leprosy, cholera, smallpox, typhoid, tuberculosis, and yellow fever devastated communities, were not understood, could not be controlled, and simply had to be endured. Death from these diseases was almost unimaginably horrible and unbearable compared with what most people experience today. Starting with the Scientific Revolution, however, diseases gradually began to be understood, and the public health field emerged in the mid-1800s. We are still in the midst of the truly revolutionary benefits that the public health movement has had on human experience. Our physical and social lives, and even our psychological experience of life, continue to be transformed as a result of the public health field.

Human life expectancy in the U.S. in 1900 was 47 years, having risen by only small amounts over previous centuries. One century later, however, it had risen to 77 years (Arias, 2004). Infectious diseases were still the dominant threat to human health around the globe in 1900, but the scientific understanding of disease and implementation of public health measures began to dramatically reduce that threat. Edward Jenner discovered a vaccine for smallpox in 1797, and John Snow traced an outbreak of cholera to a single water well on Broad Street in London in 1854. That same year he also noticed that water drawn from the Thames River upstream from London was not associated with cholera while water drawn downstream from London was. As these findings became accepted, public health measures involving sanitary water systems and vaccinations were implemented and infectious diseases began to subside.

The death rate for infectious diseases in the U.S. fell dramatically over the course of the 20th century. The rate was approximately 800 per 100,000 individuals in 1900 and steadily declined until the influenza pandemic of 1918 when it rose to nearly 1000. It continued to drop thereafter, however, and fell to around 50 per 100,000 individuals by midcentury, where it has stayed since (CDC, 1999, 2009). Most deaths due to infectious disease now involve influenza in elderly individuals. Other infectious diseases have been nearly or completely eliminated. For example, the number of cases of measles in the U.S. was estimated at 503,282 in 1900 and fell to 43 in 2007; the number of cases of diphtheria was 175,885 in 1900 and fell to 0 in 2007; the number of cases of mumps was 152,209 in 1900 and fell to 800 in 2007; the number of smallpox infections was estimated at 48,164 in 1900 and fell to 0 in 2007; and the number of cases of paralytic poliomyelitis was 16,316 in 1900 and fell to 0 in 2007 (CDC, 1999, 2009). (The number of cases of measles and mumps has risen slightly over the last decade, however, due to a small minority of parents who refuse vaccinations for their children.)

The dramatic improvements in human health over the past century and a half are often mistakenly attributed to improvements in medicine. But public health measures have actually played a much larger role. In 1959, the biologist Dubos noted that "No major disease in the history of mankind has been conquered by therapists and rehabilitative modes alone, but ultimately only through prevention." McKeown (1965) similarly concluded that "health has advanced significantly only since the late 18th century and until recently owed little to medical advances." Bunker, Frazier, and Mosteller (1994) found that only 5 years of the 30-year increase in life span over the 20th century was the result of improved medical treatment—the rest was attributable to prevention efforts. In a study of years of life gained in England and Wales from 1981 to 2000, 79% of the increase was attributed to reductions in risk factors, whereas only 21% was attributed to modern medical treatments (Unal, Critchley, Fidan, & Capewell, 2005).

Another concern that heightens the importance of prevention involves the very high cost of health care, particularly in the U.S. The average per capita amount spent on health care across the 36 countries in the Organisation for Economic Co-operation and Development (OECD) was $3992 in 2018 (OECD, 2019). (The 36 OECD member countries are among the high-income nations in the world, mostly in Europe and North America). Far more money is spent on health care in the U.S. per capita ($10,586 in 2018; the next closest country was Switzerland at $7317) and as a proportion of gross domestic product (16.9% in 2018; the next closest country was Switzerland at 12.2%) than in any of the other 35 nations in the OECD (2019). This level of spending is widely viewed as unsustainable.[1]

Despite having the most expensive health care in the world, outcomes involving population morbidity and mortality in the U.S. are nonetheless relatively low. Fig. 13.1 plots the average life expectancy in the 36 OECD countries against per capita expenditures on health care in "international dollars" (i.e., purchasing-power parity dollars adjusted for relative purchasing power across countries; OECD, 2019). The average life expectancy in the U.S. in 2018 was 78.6 years, which ranked 28th out of the 36 OECD countries. Other indicators of long, healthy, and productive lives are also lower for the U.S. than those for many other developed countries. The *World*

[1] This concern has received less attention in the news media in the U.S. since the passage of the Affordable Care Act in 2010, in part because the law included provisions designed to reduce increases in health care costs. Nonetheless, the sustainability of the level of spending on health remains a major concern in the U.S. and most of the OECD countries.

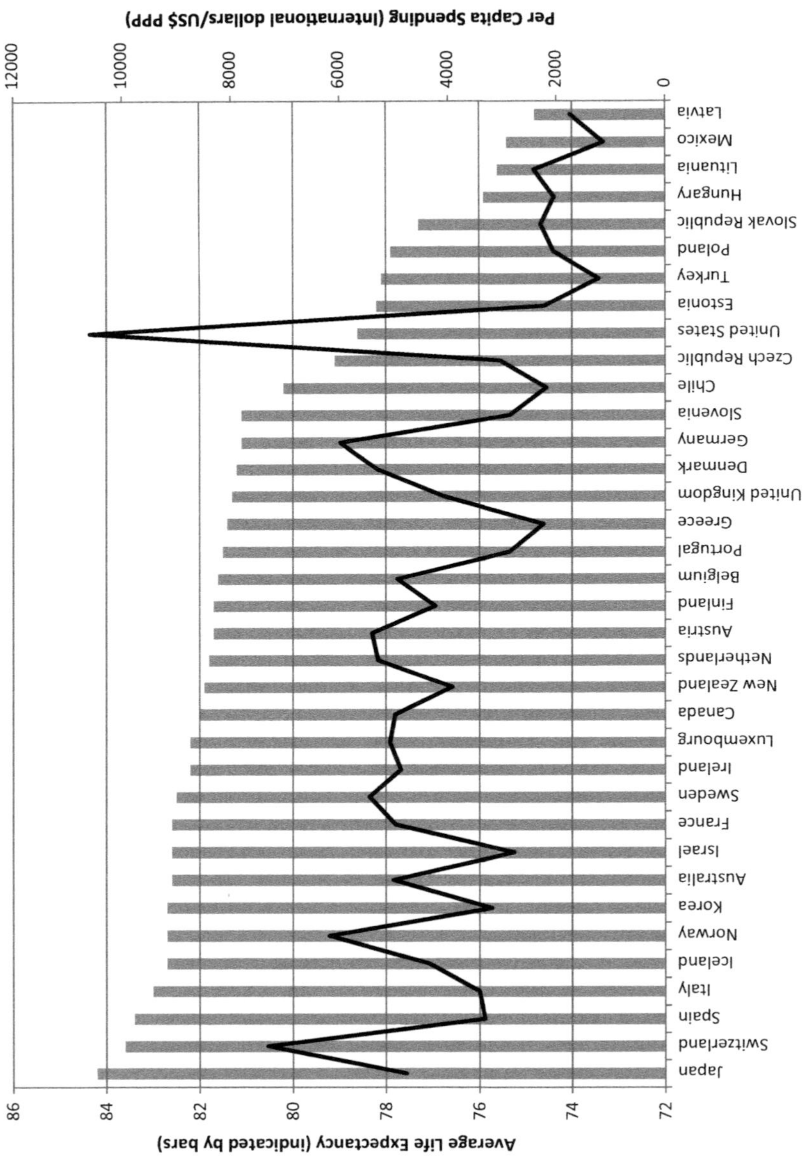

Figure 13.1 Average life expectancy and per capita health care spending in 2018 for Organisation for Economic Co-operation and Development (OECD) countries (OECD, 2019).

Health Report 2000 found that the U.S. ranked 37th in overall health among all countries in the world (World Health Organization, 2000).

Key features of public health

Several key features of public health make it a unique and complex field. First, it is grounded squarely in science. Unlike medicine or psychology (which was studied as "mental philosophy" for many centuries before the term "psychology" was used), public health did not exist before the 19th century. Epidemiology, the basic science of public health that involves the quantitative analysis of disease patterns, was an entirely new science with no history of past practices, conventions, or traditions. Instead of having prescientific origins, the field of public health was established after the experimental methods of science were invented and so has always been entirely science-based.

A second key feature of public health is that its primary purpose has been prevention (Turnock, 2015). Prevention is widely valued and appreciated, but it involves making things **not** happen. As a result, the field suffers from having no large natural constituency that advocates for prevention. The main beneficiaries of many preventive interventions are very young or have not yet been born.

A third important feature of public health is its foundation in social justice (Beauchamp, 1976; Krieger & Brin, 1998; Turnock, 2015). Social justice views public health as a public good. As discussed in Chapter 4, justice is concerned with the equitable distribution of the benefits and burdens of society. Health and access to health services are generally considered social benefits, and both require collective action on the part of others to provide them.

The social justice underpinnings of public health lead to a fourth important feature, which is its inherently political nature. The social justice foundations of the field inevitably lead to political conflict. Public health requires collective action to serve populations, and there are major political differences in how these actions and goals are valued. Public health measures require government to enforce public policies regarding sewage and water systems, pollution control, infectious disease control, drug efficacy and safety, food production and sale, workplace safety, gun and public safety, and many other issues that are frequently politically contentious. Individuals often agree regarding the general goals of greater public health and safety but disagree strongly regarding the means to achieving those goals.

A fifth feature of public health is its expanding agenda and scope (Institute of Medicine, 1994, 2002). Before 1900, infectious diseases were the focus of public health measures. The health problems and needs of mothers and children were added to that agenda in the early 20th century, and chronic disease prevention and medical care became important foci in the middle of the century. Later, substance abuse, teen pregnancy, mental illness, HIV infection, and violence were added to the agenda. After the terrorist events that occurred on September 11, 2001, including the anthrax scare that followed, bioterrorism preparedness became another public health priority in the U.S. The importance of behavior and lifestyle in public health has grown steadily over the history of the field.

This expanding scope and agenda of the public health field is reflected in a sixth feature, which is its highly diverse interdisciplinary culture. The field relies heavily on epidemiologists and biostatisticians, but a wide variety of other professionals play important roles, including physicians, nurses, dieticians, economists, political scientists, lawyers, sociologists, anthropologists, psychologists, social workers, engineers, gerontologists, and disability specialists. The large majority of professionals working in public health do not hold public health degrees, and so the field could be viewed more as a movement than a profession (Turnock, 2015).

Measuring the health of the public

Epidemiology requires accurate data, but measuring the health of the public is not straightforward. Measuring infectious and acute diseases is relatively easy because these diseases typically are objectively defined states. Measuring positive states of health and well-being, however, include subjective components that go well beyond the absence of disease and disability. Both the *quality* of health and the *quantity* of life span and disease are essential considerations.

Morbidity and mortality

Mortality is the most commonly reported indicator of health because these data are usually the easiest to obtain. This is ironic, however, because mortality (i.e., death) is neither a measure of health nor disease and is only an indirect indicator of the health of a living population (Turnock, 2015). Data on morbidity (i.e., illnesses, injuries, and functional limitations) provide another important perspective on the health of a population but are not as readily available as mortality data. Although morbidity and mortality data provide critical perspectives on the health of a population, they both provide only indirect indications of quality of health. As has been mentioned several times before in this volume, the absence of disease and disability (and death) does not imply health.

Alternative measures

Years of potential life lost (YPLL). A variety of alternative measures of health have been developed to compensate for the limitations of the indirect measures of morbidity and mortality. One of the most common involves computing YPLL, a summary measure of premature mortality. This measure is based on mortality data but gives greater weight to deaths that occur at a younger age. Based on an arbitrary age (75 is the most commonly used), years of life lost due to different causes of death are computed. An infant death contributes 75 years to the measure, a suicide at age 20 contributes 55 years to the measure, and death by cardiac arrest that occurs at age 73 contributes just 2 years to the measure. This measure gives a different perspective on the health of a population than a simple ranking of the most frequent causes of death. As seen in Table 13.1, unintentional injuries, comprising primarily drug overdoses and motor vehicle deaths, rise to the top in terms of YPLL because these accidental deaths tend to occur at relatively young ages. But unintentional injuries actually rank fourth in terms of the frequency with which they occur in the population without adjusting for YPLL. Suicide and homicide also rise to the top five using this measure, whereas they are ranked 9th and 12th when using a simple count of their frequency in the population.

Disability-adjusted life-year (DALY) and burden of disease. Another measure that attempts to capture quality-of-life considerations is the DALY, which combines self-reported health status and activity limitations with mortality data. This measure is often discussed in terms of the *burden* that disease has on a population. This perspective is very useful because many conditions have a serious impact on functioning but do not cause death (e.g., schizophrenia, cerebral palsy, arthritis).

The first major use of the DALY measure was in the Global Burden of Disease study by Murray and Lopez (1996) that provided a very different view of the impact of disease and of mental illness in particular. The study was updated by WHO in 2008,

Table 13.1 Years of potential life lost (YPLL) before age 75 in the U.S. in 2016 by cause of death, and ranks for YPLL and number of deaths (National Center for Health Statistics, 2018).

Cause of death	YPLL	Rank by YPLL	Rank by number of deaths
Unintentional injuries	1,334,000	1	4
Drug overdose	663,000		
Motor vehicle deaths	432,200		
Cancer	1,262,400	2	2
Heart disease	958,900	3	1
Suicide	438,900	4	9
Homicide	275,000	5	12
Chronic liver disease and cirrhosis	188,000	6	11
Diabetes mellitus	177,700	7	21
Chronic lower respiratory disease	175,800	8	3
Cerebrovascular diseases (stroke)	164,200	9	5
Influenza and pneumonia	79,900	10	8

Note: Years lost before age 75 per 100,000 individuals younger than 75 years of age. See Table 7.1 for data on number of deaths.

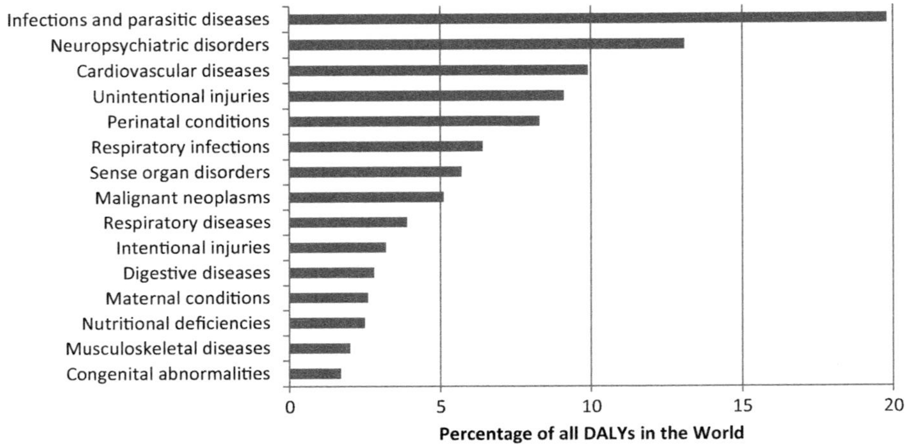

Figure 13.2 Disability-adjusted life-years (DALYs) by category in the world, 2004 (World Health Organization, 2008b).

and its findings are summarized in Fig. 13.2 by disease category. For the world as a whole, infectious and parasitic diseases accounted for 19.8% of all DALYs followed by neuropsychiatric conditions, which accounted for 13.1%.

Another approach to measuring the DALY concept finds that Americans on average have a life expectancy of 78, living their last 9 years with poor health, 12 years with activity limitations, and 35 years with a chronic disease. The same pattern emerges for life expectancy at age 65—Americans who reach age 65 live on average another 19 years, 5 of those years in poor health, 7 years with activity limitations, and 16 years with a chronic disease (National Center for Health Statistics, 2012).

Prevention

The primary purpose of public health is the prevention of problems and disease that threaten the health and well-being of the population. Epidemiology is the basic science that provides information about the prevalence and distribution of these problems. But in order to be useful for prevention, epidemiology must also provide information about risk factors that can be targeted for prevention and whether preventive interventions are successful in reducing the prevalence of a disease or disorder.

The term "risk factor" was invented in the 1950s when the Framingham (Massachusetts) Heart Study found that cardiovascular disease did not have a single cause but many different contributing factors that increased risk for the disease. Some risk factors are generally not malleable to change, such as genetic inheritance or gender, while some are relatively easily changed, such as lack of social support or being victimized by bullying (Durlak & Wells, 1997). Even disorders with very high heritability are sometimes modifiable as a result of changing the environment. For example, phenylketonuria is one of the few genetic disorders that can be very effectively controlled in this way. Unidentified and untreated phenylketonuria can lead to serious irreversible brain damage including behavioral retardation and seizures, but early detection and avoiding foods high in phenylalanine (e.g., breast milk, dairy products) can be completely successful for avoiding these problems (Centerwall & Centerwall, 2000). Most behavioral disorders, however, have a far more complex etiology, and identifying the causal risk factors involved is much more complicated.

Protective factors are internal or external influences that improve an individual's response to a risk factor. Supportive parents or other adults from the community are important external protective factors against the development of many maladaptive outcomes in children (National Research Council and Institute of Medicine, 2009). Resilience is an important internal protective factor that improves individuals' responses to stressors or traumatic events across their life spans (Garmezy & Rutter, 1983).

Many behavioral health problems share many of the same risk factors, and experiencing multiple risk factors has particularly negative effects for individuals' development and functioning (see Chapter 8). Rutter (1979) was the first to show that as the number of risks children face increases, their developmental status decreases. In a nationally representative sample of infants and toddlers investigated for child maltreatment, only 5% of children who experienced maltreatment alone or with one additional risk factor had a measurable developmental delay in their cognitive, language, or emotional functioning (Barth et al., 2008). But as the number of risk factors increased, the proportion with developmental delays rose quickly: 44% of those exposed to four risk factors had developmental delays; 76% of those exposed to five risk factors had developmental delays; and 99% of those exposed to seven risk factors had measurable developmental delays (see Fig. 8.1).

Prevention efforts often aim to reduce risk factors (Institute of Medicine, 1994). After the interaction of risk and protective factors for particular problems has been clarified, research generally focuses on identifying the causal risk factors that are malleable and potentially alterable through intervention. Once these factors are identified, preventive interventions can be designed and the effects of those interventions can be evaluated, ideally through preventive intervention trials.

Basic approaches to prevention

The principles of prevention were first applied to control infectious diseases through the use of mass vaccination, water safety, and other public health measures. These principles were later applied to chronic diseases and behavioral disorders (Institute of Medicine, 1994). The prevention of chronic diseases and behavioral disorders is typically much more complicated than preventing infectious diseases, however, because infectious diseases have specific causes while the causes of chronic and behavioral disorders tend to be far more multifactorial and complex.

Definitions of the general categories of public health preventive interventions were developed over a half century ago (Commission on Chronic Illness, 1957). Primary prevention referred to the prevention of a disease before it occurred; secondary prevention referred to the prevention of recurrences or exacerbations of a disease that had already been diagnosed; and tertiary prevention referred to the attempt to reduce the amount of disability caused by a disease.

These definitions are less applicable in the case of behavioral health, however, so the Institute of Medicine in 1994 recommended modified definitions of the different levels and types of prevention. They made essentially no change to the definition of *primary prevention*, which refers to interventions that help prevent the initial onset of behavioral disorders. Instead of secondary prevention, *treatment* was used to refer to the identification and treatment of individuals with behavioral disorders. In addition, *maintenance* was used to refer to interventions designed to reduce relapse and provide rehabilitation for those with behavioral disorders. The Institute of Medicine further distinguished between *universal*, *selective*, and *indicated* preventive interventions. These are distinguished by the population groups targeted for intervention, namely (1) the population in general; (2) groups at greater-than-average risk for developing problems, or (3) groups identified through a screening process designed to detect individuals who exhibit early signs of the problem. These different types of prevention strategies and interventions are summarized in Table 13.2.

The first two levels of primary prevention strategies noted above are well known (e.g., a universal prevention program offered to all children in a school to resist substance use or bullying; a selective prevention program offered to children who

Table 13.2 Basic types of preventive strategies and interventions.

Commission on Chronic Illness (1957) definitions:

- Primary prevention—interventions to prevent a disease before it occurs
- Secondary prevention—interventions to prevent recurrences or exacerbations of a disease that has already been diagnosed
- Tertiary prevention—interventions to reduce the amount of disability caused by a disease

Institute of Medicine (1994) definitions applied to behavioral health:

- Primary prevention—same as above—interventions to prevent a disease before it occurs
- Treatment—the identification and treatment of individuals with behavioral disorders
- Maintenance—interventions to reduce relapse and provide rehabilitation for those with behavioral disorders

Types of primary preventive interventions based on target group:

- Universal—the population in general
- Selective—groups at greater-than-average risk for developing problems
- Indicated—groups identified through a screening process designed to detect individuals with early signs of a problem

National Research Council and Institute of Medicine (2009) addition to the above:

- Health promotion—interventions to enhance individuals' abilities to achieve developmental competence and well-being experienced child abuse or community violence). One of the best-known indicated preventive interventions is the SBIRT model (mentioned in Chapter 5 in terms of stepped models of intervention) used to identify and assist individuals at risk for substance abuse. (SBIRT stands for ***S**creen, **B**rief **I**ntervention, Brief Treatment, and **R**eferral for **T**reatment.*) This intervention is being used with all patients in a growing number of inpatient and outpatient medical settings so that early intervention can be provided for those who are not dependent on substances but who may be engaging in problematic substance use (SAMHSA, 2019a). As part of routine medical practice, brief substance abuse screening instruments are used to identify those at moderate risk for substance abuse. Brief interventions are then provided to increase awareness of substance use patterns and consequences and to motivate people to reduce harmful drinking. More comprehensive brief treatment is provided when moderate to high risks are identified, and a referral to specialty treatment is provided when severe risk or dependence is identified.

As the prevalence of infectious disease was reduced dramatically in the first half of the last century, attention began to shift toward health and well-being. Focusing on well-being in addition to the prevention of illness and disorder became more widely accepted, and the National Research Council and Institute of Medicine added *health promotion* in 2009 to reflect the growing interest in developing competency and resilience and in fostering well-being. They offered the following definition: "Mental health promotion includes efforts to enhance individuals' ability to achieve developmentally appropriate tasks (developmental competence) and a positive sense of self-esteem, mastery, well-being, and social inclusion and to strengthen their ability to cope with adversity" (p. 67). Health promotion strategies aim to identify and strengthen protective factors such as supportive family, school, and community environments that enhance well-being and help children and adults avoid adverse emotions and behaviors (National Research Council and Institute of Medicine, 2009). As competence, resilience, and psychological well-being improve, individuals are better able to respond adaptively to stressors and influences that might otherwise lead to dysfunction.

Effectiveness of preventive interventions

The effectiveness of preventive interventions for reducing mental health disorders and maladaptive behavior was controversial for decades, similar to how the effectiveness of psychotherapy had been debated. Skepticism about the effectiveness of preventive interventions for behavioral health problems persisted until the late 1990s when, as in the case of psychotherapy, a meta-analysis was conducted that finally answered the question.

In 1997, Durlak and Wells conducted the first large-scale meta-analysis of controlled outcome studies of preventive interventions. They examined 177 studies designed to reduce adjustment problems and promote behavioral health in children and youth by focusing on parent training, divorce adjustment, school adjustment, awareness and expression of emotions, and interpersonal problem-solving skills.

They found that all categories of programs were associated with positive effects with mean effect sizes ranging from 0.24 to 0.93 (which are similar to, and often higher than, those achieved by many educational, medical, and psychotherapeutic interventions). Meta-analyses conducted since then have found that preventive interventions are effective with diverse problem behaviors. After conducting a comprehensive review, the National Research Council and Institute of Medicine (2009) concluded:

> *"A number of specific preventive interventions can modify risk and promote protective factors that have been linked to important determinants of mental, emotional, and behavioral health, especially in such areas as family functioning, early childhood experiences, and social skills. Interventions are also available to reduce the incidence of common disorders or problem behaviors, such as depression, substance use, and conduct disorder. Some interventions reduce multiple disorders and problem behaviors as well as increase healthy functioning" (pp. 2–3).*

The United Kingdom undertook a pioneering effort a decade ago to decrease depression and anxiety disorders on a nationwide basis (see Chapter 10). The program screens all individuals entering the health care system and then offers evidence-based psychological treatments to those with depressive and anxiety symptoms (Clark et al., 2009). Systematic assessment and a stepped level of care model are used to inform the level of intervention implemented. At low levels of depression, self-help activities with guidance from a *psychological wellbeing practitioner*, computer-assisted cognitive behavior therapy, psychoeducational groups, and structured physical activities are available. Higher-intensity services for moderate to severe depression can include cognitive behavior therapy, interpersonal therapy, and medication (Clark, 2011). Preliminary data on the effectiveness of this initiative are promising (e.g., effect sizes of 0.98–1.26 have been found across a range of outcome measures; Clark et al., 2009; Fonagy & Clark, 2015). Of those who had at least two contacts with a health care provider, 55% were considered recovered in terms of their depression and anxiety scores both falling below the clinical cutoff at posttreatment.

The suffering and pain experienced by individuals and families dealing with behavioral health disorders are of course enormous, and these disorders are also very costly in monetary terms. Focusing on only the costs of mental, emotional, and behavioral disorders among young people up to age 24, an analysis conducted for the National Research Council and Institute of Medicine (2009) found that the total cost of these disorders was approximately $247 billion in 2007. The estimated cost of providing mental health services was $45 billion, and the rest was attributable to costs related to health, productivity, and crime. Focusing only on lost income, Kessler et al. (2008) found that individuals with serious mental illness had personal incomes far below those with no mental illness. They estimated the loss of personal earnings associated with serious behavioral illness at $193.2 billion in 2002. Considering only the direct costs of treating mental illness and the personal income loss associated with mental illness, these two factors combined equaled approximately 2% of the entire gross domestic product of the U.S.

Research on the cost-effectiveness of preventive interventions suggests they can be very beneficial. Durlak and Wells (1997) found that preventive interventions focused on physical health promotion, early childhood education, and childhood injury saved between $8 and $45 for every dollar spent. More recent investigations have found smaller but still-substantial economic benefit from these types of programs. Three long-term studies of early childhood programs for low-income children found returns of $4 to $9 for every dollar invested (Heckman, Moon, Pinto, Savelyev, & Yavitz, 2010, p. 17; Karoly, Kilburn, & Cannon, 2005; Masse & Barnett, 2002). Savings for the public included reduced special education, welfare, and crime costs, while participants followed into adulthood had increased earnings. After reviewing the available research, the National Research Council and Institute of Medicine (2009) concluded that "Of those few intervention evaluations that have included some economic analysis, most have presented cost-benefit findings and demonstrate that intervention benefits exceed costs, often by substantial amounts" (p. 259).

Integrated primary care

Despite the dramatic success of public health measures for reducing disease and improving health in the U.S., the extraordinary cost and disappointing outcomes of American health care became a widespread concern as the last century came to a close. The Institute of Medicine's reports of the early 2000s (IOM, 2000, 2001, 2003a, 2003b) brought attention to widespread problems with patient safety, and many of these could be attributed to lack of communication and collaboration among health care providers. The Institute of Healthcare Improvement succinctly captured the concerns about problems with American health care into three priorities that they referred to as the *Triple Aim.* This approach has since become widely known and the three priorities are (1) improve the patient experience of care; (2) improve the health of populations; and (3) reduce the per capita cost of health care.

Integrated care models have been widely advocated as potential solutions for making progress on the Triple Aim. The Institute of Medicine's reports (2000, 2001, 2003a) called for better coordination and team-based care. The World Health Organization (2008a, 2018) also concluded that integrated primary care is the best approach for meeting individuals' health care needs in developing as well as wealthy countries around the world. The Affordable Care Act passed in 2010 also prioritized integrated care as a solution to problems with health care cost, quality, and access.

The passage of the Patient Protection and Affordable Care Act of 2010 represented the largest expansion and regulatory overhaul of the American health care system since the passage of Medicare and Medicaid in the 1960s. This legislation is also having a dramatic effect on behavioral health care. The Affordable Care Act specifically encourages integrated primary health care approaches where behavioral health care is provided as part of comprehensive care in the same setting. Integrated health care has a long history in the U.S. but had limited influence until the passage of this legislation. Integrated care is now beginning to be viewed as a necessary transition for addressing the problems with cost and effectiveness in health care.

Origins of integrated care in the United States

The history of integrated care in the U.S. begins with the Mayo Clinic. A devastating tornado struck Rochester, Minnesota in 1883, and Dr. Mayo and others in the city realized that the local medical care systems were completely inadequate for meeting the health care needs of the area. To address those needs, a hospital was built over the next several years and Dr. Mayo's sons, who had entered medicine in the 1880s, began working closely with their father in their new clinic and hospital. The sons later invited several other physicians to join them, and the group eventually developed the world's first integrated, team-based approach to health care focused on providing the best quality of care possible. The physicians were salaried to reduce the financial incentive to see large numbers of patients, and their clinics and hospitals went on to provide some of the best-quality medical care in the nation (Fye, 2010).

Mental health was not included in early health care plans in the U.S. In fact, up through the 1950s, no health plan paid for psychotherapy. Kaiser Permanente offered a large integrated health care plan starting in the 1940s in California. The organization instituted the first prepaid psychotherapy benefit in the late 1950s after finding that 60% of patient visits to a physician were for somatic stress and other emotional factors (Follette & Cummings, 1967). The psychologist Nicholas Cummings wrote that first benefit plan, and Kaiser Permanente later found it to be remarkably successful, resulting in a 65% reduction in cost utilization (Cummings, Cummings, & Johnson, 1997). Other plans soon followed, and mental health care became routinely covered in both public and private health care plans across the country.

Mayo Clinic and Kaiser Permanente are very large systems that provide health care to millions of individuals, but the largest provider of integrated health care in the U.S. has been the Department of Veterans Affairs (Trivedi & Grebla, 2011). (There are about 18 million veterans in the U.S., and the Veterans Administration serves about half of those.) As a result of the successes of those systems and the requirements of the Affordable Care Act, a large number of public and private health care systems began to offer integrated care over the last decade.

Primary care as the de facto behavioral health care system

As the data from previous chapters amply show, behavioral health conditions have a major impact on individuals' health and well-being and are a major reason that people seek health care services. Half of all Americans meet the criteria for a mental disorder during their lifetimes, and one-quarter during the previous year (Kessler et al., 2005). Chronic medical conditions are also highly prevalent and often associated with co-occurring behavioral disorders as well. Over one-half of the American population (and 60% of adults) deals with a chronic medical condition (Buttorff, Ruder, & Bauman, 2017). The Institute of Medicine (2004) concluded that approximately half of all morbidity and mortality in the U.S. is caused by behavior and lifestyle. Not only are behavioral health disorders highly prevalent, but behavior and lifestyle are also major parts of the clinical picture for many individuals with medical disease. From the biopsychosocial perspective, these findings are not surprising.

To appreciate the role of primary care in meeting the health needs of the population, one needs to be aware of the distinctions between primary, secondary, and tertiary care. Primary care refers to the services normally provided when patients first have a health problem. This level of care is usually offered in community-based clinics where care is provided by general practitioners who are focused on all the health needs of the whole person. When primary care providers have patients with more complicated and serious problems, they may refer them to specialists who can provide more intensive and specialized secondary care. This would include the services of cardiologists, rheumatologists, obstetricians, physical therapists, psychotherapists, and psychiatrists. Secondary care also includes acute hospital care such as visits to an emergency department or services for childbirth, medical imaging, and intensive care. Tertiary care provides even higher levels of specialized care that are usually hospital-based and requires more complicated procedures and equipment (e.g., cardiac surgery, cancer treatment, burn treatment, neurosurgery). Health psychologists have long worked as part of the teams offering secondary and tertiary care because of the major psychological aspects of the problems addressed and treatments provided. But relatively few psychologists have worked in integrated primary care settings.

Large numbers of psychologists have provided specialty mental health services (i.e., secondary care), but the majority of individuals with mental health problems who receive treatment actually rely on primary care providers for meeting their behavioral health needs. In fact, the role of nonpsychiatric mental health specialists in providing treatment actually declined from the early 1990s to the early 2000s while the proportion of patients with behavioral health issues treated by general primary care providers increased (Kessler, Demler, et al., 2005; Wang, Demler, Olfson, Wells, & Kessler, 2006). Out of the total number of individuals who received outpatient mental health care, the proportion who received psychotherapy alone declined form 16% in 1998 to 11% in 2007, while those who received medications alone increased from 44% to 57% (Olfson & Marcus, 2010). In addition, as many as 80% of all psychotropic medications are prescribed by nonpsychiatric physicians, nurse practitioners, and physician assistants (Mark, Levit, & Buck, 2009).

Primary care has long been recognized as the de facto behavioral health care system in the U.S. (Bray, 1996; Regier, Goldberg, & Taube, 1978). A 2010 CDC survey found that 20% of all primary care physician visits were associated with mental health care (i.e., a mental health screen or treatment was provided, a mental health diagnosis or "reason for visit" was made, or a psychotropic medication was prescribed). The percent varied from less than 6% for children younger than 12% to 31% for adults aged 75 years or older (Cherry & Schappert, 2014). Although many patients have mental health concerns, psychologists and other behavioral health care professionals provide relatively little of this care, and many patients' behavioral health problems are undiagnosed or undertreated as a result (Blount et al., 2007). Physicians, physician assistants, and nurse practitioners provide the vast majority of the behavioral health care in primary care settings. These professionals are very well trained in physical medicine, but their training in the evaluation, treatment, and management of behavioral health problems is often limited. Consequently, there are major needs for health service psychologists to become more involved in primary care settings. Given the potential of integrated, collaborative health care to address problems with cost, patient satisfaction, and quality, it is likely that integrated care will continue to grow.

Integrated care is especially important for individuals with serious mental illness. Rates of morbidity and mortality among those with serious mental illness in the U.S. are tragically high, particularly in the public health system where the average lifespan is 25 years shorter than in the general population (National Association of State Mental Health Program Directors, 2006). The National Association of State Mental Health Program Directors (Miller & Prewitt, 2012) identified integrated health care as a top priority for addressing this alarming state of affairs. They noted that "Evidence demonstrates that physical and behavioral health problems often occur at the same time. Integrating services to treat both will yield improvement in clinical outcomes and quality of life and the best possible results, and the most acceptable and effective approach for those being served" (p. viii). They further emphasize that co-occurring substance abuse treatment needs to be integrated into primary care because of the high prevalence of co-occurring mental health and substance use disorders among individuals with serious mental illness.

Coordinated, integrated health care models

Several different approaches to collaborative and integrative health care have been used across health care systems. Hunter, Goodie, Oordt, and Dobmeyer (2009) describe these as falling on a continuum. At one end is the *coordinated care model* where primary care providers and behavioral health specialists work in separate facilities delivering separate care and exchanging information regarding patients as needed. In the middle of the continuum is the on-site or *co-located care* model where behavioral health and primary care providers deliver separate care but work in the same set of offices or in the same building, sometimes sharing office staff and waiting rooms and communicating with other providers face-to-face regarding patients. In this and the coordinated care models, primary care providers typically refer patients for behavioral health care treatment and separate records and treatment plans are maintained, and the multidisciplinary professionals working with patients do not work as a cohesive team and do not intentionally integrate their care (Kelly & Coons, 2012). At the high end of the collaborative continuum described by Hunter et al. (2009) is the *integrated care model* where behavioral health providers are full members of the primary care team, all of whom communicate, collaborate, and coordinate on all aspects of patient care. The team addresses the full spectrum of the patient's needs and one treatment plan and medical record are maintained.

In 2010, the U.S. Congress passed the Patient Protection and Affordable Care Act to address the fragmented and uncoordinated health care delivery system in the U.S. and improve health outcomes, improve quality and efficiency, and reduce the rate of growth in health care costs. The survival of this milestone legislation has been in doubt, but implementing the legislation has already resulted in a significant transformation of the U.S. health care system. This legislation preserves the U.S. system of private, employer-based health coverage, but it includes several major changes such as government-financed testing of new, more efficient health care delivery models; revamped payment systems; expansion of pay-for-performance; wellness and preventive care; and levels of transparency and accountability that were never before required.

Central to the Affordable Care Act are new health care delivery models. The legislation strongly supports the development of Accountable Care Organizations and patient-centered medical homes (PCMHs). These two innovations are both designed to achieve the Triple Aim of improved population health, lower costs, and better patient experiences in health care (Berwick, Nolan, & Whittington, 2018). The PCMH model is the most widely implement approach to improve primary care and seeks to increase the focus on patient-centered, coordinated, team-based care (Kazak, Nash, Hiroto, & Kaslow, 2017). A 2017 survey found that nearly half (49%) of family physicians are now working in a PCMH practice (American Academy of Family Physicians, 2017). Research evaluating the effectiveness of the PCMH model is still limited, but a recent review found that use of the approach did generate cost savings and higher quality in terms of health status, health promotion, preventive services, and chronic disease management (Jabbarpour et al., 2018).

Psychotherapists' views regarding the purpose and nature of primary health care are beginning to change. Although very large numbers of Americans receive behavioral health care from their primary care providers, many psychotherapists still view primary care as mainly responsible for physical health care. Many psychologists see themselves as specialists who accept referrals for mental health treatment and provide their services separately from medical care, ordinarily with only limited consultation with primary care providers in some cases. Education and training in behavioral health care typically takes this perspective as well. But primary care is increasingly viewed as a biopsychosocial (rather than a biomedical) field responsible for both behavioral and physical health care needs. From this perspective, individuals with behavioral health needs receive their care within the primary care setting unless their problems required more intensive treatment and a referral to secondary or specialist care (Bluestein & Cubic, 2009; Nordal, 2012).

Behavioral health professionals interested in working in integrated primary care settings also need to appreciate that the practice setting is very different from specialized mental health care (Bluestein & Cubic, 2009; Bray et al., 2009; Cummings et al., 1997; Hunter et al., 2009; Kelly & Coons, 2012). Caseloads are normally large and involve diverse concerns, including highly complex cases and disorders. Patients are often routinely screened with brief assessment instruments for common issues such as depression, anxiety, and substance abuse, and the results are quickly scored and brief interventions and/or referrals are made. Assessment and treatment sessions may last only 15 minutes and follow-up sessions may take place when the patient returns for appointments with another member of the team. Sometimes other team members conduct the follow-up sessions. Patients may be seen in examination rooms shared between team members instead of in one's own consultation office. Interruptions may be common. Recommendations to patients are often problem-focused and handouts for handling common issues are frequently provided. Interactions between providers are often fast paced, and communication and documentation are typically very succinct and require familiarity with medical terms and abbreviations. The conceptualization of cases is biopsychosocial in orientation with strong emphasis on evidence-based practice. This approach to practice is quite different from the training received in many behavioral health care programs.

Interprofessional training

In order to provide effective integrated care, health care professionals need to collaborate and coordinate their efforts in well-functioning teams centered around the needs of patients. With the exception of Mayo Clinics and some other health systems, this approach to practice has not been the norm in American health care. In order for professionals from a variety of disciplines to effectively provide integrated care for patients' physical and behavioral health needs, open communication and true collaboration are essential. This requires improved interprofessional training across all the professions involved.

To help develop interprofessional skills for providing effective integrated care, the Interprofessional Education Collaborative (2011) developed a list of core competencies for all health care professionals. These competencies fall within the domains of values and ethics for interprofessional practice, roles and responsibilities, interprofessional communication, and teams and teamwork. A variety of professions incorporated these competencies into their accreditation guidelines and standards. The Interprofessional Education Collaborative began with 6 national health care education associations and grew to 21 by 2017, including the APA. In 2017, the APA Commission on Accreditation incorporated interprofessional education competencies into the latest version of its Standards of Accreditation for health service psychology programs.

Improving human health and functioning

The population health perspectives discussed in this chapter have great potential for further improving human health and functioning. The public health field has already played a transformative role with regard to health and disease around the world. The remarkable effectiveness of public health measures for reducing acute and infectious disease has resulted in what has been referred to as the *epidemiological transition* (Gribble & Preston, 1993), and the benefit to humankind has been enormous. No other intervention has had a comparable effect in reducing suffering, disease, disability, and death. This is certainly true with regard to physical health, but the role of public health measures could be much greater for behavioral health as well. No widespread disease or disorder has ever been controlled or eliminated through the individual treatment of those who had the disease or disorder (Dubos, 1959; McKeown, 1965). Given that more than one-quarter of Americans have a behavioral health disorder in any given year, and one-half have one or more disorders over their lifetimes (Kessler et al., 2005), a massive amount of resources would be needed to treat all those individuals.

And even if those resources could be made available, the evidence does not suggest that behavioral disorders would be controlled or eliminated as a result. Instead, major reductions in behavioral problems and disorders may depend on the implementation of preventive public health measures.

There was enthusiasm about the potential of public health to reduce behavioral health problems in the U.S. in the late 1980s and early 1990s as prevention research advanced and behavioral health prevention became a national priority. That excitement soon abated, however, as the political climate shifted and prevention became a lower priority for the federal government in the second half of the 1990s (Mrazek & Hall, 1997). Although federal funding for prevention research and intervention stalled at that point, the potential of public health measures to reduce behavioral health problems remains. Preventing the huge costs and burdens of behavioral problems and disorders should be both a humanitarian and economic priority for the health care professions and for society in general. George Albee, the leading researcher and advocate in the behavioral health prevention field, argued this case for a half century. Two years before he died in 2006, Albee addressed the Third World Conference on the Promotion of Mental Health and Prevention of Mental and Behavioral Disorders and presented his conclusions about the importance of behavioral health prevention:

1. "One-on-one treatment, while humane, cannot reduce the rate of behavioral disorders …
2. Only primary prevention, which includes strengthening resistance, can reduce the rate of disorders. Positive infant and childhood experience are crucial. Reducing poverty and sexism are urgent strategies.
3. Ensuring that each child is welcomed into life with good nutrition, a supportive family, good education, and economic security will greatly reduce emotional distress …
4. Cultural differences in diagnoses must be understood and be part of program planning.
5. Strong differences of opinions about causes—particularly brain disease versus social injustice—must be resolved by unbiased scientific judgment before real progress can be made." (Albee, 2006, p. 455, p. 455.)

Specifically becoming more involved in primary care presents health service psychology with a tremendous opportunity to provide more prevention and early intervention services for behavioral health problems as well as participate more in the treatment of physical health problems and promote biopsychosocial health and well-being in general. Psychologists have long been engaged in providing secondary specialist care. But primary care has been the de facto behavioral health care system in the U.S., and it is likely to become even more so as health care becomes more biopsychosocial in orientation. Medical health care was still heavily biomedical in orientation a couple decades ago but has shifted significantly toward a more holistic biopsychosocial orientation that integrates behavior and psychological functioning under the umbrella of care. During this time, the role of behavior and lifestyle in physical health has also become clearer. Cognition, affect, and behavior play critical roles in health and functioning across the biopsychosocial domains, and the need for a fuller integration of psychosocial factors into all of health care is urgent.

Psychologists have long been involved in integrated health care within the Veterans Administration, Kaiser Permanente, and other organizations, but they were not included in many of the other integrated primary care models that have proliferated in American health care in recent years (Kelly & Coons, 2012). It is critical that health service psychologists advocate for the interests of patients and get involved in these systems. Medical professionals are well trained to meet patients' physical health needs but receive less training in behavioral health care. Patients' behavioral health problems and needs can go unnoticed and undertreated as a result. Getting more involved in primary care presents health service psychologists with a huge opportunity to help improve the prevention and treatment of psychosocial problems as well as improve maintenance care for those with chronic mental health disorders (Kazak et al., 2017). Psychologists can also help improve patient adherence to medical treatments for physical health problems. Opportunities for improving the health and well-being of the whole person and the whole population are substantial. Failing to get more involved in primary care will result in a diminished role for health service psychology in health care as other professions take more responsibility for assessing and treating patients' behavioral health needs. This would, of course, result in fewer employment opportunities for psychologists as well.

As the movement toward integrated care proceeds, psychology also needs to reconsider the education and training of its practitioners so that psychologists develop the interprofessional knowledge, skills, and dispositions needed to work in integrated care settings while our unique expertise and perspective are maintained (Belar, 2012; Bray et al., 2009; Johnson, 2013; Rozensky, 2011). There will continue to be an important role for independent specialty psychotherapy practice. But as more people receive health care through accountable care organizations and PCMHs, these opportunities may decrease. To remain relevant and vital, health service psychology needs to get involved and adapt to the evolving nature of health care.

The science-based biopsychosocial approach to behavioral health care education and practice advocated in this volume provides the conceptual perspective needed for providing preventive services and practicing in integrated primary care settings. On the other hand, adherence to traditional orientations for providing psychotherapy does not provide the necessary perspective for providing these services or working in these settings. Knowledge of health, dysfunction, and disorder has grown dramatically, and health care is becoming increasingly biopsychosocial in orientation. Health service psychology has a great deal to offer in terms of preventing health problems from developing, assessing and treating them when they do occur, improving health care quality and efficiency, and promoting the health and well-being of the whole person and the population as a whole.

A new era for health service psychology

14

The behavioral sciences have progressed dramatically in recent decades. For millennia, comprehensively understanding human psychology was seemingly beyond our grasp. Ever since the cognitive revolution about 70,000 years ago when we developed language, humans undoubtedly debated things like, for example, why one's cousin treated one's brother the way she did, why he then reacted the way he always does, and why they keep causing so much trouble for each other. They undoubtedly argued about whether women and men were really inherently different psychologically, and whether the differences they saw were merely the result of different life experiences or were true biological differences. Since they lived very close to other animals, both physically and in terms of their life circumstances as hunter-gatherers, they undoubtedly discussed how different they actually were from other animals. They probably wondered about meaning, purpose, and the nature of a good life. Before the distractions of modern culture and technology, one can imagine that their conversations were often very lengthy.

After the Neolithic Age when agriculture was invented (about 10,000 years ago), society and culture of course changed again dramatically as we began to leave our hunter-gatherer lifestyle behind. More organized, doctrinal versions of religions were invented (as opposed to the experiential, shamanic religions typical of hunter-gatherers) that allowed strangers to trust each other at a basic level for the first time in human history. This allowed humans to cooperate for the first time on very large scales between thousands and eventually even millions of strangers. Life began changing at a much faster pace as more and more plants and animals were successfully domesticated, technology developed, and economies grew.

After several millennia of gradual progress in technology and culture, the Scientific Revolution occurred and human life began changing far faster. When we were hunter-gatherers, life went on for generations with basic things literally never changing. After the discovery of agriculture and civilization, gradual change occurred, although much remained the same from one century to the next. But things started changing dramatically with the Scientific Revolution—our understanding of the world changed with the publication of each new major scientific paper or book! Those who were clever and entrepreneurial enough were also turning scientific discoveries into new technologies, goods, and services, some of which were very useful or popular and sometimes very profitable as well, and the wealth that was generated was simply amazing. Whereas all of nature once seemed completely mysterious and often foreboding, physics, chemistry, and biology began unlocking nature's secrets, and nature turned out to be much less threatening than people had believed. A new, positive Enlightenment attitude emerged that viewed progress and improvement in the human experience as real possibilities.

Foundations of Health Service Psychology. https://doi.org/10.1016/B978-0-12-816426-6.00014-1

As the 19th century came to a close, even the nature of the human mind and brain seemed like it might be uncovered. Darwin had explained the development of the animal world in a fascinating new manner that was consistent with the evidence. If evolution was accurate and humans evolved from the apes, what did that imply for human psychology? (Darwin (1859) also predicted that an evolutionary perspective was necessary for understanding the nature of human psychology.) We now understand the human mind and consciousness as emergent properties of the biological brain, but across history, higher-order mental processes remained nearly total mysteries to us. Human behavior was simply inexplicable. We humans are amazingly intelligent *and* unintelligent, not only across individuals but often *within* the same person as well. We are also the nicest *and* the nastiest species on earth. We are often amazingly kind and generous to family, friends, and sometimes complete strangers and even enemies, but our cruelty at other times seems to know no boundaries, sometimes even for those we love. We are so varied in our talents, interests, proclivities, personalities, and psychopathology that it is difficult to even talk about *human* nature (in the singular) because we seem to have so many different *natures*.

But science was beginning to uncover the structure and function of the human mind and brain. Wilhelm Wundt, William James, Sigmund Freud, and the other early scholars of human psychology in the late 1880s may have been reminded that the nature of the sun, moon, and stars were nearly total mysteries until Copernicus and Galileo had explained them just three centuries before; the nature of gravity, light, and motion were mysteries until Newton had explained them two centuries previously; and the similarities and differences between the species were a mystery until Darwin had explained them just a quarter-century before. Perhaps science would allow the nature of the human mind and brain to be revealed as well.

The achievements of Wundt, James, Freud, and others were certainly remarkable, and their work can still offer insights to readers who encounter them for the first time even now, more than a century later. But the inadequacies of the first theoretical orientations proposed for explaining human psychology are not surprising in retrospect. The higher operations of the human mind and brain were simply too complex to explain using the scientific tools available at the time. It was not reasonable to expect the first scientists to unravel the unimaginably complicated interrelationships among the 86 billion neurons and their 100 trillion dendritic connections in what is now understood to be the most complicated system in the universe. This would be like expecting Newton and his contemporaries to explain the subatomic structure of atoms or expecting Darwin and his colleagues to explain the human genome using the scientific knowledge and instruments available during the time they lived. Although Wundt, James, and the other founders of scientific psychology were well aware of this problem, it was perhaps inevitable that a diverse array of theories for explaining human psychology would be proposed because of the strong urge to understand mental life, alleviate distress and suffering, pursue excellence, and optimize well-being. The theories proposed sometimes provided important insights into human emotion, thought, and behavior, but it was perhaps inevitable that the early ones were incomplete and sometimes completely mistaken.

The scientific understanding of the human mind and brain that has recently emerged continues to grow steadily. We now have proximate and ultimate explanations for a large number of psychological processes. These explanations have revealed an amazingly intricate and wonderfully complicated system that is simply astoundingly complex. But that is because human nature is so tremendously complex. An important starting point for understanding this body of literature is the biopsychosocial framework that captures the fundamental levels of natural organization necessary for understanding human psychology. Almost all psychological outcomes are multifactorially determined based on complex biopsychosocial developmental processes. Understanding physical, psychological, and social health and functioning all require this basic perspective. Given that psychological outcomes are multifactorially determined, it is also not surprising that multiple psychologically, socially, and biologically based interventions have been shown to result in improved psychological functioning.

Of course, many aspects of human psychology are not well understood at this point, and it is critical not to overstate what is known about the human mind and brain. Many processes are only understood in outline form, and detailed knowledge of the mechanisms and tremendously complex interactions that produce those processes may take decades to unravel. (The same is true of many aspects of biology and medicine as well.) It would, of course, be completely irresponsible to overstate the level of our present knowledge. Humans (including psychologists) have done this many times before, frequently with very negative consequences, and we need to guard against repeating these human tendencies. Psychologists have specifically incorporated requirements to accurately convey psychological knowledge and information into our ethics code (APA, 2010 Ethics Code 2.03, 5.01, 7.03(b)).

But it is also important not to understate what is currently known about human psychology. A survey of current scientific knowledge reveals that a great deal is known about many aspects of development, cognition, emotion, neuropsychological functioning, the factors that give rise to healthy development and psychopathology, and many other processes. The field has also developed a range of prevention and early-intervention strategies and psychotherapeutic treatments that are quite effective for preventing and relieving distress, promoting health, and improving functioning. Indeed, the effectiveness of these interventions compares favorably with many medical and other human services interventions. Applying these strategies and interventions appropriately in clinical practice and as part of public health interventions can prevent and alleviate major amounts of distress and suffering and improve functioning for large numbers of people. The ethical principles underlying health care suggest that these interventions should be made as accessible as possible. The profession has a lot to offer the public in this regard.

To offer health care in a responsible, ethical manner as a clinical science, practitioners must ensure that their practice rests squarely on the scientific and ethical foundations of the field. Extensive research into moral reasoning and behavior demonstrates the ease with which humans engage in automatic biased thinking, cheating, and dishonest behavior; the relative difficulty of rational analytical thinking; and the importance of practices and structures that help limit those tendencies. It is therefore critical that the principles of respect for autonomy, nonmaleficence, beneficence, and justice along with moral character are integrated into all aspects of behavioral health care education, practice, and research. The clinical sciences, along with all human services professions and institutions, need to have very solid foundations in professional ethics.

Health service psychology also needs to be firmly grounded in science. The preceding chapters show how this might be accomplished based on the current state of the scientific literature. The reader is reminded that the evidence-based biopsychosocial approach advocated here is fundamentally different from traditional practices involving the personal selection and application of a theoretical orientation to case conceptualization and clinical practice. The traditional theoretical orientations are no longer viewed as sufficient for providing comprehensive scientific explanations of human development or functioning. But many of these orientations are nonetheless still very useful as part of the explanation for midlevel psychological processes (e.g., unlearning maladaptive behaviors) and for conceptualizing therapeutic treatments (e.g., behavior therapy). Standards for reliable and valid measurement and for experimentally testing psychological theories are now much higher than they were when the traditional theoretical orientations were proposed. Theories must now withstand rigorous experimental tests aimed at verification and falsification and also must be consistent with knowledge from across the biological and behavioral sciences. Addressing both ultimate and proximate explanations of human behavior is also expected. As the anatomy and physiology of the human body is unintelligible without evolutionary theory, it is now evident that the same is true for human psychology. Scientific knowledge in the field is now cumulative and consistent across levels of natural organization in a manner it never was before. Psychology has become consistent with the other natural and social sciences precisely as one would expect of any young scientific discipline.

Health service psychology is now ready to proceed based on a unified, scientific understanding of human psychology. Reaching this point represents a true milestone for the field. It allows the field to leave behind much of the divisiveness of the pre-paradigmatic era and move forward under a unified clinical science approach. This has major implications for the future of health service psychology as well.

Implications of a unified clinical science approach to health service psychology

Coming together around a unified clinical science approach to health service psychology will allow psychologists and other behavioral health professionals to address challenges and approach opportunities in a more cohesive, less fragmented manner. It is impossible to predict how this approach will play out. But embracing a unified clinical science approach to health service psychology could result in several exciting developments for the field and for the behavioral health of the general public.

Less competition and greater cohesiveness within the field

The historical practice of selecting one or some combination of the traditional theoretical orientations to guide one's clinical practice naturally led to competition between the theoretical camps. The science-based biopsychosocial approach, on the other hand, quickly renders much of that competition obsolete. From the biopsychosocial perspective, all biological, psychological, and sociocultural processes are important, as are all treatments that have been demonstrated to relieve distress and improve functioning. The perennial conflicts within the field regarding the superiority of particular theoretical orientations, the relevance of research to practice, the superiority of qualitative versus quantitative research, and untested hypotheses regarding the etiology of psychopathology or the mechanisms that account for behavior change all fade in importance when a science-based biopsychosocial approach is applied.

Without the traditional conflicts between the different theoretical camps and schools of thought in psychology, it should be easier to pursue more collaborative approaches to challenges facing the field as well as opportunities to better serve the public. In the past, a huge amount of time and energy was spent arguing for the superiority of favored orientations and the weaknesses of competing approaches. A unified science-based approach avoids these arguments. Hypotheses that cannot be supported through verified, replicated experimental tests are simply not endorsed; they may be interesting possibilities but they do not need to be argued about until they receive empirical support. The overwhelming amount of evidence in support of evolutionary theory and the research that provides ultimate and proximate explanations of human behavior quickly renders many historical conflicts between the theoretical schools moot. Conflicts between advocates of the influence of nature versus nurture, the importance of quantitative versus qualitative research, and the different traditional theoretical orientations quickly become irrelevant in light of current scientific knowledge about human psychology.

Serving more individuals through greater integration into primary care

The evidence-based biopsychosocial approach to health service psychology is compatible with greater integration into health care generally. The big opportunity here involves integration into primary care. Primary care is the de facto behavioral health care system for most individuals with behavioral health care needs. The medical field is also becoming more biopsychosocial in orientation as the role of behavior and lifestyle in physical health becomes clearer. The fact that most people get their behavioral needs met through primary care is therefore perhaps appropriate and natural at this point. But most behavioral health care in these settings is provided by medical professionals, whereas behavioral health care professionals have not been heavily involved. (Health psychologists have often been integrated into secondary, specialist care for many medical problems, and psychologists obviously provide large amounts of specialist care for mental health problems. But psychologists' involvement in primary care has not been widespread.) It is possible that the behavioral health care provided in primary care settings could be improved if more behavioral health professionals were integrated into primary care teams. Large numbers of individuals whose mental health and addiction problems presently go untreated or undertreated might receive better care as a result.

The future of health service psychology will be significantly affected by initiatives to integrate behavioral health care into primary health care settings (see Chapter 13). The Affordable Care Act of 2010 promoted new health care delivery models such as the patient-centered medical home that involve interprofessional team-based care to treat behavioral health disorders, manage chronic conditions, improve medical treatment adherence, and provide preventive interventions. There have been many attempts to repeal or weaken that legislation, so its future remains uncertain. But to the extent that integrated-care models continue to proliferate, psychologists have a lot to offer. The science-based biopsychosocial approach provides a framework that facilitates effective collaboration and communication for working within integrated primary care, whereas traditional theoretical orientations can be very difficult or impossible to implement in primary care settings. The biopsychosocial approach is already familiar to medical professionals, insurers, and other stakeholders. Sharing a general conceptual framework is important for the successful integration of health service psychologists into primary health care.

Greater involvement in prevention and health promotion

Prevention has played a key role in improving the health of humankind. Over the past century and a half, humankind went through the *epidemiological transition*, where the primary causes of disease and death shifted from acute and infectious disease to chronic diseases associated with behavior and lifestyle. The experiences of health, disease, and death have been completely transformed in just the wink of an eye in terms of evolutionary time. But as the prevalence of infectious disease has declined, the prevalence of chronic diseases has risen dramatically.[1] Research suggests that intervention after chronic diseases have developed may play a small role in reducing the overall prevalence of those problems. Prevention, on the other hand, can make a large difference.

The potential of prevention and health promotion in behavioral health is still largely untested. For example, research on trauma and adverse childhood experiences points out the pervasive and highly negative effects of these experiences on mental and physical as well as social, educational, and vocational functioning. What appears to be needed is a thorough paradigm shift toward embracing prevention as a means to reduce the prevalence and impact of behavioral health problems (National Research Council and Institute of Medicine, 2009). This approach was dramatically effective in terms of infectious disease, and research suggests that behavioral health prevention and promotion strategies are effective even though there have been few attempts to implement them on a large scale. The science-based biopsychosocial approach easily

[1] Although recent epidemics of chronic disease around the world are very discouraging, it is important to recall that it is a blessing to be able to develop chronic diseases that result from an overabundance of food, a minimum of physical exertion, and the eradication of infectious disease in comparison to the previous era when few people developed chronic disease.

accommodates the principles of prevention and health promotion, whereas there was not a natural fit between traditional theoretical orientations and the public health perspective. This is an area of great potential for improving the health and well-being of the general population, particularly within the context of primary care. The biggest challenge to moving forward in this way is political will; the scientific knowledge base is already fairly well established.

Improved treatment effectiveness

Research has provided several suggestions for how the effectiveness of treatment can be improved. One line of research finds that treatment effectiveness can be improved through systematic outcomes monitoring (see Chapters 11 and 12). Providing outcomes assessment data to therapists and patients results in more attention being given to cases where no improvement or deterioration is occurring, and significant numbers of these cases consequently turn around. There is also evidence that some patients are not helped due to negative therapist attitudes or personality characteristics, the inept application of treatment, or other negative therapist factors. Graduate training faculty, clinical supervisors, and managers can use evidence-based tools and procedures to address these issues, and the effectiveness of behavioral health treatment will likely improve as a result.

There is also extensive evidence that psychotherapy can be effective over the long term (see Chapter 11). Several meta-analyses have even found that the effect sizes of some therapies were actually larger at follow-up than at treatment termination. Alleviating distress and symptomatology over the short term is certainly an important treatment goal, but resolving problems and improving functioning over the long term is normally the desired goal. More research should be focused on identifying the methods and processes for reliably producing those types of outcomes. Growing concerns about the effectiveness and side effects of some psychotropic medications place priority on treatments that are safe and effective over the long term.

Greater emphasis on well-being

The fundamental changes in human experience associated with the *epidemiological transition* involve fascinating questions that have not yet been thoroughly examined. Nearly a century ago, the eminent economist John Maynard Keynes (1930) noted that the challenge was to figure out how "to live wisely and agreeably and well" (p. 328) once desperation and deprivation are no longer the driving forces of human existence. This challenge has daunting implications for each of us, but answers are still elusive almost a century later.

A very personal measurement can remind us of the seriousness of Keynes's challenge. A typical human heart beats 60 to 100 times a minute, which means we have approximately three billion heartbeats during our life spans. (All mammals on earth live for about 1.5 billion heartbeats. But we modern humans live for about three billion heartbeats, twice the normal number, due to modern medical and public health measures that have roughly doubled our expected life span.[2]) Three billion is a very large number, but it is still limited, and we can be reminded of that number at any moment in our lives by simply paying attention to our heartbeat. (Most readers of this volume have already used up one billion or more of their heartbeats.) This raises the question of what we each will do with our heartbeats.

We are still in the midst of gaining a comprehensive scientific understanding of human health and well-being, so we cannot satisfactorily answer questions about these issues at this point. Particularly when it comes to questions regarding the nature of human wellness and flourishing, we may still be at the early stages of figuring these issues out with certainty. For example, on the one hand, some initial data on those questions present a very discouraging picture. Keyes (2007) estimated that only two in 10 Americans are flourishing and enjoying positive physical and mental health (see Chapter 8). The rest fall on a continuum of moderately poor to very poor health and well-being, certainly a less-than-desirable state for the population as a whole. On the other hand, the research on meaning and purpose in life presents a very different perspective. Heintzelman and King (2014) found that roughly 9 in 10 individuals from societies around the world report that their lives are meaningful, and they feel a sense of meaning and purpose based on their social relationships, experiencing positive emotion, and viewing life as making sense.

Empirical research on this subject is still in its early stages, and there is still much to learn. Disagreements about the nature of wellness and the good life over the last two-and-a-half millennia in the Western world have tended to revolve around the hypotheses put forward by the ancient Greeks. The two main schools of thought revolved around the importance of pursuing pleasure (i.e., hedonia, primarily associated with Epicurus in Ancient Greece) versus the pursuit of a virtuous and fulfilling life where one is able to achieve one's full potential (i.e., eudaemonia, typically associated with Aristotle). But recent research suggests that both perspectives are incomplete. Evolutionary theory suggests that the ultimate goal of living organisms is survival and reproduction, not maximizing happiness, virtue, or fulfillment. If organisms with particular characteristics have greater reproductive success, they leave more descendants, and their characteristics will eventually dominate in a population. The attainment of happiness, virtuousness, or fulfilling one's potential does not necessarily result in adaptive advantages and greater reproductive success (Von Hippel, 2018; Wrangham, 2019). Hedonism and eudaemonia have long been central to debates about well-being and the good life, but evolutionary research shows that humans are highly social animals very focused on a variety of social and other survival goals. As it has with everything else in the organic world, evolutionary theory may overturn centuries of conventional thinking regarding the nature of well-being in human life. More

[2] The average lifespan for all mammals is roughly 1.5 billion heartbeats. West, Woodruff, and Brown (2002) discovered that the speed of mammals' heartbeats is proportional to their physical size (mass). Small mammals' hearts beat very fast and so their 1.5 billion heartbeats occur over a much shorter time period. West's "scaling laws" predict that the human lifespan would be 1.5 billion heartbeats, but our modern average lifespan is roughly twice that length primarily due to modern public health measures. We are the only mammal that does not fall on the normal scale with regard to length of lifespan in heartbeats.

research is needed before these questions can be answered, but the potential benefits from exploring these questions more thoroughly could be monumental and certainly warrant the effort.

Changing human self-identity

The new scientific understanding of human nature is quite different from the ways that human beings have generally viewed themselves in the past. Instead of being special creatures created by a divine being as the creation stories of most cultures have told us, we are merely a human animal similar to other mammals in many ways. We are a very special animal, no doubt! Evolution provided us with a large brain and then language, which allowed us to plan and cooperate far better than any other species. And this, of course, changed everything. We came to dominate all other species on earth, actually causing the extinction of many of them. We have recently burned so much carbon-based fuel that we might even kill off ourselves as well.

This new scientific understanding of human psychology will be profound once its implications fully sink in. For example, one of the most striking characteristics of human animals, like all social species, is that we feel very strong bonds to each other. Before the invention of agriculture, the size of the groups in which we lived was small: camps of around 50 individuals, clans of around 150 individuals, bands of around 500, and a tribe (that shared the same language) of 1500 individuals (Dunbar, 2016). After the emergence of doctrinal religions in the Neolithic Age that allowed strangers of the same faith to hold a basic level of trust in one another, humans could form much larger groups of cooperating strangers that eventually grew to thousands, and in recent centuries to hundreds of millions, of people. Our tendency toward tribalism, to ally within groups, is still *very* strong, be they families, neighborhoods, schools and colleges, states and nations, religions, political parties, vocational and avocational groups, or even athletic teams. A number of especially inspired individuals throughout history have felt and worked for *all* people as members of a single universal group. This was also the aspiration of the political leaders who formed the United Nations and the World Health Organization following the end of World War II, a shocking conflict that demonstrated the potential of our species to end human life on earth through nuclear war. But, sadly, it has been very difficult to persuade more people to this perspective. Nonetheless, clearly humankind has been making great progress in expanding past the bounds of our "natural" inclinations. Further progress along these lines, if ever realized, will dramatically transform life on earth.

Health service psychologists are still in the process of absorbing the implications of the new scientific understanding of human nature. Historically, we too have tended to ally with theoretical camps that often have believed in the superiority of their perspective and concentrated on the faults and weaknesses of other theoretical orientations and methodological approaches. Although we knew that people in general were prone to biases and cognitive heuristics that greatly distorted their perceptions of others and reality, we were slow to see these same mechanisms at work in ourselves. As research over the next decade uncovers more detail about the functioning of the human mind and brain, behavioral health care professionals and society in general may struggle to accept the nature of our highly fallible and vulnerable species. We already know how easily we can be manipulated and deceived, but it may be difficult to incorporate knowledge of these flaws into our social and personal identities.

Addressing urgent challenges of the contemporary world

The future is coming fast, and psychology should feel great responsibility to participate in the decision-making about how to proceed. The popular historian Harari (2018) has identified three urgent existential threats that now face humanity: nuclear war, climate change, and technological disruption. Nuclear war and climate change obviously need to be avoided, whereas scientific and technological advances present many opportunities as well as threats. For example, artificial intelligence and biotechnology are likely to greatly improve medical testing, monitoring, and treatment. Just one example is the use of microsensors placed in our bloodstream to detect cancer well before it causes damage and while it is still easy to treat. Technologies that monitor various biological processes might become relatively inexpensive and could be used universally within populations to monitor the health of individuals and greatly improve early intervention and treatment. But artificial intelligence and robotics will also replace large numbers of workers in many fields, resulting in a class of people with potentially very limited economic and political power.[3]

Scientific and technological changes over the coming decades will present many opportunities and challenges that directly involve human psychology. We will likely learn much more about physical and psychosocial health and well-being, and the potential exists for major improvements in the human condition across the biopsychosocial domains. There will also be developments that present great opportunities but unknown challenges. For example, how might one experience life satisfaction, meaning, and purpose in life if one could live to 150 years of age in good health? Robotics and artificial intelligence are already replacing workers in both low-skilled and high-skilled occupations. Is universal income a viable solution for displaced workers? What might be the implications if people do not need to develop skills or motivations to achieve and excel? Might this work better in adulthood than in childhood? How would one's identity be affected if one's intelligence, mental health, and appearance were chosen through genetic editing (e.g., using CRISPR technology for "designer" babies)? What would be the implications if medications or brain–computer interfaces were used to enhance intelligence and mental performance? Might the biggest class divide in the future be between those who were enhanced compared with those who were "natural"? The psychological implications of these technological advances could hardly be greater. There is certainly great opportunity associated with these coming developments, but also major risks and challenges. Psychology has a

[3] Harari (2018) intentionally referred to this group of people as a "useless class" to be provocative in order to draw people's attention to the seriousness of the issue. He is very concerned about the ramifications of advanced technology for humankind and that politicians, civic and business leaders, and society in general are not discussing these issues with the seriousness they deserve.

great deal to offer in the decision-making about how to move forward in the safest, healthiest, and most effective manner possible.

Interconnectedness of all life and existence

Perhaps the most profound implication of the scientific understanding of human psychology involves the connections it has uncovered to all of humanity, the rest of the organic world, and even the whole of existence. Some of the most remarkable findings of science involve the interconnectedness of life. It was evident to Darwin (1859) that all of life must be interrelated, although it took many decades of research to identify the precise nature of those interrelationships. It has now been verified that all human beings in fact share a common ancestry and consequently also share a common psychology that accounts for both our remarkable strengths and weaknesses as a species. Although culture has changed dramatically in recent centuries, our basic biology, genetic inheritance, and psychological functioning have not changed a great deal. And this is why our brilliant intelligence and ingenuity, but also our major irrationality and neuroticism, are shared by all peoples across the human family. We are only the first generation of humans to understand human psychology from a scientific perspective, and this understanding reveals that humans throughout history have shared many of the very same basic thoughts, feelings, and behaviors.

Science has revealed not only that all humans are related to each other, but also that all animals that have ever lived on earth are related as well. And further, all living organisms, plant and animal, are related as well. Science has shown that life's smallest components, such as proteins and nucleic acids, are universal components of life on earth, and that the genetic code is written the same way across living organisms (see Chapter 3). Darwin's (1859) prediction that every living creature could trace its lineage back to one source has now been verified to a very high degree of certainty (Theobald, 2010). All of life that has ever existed on this earth is actually related at this fundamental level.

And not only is all life on earth descended from a common universal ancestor, but science also shows that the whole universe is fundamentally connected as well. During the Big Bang, tiny particles bound together to form hydrogen and helium. When the early stars became unstable and collapsed, the intense heat and pressure formed heavier particles such as oxygen and carbon that were then spewed out into the universe when the stars exploded. As this process continued, heavier elements such as nitrogen, iron, and all other elements that make up life on earth were formed and dispersed throughout the universe. The most common elements in the universe also turn out to be the most common elements in the human body (Tyson & Goldsmith, 2004). So all the atoms that comprise the mind and body now reading this sentence participated in the Big Bang. If you trace the ancestry of our atoms back far enough, all humans, animals, heavenly bodies, and matter were long ago members of the same "atomic family" that experienced the same celestial spectacle before splitting up to pursue their different life trajectories.

Several religions and philosophies have emphasized the interconnectedness of humanity and all life, but science has now demonstrated this as fact. One can hope that absorbing this knowledge will have a positive, transformative effect on humanity. This knowledge almost necessarily forces one to consider how truly *precious* human consciousness is. The fact that conscious life evolved on this earth is simply astounding. And the fact that human beings further used that consciousness to reveal the extraordinary chain of events that led to the evolution of conscious life turns our existence into something that borders on the miraculous! The significance of these facts strains one's comprehension: that the Big Bang resulted in a planet that could support organic life; that organic life on earth evolved; that we share our fundamental biological components with all other plants and animals on earth; that our hominin ancestors evolved consciousness; and that all human beings are related to each other and actually descended from the same parents. And that the very same stardust that comprises each of us also comprises everything else in the universe. What a truly amazing thing it is to be aware of these facts! The sequence of events that led to us having this awareness is simply astounding. The teeming, restless churning of the human mind has resulted in a great deal of misery, tragedy, and suffering but has also given rise to endlessly fascinating human abilities including exquisite sensibilities and a soaring intellect, the limits of which are still unknown. The rise of conscious life on this earth is certainly one of the most wondrous developments to ever have occurred, at least in our part of the universe. To be able to participate in further realizing the potential of human consciousness is also a true privilege for behavioral health care professionals.

References

Abramowitz, J. S. (1996). Variants of exposure and response prevention in the treatment of obsessive-compulsive disorder: A meta-analysis. *Behavior Therapy, 27*, 385–600. https://doi.org/10.1016/S0005-7894(96)80045-1.

Achenbach, T. M., & Edelbrock, C. S. (1983). *Manual for the child behavior checklist and revised child behavior profile*. Burlington, VT: Department of Psychiatry, University of Vermont.

Acierno, R., Hernandez, M. A., Amstadter, A. B., Resnick, H. S., Steve, K., Muzzy, W., et al. (2010). Prevalence and correlates of emotional, physical, sexual, and financial abuse and potential neglect in the United States: The National Elder Mistreatment Study. *American Journal of Public Health, 100*(2), 292–297.

Ainsworth, M. C. S., Blehar, M. C., Waters, E., & Wall, S. (1978). *Patterns of attachment: A psychological study of the strange situation*. Hillsdale, NJ: Erlbaum.

Albee, G. W. (2006). Historical overview of primary prevention of psychopathology: Address to the 3rd world Conference on the promotion of mental health and prevention of mental and behavioral disorders, September 15–17, 2004, Auckland, New Zealand. *Journal of Primary Prevention, 27*, 449–456. https://doi.org/10.1007/s10935-006-0047-7.

Alchon, S. A. (2003). *A pest in the land: New world epidemics in a global perspective*. Albequerque, NM: University of New Mexico Press.

Altman, J., & Das, G. (1965). Autoradiographic and histological evidence of postnatal hippocampal neurogenesis in rats. *Journal of Comparative Neurology, 124*, 319.

American Academy of Family Physicians. (2017). *Value-based payment study*. Retrieved from http://humananews.com/wp-content/uploads/2017/11/Data-Brief2017_Value-Base_FINAL4.pdf.

American Association of Community Psychiatrists. (2016). *LOCUS: Level of Care Utilization System for Psychiatric and Addiction Services*. Retrieved from https://sites.google.com/view/aacp123/resources/locus.

American Counseling Association. (2014). *Code of ethics and standards of practice*. Retrieved from https://www.counseling.org/resources/aca-code-of-ethics.pdf.

American Medical Association. (1994). Ethical issues in health care systems reform: The provision of adequate Health care. *Journal of the American Medical Association, 272*, 1056–1062.

American Psychiatric Association. (1980). *Diagnostic and statistical manual of mental disorders* (3rd ed.). Washington, DC: American Psychiatric Association.

American Psychiatric Association. (2006). *Practice guidelines for the treatment of psychiatric disorders: Compendium 2006*. Arlington, VA: American Psychiatric Association.

American Psychological Association. (2006). *Health care for the whole person statement of vision and principles*. Retrieved from www.apa.org/practice/hcwp_statement.html.

American Psychological Association. (2009). *Resolution on appropriate affirmative responses to sexual orientation distress and change efforts*. Retrieved from http://www.apa.org/about/policy/sexual-orientation.pdf.

American Psychological Association. (2010). *Ethical principles of psychologist and code of conduct*. Retrieved from https://www.apa.org/ethics/code/.

American Psychological Association. (2012). *Recognition of psychotherapy effectiveness*. Retrieved from https://www.apa.org/about/policy/resolution-psychotherapy.

American Psychiatric Association. (2013). *Diagnostic and statistical manual of mental disorders* (5th ed.). Washington, DC: American Psychiatric Association.

American Psychological Association. (2017a). *Clinical practice guideline for the treatment of posttraumatic stress disorder (PTSD)*. Retrieved from https://www.apa.org/ptsd-guideline.

American Psychological Association. (2017b). *Standards of accreditation for health service psychology and accreditation operating procedures*. Retrieved from https://www.apa.org/ed/accreditation/about/policies/standards-of-accreditation.pdf.

American Psychological Association. (2018). *APA resolution for the use of the term patient in American Psychological Association policies, rules, and public relations activities when referring to the health-related and scientific activities of health service psychologists and scientists in health care services and settings*. Washington, DC: American Psychological Association. Retrieved from https://www.apa.org/about/policy/resolution-term-patient.pdfhttps://www.apa.org/about/policy/resolution-term-patient.pdf.

American Psychological Association. (October 2018c). *Stress in America: Generation Z*. Washington, DC: American Psychological Association. Retrieved from https://www.apa.org/news/press/releases/stress/2018/stress-gen-z.pdf.

American Psychological Association. (2019). *APA clinical practice guideline development*. Retrieved from https://www.apa.org/about/offices/directorates/guidelines/clinical-practice.

American Psychological Association Center for Workforce Studies. (2011). *2011 APA member profiles*. Retrieved from http://www.apa.org/workforce/publications/11-member/index.aspx.

American Psychological Association Commission on Accreditation. (2009). *Guidelines and principles for accreditation of programs in professional psychology*. Washington, DC: American Psychological Association.

American Psychological Association Presidential Task Force on Evidence-Based Practice. (2006). Evidence-based practice in psychology. *American Psychologist, 61*, 271–285. https://doi.org/10.1037/0003-066X.61.4.271.

American Psychological Association Presidential Task Force on the Future of Psychology Practice. (2009). *Final report*. Washington, DC: American Psychological Association.

Anderson, P. W. (1972). More is different. *Science, 177*(4047), 393–396.

Annon, J. S. (1976). *Behavioral treatment of sexual problems*. Hagerstown, MD: Harper & Row.

Antonsen, B. T., Kvarstein, E. H., Urnes, O., Hummelen, B., Karterud, S., & Wilberg, T. (2017). Favourable outcome of long-term combined psychotherapy for patients with borderline personality disorder: Six-year follow-up of a randomized study. *Journal of Psychotherapy Research, 27*(1), 51–63.

Arias, E. (2004). United States life tables, 2001. *National Vital Statistics Reports, 52*(14).

Ariely, D. (2012). *The (honest) truth about dishonesty: How we lie to everyone—especially ourselves*. New York: HarperCollins.

Association for Psychology Postdoctoral and Internship Centers. (2018). *APPIC application for psychology internship*. Retrieved from http://appic.org/match/5_3_match_application.html#PREVIOUSAAPI.

Atherly, A. (2006). In R. L. Kane (Ed.), *Understanding health care outcomes research* (2nd ed., pp. 123–164). Sudbury, MA: Jones and Barlett Publishers.

Bae, C. J., Douka, K., & Petraglia, M. D. (2017). On the origin of modern humans: Asian perspectives. *Science, 358*(6368). eaai9067.

Baldwin, S. A., & Imel, Z. E. (2013). Therapist effects: Findings and methods. In M. J. Lambert (Ed.), *Bergin and Garfield's Handbook of psychotherapy and behavior change* (6th ed., pp. 258–297). Hoboken, NJ: John Wiley and Sons.

Bandolier. (2008). *Statin effectiveness: ASCOT update*. Retrieved from http://www.medicine.ox.ac.uk/bandolier/booth/cardiac/statascot.html.

Bargh, J. (2017). *Before you know it: The unconscious reasons we do what we do*. New York: Touchstone.

Barlow, D. H. (2004). Psychological treatments. *American Psychologist, 59*, 869–878. https://doi.org/10.1037/0003-066X.59.9.869.

Barlow, D. H. (2010). Negative effects from psychological treatments: A perspective. *American Psychologist, 65*, 13–20. https://doi.org/10.1037/a0015643.

Barnes, P. M., Bloom, B., & Nahin, R. L. (December 10, 2008). Complementary and alternative medicine use among adults and children: United States, 2007. *National Health Statistics Report, 12*, 1–23.

Barnett, J. E., & Shale, A. J. (2012). The integration of complementary and alternative medicine (CAM) into the practice of psychology: A vision for the future. *Professional Psychology: Research and Practice, 43*, 576–585.

Barth, R. P., Scarborough, A. A., Lloyd, E. C., Losby, J. L., Casanueva, C., & Mann, T. (2008). *Developmental status and early intervention service needs of maltreated children*. Washington, DC: U.S. Department of Health and Human Services, Office of the Assistant Secretary for Planning and Evaluation.

Bateman, A., & Fonagy, P. (2008). 8-Year follow-up of patients treated for borderline personality disorder: Mentalization-based treatment versus treatment as usual. *American Journal of Psychiatry, 165*, 631–638. https://doi.org/10.1176/appi.ajp.2007.07040636.

Baumard, N., Hyafil, A., Morris, L., & Boyer, P. (2015). Increased affluence explains the emergence of ascetic wisdoms and moralizing religions. *Current Biology, 25*, 10–15.

Baumeister, R. F., & Landau, M. J. (2018). Finding the meaning of meaning: Emerging insights on four grand questions. *Review of General Psychology, 22*, 1–10.

Baxter, L. R., Jr., Schwartz, J. M., Bergman, K. S., Szuba, M. P., Guze, B. H., Mazziotta, J. C., et al. (1995). Caudate glucose metabolic rate changes with both drug and behavior therapy for obsessive-compulsive disorder. *Archives of General Psychiatry, 49*, 681–689.

Beauchamp, D. E. (1976). Public health as social justice. *Inquiry, 13*, 3–14.

Beauchamp, T. L., & Childress, J. F. (1977). *Principles of biomedical ethics*. New York: Oxford University Press.

Beauchamp, T. L., & Childress, J. F. (2013). *Principles of biomedical ethics* (7th ed.). New York: Oxford University Press.

Beauchamp, T. L., Walters, L., Kahn, J. P., & Mastroianni, A. C. (2008). *Contemporary issues in bioethics*. Belmont, CA: Thomson Wadsworth.

Beck, A. T. (1967). *Depression: Causes and treatment*. Philadelphia: University of Pennsylvania Press.

Beck, A. T., Emery, G., & Greenberg, R. (1985). *Anxiety disorders and phobias: A cognitive perspective*. New York: Basic Books.

Beck, A. T., Freeman, A., Davis, D. D., & Associates. (2004). *Cognitive therapy of personality disorders* (2nd ed.). New York: Guilford.

Beck, A. T., Steer, R. A., & Brown, G. K. (1996). *Manual for the beck depression inventory-II*. San Antonio, TX: Psychological Corporation.

Belar, C. D. (2012). Reflections on the future: Psychology as a health profession. *Professional Psychology: Research and Practice, 43*, 545–550.

Belsky, J. (2007). Childhood experiences and reproductive strategies. In R. I. M. Dunbar, & L. Barrett (Eds.), *Oxford handbook of evolutionary psychology* (pp. 237–254). Oxford, UK: Oxford University Press.

Benjamin, L. T., Jr. (2001). American psychology's struggles with its curriculum: Should a thousand flowers bloom? *American Psychologist, 56*, 735–742.

Benjamin, L. T., Jr. (2014). *A brief history of modern psychology* (2nd ed.). Malden, MA: Blackwell.

Bentham. (1834). In J. Bowring (Ed.), *Deontology or, the science of morality*. London: Longman, Rees, Orme, Brown, Green and Longman.

Bergin, A. E. (1966). Some implications of psychotherapy: Negative results revisited. *Journal of Counseling Psychology, 10*, 224–250.

Berlin, L. J., Cassidy, J., & Appleyard, K. (2008). The influence of early attachments on other relationships. In J. Cassidy, & P. R. Shaver (Eds.), *Handbook of attachment: Theory, research, and clinical applications* (2nd ed., pp. 333–347). New York: Guilford Press.

Berwick, D. M., Nolan, T. W., & Whittington, J. (2018). The triple aim: Care, health, and cost. *Health Affairs, 27*(3), 759–769.

Bethell, C. D., Newacheck, P., Hawes, E., Halfon, N., et al. (2014). Adverse childhood experiences: Assessing the impact of health and school engagement and the mitigating role fo resilience. *Health Affairs, 33*(12), 2106–2115.

Beutler, L. E., Malik, M., Talebi, H., Fleming, J., & Moleiro, C. (2004). Use of psychological tests/instruments for treatment planning. In M. E. Maruish (Ed.), *The use of psychological testing for treatment planning and outcomes assessment* (3rd ed., pp. 11–146). Mahwah, NJ: Lawrence Erlbaum.

Biglan, A., Flay, B. R., Embry, D. D., & Sandler, I. N. (2012). The critical role of nurturing environments for promoting human well-being. *American Psychologist, 67*, 257–271.

Blackhall, L. J., Murphy, S. T., Frank, G., et al. (1995). Ethnicity and attitudes toward patient autonomy. *Journal of the American Medical Association, 274*, 820–825.

Blaisure, K. R., & Geasler, M. J. (2006). Educational interventions for separating and divorcing parents and their children. In M. A. Fine, & J. H. Harvey (Eds.), *Handbook of divorce and relationship dissolution* (pp. 575–602). Mahwah, NJ: Lawrence Erlbaum.

Bloom, P. (2016). *Against empathy: The case for rational compassion*. New York: Harper Collins Publishers.

Blount, A., Schoenbaum, M., Kathol, R., Rollman, B. L., Thomas, M., O'Donohue, W., et al. (2007). The economics of behavioral health services in medical settings: A summary of the evidence. *Professional Psychology: Research and Practice, 38*, 290–297. https://doi.org/10.1037/0735-7028.38.3.290.

Bluestein, D., & Cubic, B. A. (2009). Psychologists and primary care physicians: A training model for creating collaborative relationships. *Journal of Clinical Psychology in Medical Settings, 16*, 101–112. https://doi.org/10.1007/s10880-009-9156-9.

Bonham, V. L., Warshauer-Baker, E., & Collins, F. S. (2005). Race in the genome era: The complexity of the constructs. *American Psychologist, 60*, 9–15.

Bonnano, G. A., & Lilienfeld, S. O. (2008). Let's be realistic: When grief counseling is effective and when it's not. *Professional Psychology: Research and Practice, 39*, 377–380.

Bonow, R. O., Mann, D. L., Zipes, D. P., & Libby, P. (2012). *Braunwald's heart disease: A textbook of cardiovascular medicine* (9th ed.). Philadelphia: Elsevier Saunders.

Bowlby, J. (1969). Attachment and loss. In *Attachment* (Vol. 1). New York: Basic Books.

Bowlby, J. (1973). Attachment and loss. In *Separation* (Vol. 2). New York: Basic Books.

Bowlby, J. (1980). Attachment and loss. In *Sadness and depression* (Vol. 3). New York: Basic Books.

Boyd, R., Gintis, H., Bowles, S., & Richerson, P. J. (2003). The evolution of altruistic punishment. *Proceedings of the National Academy of Sciences USA, 100*, 3531–3535.

Bray, J. H. (1996). Psychologists as primary care practitioners. In R. J. Resnick, & R. H. Rozensky (Eds.), *Health psychology through the life span: Practice and research opportunities* (pp. 89–99). Washington, DC: American Psychological Association.

Bray, J. H., Goodheart, C., Heldring, M., Brannick, J., Gresen, R., Hawley, G., et al. (2009). *2009 presidential task force on the future of psychology practice final report*. Washington, DC: American Psychology Association. Retrieved from www.apa.org/pubs/info/reports/future-practice.pdf.

Bringhurst, D. L., Watson, C. W., Miller, S. D., & Duncan, B. L. (2006). The reliability and validity of the outcome rating scale: A replication study of a brief clinical measure. *Journal of Brief Therapy, 5*, 23–30.

Bronfenbrenner, U. (1979). *The ecology of human development*. Cambridge, MA: Harvard University Press.

Bronfenbrenner, U. (2001). The bioecological theory of human development. In N. J. Smelser & P. B. Baltes (Eds.), *International encyclopedia of the social and behavioral sciences* (Vol. 10, pp. 6963–6970). New York: Elsevier.

Brown, A. S., & Susser, E. S. (2008). Prenatal nutritional deficiency and risk of adult schizophrenia. *Schizophrenia Bulletin, 34*(6), 1054–1063.

Brown, D. W., Anda, R. F., Tiemeier, H., Felitti, V. J., Edwards, V. J., Croft, J. B., et al. (2009). Adverse childhood experiences and the risk of premature mortality. *American Journal of Preventive Medicine, 37*(5), 389–396.

Buckley, C. (January 3, 2007). *Man is rescued by stranger on subway tracks*. New York Times.

Bullough, V. L. (1976). *Sexual variance in society and history*. Chicago: University of Chicago Press.

Bunker, J. P., Frazier, H. S., & Mosteller, F. (1994). Improving health: Measuring effects of medical care. *The Milbank Quarterly, 72*, 225–258.

Burlingame, G. M., Seebeck, J. D., Janis, R. A., Whitcomb, K. E., Barkowski, S., Rosendahl, J., et al. (2016). Outcome differences between individual and group formats when identical and nonidentical treatments, patients, and doses are compared: A 25-year meta-analytic perspective. *Psychotherapy, 53*(4), 446–461.

Buss, D. M. (1991). Evolutionary personality psychology. *Annual Review of Psychology, 42*, 459–491.

Buss, D. M. (Ed.). (2005a). *The handbook of evolutionary psychology*. Hoboken, NJ: John Wiley & Sons.

Buss, D. M. (2005b). Introduction. In D. M. Buss (Ed.), *The handbook of evolutionary psychology* (pp. xxiii–xxv). Hoboken, NJ: John Wiley & Sons.

Butler, J. (1990). *Gender trouble: Feminism and the subversion of identity*. New York: Routledge.

Buttorff, C., Ruder, T., & Bauman, M. (2017). *Multiple chronic conditions in the United States*. Santa Monica, CA: Rand Corporation. Retrieved from https://www.rand.org/pubs/tools/TL221.html.

Callahan, R. J., & Callahan, J. (2000). *Stop the nightmares of trauma*. Chapel Hill: Professional Press.

Cann, R. L., Stoneking, M., & Wilson, A. C. (1987). Mitochondrial DNA and human evolution. *Nature, 329*, 111–112.

Carey, J. (January 16, 2008). *Do cholesterol drugs do any good?* Business Week. Retrieved from hppt://www.businessweek.com/stories/2008-01-16/do-cholesterol-drugs-do-any-good.

Carroll, S. (2016). *The big picture: On the origins of life, meaning, and the universe itself*. New York: Dutton.

Cassidy, J., & Shaver, P. R. (Eds.). (2008). *Handbook of attachment: Theory, research, and clinical applications* (2nd ed.). New York: Guilford.

Causadias, J. M., Vitriol, J. A., & Atkin, A. L. (2018). Do we overemphasize the role of culture in the behavior of racial/ethnic minorities? Evidence of a cultural (mis)attribution bias in American psychology. *American Psychologist, 73*, 243–255.

Centers for Disease Control and Prevention. (1999). Public health achievements, United States, 1900-1999. *Morbidity and Mortality Weekly Report, 48*, 621–629.

Centers for Disease Control and Prevention. (2009). Summary of notifiable diseases, United States, 2009. *Morbidity and Mortality Weekly Report, 56*, 1–94.

Centers for Disease Control and Prevention. (2017). *WISQARS Ten leading causes of death.* United States. Retrieved from: https://webappa.cdc.gov/sasweb/ncipc/leadcause.html.

Centers for Disease Control and Prevention. (2018). *Marriage and divorce.* Retrieved from https://www.cdc.gov/nchs/fastats/marriage-divorce.htm.

Centerwall, S. A., & Centerwall, W. R. (2000). The discovery of phenylketonuria: The story of a young couple, two affected children, and a scientist. *Pediatrics, 105*, 89–103. https://doi.org/10.1542/peds.105.1.89.

Chaffin, M., Hanson, R., Saunders, B. E., Nichols, T., Barnett, D., Zeanah, C., et al. (2006). Report of the APSAC task force on attachment therapy, reactive attachment disorder, and attachment problems. *Child Maltreatment, 11*, 76–89. https://doi.org/10.1177/1077559505283699.

Chen, H., Cohen, P., & Chen, S. (2010). How big is a big odds ratio? Interpreting the magnitudes of odds ratios in epidemiological studies. *Journal of Communications in Statistics, 39*(4), 860–864.

Cherry, D. K., & Schappert, S. M. (November 28, 2014). QuickStats: Percentage of mental health-related primary are office visits, by age group—National Ambulatory Medical Care Survey, United States, 2010. *Morbidity and Mortality Weekly Report, 63*(47), 1118.

Chiles, A., & Strosahl, D. (2005). *Clinical manual for assessment and treatment of suicidal patients.* Washington, DC: American Psychiatric Publishing.

Chopik, W. J., Edelstein, R. S., & Grimm, K. J. (2019). Longitudinal changes in attachment orientation over a 59-year period. *Journal of Personality and Social Psychology, 116*(4), 598–611.

Christakis, N. A. (2019). *Blueprint: The evolutionary origins of a good society.* New York: Little Brown Spark.

Cicchetti, D., & Rogosch, R. A. (1996). Equifinality and multifinality in developmental psychology. *Development and Psychopathology, 8*, 597–600.

Cicchetti, D., & Toth, S. L. (1992). The role of developmental theory in prevention and intervention. *Development and Psychopathology, 4*, 489–493.

Cigna. (2018). *New Cigna study reveals loneliness at epidemic levels in America.* Bloomfield, CN: Cigna. Available from: http://cigna.newshq.business.com/press-release/new-cigna-study-reveals-loneliness-epidemic-levels-america.

Cipriani, A., Furukawa, T. A., Salanti, G., Chaimani, A., Atkinson, L. Z., Ogawa, Y., et al. (2018). Comparative efficacy and acceptability of 21 antidepressant drugs fo rthe acute treatment of adults with major depressive disorder: A systematic review and network meta-analysis. *Lancet, 392*(10128), 1356–1366.

Clark, D. M. (2011). Implementing NICE guidelines for the psychological treatment of depression and anxiety disorders: The IAPT experience. *International Review of Psychiatry, 23*, 318–327.

Clark, D. M., Layard, R., Smithies, R., Richards, D. A., Suckling, R., & Wright, B. (2009). Improving access to psychological therapy: Initial evaluation of two UK demonstration sites. *Behavior Research and Therapy, 47*, 910–920. https://doi.org/10.1016/j.brat.2009.07.010.

Clarke, T. C., Norris, T., & Schiller, J. S. (March 2019). *Early release of selected estimates based on data from the National Health Interview Survey*. National Center for Health Statistics. Available from: https://www.cdc.gov/nchs/nhis.htm.

Clement, P. W. (1999). *Outcomes and incomes: How to evaluate, improve, and market your psychotherapy practice by measuring outcomes*. New York: Guilford.

Cochrane, A. (1972). *Effectiveness and efficiency: Random reflections on health services*. London: Royal Society of Medicine Press.

Cohen, E. D., & Cohen, G. S. (1999). *The virtuous therapist: Ethical practice of counseling and psychotherapy*. Belmont, CA: Brooks/Cole Wadsworth.

Cohen, J. (1988). *Statistical power analysis for the behavioral sciences* (2nd ed.). Hillsdale, NJ: Lawrence Erlbaum.

Cohen, N. (2007). *What's left? How the left lost its way*. London: Harper Perrenial.

Colby, S. L., & Ortman, J. M. (2015). *Projection of the size and composition of the U.S. Population: 2014 to 2060 (report No. P25-1143)*. Washington, DC: U.S. Census Bureau.

Columbia Lighthouse Project. (2019). *Columbia-Suicide severity rating scale (C-SSRS). (2019)*. New York: Columbia University. Retrieved from http://cssrs.columbia.edu/the-columbia-scale-c-ssrs/about-the-scale/.

Commission on Chronic Illness. (1957). *Chronic illness in the United States* (Vol. 1). Cambridge, MA: Harvard University Press.

Cooper, C., Selwood, A., & Livingston, G. (2008). The prevalence of elder abuse and neglect: A systematic review. *Age and Aging, 37*, 151–160.

Corbin, J., Gottdiener, W. J., Sirikantraporn, S., Armstrong, J. L., & Probber, S. (2013). Prevalence of training in addiction psychology and treatment in APA-accredited clinical and counseling psychology doctoral programs. *Addiction Research and Theory, 21*(4), 269–272.

Cordain, L., Eaton, S. B., Sebastian, A., Mann, N., Lindeberg, S., Watkins, B. A., et al. (2005). Origins and evolution of the Western diet: Health implications for the 21st century. *American Journal of Clinical Nutrition, 81*(2), 341–354.

Corsini, R. J., & Wedding, D. (2008). *Current psychotherapies* (8th ed.). Belmont, CA: Thomson Brooks/Cole.

Council for the Parliament of the World's Religions. (1993). *Declaration toward a global ethic*. Retrieved from http://www.parliamentofreligions.org/index.cfm?n=4&sn=4.

Crenshaw, K. W. (1991). Mapping the margins: Intersectionality, identity politics, and violence against women of color. *Stanford Law Review, 43*(6), 1241–1299.

Cruciani, F., Trombetta, B., Massaia, A. G., Destro-Bisol, G., Sellitto, D., et al. (2011). A revised root for the human Y chromosomal phylogenetic tree: The origin of patrilineal diversity in Africa. *The American Journal of Human Genetics, 88*, 814–818.

Crump, T. (2001). *A brief history of science: As seen through the development of scientific instruments*. London: Constable.

Cuijpers, P., Driessen, E., Hollon, S. D., van Oppen, P., Barth, J., & Andersson, G. (2012). The efficacy of non-directive supportive psychotherapy for adult depression: A meta-analysis. *Clinical Psychology Review, 32*, 280–291.

Cuijpers, P., Hollon, S. D., van Straten, A., Blockting, C., Berking, M., & Andersson, G. (2013). Does cognitive behaviour therapy have an enduring effect that is superior to keeping patients on continuation pharmacotherapy? A meta-analysis. *BMJ Open, 3*, e002542.

Cummings, N. A., Cummings, J. L., & Johnson, J. N. (1997). *Behavioral health in primary care: A guide for clinical integration*. Madison, CT: Psychosocial Press.

Cuthbert, B. N., & Kozak, M. J. (2013). Constructing constructs for psychopathology: The NIMH research domain criteria. *Journal of Abnormal Psychology, 122*(3), 928–937.

Darwin, C. R. (1859). *The origin of species*. London: John Murray.

Davidson, D. J., & Begley, S. (2012). *The emotional life of your brain*. New York: Hudson Street Press.

Davidson, R. J., Kabat-Zinn, J., Schumacher, J., Rosenkranz, M. A., Muller, D., Santorelli, S. F., et al. (2003). Alterations in brain and immune function produced by mindfulness meditation. *Psychosomatic Medicine, 65*, 564–570.

Dawkins, R. (1976). *The selfish gene*. New York: Oxford University Press.

Dawkins, R. (2004). *The ancestor's tale: A pilgrimage to the dawn of life*. New York: Houghton Mifflin.

DeKlyen, M., & Greenberg, M. T. (2008). Attachment and psychopathology in childhood. In J. Cassidy, & P. R. Shaver (Eds.), *Handbook of attachment: Theory, research, and clinical applications* (2nd ed., pp. 637–665). New York: Guilford Press.

Derogatis, L. R., & Melisaratos, N. (1983). The brief symptom inventory: An introductory report. *Psychological Medicine, 13*, 595–605. https://doi.org/10.1017/S0033291700048017.

Deutsch, D. (2011). *The beginning of infinity: Explanations that transform the world*. New York: Viking.

Dobzhansky, T. (1973). Nothing in biology makes sense except in the light of evolution. *The American Biology Teacher, 35*(3), 125–129.

Donagan, A. (1977). *The theory of morality*. Chicago: University of Chicago Press.

Dowbiggin, I. (2008). *The sterilization movement and global fertility in the twentieth century*. New York: Oxford University Press.

Drum, D. J., Brownson, C., Denmark, A. B., & Smith, S. E. (2009). New data on the nature of suicidal crises in college students: Shifting the paradigm. *Professional Psychology: Research and Practice, 40*, 213–222. https://doi.org/10.1037/a0014465.

Druss, B. G., et al. (2011). Understanding excess mortality in persons with mental illness. *Medical Care, 49*, 599–604.

Dubos, R. (1959). *Mirage of health*. New York: Harper & Row.

Duignan, B. (2017). *Postmodernism. Encyclopedia britannica*. Retrieved from https://www.britannica.com/topic/postmodernism-philosophy.

Dunbar, R. (2016). *Human evolution: Our brains and behavior*. Oxford, England: Oxford University Press.

Dunbar, R. I. M., & Barrett, L. (Eds.). (2007b). *Oxford handbook of evolutionary psychology*. New York: Oxford University Press.

Durbin, J., Goering, P., Cochrane, J., Macfarlane, D., & Sheldon, T. (2004). Needs-based planning for persons with schizophrenia residing in board-and-care homes. *Schizophrenia Bulletin, 30*, 123–132.

Durlak, J. A., & Wells, A. M. (1997). Primary prevention mental health programs for children and adolescents: A meta-analytic review. *American Journal of Community Psychology, 25*, 115–152. https://doi.org/10.1023/A:1024654026646.

Dworkin, R. (1977). *Taking rights seriously*. Cambridge, MA: Harvard University Press.

Ecker, B., & Hulley, L. (2006). *Coherence therapy practice manual and training guide*. Oakland, CA: Pacific Seminars.

Egger, H. L., & Emde, R. N. (2011). Developmentally sensitive diagnostic criteria for mental health disorders in early childhood: The diagnostic and statistical manual of mental disorders-IV, the research diagnostic criteria—preschool age, and the diagnostic classification of mental health and developmental disorders in infancy and early childhood-revised. *American Psychologist, 66*, 95–106. https://doi.org/10.1037/a0021026.

Elbert, T., Pantev, C., Wienbruch, C., Rockstroh, B., & Taub, E. (1995). Increased cortical representation of the fingers of the left hand in string players. *Science, 270*, 305–307.

Ellis, A. (1957). Rational psychotherapy and individual psychology. *Journal of Individual Psychology, 13*, 38–44.

Emotional Well-Being Roundtable. (2018). *Emotional well-being: Emerging insights and questions for future research*. National Center for Complementary and Integrative Health. Retrieved from https://files.nccih.nih.gov/s3fs-public/Emotional%20Well-Being%20Roundtable%20Summary%20MASTER%20FINAL%20September2018_508.pdf?eq0JqgpH_u5wb.rYnOoikp6Il2Th05Wh.

Engel, G. L. (1977). The need for a new medical model: A challenge for biomedicine. *Science, 196*(4286), 129–136.

Englich, B., Mussweiler, T., & Strack, F. (2006). Playing dice with criminal sentences: The influence of irrelevant anchors on experts' judicial decision making. *Personality and Social Psychology Bulletin, 32*, 188–200.

Eysenck, H. J. (1952). The effects of psychotherapy: An evaluation. *Journal of Consulting Psychology, 16*, 319–324. https://doi.org/10.1037/h0063633.

Eysenck, H. J. (1970). A mish-mash of theories. *International Journal of Psychiatry, 9*, 140–146.

Felitti, J., Anda, R. F., Nordenberg, D., Williamson, D. F., Spitz, A. M., Edwards, V., et al. (1998). Relationship of childhood abuse and household dysfunction to many of the leading causes of death in adults: The Adverse Childhood Experiences (ACE) study. *American Journal of Preventive Medicine, 14*(4), 245–258.

Feyerabend, P. (1975). *Against method: Outline of an anarchistic theory of knowledge*. Humanities Press.

Finkelhor, D. (2008). *Childhood victimization: Violence, crime, and abuse in the lives of young people*. New York: Oxford University Press.

Finkelhor, D., Vanderminden, J., Turner, H., Hamby, S., & Shattuck, A. (2014). Child maltreatment rates assessed in a national household survey of caregivers and youth. *Child Abuse & Neglect, 39*, 1421–1435.

Fisher, H. (2016). *Anatomy of love: A natural history of mating, marriage, and why we stray*. New York: Norton.

Follette, W. T., & Cummings, N. A. (1967). Psychiatric services and medical utilization in a prepaid health plan setting. *Medical Care, 5*, 24–35.

Fonagy, P., & Clark, D. M. (2015). Update on the improving access to psychological therapies programme in england: Commentary on ... Children and young people's improving access to psychological therapies. *BJPsych Bulletin, 39*(5), 248–251.

Fontenot, K., Semega, J., & Kollar, M. (September 2018). *Income and poverty in the United States: 2017. Current population reports (P60-263)*. Washington, DC: U.S. Census Bureau. Retrieved from https://www.census.gov/library/publications/2018/demo/p60-263.html.

Food and Drug Administration. (2018). *Mobile medical applications*. Retrieved from https://www.fda.gov/medicaldevices/digitalhealth/mobilemedicalapplications/default.htm.

Forand, N. R., DeRubeis, R. J., & Amsterdam, J. D. (2013). Combining medication and psychotherapy in the treatment of major mental disorders. In M. Lambert (Ed.), *Bergin and Garfield's handbook of psychotherapy and behavior change* (6th ed., pp. 735–774). Hoboken, NJ: John Wiley and Sons.

Fortney, J. C., Unützer, J., Wrenn, G., Pyne, J. M., Smith, G. R., Schoenbaum, M., et al. (2017). A tipping point for measurement-based care. *Psychiatric Services, 68*(2), 179–188.

Fouad, N. A., Grus, C. L., Hatcher, R. L., Kaslow, N. J., Hutchings, P. S., Madson, M. B., et al. (2009). Competency benchmarks: A model for understanding and measuring competence in professional psychology cross training levels. *Training and Education in Professional Psychology, 3*(No. 4 Suppl. l.), S5–S26.

Fournier, J. C., DeRubeis, R. J., Hollon, S. D., Dimidgian, S., Amsterdam, J. D., Shelton, R. C., et al. (2010). Antidepressant drug effects and depression severity: A patient-level meta-analysis. *Journal of the American Medical Association, 303*, 47–53. https://doi.org/10.1001/jama.2009.1943.

Fournier, J. C., DeRubeis, R. J., Hollon, S. D., Gallop, R., Shelton, R. C., & Amsterdam, J. D. (2013). Differential change in specific depressive symptoms during antidepressant medication or cognitive therapy. *Behaviour Research and Therapy, 51*(7), 392–398.

Frances, A. (2009). A warning sign on the road to DSM-V: Beware of its unintended consequences. *Psychiatric Times, 26*, 3–9.

Francis, D., Diorio, J., Liu, D., & Meaney, M. J. (1999). Nongenomic transmission across generations of maternal behavior and stress response in the rat. *Science, 286*(5442), 1155–1158.

Frankel, R. M., Quill, T. E., & McDaniel, S. H. (Eds.). (2003). *The biopsychosocial approach: Past, present, and future*. Rochester, NY: University of Rochester Press.

Freeman, A., Beck, A. T., et al. (1990). *Cognitive therapy of personality disorders*. New York: Guilford.

Freeman, D., Reeve, S., Robinson, A., Ehlers, A., Clark, D., Spanlang, B., et al. (2017). Virtual reality in the assessment, understanding, and treatment of mental health disorders. *Psychological Medicine, 47*(14), 2393–2400.

Freeman, S. J. (2000). *Ethics: An introduction to philosophy and practice*. Belmont, CA: Wadsworth.

Fye, W. B. (2010). The origins and evolution of the mayo clinic from 1864 to 1939: A Minnesota family practice becomes an international 'medical mecca'. *Bulletin of the History of Medicine, 84*, 323–357.

Galbraith, J. K. (1955). *The great crash, 1929*. New York: Houghton Mifflin.

Garb, H. N. (1998). *Studying the clinician: Judgment research and psychological assessment*. Washington, DC: American Psychological Association.

Garfield, S. L. (1994). Research on client variables in psychotherapy. In A. E. Bergin, & S. L. Garfield (Eds.), *Handbook of psychotherapy and behavior change* (4th ed., pp. 190–228). New York: Wiley.

Garmezy, N., & Rutter, M. (Eds.). (1983). *Stress, coping, and development in children*. Baltimore, MD: Johns Hopkins University Press.

Gay, P. (1988). *Freud: A life for our times*. New York: Norton.

Gazzaniga, M. S. (2011). *Who's in charge? Free will and the science of the brain*. New York: Harper Collins.

Gert, B., Culver, C. M., & Clouser, K. D. (1997). *Bioethics: A return to fundamentals*. New York: Oxford University Press.

Gert, B., Culver, C. M., & Clouser, K. D. (2006). *Bioethics: A systematic approach* (2nd ed.). New York: Oxford University Press.

Ghaemi, S. N. (2010). *The rise and fall of the biopsychosocial model: Reconciling art and science in psychiatry*. Baltimore, MD: Johns Hopkins University Press.

Gilbert, L. K., Breiding, M. J., Merrick, M. T., Parks, S. E., Thompson, W. W., Dhingra, S. S., et al. (2015). Childhood adversity and adult chronic disease: An update from ten states and the District of Columbia. *American Journal of Preventive Medicine, 48*(3), 345–349.

Gilligan, C. (1982). *In a different voice: Psychological theory and women's development.* Cambridge, MA: Harvard University Press.

Gino, F., Ayal, S., & Ariely, D. (2009). Contagion and differential in unethical behavior: The effect of one bad apple on the barrel. *Psychological Science, 20*, 393–398.

Gino, F., Norton, M. I., & Ariely, D. (2010). The counterfeit self: The deceptive costs of faking it. *Psychological Science, 21*, 712–720.

Gintis, H., Bowles, S., Boyd, R., & Fehr, E. (2007). Explaining altruistic behaviour in humans. In R. I. M. Dunbar, & L. Barrett (Eds.), *Oxford handbook of evolutionary psychology* (pp. 605–619). New York: Oxford University Press.

Goldacre, B. (2012). *Bad pharma: How drug companies mislead doctors and harm patients.* Faber and Faber.

Goldapple, K., Segal, Z., Garson, C., Lau, M., Bieling, P., Kennedy, S., et al. (2004). Modulation of cortical limbic pathways in major depression: Treatment-specific effects of cognitive behavior therapy. *Archives of General Psychiatry, 61*, 34–41.

Goodheart, C. D., & Carter, J. A. (2008). The proper focus of evidence-based practice in psychology: Integration of possibility and probability. In W. B. Walsh (Ed.), *Biennial review of counseling psychology* (Vol. 1, pp. 47–70). New York: Taylor & Francis Group. https://doi.org/10.1037/a0019498.

Gould, R. A., Otto, M. W., & Pollack, M. H. (1995). A meta-analysis of treatment outcome for panic disorder. *Clinical Psychology Review, 15*, 819–844. https://doi.org/10.1016/0272-7358(95)00048-8.

Gould, R. A., Otto, M. W., Pollack, M. H., & Yap, L. (1997). Cognitive behavioral and pharmacological treatment of generalized anxiety disorder: A preliminary meta-analysis. *Behavior Therapy, 28*, 285–305. https://doi.org/10.1016/S0005-7894(97)80048-2.

Grant, B. F., et al. (2004). Prevalence and co-occurrence of substance use disorders and independent mood and anxiety disorders: Results from the National Epidemiologic Survey on Alcohol and Related Conditions. *Archives of General Psychiatry, 29*, 107–120.

Greene, J. (2003). From neural "is" to moral "ought": What are the moral implications of neuroscientific moral psychology? *Nature Reviews Neuroscience, 4*, 847–850. https://doi.org/10.1038/nrn1224.

Greene, J. (2013). *Moral tribes: Emotion, reason, and the gap between us and them.* New York: Penguin.

Greene, J. D., Nystrom, L. E., Engell, A. D., Darley, J. M., & Cohen, J. D. (2004). The neural bases of cognitive conflict and control in moral judgment. *Neuron, 44*, 389–400. https://doi.org/10.1016/j.neuron.2004.09.027.

Gribble, J. H., & Preston, S. H. (Eds.). (1993). *The epidemiological transition: Policy and planning implications for developing countries.* Washington, DC: National Academies Press.

Griffin, J. (1986). *Well-being: Its meaning, measurement and moral importance.* Oxford: Clarendon.

Grissom, R. J. (1996). The magical number 7 +- 2: Meta-meta-analysis of the probability of superior outcome in comparisons involving therapy, placebo, and control. *Journal of Consulting and Clinical Psychology, 64*, 973–982. https://doi.org/10.1037/0022-006X.64.5.973.

Groth-Marnat, G., & Wright, A. J. (2016). *Handbook of psychological assessment* (6th ed.). Hoboken, NJ: John Wiley & Sons.

Guarner, F., & Malagelada, J. R. (2003). Gut flora in health and disease. *Lancet, 361*, 512–519.

Gutting, G. (Ed.). (1980). *Paradigms and revolutions: Applications and appraisals of Thomas Kuhn's philosophy of science*. South Bend, IN: University of Notre Dame Press.

Haas, E., Hill, R., Lambert, M. J., & Morrell, B. (2002). Do early responders to psychotherapy maintain treatment gains? *Journal of Clinical Psychology, 58*, 1157–1172. https://doi.org/10.1002/jclp.10044.

Haidt, J. (2001). The emotional dog and its rational tail: A social intuitionist approach to moral judgment. *Psychological Review, 108*, 814–834. https://doi.org/10.1037/0033-295X.108.4.814.

Haidt, J. (2012). *The righteous mind: Why good people are divided by politics and religion*. New York: Vintage Books.

Hamilton, W. D. (1963). The evolution of altruistic behavior. *The American Naturalist, 97*, 354–356.

Hamilton, W. D. (1964). The genetic evolution of social behavior. *Journal of Theoretical Biology, 7*, 1–52.

Hannan, C., Lambert, M. J., Harmon, C., Nielsen, S. L., Smart, D. W., Shimokawa, K., et al. (2005). A lab test and algorithms for identifying clients at risk for treatment failure. *Journal of Clinical Psychology: In Session, 61*, 155–163.

Harari, Y. N. (2011). *Sapiens: A brief history of humankind*. London: Vintage Books.

Harari, Y. N. (2015). *Homo deus: A brief history of tomorrow*. London: Harvill Secker.

Harari, Y. N. (2018). *21 lessons for the 21st century*. New York: Spiegel & Grau.

Harris, N. B. (2018). *The deepest well: Healing the long-term effects of childhood adversity*. New York: Houghton Mifflin Harcourt.

Harwood, H. J., Kowalski, J., & Ameen, A. (2004). The need for substance abuse training among mental health professionals. *Administration and Policy in Mental Health, 32*, 189–205.

Hatfield, D. R., McCullough, L., Plucinski, A., & Krieger, K. (2009). Do we know when our clients get worse? An investigation of therapists' ability to detect negative client change. *Clinical Psychology & Psychotherapy, 17*(1), 25–32.

Hauser, M. (2006). *Moral minds*. New York: Ecco.

Hayes, S. C., & Follette, W. C. (1992). Can functional analysis provide a substitute for syndromal classification? *Behavioral Assessment, 14*, 345–365.

Hazelton. (December 2008). *Research update: The importance of continuing care*. Center City, MN: Butler Center for Research.

Health Service Psychology Education Collaborative (HSPEC). (2013). Professional psychology in health care services: A blueprint for education and training. *American Psychologist, 68*, 411–426.

Healy, D. (2012). *Pharmageddon*. Berkeley, CA: University of California Press.

Hebb, D. O. (1958). *Textbook of psychology*. Philadelphia, PA: Saunders.

Heckman, J. J., Moon, S. H., Pinto, R., Savelyev, P., & Yavitz, A. (2010). *A new cost-benefit and rate of return analysis for the perry preschool program: A summary* (p. 17). IZA Policy Papers.

Heintzelman, S. J., & King, L. A. (2014). Life is pretty meaningful. *American Psychologist, 69*, 561–574.

Hempel, C. G., & Oppenheim, P. (1948). Studies in the logic of explanation. *Philosophy of Science, 15*, 135–175.

Henrique, G. (2011). *A new unified theory of psychology*. New York: Springer.

Hersen, M., & Rosqvist, J. (2008). *Handbook of psychological assessment, case conceptualization, and treatment*. Hoboken, NJ: John Wiley & Sons. https://doi.org/10.1002/jclp.20034.

Hiatt, M. D., & Stockton, C. G. (2003). The impact of the Flexner Report on the fate of medical schools in North America after 1909. *Journal of American Physicians and Surgeons, 8*, 37–40.

Hicks, S. R. C. (2004). *Explaining postmodernism: Skepticism and socialism from Rousseau to Foucault*. Tempe, AZ: Scholargy Publishing.

Hickson, G. B., Clayton, E. W., Entman, S. S., Miller, C. S., Githens, P. B., Whetten-Goldstein, K., et al. (1994). Obstetricians' prior malpractice experience and patients' satisfaction with care. *Journal of the American Medical Association, 272*, 1583–1587. https://doi.org/10.1001/jama.272.20.1583.

Hinshaw, S. P., & Stier, A. (2008). Stigma as related to mental disorders. *Annual Review of Clinical Psychology, 4*, 367–393. https://doi.org/10.1146/annurev.clinpsy.4.022007.141245.

Hobbes, T. (1651/2002). *Leviathan, or the matter, forme, and power of a commonwealth, ecclesiasticall and civil*. Project Gutenberg.

Hollon, S. D., & Beck, A. T. (2004). Cognitive and cognitive-behavioral therapies. In M. J. Lambert (Ed.), *Garfield and Bergin's handbook of psychotherapy and behavior change: An empirical analysis* (5th ed., pp. 447–492). New York: Wiley.

Holmes, O. W. (1939). In F. Frankfurter (Ed.), *Mr. Justice Holmes and the Supreme Court*. Cambridge, MA: Harvard University Press.

Holt-Lundstad, J., Smith, T. B., Baker, M., Harris, T., & Stephenson, D. (2015). Loneliness and social isolation as risk factors for mortality: A meta-analytic review. *Perspectives on Psychological Science, 10*, 227–237.

Hughes, K., Bellis, M. A., Hardcastle, K. A., Sethi, D., Butchart, A., Mikton, C., et al. (2017). The effect of multiple adverse childhood experiences on health: A systematic review and meta-analysis. *Lancet Public Health, 2*, e356–366.

Hunter, C. L., Goodie, J. L., Oordt, M. S., & Dobmeyer, A. C. (2009). *Integrated behavioral health in primary care: Step-by-step guidance for assessment and intervention*. Washington, DC: American Psychological Association.

Hursthouse, R. (2001). *On virtue ethics*. Oxford: Oxford University Press.

Institute of Medicine. (1972). *Educating for the health team*. Washington, DC: National Academies of Sciences.

Institute of Medicine. (1994). *Reducing risks for mental disorders: Frontiers for preventive intervention research*. Washington, DC: National Academy Press.

Institute of Medicine. (2000). *To err is human: Building a safer health system*. Washington, DC: National Academies Press.

Institute of Medicine. (2001). *Crossing the quality chasm: A new health system for the 21st century*. Washington, DC: National Academies Press.

Institute of Medicine. (2002). *The future of the public's health in the 21st century*. Washington, DC: National Academies Press.

Institute of Medicine. (2003a). *Health professions education: A bridge to quality*. Washington, DC: National Academies Press.

Institute of Medicine. (2003b). *Unequal treatment: What healthcare providers need to know about racial and ethnic disparities in healthcare*. Washington, DC: National Academies Press.

Institute of Medicine. (2004). *Improving medical education: Enhancing the behavioral and social science content of medical school curricula*. Washington, DC: National Academies Press.

Institute of Medicine. (2011). *Finding what works in health care: Standards for systematic reviews*. Washington, DC: National Academies Press.

Interprofessional Education Collaborative Expert Panel. (2011). *Core competencies for interprofessional collaborative practice: Report of an expert panel*. Washington, DC: Interprofessional Education Collaborative. Retrieved from https://www.aamc.org/download/186750/data/core)_competencies.pdf.

IsHak, W. W. (2020). *Handbook of wellness medicine*. Cambridge, UK: Cambridge University Press.

Jabbarpour, Y., Coffman, M., Habib, A., Chung, Y., Liaw, W., Gold, S., et al. (2018). *Advanced primary care: A key contributor to successful ACOs. Patient-centered primary care collaborative*. Retrieved from https://www.pcpcc.org/sites/default/files/resources/PCPCC%202018%20Evidence%20Report.pdf.

James, W. (1890). *The principles of psychology, in two volumes*. New York: Henry Holt.

Jaspers, K. (1953). *The origin and goal of history*. New Haven: Yale University Press.

Jecker, N. S., Jonsen, A. R., & Pearlman, R. A. (2007). *Bioethics: An introduction to the history, methods, and practice* (2nd ed.). Sudbury, MA: Jones and Bartlett.

Johanson, D. C., & Wong, K. (2009). *Lucy's legacy: The quest for human origins*. New York: Harmony Books.

Johnson, S. B. (2013). Increasing psychology's role in health research and health care. *American Psychologist, 68*, 311–321.

Joiner, T. E. (2005). *Why people die by suicide*. Cambridge, MA: Harvard University Press.

Jonas, B. S., Albertorio-Diaz, J. R., & Gu, Q. (2012). *Trends in psychotropic medication use in the noninstitutionalized adolescent population: An NHANES analysis*. Hyattsville, MD: National Center for Health Statistics. Retrieved from http://www.cdc.gov/nchs/ppt/nchs2012/SS-22_JONAS.pdf.

Jones, R., & Cox, D. (2017). *2017 America's changing religious identity: Findings from the 2016 American Values Atlas*. Washington, DC: Public Religion Research Institute. Retrieved from https://www.jewishdatabank.org/content/upload/bjdb/PRRI-America's_Changing_Religious_Identity_2017_Complete_Report.pdf.

Judd, L. L. (1997). The clinical course of unipolar major depressive disorders. *Archives of General Psychiatry, 54*, 989–991.

Jutapakdeegul, N., Casalotti, S. O., Govitrapong, P., & Kotchabhakdi, N. (2003). Postnatal touch stimulation acutely alters corticosterone levels and glucocorticoid receptor gene expression in the neonatal rat. *Developmental Neuroscience, 25*, 26–33.

Kahneman, D. (2012). *Thinking, fast and slow*. New York: Farrar, Straus & Giroux.

Kahneman, D., & Deaton, A. (2012). High income improves evaluation of life but not emotional well-being. *PNAS Proceedings of the National Academy of Sciences, 107*(38), 16489–16493.

Kaplan, A. (1964). *The conduct if inquiry: Methodology for behavioral science*. San Francisco: Chandler Publishing.

Karoly, L. A., Kilburn, M. R., & Cannon, J. (2005). *Early childhood interventions: Proven results, future promise*. Santa Monica, CA: RAND Corporation.

Kazak, A. E., Hoagwood, K., Weisz, J. R., Hood, K., Kratochwill, T. R., Vargas, L. A., et al. (2010). A meta-systems approach to evidence-based practice with children and adolescents. *American Psychologist, 65*, 85–97. https://doi.org/10.1037/a0017784.

Kazak, A. E., Nash, J. M., Hiroto, K., & Kaslow, N. J. (2017). Psychologists in patient-centered medical homes (PCMHs): Roles, evidence, opportunities, and challenges. *American Psychologist, 72*(1), 1–12.

Kazdin, S. E. (2007). Mediators and mechanisms of change in psychotherapy research. *Annual Review of Clinical Psychology, 3*, 1–27. https://doi.org/10.1146/annurev.clinpsy.3.022806.091432.

Kellam, S. G., & Rebok, G. W. (1992). Building developmental and etiological theory through epidemiologically based preventive intervention trials. In J. McCord, & R. E. Tremblay (Eds.), *Preventing antisocial behavior: Interventions from birth through adolescence* (pp. 162–195). New York: Guilford Press.

Kelly, J. F., & Coons, H. L. (2012). Integrated health care and professional psychology: Is the setting right for you? *Professional Psychology: Research and Practice, 43*(6), 586–595.

Kempe, C. H., Silverman, F. N., Steele, B. F., Droegemuller, W., & Silver, H. K. (1962). The battered child syndrome. *Journal of the American Medical Association, 181*, 17–24.

Kempermann, G., Kuhn, H. G., & Gage, F. H. (1997). More hippocampal neurons in adult mice living in an enriched environment. *Nature, 386*(6624), 493–495.

Kessler, R. C., Demler, O., Frank, R. G., Olfson, M., Pincus, H. A., Walters, E. E., et al. (2005). Prevalence and treatment of mental disorders, 1990 to 2003. *New England Journal of Medicine, 352*, 2515–2524. https://doi.org/10.1056/NEJMsa043266.

Kessler, R. C., Heeringa, S., Lakoma, M. D., Petukhova, M., Rupp, A. E., Schoenbaum, M., et al. (2008). Individual and societal effects of mental disorders on earnings in the United States: Results from the national comorbidity survey replication. *American Journal of Psychiatry, 165*, 703–711. https://doi.org/10.1176/appi.ajp.2008.08010126.

Kessler, R. C., McGonagle, K. A., Zhao, S., Nelson, C. B., Hughes, M., Eshleman, H. U., et al. (1994). Lifetime and 12-month prevalence of DSM-III-R disorders in the United States: Results from the national comorbidity study. *Archives of General Psychiatry, 51*, 8–19.

Keyes, C. L. M. (2007). Promoting and protecting mental health as flourishing: A complementary strategy for improving national mental health. *American Psychologist, 62*, 95–108. https://doi.org/10.1037/0003-066X.62.2.95.

Keynes, J. M. (1930/1972). Economic possibilities for our grandchildren. In *The collected writings of John Maynard Keynes*. London: Macmillan.

Kindig, D. A., & Stoddart, G. (2003). What is population health? *American Journal of Public Health, 93*, 366–369.

Klein, R. G. (2000). Archaeology and the evolution of human behavior. *Evolutionary Anthropology, 9*, 17–36.

Kluckhohn, Clyde, & Murray, Henry (1953). *Personality in nature, society, and culture* (2nd ed.). New York: Knopf.

Knapp, S., & VandeCreek, L. (2007). When values of different cultures conflict: Ethical decision making in a multicultural context. *Professional Psychology: Research and Practice, 388*, 660–666. https://doi.org/10.1037/0735-7028.38.6.660.

Koestler, A. (1967). *The ghost in the machine*. New York: Macmillan.

Kohlberg, L. (1971). *From is to ought: How to commit the naturalistic fallacy and get away with it in the study of moral development*. New York: Academic Press.

Kolodny, et al. (2015). The prescription opioid and heroin crisis: A public health approach to an epidemic of addiction. *Annual Review of Public Health, 36*, 559–574.

Koocher, G. P., & Keith-Spiegel, P. (2008). *Ethics in psychology and the mental health professions: Standards and cases* (3rd ed.). New York: Oxford University Press.

Kraemer, H.,C., Kazdin, A. E., & Offord, D. R. (1997). Coming to terms with terms of risk. *Archives of General Psychiatry, 54*, 337–343.

Kramer, P. D. (2008). Compared to what? *Psychology Today*. Retrieved from http://www.psychologytoday.com/node/1022.

Krebs, D. (2005). The evolution of morality. In D. M. Buss (Ed.), *The handbook of evolutionary psychology* (pp. 747–775). Hoboken, NJ: John Wiley and Sons.

Krieger, N., & Brin, A. E. (1998). A vision of social justice as the foundation of public health: Commemorating 150 years of the spirit of 1848. *American Journal of Public Health, 88*, 1603–1606.

Kroenke, K. (2003). Patients presenting with somatic complaints: Epidemiology, psychiatric co-morbidity and management. *International Journal of Methods in Psychiatric Research, 12*, 34–43.

Kroenke, K., Spitzer, R. L., & Williams, J. B. (2001). The PHQ-9: Validity of a brief depression severity measure. *Journal of General Internal Medicine, 16*, 603–613. https://doi.org/10.1046/j.1525-1497.2001.016009606.x.

Krupnick, J. L., Stotsky, S. M., Simmons, S., Moyer, J., Watkins, J., Elkin, I., et al. (1996). The role of the therapeutic alliance in psychotherapy and pharmacotherapy outcome: Findings in the national institute of mental health treatment of depression collaborative research program. *Journal of Consulting and Clinical Psychology, 64*, 532–539. https://doi.org/10.1037/0022-006X.64.3.532.

Kuhn, T. S. (1962). *The structure of scientific revolutions*. Chicago: University of Chicago Press.

Kuhn, T. S. (1977). Second thoughts on paradigms. In F. Suppe (Ed.), *The structure of scientific theories* (2nd ed., pp. 459–499). Urbana, IL: University of Illinois Press.

Lambert, M. J. (1992). Implications of outcome research for psychotherapy integration. In J. C. Norcross, & M. R. Goldstein (Eds.), *Handbook of psychotherapy integration* (pp. 94–129). New York: Basic Books.

Lambert, M. J. (2007). Presidential address: What we have learned from a decade of research aimed at improving psychotherapy outcome in routine care. *Psychotherapy Research, 17*, 1–14. https://doi.org/10.1080/10503300601032506.

Lambert, M. J. (2010). *Prevention of treatment failure: The use of measuring monitoring and feedback in clinical practice*. Washington, DC: American Psychological Association.

Lambert, M. J. (2013). The efficacy and effectiveness of psychotherapy. In M. J. Lambert (Ed.), *Bergin and Garfield's Handbook of psychotherapy and behavior change* (6th ed.). Hoboken, NJ: John Wiley and Sons (pp. 269–218).

Lambert, M. J., & Archer, A. (2006). Research findings on the effects of psychotherapy and their implications for practice. In C. D. Goodheart, A. E. Kazdin, & R. J. Sternberg (Eds.), *Evidence-based psychotherapy: Where practice and research meet* (pp. 111–130). Washington, DC: American Psychological Association. https://doi.org/10.1037/11423-005.

Lambert, M. J., & Bergin, A. E. (1994). The effectiveness of psychotherapy. In A. E. Bergin, & S. L. Garfield (Eds.), *Handbook of psychotherapy and behavior change* (4th ed., pp. 143–189). New York: Wiley.

Lambert, M. J., Burlingame, G. M., Umphress, V. J., Hansen, N. B., Vermeersch, D., Clouse, G., et al. (1996). The reliability and validity of the Outcome Questionnaire. *Clinical Psychology & Psychotherapy, 3*, 106–116.

Laupacis, A., Sackett, D. L., & Roberts, R. S. (1988). An assessment of clinically useful measures of the consequences of treatment. *New England Journal of Medicine, 318*, 1728–1733. https://doi.org/10.1056/NEJM198806303182605.

Lazarus, A. A., Beutler, L. E., & Norcross, J. C. (1992). The future of technical eclecticism. *Psychotherapy, 29*, 11–20.

Lechner, S. C., Tennen, H., & Affleck, G. (2009). Benefit-finding and growth. In C. J. Lopez, & C. R. Snyder (Eds.), *The Oxford handbook of positive psychology* (2nd ed.). New York: Oxford University Press.

Leucht, S., Helfer, B., Gartlehner, G., & Davis, J. M. (2015). How effective are common medications: A perspective based on meta-analyses of major drugs. *BMC Medicine, 13*, 253.

Lezak, M. D., Howieson, D. B., Bigler, E. D., & Tranel, D. (2012). *Neuropsychological assessment* (5th ed.). New York: Oxford University Press.

Lieberman, D. E. (2011). Epigenetic integration, complexity, and evolvability of the head: Rethinking the functional matrix hypothesis. In B. Hallgrimsson, & B. K. Hall (Eds.), *Epigenetics: Linking genotype and phenotype in development and evolution* (pp. 271–289). Berkley, CA: University of California Press.

Lieberman, D. E. (2013). *The story of the human body: Evolution, health, and disease*. New York: Pantheon.

Lieberman, J., & Insel, T. (May 14, 2013). *Lieberman, Insel issue joint statement about DSM-5 and RDoC*. Psychiatric News. Retrieved from http://alert.psychnews.org/2013/05/lieberman-insel-issue-joint-statement.html.

Lilienfeld, S. O. (2007). Psychological treatments that cause harm. *Perspectives on Psychological Science, 2*, 53–70. https://doi.org/10.1111/j.1745-6916.2007.00029.x.

Lilienfeld, S. O., Lynn, S. J., & Lohr, J. M. (2015). *Science and pseudoscience in clinical psychology*. New York: Guilford.

Linehan, M. M., & Dexter-Mazza, E. T. (2008). Dialectical behavior therapy for borderline personality disorder. In D. H. Barlow (Ed.), *Clinical handbook of psychological disorders: A step-by-step treatment manual* (pp. 365–420). New York: Guildford.

Lipsey, M. W., & Wilson, D. B. (1993). The efficacy of psychological, educational, and behavior treatment: Confirmation from meta-analysis. *American Psychologist, 48*, 1181–1209. https://doi.org/10.1037/0003-066X.48.12.1181.

Loftus, E. F., & Davis, D. (2006). Recovered memories. *Annual Review of Clinical Psychology, 2*, 469–498. https://doi.org/10.1146/annurev.clinpsy.2.022305.095315.

Luthar, S. S. (2003). *Resilience and vulnerability: Adaptation in the context of childhood adversities*. New York: Cambridge University Press.

De Maat, S., Dekker, J., Schoevers, R., & De Jonghe, F. (2006). Relative efficacy of psychotherapy and pharmacotherapy in the treatment of depression: A meta-analysis. *Psychotherapy Research, 16*, 562–572. https://doi.org/10.1080/10503300600756402.

Maciejewski, M. L. (2006). Generic measures. In R. L. Kane (Ed.), *Understanding health care outcomes research* (2nd ed., pp. 123–164). Sudbury, MA: Jones and Barlett Publishers.

MacIntyre, A. (1982). *After virtue: A study in moral theory*. Notre Dame, IN: University of Notre Dame Press.

Magnavita, J., & Anchin, J. (2014). *Unifying psychotherapy: Principles, methods, and evidence from clinical science*. New York: Springer.

Main, M., Kaplan, N., & Cassidy, J. (1985). Security in infancy, childhood and adulthood: A move to the level of representation. In I. Bretherton, & E. Waters (Eds.), *Growing points of attachment theory and research* (pp. 66–104). Chicago: University of Chicago Press.

Mameli, M. (2007). Evolution and psychology in philosophical perspective. In R. I. M. Dunbar, & L. Barrett (Eds.), *Oxford handbook of evolutionary psychology* (pp. 21–34). New York: Oxford University Press.

Manderscheid, R. W., & Henderson, M. J. (2004). Mental health, United States, 2002 executive summary. *Administration and Policy in Mental Health, 32*(1), 49–55.

Mark, T. L., Levit, K. R., & Buck, J. A. (2009). Psychotropic drug prescriptions by medical speciality. *Psychiatric Services, 60*, 1167. https://doi.org/10.1176/appi.ps.60.9.1167.

Marks, I. M., & Matthews, A. M. (1978). Brief standard self-rating for phobic patients. *Behavior Research and Therapy, 17*, 263–267. https://doi.org/10.1016/0005-7967(79)90041-X.

Martin, P. R., Weinberg, B. A., & Bealer, B. K. (2007). *Healing addiction: An integrated pharmacopsychosocial approach to treatment*. Hoboken, NJ: Wiley.

Maruish, M. E. (2004a). Introduction. In M. E. Maruish (Ed.), *The use of psychological testing for treatment planning and outcomes assessment* (3rd ed., pp. 1–64). Mahwah, NJ: Lawrence Erlbaum.

Maruish, M. E. (2004b). Development and implementation of a behavioral health outcomes program. In M. E. Maruish (Ed.), *The use of psychological testing for treatment planning and outcomes assessment* (3rd ed., pp. 215–272). Mahwah, NJ: Lawrence Erlbaum.

Maslow, A. H. (1943). A theory of human motivation. *Psychological Review, 50*, 370–396. https://doi.org/10.1037/h0054346.

Maslow, A. H. (1966). *The psychology of science: A reconnaissance*. Maurice Bassett.

Masse, L. N., & Barnett, W. S. (2002). A benefit-cost analysis of the Abecedarian early childhood intervention. In H. Levin, & P. McEwan (Eds.), *Cost effectiveness and educational policy: 2002 yearbook of the American Education Finance Association* (pp. 157–176). Larchmont, NY: Eye on Education.

Masten, A. S., Burt, K., & Coatsworth, J. D. (2006). Competence and psychopathology in development. In D. Cicchetti, & D. J. Cohen (Eds.), *Developmental psychopathology risk, disorder, and adaptation* (Vol. 3, pp. 696–738). New York: Wiley.

Masten, A. S., Faden, V. B., Zucker, R. A., & Spear, L. P. (2008). Underage drinking: A developmental framework. *Pediatrics, 121*(Suppl. 4), S235–S251.

Mayou, R. A., Ehlers, A., & Hobbs, M. (2000). Psychological debriefing for road traffic accident victims: Three-year follow-up of randomized controlled trial. *British Journal of Psychiatry, 176*, 589–593. https://doi.org/10.1192/bjp.176.6.589.

Mazar, N., Amir, O., & Ariely, D. (2008). The dishonesty of honest people: A theory of self-concept maintenance. *Journal of Marketing Research, 45*, 633–644.

Mazza, J. J., Catalano, R. D., Abbott, R. F., & Haggerty, K. P. (2011). An examination of the validity of retrospective measures of suicide attempts in youth. *Journal of Adolescent Health, 49*, 532–537.

McClain, T., O'Sullivan, P. S., & Clardy, J. A. (2004). Biopsychosocial formulation: Recognizing educational shortcomings. *Academic Psychiatry, 28*, 88–94. https://doi.org/10.1176/appi.ap.28.2.88.

McGowen, P. O., Sasaki, A., D'Alessio, A. C., Dymov, S., Labonte, B., Szyf, M., et al. (2009). Epigenetic regulation of the glucocorticoid receptor in human brain associates with childhood abuse. *Nature Neuroscience, 12*, 342–348. https://doi.org/10.1038/nn/2270.

McHugh, R. K., Whitton, S. W., Peckham, A. D., Welge, J. A., & Otto, M. W. (2013). Patient preference for psychological vs. pharmacological treatment of psychiatric disorders: A meta-analytic review. *Journal of Clinical Psychiatry, 74*(6), 595–602.

McKeown, T. (1965). *Medicine in modern society*. London: Allen and Unwin.

McLaren, N. (2007). *Humanizing madness*. Ann Arbor, MI: Loving Healing Press.

Mead, M. L., Baumeister, R. F., Gino, F., Schweitzer, M. E., & Ariely, D. (2009). Too tired to tell the truth: Self-control resource depletion and dishonesty. *Journal of Experimental Social Psychology, 45*, 594–597.

Meaney, M. J. (2001). Maternal care, gene expression, and the transmission of individual differences in stress reactivity across generations. *Annual Review of Neuroscience, 24*, 1161–1192.

Mee-Lee, D. (Ed.). (2013). *The ASAM criteria: Treatment criteria for addictive, substance-related, and co-occurring conditions*. Rockville, MD: American Society of Addiction Medicine.

Melchert, T. P. (2011). *Foundations of professional psychology: The end of theoretical orientations and the emergence of the biopsychosocial approach*. London: Elsevier.
Melchert, T. P. (2015). *Biopsychosocial practice: A science-based framework for behavioral health care*. Washington, DC: American Psychological Association.
Melchert, T. P. (2016). Leaving behind our preparadigmatic past: Professional psychology as a unified clinical science. *American Psychologist, 71*, 486−496.
Melchert, T. P. (2020). Measuring wellness. In W. W. IsHak (Ed.), *Handbook of wellness medicine*. Cambridge, UK: Cambridge University Press.
Mellars, P. A., & Stringer, C. (Eds.). (1989). *The human revolution: Behavioural and biological perspectives in the origins of modern humans*. Edinburgh: Edinburgh University Press.
Merrick, M. T., Ford, D. C., Ports, K. A., & Guinn, A. S. (2018). Prevalence of adverse childhood experiences from the 2011-2014 behavioral risk factor surveillance system in 23 states. *JAMA Pediatrics, 172*(11), 1038−1044.
Mesoudi, A., & Jensen, K. (2012). Culture and the evolution of human sociality. In J. Vonk, & T. K. Shackelford (Eds.), *The Oxford handbook of comparative evolutionary psychology* (pp. 419−433). New York: Oxford University Press.
Messer, S. B., & Winokur, M. (1980). Some limits to the integration of psychoanalytic and behavior therapy. *American Psychologist, 35*, 818−827. https://doi.org/10.1037/0003-066x.35.9.818.
Meyer, G. J., Finn, S. E., Eyde, L. D., Kay, G. G., Moreland, K. L., Dies, R. R., et al. (2001). Psychological testing and psychological assessment: A review of evidence and issues. *American Psychologist, 56*, 128−165. https://doi.org/10.1037/0003-066X.56.2.128.
Meyer, L. (2008). *The use of a comprehensive biopsychosocial framework for intake assessment in mental health practice*. Doctoral dissertation. Milwaukee, WI: Marquette University.
Meyer, L., & Melchert, T. P. (2011). Examining the content of mental health intake assessments from a biopsychosocial perspective. *Journal of Psychotherapy Integration, 21*, 70−89.
Micozzi, M. S. (2018). *Fundamentals of complementary, alternative, and integrative medicine* (6th ed.). St. Louis, MO: Elsevier.
Mikulincer, M., & Shaver, P. R. (2007). *Attachment in adulthood: Structure, dynamics, and change*. New York: Guilford.
Mikulincer, M., & Shaver, P. R. (2012). *The social psychology of morality: Exploring the causes of good and evil*. Washington, DC: American Psychological Association.
Miller, J. E., & Prewitt, E. (2012). *Reclaiming lost decades: The role of state behavioral health agencies in accelerating the integration of behavioral health care and primary care to improve the health of people with serious mental illness*. Alexandria, VA: National Association of State Mental Health Program Directors.
Miller, R. C., & Berman, J. S. (1983). The efficacy of cognitive behavior therapies: A quantitative review of the research evidence. *Psychological Bulletin, 94*, 39−53. https://doi.org/10.1037/0033-2909.94.1.39.
Mojtabai, R., & Olfson, M. (2008). National trends in psychotherapy by office-based psychiatrists. *Archives of General Psychiatry, 65*, 962−970.
Mokdad, A. H., Marks, J. S., Stroup, D. F., & Gerberding, J. L. (2004). Actual causes of death in the United States, 2000. *Journal of the American Medical Association, 291*, 1238−1245. https://doi.org/10.1001/jama.291.10.1238.
Moll, J., de Oliveira-Souza, R., & Zahn, R. (2008). The neural basis of moral cognition: Sentiments, concepts, and values. *Annals of the New York Academy of Sciences, 1124*, 161−180.
Montague, A. (1942). *Man's most dangerous myth: The fallacy of race*. New York: Columbia University Press.

Moore, A. (2009). *What is an NNT? Kent*. UK: Hayward Medical Group. Retrieved from http://meds.queensu.ca/medicine/obgyn/pdf/what_is/WhatisanNNT.pdf.

Morris, I. (2013). *The measure of civilization: How social development decides the fate of nations*. Princeton, NJ: Princeton University Press.

Mrazek, P. J., & Hall, M. (1997). A policy perspective on prevention. *American Journal of Community Psychology, 25*, 221–226. https://doi.org/10.1001/jama.291.10.1238.

Munder, T., Fluckiger, C., Leichsenring, F., Abbass, A. A., Hilsenroth, M. J., Luyten, P., et al. (2019). Is psychotherapy effective? A re-analysis of treatments for depression. *Epidemiology and Psychiatric Sciences, 28*(3), 268–275.

Murray, C. J. L., & Lopez, A. D. (Eds.). (1996). *The global burden of disease: A comprehensive assessment of mortality and disability from diseases, injuries, and risk factors in 1990 and projected to 2020*. Cambridge, MA: Harvard School of Public Health.

Myers, J. E. B. (Ed.). (2011). *The APSAC handbook on child maltreatment* (3rd ed.). Thousand Oaks, CA: Sage.

Nagel, T. (1986). *The view from nowhere*. New York: Oxford University Press.

Nagel, T. (2012). *Mind and cosmos: Why the materialist Neo-Darwinian conception of nature is almost certainly false*. Oxford University Press.

National Association of Social Workers. (2017). *Code of ethics*. Retrieved from http://www.socialworkers.org/pubs/code/code.asp.

National Association of State Mental Health Program Directors. (2006). *Morbidity and mortality in people with serious mental illness*. Alexandria, VA. Retrieved from http://www.nasmhpd.org/general_files/publications/med_directors_pubs/Technical%20Report%20on%20Morbidity%20and%20Mortaility%20-%20Final%2011-06.pdf.

National Center for Educational Statistics. (2008). *National assessment of adult literacy*. Retrieved from nces.ed/gov/naal/estimates/overview.aspx.

National Center for Health Statistics. (2012). *Healthy people 2010 final review*. Hyattsville, MD: National Center for Health Statistics.

National Center for Health Statistics. (2018). *Health, United States, 2017*. Hyattsville, MD: National Center for Health Statistics.

National Research Council and Institute of Medicine. (2000). From neurons to neighborhoods: The science of early childhood development. In J. P. Shonkoff, & D. A. Phillips (Eds.), *Committee on integrating the science of early childhood development, board on children, youth, and families*. Washington, DC: National Academy Press.

National Research Council and Institute of Medicine. (2009). Preventing mental, emotional, and behavioral disorders among young people: Progress and Possibilities. In M. E. O'Connell, T. Boat, & K. E. Warner (Eds.), *Committee on the prevention of mental disorders and substance abuse among children, youth, and young adults, board on children, youth, and families*. Washington, DC: National Academy Press.

Nettle, D. (2006). The evolution of personality variation in humans and other animals. *American Psychologist, 61*, 622–631.

Newport, F. (2017). *2017 update on Americans and religion*. Princeton, NJ: Gallup. Retrieved from https://news.gallup.com/poll/224642/2017-update-americans-religion.aspx?g_source=link_NEWSV9&g_medium=TOPIC&g_campaign=item_&g_content=2017%2520Update%2520on%2520Americans%2520and%2520Religion.

Newport, F. (2018). *In U.S., estimate of LGBT population rises to 4.5%*. Princeton, NJ: Gallop. Retrieved from https://news.gallup.com/poll/234863/estimate-lgbt-population-rises.aspx.

Nietzel, M. T., Russell, R. L., Hemmings, K. A., & Gretter, M. L. (1987). Clinical significance of psychotherapy for unipolar depression: A meta-analytic approach to social comparison. *Journal of Consulting and Clinical Psychology, 55*, 156–161. https://doi.org/10.1037/0022-006X.55.2.156.

Norcross, J. C. (Ed.). (2011). *Psychotherapy relationships that work: Evidence-based responsiveness* (2nd ed.). New York: Oxford University Press.

Norcross, J. C., Koocher, G. P., & Garofalo, A. (2006). Discredited psychological treatments and tests: A delphi poll. *Professional Psychology: Research and Practice, 37*, 515–522. https://doi.org/10.1037/0735-7028.37.5.515.

Norcross, J. C., & Wampold, B. E. (2011). Evidence-based therapy relationships: Research conclusions and clinical practices. In J. C. Norcross (Ed.), *Psychotherapy relationships that work: Evidence-based responsiveness* (2nd ed., pp. 423–430). New York: Oxford University Press.

Nordal, K. C. (2012). Health care reform: Implications for independent practice. *Professional Psychology: Research and Practice, 43*, 535–544.

O'Donovan, A., Epel, E., Wolkowitz, O., Cohen, B., Maguen, S., Metzler, T., et al. (2011). Childhood trauma associated with short leukocyte telomere length in posttraumatic stress disorder. *Biological Psychiatry, 70*(5), 465–471.

Ogles, B. M. (2013). Measuring change in psychotherapy research. In M. J. Lambert (Ed.), *Bergin and Garfield's handbook of psychotherapy and behavior change* (6th ed., pp. 134–166). Hoboken, NJ: John Wiley and Sons.

Okiishi, J. C., Lambert, M. J., Eggett, D., Nielsen, S. L., Dayton, D. D., & Vermeersch, D. A. (2006). An analysis of therapist treatment effects: Toward providing feedback to individual therapists on their patients' psychotherapy outcome. *Journal of Clinical Psychology, 62*, 1157–1172. https://doi.org/10.1002/jclp.20272.

Okiishi, J. C., Lambert, M. J., Nielsen, S. L., & Ogles, B. M. (2003). In search of supershrink: Using patient outcome to identify effective and ineffective therapists. *Clinical Psychology & Psychotherapy, 10*, 361–373. https://doi.org/10.1002/cpp.383.

Olfson, M., & Marcus, S. C. (2010). National trends in outpatient psychotherapy. *American Journal of Psychiatry, 167*(12), 1456–1463.

Omi, M. (2001). The changing meaning of race. In N. J. Smelser, W. J. Wilson, & F. Mitchell (Eds.), *American becoming: Racial trends and their consequences* (p. 243). Washington, DC: National Academy Press.

Oregon Department of Human Services, Addiction and Mental Health Division. (June 6, 2008). *Measuring premature mortality among Oregonians*. Retrieved from http://www.oregon.gov/oha/amh/Documents/msur_pre_mort_6_2008.pdf.

Organization of Economic Co-operation and Development Health Division. (July 2, 2019). *OECD.Stat*. Paris: Organization of Economic Co-operation and Development. Retrieved from https://stats.oecd.org/index.aspx?DataSetCode=HEALTH_STAT#.

Otto, M. W., Smits, J. A. J., & Reese, H. E. (2005). Combined psychotherapy and pharmacotherapy for mood and anxiety disorders in adults: Review and analysis. *Clinical Psychology: Science and Practice, 12*, 72–86. https://doi.org/10.1093/clipsy/bpi009.

Ouellette, J. (2014). *Me, myself, and why: Searching for the science of self*. New York: Penguin Books.

Painter, R. C., Osmond, C., Gluckman, P., Hanson, M., Phillips, D. I., & Roseboom, T. J. (2008). Transgenerational effects of prenatal explosure to the Dutch famine on neonatal adiposity and health in later life. *BJOG: An International Journal of Obstetrics and Gynaecology, 115*(10), 1243–1249.

Pascual-Leone, A., Amedi, A., Fregni, F., & Merabet, L. B. (2005). The plastic human brain cortex. *Annual Review of Neuroscience, 28*, 377–401.

Pascual-Leone, A., & Hamilton, R. (2001). The metamodal organization of the brain. *Progress in Brain Research, 134*, 427–445.

Patrick, D. L., & Deyo, R. A. (1989). Generic and disease-specific measures in assessing health status and quality of life. *Medical Care, 27*, 5217–5232. https://doi.org/10.1097/00005650-198903001-00018.

Patterson, O. (1985). *Slavery and social death.* Cambridge, MA: Harvard University Press.

Penfield, W., & Rasmussen, T. (1950). *The cerebral cortex of man: A clinical study of localization of function.* Oxford, England: Macmillan.

Persons, J. B., & Tompkins, M. A. (2007). Cognitive-behavioral case formulation. In T. D. Eells (Ed.), *Handbook of psychotherapy case formulation* (2nd ed., pp. 290–316). New York: Guilford.

Pinker, S. (2018). *Enlightenment now: The case for reason, science, humanism, and progress.* New York: Viking.

Pluckrose, H. (February 7, 2018). No, postmodernism is not dead (and other misconceptions). *Areo Magazine*. Retrieved from https://areomagazine.com/2018/02/07/no-postmodernism-is-+not-dead-and-other-misconceptions/.

Pollard, J. A., Hawkins, J. D., & Arthur, M. W. (1999). Risk and protection: Are both necessary to understand diverse behavioral outcomes in adolescence. *Social Work Research, 23*, 145–158.

Pons, T. P., Garraghty, P. E., Ommaya, A. K., Kaas, J. H., Taub, E., & Mishkin, M. (1991). Massive cortical reorganization after sensory deafferentation in adult macaques. *Science, 252*, 1857–1860.

Popper, K. (1963). *Conjectures and refutations: The growth of scientific knowledge.* London: Routledge.

Porter, R. (1997). *The greatest benefit to mankind: A medical history of humanity.* New York: Norton.

Powers, M., & Faden, R. (2006). *Social justice: The moral foundations of public health and health policy.* New York: Oxford University Press.

Pratt, L. A., Brody, D. J., & Gu, Q. (2011). *Antidepressant use in persons aged 12 and over: United States, 2005 – 2008.* NCHS data brief, no. 76. Hyattsville, MD: National Center for Health Statistics. Retrieved from http://www.cdc.gov/nchs/data/databriefs/db76.pdf.

Price, M. E. (2011). Cooperation as a classic problem in behavioral biology. In V. Swami (Ed.), *Evolutionary psychology: A critical introduction* (pp. 73–106). West Sussex, UK: BPS Blackwell.

Prochaska, J. O., & Norcross, J. C. (2018). *Systems of psychotherapy: A transtheoretical analysis* (9th ed.). New York: Oxford University Press.

Project release v. Prevost, 722 F.2d 960 (2nd Cir., 1983).

Puterman, E., Gemmill, A., Karasek, D., Weir, D., Adler, N. E., Prather, A. A., et al. (2016). Lifespan adversity and later adulthood telomere length in the nationally representative US Health and Retirement Study. *Proceedings of the National Academy of Sciences, 113*(42), e6335–6342.

Raghupathi, W., & Raghupathi, V. (2014). Big data analytics in health care: Promise and potential. *Health Information Science and Systems, 2*, 3.

Ramachandran, V. S. (2011). *The tell-tale brain: A neuroscientist's quest for what makes us human.* New York: W. W. Norton.

Rawls, J. (1999). *A theory of justice* (2nd ed.). Cambridge, MA: Harvard University Press.

Redelmeier, D. A., & Kahneman, D. (1996). Patients' memories of painful medical treatments: Real-time and retrospective evaluations of two minimally invasive procedures. *Pain, 66*, 3–8.

Redfield, R. R. (November 29, 2018). *CDC Director's media statement on U.S. life expectancy (Media Statement).* Atlanta, GA: Center for Disease Control and Prevention. Retrieved from https://www.cdc.gov/media/releases/2018/s1129-US-life-expectancy.html.

Reed, G. M., & Eisman, E. J. (2006). Uses and misuses of evidence: Managed care, treatment guidelines, and outcomes measure in professional practice. In C. D. Goodheart, A. E. Kazdin, & R. J. Sternberg (Eds.), *Evidence-based psychotherapy: Where practice and research meet* (pp. 13–36). Washington, DC: American Psychological Association.

Regier, D. A., Goldberg, I. D., & Taube, C. A. (1978). The de factor U.S. Mental health services system: A public health perspective. *Archives of General Psychiatry, 35*, 685–693. https://doi.org/10.1001/archpsyc.1978.01770300027002.

Rescher, N. (1966). *Distributive justice*. Indianapolis, IN: Bobbs-Merrill.

Resick, P. A., Williams, L. F., Suvak, M. K., Monson, C. M., & Gradus, J. L. (2012). Long-term outcomes of cognitive-behavioral treatments for posttraumatic stress disorder among female rape survivors. *Journal of Consulting and Clinical Psychology, 80*, 201–210.

Roberts, S. C. (2012). *Applied evolutionary psychology*. New York: Oxford University Press.

Roder, B., Teder-Salejarvi, W., Sterr, A., Rosler, F., Hillyard, S. A., & Neville, H. J. (1999). Improved auditory spatial tuning in blind humans. *Nature, 400*, 162–166.

Rogers, C. R. (1951). *Client-centered therapy: Its current practice, implications, and theory*. Boston: Houghton Mifflin.

Rorty, R. (1991). *Objectivity, relativism, and truth*. Cambridge, UK: Cambridge University Press.

Rosenberg, A. (2012). *Philosophy of science: A contemporary introduction* (*3rd* ed.). New York: Routledge.

Rozensky, R. H. (2011). The institution of the institutional practice of psychology: Health care reform and psychology's future workforce. *American Psychologist, 66*, 797–808.

Rudd, M. D. (2006). *The assessment and management of suicidality*. Sarasota, FL: Professional Resource Press.

Ruse, M. (2005). Entry for "reductionism.". In Ted honderich, *The Oxford Companion to Philosophy* (p. 793). Oxford University Press.

Rutter, M. (1979). Protective factors in children's responses to stress and disadvantage. *Annals Academy of Medicine Singapore, 8*, 324–338.

Ryan, C. L., & Bauman, K. (March 2016). *Educational attainment in the United States: 2015. Current population reports* (P20-578). Washington, DC: US Census Bureau. Retrieved from https://www.census.gov/content/dam/Census/library/publications/2016/demo/p20-578.pdf.

Sackett, D. L., Rosenberg, W. M. C., Gray, J. A. M., Haynes, R. B., & Richardson, W. S. (1996). Evidence based medicine: What it is and what is isn't. *British Medical Journal, 312*, 71–72.

Sadato, N., Pascual-Leone, A., Grafman, J., Ibanez, V., Deiber, M. P., Dold, G., et al. (1996). Activation of the primary visual cortex by Braille reading in blind subjects. *Nature, 380*, 526–528.

Said, E. W. (1978). *Orientalism*. New York: Vintage Books.

Salmon, W. S. (1984). *Scientific explanation and the causal structure of the world*. Princeton, NJ: Princeton University Press.

Salvatore, J. E., Kuo, S. I., Steele, R. D., Simpson, J. A., & Collins, W. A. (2011). Recovering from conflict in romantic relationships: A developmental perspective. *Psychological Science, 22*, 376–383.

Sapolsky, R. M. (2017). *Behave: The biology of humans at our best and worst*. New York: Penguin.

Saxon, D., & Barkham, M. (2012). Patterns of therapist variability: Therapist effects and the contribution of patient severity and risk. *Journal of Consulting and Clinical Psychology, 80*, 535–546.

Schiller, J. S., Lucas, J. W., & Peregoy, J. A. (2012). *Summary health statistics for U.S. adults: National health interview survey, 2011. Vital Health Stat 10*(256). 2012. Hyattsville, MD: National Center for Health Statistics.

Schmitz, W. M., Jr., Allen, M. H., Feldman, B. N., Gutin, N. J., Jahn, D. R., Kleespies, P. M., et al. (2012). Preventing suicide through improved training in suicide risk assessment and care: An American Association of Suiciology task force report addressing serious gaps in U.S. mental health training. *Suicide and Life-Threatening Behavior, 42*(3), 292–304.

Scholl, L., Seth, P., Kariisa, M., Wilson, N., & Baldwin, G. (December 21, 2018). Drug and opioid-involved overdose deaths—United States, 2013-2017. *WR Morbidity and Mortality Weekly Report*, ePub. Atlanta, GA: Center for Disease Control and Prevention.

Schone-Seifert, B. (2006). Danger and merits of principlism: Meta-theoretical reflections on the Beauchamp/Childress approach to biomedical ethics. In C. Rehmann-Sutter, M. Duwell, & D. Mieth (Eds.), *Bioethics on cultural contexts: Reflections on methods and finitude* (pp. 109–119). Dordrecht, Netherlands: Springer. https://doi.org/10.1007/1-4020-4241-8_8.

Schwartz, J. M., & Begley, S. (2002). *The mind and the brain: Neuroplasticity and the power of mental force*. New York: Regan Books.

Scott, R. A. (2010). *Miracle cures: Saints, pilgrimage, and the healing powers of belief.* Berkeley: University of California Press.

Seagull, E. A. (2000). Beyond mothers and children: Finding the family in pediatric psychology. *Journal of Pediatric Psychology, 25*, 161–169. https://doi.org/10.1093/jpepsy/25.3.161.

Seikkula, J., Aaltonen, J., Alakare, B., Haarakangas, K., Keranen, J., & Lehtinen, K. (2006). Five-year experience of first-episode nonaffective psychosis in open-dialogue approach: Treatment principles, follow-up outcomes, and two case studies. *Psychotherapy Research, 16*, 214–228.

Seligman, M. E. P., & Csikszentmihalyi, M. (2000). Positive psychology: An introduction. *American Psychologist, 55*(1), 5–14.

Shah, S., & Reichman, W. E. (2006). Psychiatric intervention in long-term care. In L. Hyer, & R. C. Intrieri (Eds.), *Geropsychological interventions in long-term care* (pp. 85–107). New York: Springer.

Sharot, T. (2017). *The influential mind: What the brain reveals about our power to change minds*. New York: Henry Holt.

Sharpe, V. A., & Faden, A. I. (1998). *Medical harm: Historical, conceptual, and ethical dimensions of iatrogenic illness*. Cambridge: Cambridge University Press. https://doi.org/10.1017/CBO9780511527029.

De Shazer, S. (1985). *Keys to solution in brief therapy*. New York: Norton.

Shedler, J. (2010). The efficacy of psychodynamic psychotherapy. *American Psychologist, 65*, 98–109. https://doi.org/10.1037/a0018378.

Shubing, N. (2008). *Your inner fish: A journey into the 3.5-billion-year history of the human body*. New York: Pantheon Books.

Simpson, J. A., & Belsky, J. (2008). Attachment theory within a modern evolutionary framework. In J. Cassidy, & P. R. Shaver (Eds.), *Handbook of attachment: Theory, research, and clinical applications* (2nd ed., pp. 131–157). New York: Guilford.

Singer, P. (1981). *The expanding circle: Ethics and sociobiology*. New York: Farrar, Straus, & Giroux.

Slade, K., Lambert, M. J., Harmon, S. C., Smart, D. W., & Bailey, R. (2008). *Clinical support tool manual*. Unpublished manuscript. Provo, UT: Brigham Young University.

Smedley, B. D., Stith, A. Y., & Nelson, A. R. (Eds.). (2003). *Unequal treatment: Confronting racial and ethic disparities in health care*. Washington, DC: National Academies Press.

Smith, M. A., Schussler-Fiorenza, C., & Rockwood, T. (2006). Satisfaction with care. In R. L. Kane (Ed.), *Understanding health care outcomes research* (2nd ed., pp. 185–218). Sudbury, MA: Jones and Barlett Publishers.

Smith, M. L., & Glass, G. V. (1977). Meta-analysis of psychotherapy outcome studies. *American Psychologist, 32*, 752–760. https://doi.org/10.1037/0003-066X.32.9.752.

Smith, M. L., Glass, G. V., & Miller, T. I. (1980). *The benefits of psychotherapy*. Baltimore, MD: Johns Hopkins University Press.

Smith, S. G., Zhang, X., Basile, K. C., Merrick, M. T., Wang, J., Kresnow, M., et al. (2018). *The national intimate partner and sexual violence survey (NISVS): 2015 data brief – updated release*. Atlanta, GA: National Center for Injury Prevention and Control, Centers for Disease Control and Prevention.

Snyder, T. D., de Brey, C., & Dillow, S. A. (2016). *Digest of education statistics 2016* (*52nd* ed.). Washington, DC: National Center for Educational Statistics.

Sobell, M. B., & Sobell, L. C. (2000). Stepped care as a heuristic approach to the treatment of alcohol problems. *Journal of Consulting and Clinical Psychology, 68*, 573–579. https://doi.org/10.1037/0022-006X.68.4.573.

Sowers, W., George, C., & Thompson, K. (1999). Level of care utilization system for psychiatric and addiction services (LOCUS): A preliminary assessment of reliability and validity. *Community Mental Health Journal, 35*, 545–563. https://doi.org/10.1023/A:1018767403107.

Sowers, W., Pumariega, A., Huffine, C., & Fallon, T. (2003). Best practices: Level-of-care decision making in behavioral health services: The LOCUS and the CALOCUS. *Psychiatric Services, 54*, 1461–1463. https://doi.org/10.1176/appi.ps.54.11.1461.

Spanier, G. B. (1976). Measuring dyadic adjustment: New scales for assessing the quality of marriage and similar dyads. *Journal of Marriage and Family, 38*, 15–28. https://doi.org/10.2307/350547.

Speer, D. C. (1998). *Mental health outcome evaluation*. San Diego, CA: Academic Press.

Spielberger, C. D., Gorsuch, R. L., & Lushene, R. E. (1970). *Manual for the state-trait anxiety inventory*. Palo Alto, CA: Consulting Psychologists Press.

Spitzer, R. L., Kroenke, R., Williams, J. B., & Lowe, B. (2006). A brief measure for assessing generalized anxiety disorder: The GAD-7. *Archives of Internal Medicine, 166*, 1092–1097. https://doi.org/10.1001/archinte.166.10.1092.

Spring, B. (2007). Evidence-based practice in clinical psychology: What it is, why it matters, what you need to know. *Journal of Clinical Psychology, 63*(7), 611–631.

Sroufe, L. A., Egeland, B., Carlson, E. A., & Collins, W. A. (2005). *The development of the person: The Minnesota study of risk and adaptation from birth to adulthood*. New York: Guilford.

Sroufe, A., & Siegel, D. (2011). The verdict is in: The case for attachment theory. *Psychotherapy Networker, 35*(34–39), 52–53.

Steele, H., Steele, M., & Fonagy, P. (1996). Associations among attachment classifications of mothers, fathers, and their infants. *Child Development, 67*, 541–555. https://doi.org/10.2307/1131831.

Sternberg, R. J. (2005). Unifying the field of psychology. In R. J. Sternberg (Ed.), *Unity in psychology: Possibility or pipedream?* (pp. 3–14). Washington, DC: American Psychological Association. https://doi.org/10.1037/10847-001.

Stone, D. M., Simon, T. R., Fowler, K. A., Kegler, S. R., Yuan, K., Holland, K. M., et al. (June 8, 2018). Vital Signs: Trends in state suicide Rates—unites States, 1999-2016 and circumstances contributing to suicide—27 states, 2015. *Morbidity and Morality Weekly Report, 67*(22), 617–624.

Streim-Amit, E., et al. (2012). Reading with sounds: Sensory substitution selectively activates the visual word form area in the blind. *Neuron, 76*, 640.

Stringer, C. (2012a). *Lone survivors: How we came to be the only humans on earth*. New York: Times Books Henry Holt.

Stringer, C. (2012b). What makes a modern human. *Nature, 485*, 33–35.

Stromberg, C. D., Haggarty, D. J., Mishkin, B., Leibenluft, R. F., Rubin, B. L., McMillian, M. H., et al. (1988). *The psychologist's legal handbook*. Washington, DC: Council for the National Register of Health Service Providers in Psychology.

Strum, P. (1999). *When the Nazi's came to town: Freedom for speech we hate*. Lawrence, KS: University of Kansas Press.

Strupp, H. H., & Hadley, S. M. (1977). A tripartite model of mental health and therapeutic outcomes. *American Psychologist, 32*, 187–196. https://doi.org/10.1037/0003-066X.32.3.187.

Substance Abuse and Mental Health Services Administration. (2011). *SAMSHA's wellness initiative: Eight dimensions of wellness*. Rockville, MD: Substance Abuse and Mental Health Services Administration. Retrieved from http://samhsa.gov/wellness.

Substance Abuse and Mental Health Services Administration. (2018). *Key substance use and mental health indicators in the United States: Results from the 2017 national survey on drug use and health (HHS publication No. SMA 18-5068, NSDUH series H-53)*. Rockville, MD: Center for Behavioral Health Statistics and Quality, Substance Abuse and Mental Health Services Administration. Retrieved from https://www.samhsa.gov/data/.

Substance Abuse and Mental Health Services Administration. (2019a). *Screening, brief intervention, and Referral to treatment (SBIRT)*. Rockville, MD: Substance Abuse and Mental Health Services Administration. Retrieved from https://www.integration.samhsa.gov/clinical-practice/sbirt.

Substance Abuse and Mental Health Services Administration. (2019b). *Suicide assessment five-step evaluation and triage (SAFE-T)*. Rockville, MD: Substance Abuse and Mental Health Services Administration. Retrieved from https://store.samhsa.gov/system/files/sma09-4432.pdf.

Sue, D. W., & Sue, D. (2012). *Counseling the culturally diverse: Theory and practice* (6th ed.). New York: Wiley.

Suls, J., & Rothman, A. (2004). Evolution of the biopsychosocial model: Prospects and challenges for health psychology. *Health Psychology, 23*, 119–125. https://doi.org/10.1037/0278-6133.23.2.119.

Tarasoff v. Board or Regents of the University of California. (1976). *17 cal. 3d 425, 551 P.2d 334, 131 cal reptr. 14*.

Taubenberger, J. K., & Morens, D. M. (2006). 1918 influenza: The mother of all pandemics. *Emerging Infectious Diseases, 12*(1), 15–22.

Taub, E., Uswatte, G., King, D. K., Morris, D., Crago, J. E., & Chatterjee, A. (2006). A placebo-controlled trial of constraint-induced movement therapy for upper extremity after stroke. *Stroke, 37*, 1045–1049.

Thase, M. E., & Jindal, R. D. (2004). Combining psychotherapy and psychopharmacology for treatment of mental disorders. In M. J. Lambert (Ed.), *Garfield and Bergin's handbook of psychotherapy and behavior change: An empirical analysis* (5th ed., pp. 743–766). New York: Wiley. https://doi.org/10.1023/A:1024630205999.

The Kennedy Forum. (2016). *A core set of outcome measures for behavioral health across service settings*. Retrieved from https://chp-wp-uploads.s3.amazonaws.com/www.thekennedyforum.org/uploads/2017/06/MBC_supplement.pdf.

Theobald, D. L. (2010). A formal test of the theory of universal common ancestry. *Nature, 465*, 219–222. https://doi.org/10.1038/nature09014.

Tinbergen, N. (1963). On the aims and methods of ethology. *Zeitschrift fur Tierpsychologie, 20*, 410–433.

Tishkoff, S. A., & Kidd, K. K. (2004). Implications of biogeography of human populations for 'race' and medicine. *Nature Genetics, 36*, S21–S27. https://doi.org/10.1038/ng1438.

Trivedi, A. N., & Grebla, R. C. (2011). Quality and equity of care in the Veterans Affairs health-care system and in Medicare advantage health plans. *Medical Care, 49*, 560–568. https://doi.org/10.1097/MLR.0b013e31820fb0f6.

Trivers, R. (1971). The evolution of reciprocal altruism. *Quarterly Review of Biology, 46*, 35–57.

Trull, T. J., Nietzel, M. T., & Main, A. (1988). The use of meta-analysis to assess the clinical significance of behavior therapy for agoraphobia. *Behavior Therapy, 19*, 527–538. https://doi.org/10.1016/S0005-7894(88)80021-2.

Tsai, J. (2018). Lifetime and 1-year prevalence of homelessness in the US populations: Results from the national epidemiologic survey on alcohol and related conditions-III. *Journal of Public Health, 40*(1), 65–74.

Turner, S. M., DeMers, S. T., Fox, H. R., & Reed, G. M. (2001). Guidelines for test user qualifications: An executive summary. *American Psychologist, 56*, 1099–1113. https://doi.org/10.1037/0003-066X.56.12.1099.

Turnock, B. J. (2015). *Essentials of public health* (3rd ed.). Sudbury, MA: Jones and Bartlett Learning.

Tversky, A., & Kahneman, D. (1983). Extensional versus intuitive reasoning: The conjunction fallacy in probability judgment. *Psychological Review, 90*, 293–315.

Tyson, N. D. (2017). *Astrophysics for people in a hurry*. New York: Norton.

Tyson, N. D., & Goldsmith, D. (2004). *Origins: Fourteen billion years of cosmic evolution*. New York: W. W. Norton.

Unal, B., Critchley, J. A., Fidan, D., & Capewell, S. (2005). Life-years gained from modern cardiological treatments and populations risk factors changes in England and Wales, 1981-2000. *American Journal of Public Health, 95*, 103–108.

United Nations. (1948). *Universal declaration of human rights of the United Nations*. New York: United Nations.

U.S. Bureau of Justice Statistics. (2012a). *Criminal victimization, 2011*. Washington, DC: Bureau of Justice Statistics. Retrieved from http://bjs.gov/index.cfm?ty=pbdetail&iid=4494.

U.S. Bureau of Justice Statistics. (2012b). *State court caseload statistics*. Washington, DC: Bureau of Justice Statistics. Retrieved from http://bjs.gov/index.cfm?ty=tp&tid=30.

U.S. Census Bureau. (March 13, 2018). *Older people projected to outnumber children for first time in U.S. history (Press Release CB18-41)*. Washington, DC: U.S. Census Bureau. Retrieved from https://www.census.gov/newsroom/press-releases/2018/cb18-41-population-projections.html.

U.S. Census Bureau. (November 14, 2018b). *U.S. Census Bureau releases 2018 families and living arrangements tables (Release No. CB18-TPS.54)*. Washington, DC: U.S. Census Bureau. Retrieved from https://www.census.gov/newsroom/press-releases/2018/families.html.

U.S. Census Bureau. (2019). *QuickFacts: United States*. Washington, DC: U.S. Census Bureau. Retrieved from https://www.census.gov/quickfacts/fact/table/US/PST045218.

U.S. Department of Health and Human Services. (2013). *Framework: The vision, mission, and goals of Healthy People 2020*. Washington, DC: Department of Health and Human Services. Retrieved from http://healthypeople.gov/2020/Consortium/HP2020Framework.pdf.

U.S. Department of Health and Human Services. (2014). *The health consequences of smoking—50 years of progress: A report of the surgeon general*. U.S. Department of Health and Human Services, Centers for Disease Control and Prevention.

U.S. Department of Health and Human Services. (2019). *Healthy People 2020 leading health indicators: Progress update*. Washington, DC: Department of Health and Human Services. Retrieved from https://www.healthypeople.gov/2020/leading-health-indicators/Healthy-People-2020-Leading-Health-Indicators%3A-Progress-Update.

U.S. Department of Health and Human Services, Administration for Children and Families, Administration on Children, Youth and Families, & Children's Bureau. (2018). *Child maltreatment 2016*. Retrieved from https://www.acf.hhs.gov/sites/default/files/cb/cm2016.pdf.

U.S. Preventive Services Task Force. (2019). *About the USPSTF*. Retrieved from https://www.uspreventiveservicestaskforce.org/Page/Name/about-the-uspstf.

Valenstein, M., Adler, D. A., Berlant, J., Dixon, L. B., Dulit, R. A., Goldman, B., et al. (2009). Implementing standardized assessments in clinical care: Now's the time. *Psychiatric Services, 60*(10), 1372–1375.

Virani, A. S., Bezchlibnyk-Butler, K. Z., & Jeffries, J. J. (Eds.). (2009). *Clinical handbook of psychotropic drugs* (18th ed.). Ashland, OH: Hogrefe Publishing.

Von Foerster, H. (1972). Responsibilities of competence. *Journal of Cybernetics, 2*, 1–6.

Von Hippel, W. (2018). *The social leap: The new evolutionary science of who we are, where we come from, and what makes us happy*. New York: Harper Wave.

Vonk, J., & Shackelford, T. K. (Eds.). (2012). *The Oxford handbook of comparative evolutionary psychology*. New York: Oxford University Press.

Vyse, S. (2008). *Going broke: Why Americans can't hold on to their money*. New York: Oxford University Press.

Wachter, R. M. (2009). Entering the second decade of the patient safety movement: The field matures. *Archives of Internal Medicine, 169*, 1894–1896. https://doi.org/10.1001/archinternmed.2009.351.

Wade, N. (2006). *Before the dawn: Recovering the lost history of our ancestors*. New York: Penguin.

Wahba, A., & Bridgewell, L. (1976). Maslow reconsidered: A review of research on the need hierarchy theory. *Organizational Behavior & Human Performance, 15*, 212–240. https://doi.org/10.1016/0030-5073(76)90038-6.

Walfish, S., McAlister, B., O'Donnell, P., & Lambert, M. J. (2012). An investigation of self-assessment bias in mental health providers. *Psychological Reports, 110*, 639–644.

Wampold, B. E. (2001). *The great psychotherapy debate: The evidence for what makes psychotherapy work*. New York: Routledge.

Wampold, B. E. (2007). Psychotherapy: The humanistic (and effective) treatment. *American Psychologist, 62*, 857–873. https://doi.org/10.1037/0003-066X.62.8.857.

Wampold, B. E., & Imel, Z. E. (2015). *The great psychotherapy debate: The evidence for what makes psychotherapy work* (2nd ed.). New York: Routledge.

Wang, P. S., Demler, O., Olfson, M., Wells, K. B., & Kessler, R. C. (2006). Changing profiles of service sectors used for mental health care in the United States. *American Journal of Psychiatry, 163*, 1187–1198. https://doi.org/10.1176/appi.ajp.163.7.1187.

Wang, P. S., Lane, M., Olfson, M., Pincus, H. A., Wells, K. B., & Kessler, R. C. (2005). Twelve-month use of mental health services in the United States: Results from the national co-morbidity survey replication. *Archives of General Psychiatry, 62*, 629–640. https://doi.org/10.1001/archpsyc.62.6.629.

Ware, J. E., & Sherbourne, C. D. (1992). The MOS 36-item Short-Form Health Survey (SF-36). I. Conceptual framework and item selection. *Medical Care, 30*, 473–483. https://doi.org/10.1097/00005650-199206000-00002.

Waskow, I. E., & Parloff, M. B. (1975). *Psychotherapy change measures*. Rockville, MD: National Institute of Mental Health.

Watson, J. B. (1924). *Behaviorism*. New York: People's Institute Publishing Company.

Weaver, I. C. G., Cervoni, N., Champagne, F. A., D'Alessio, A. C., Sharma, S., Seckl, J. R., et al. (2004). Epigenetic programming by maternal behavior. *Nature Neuroscience, 7*, 847–854.

Wei, Y., et al. (2014). Paternally induced transgenerational inheritance of susceptibility to diabetes in mammals. *Proceedings of the National Academy of Sciences, 111*, 1873.

Weiss, R., Caron, A., Ball, S., Tapp, J., Johnson, M., & Weisz, J. R. (2006). Iatrogenic effects of group treatment for antisocial youth. *Journal of Consulting and Clinical Psychology, 73*, 1001–1008.

West, G. B., Woodruff, W. H., & Brown, J. H. (2002). Allometric scaling of metabolic rate from molecules and mitochondria to cells and mammals. *Proceedings of the National Academy of Sciences, 99*(Suppl. l. 1), 2473.

Whitaker, R. (2010). *Anatomy of an epidemic: Magic bullets, psychiatric drugs, and the astonishing rise of mental illness in America*. New York: Broadway Paperbacks.

Whitaker, R., & Cosgrove, L. (2015). *Psychiatry under the influence: Institutional corruption, social injury, and prescriptions for reform*. New York: Palgrave Macmillan.

White, M., & Epston, D. (1990). *Narrative means to therapeutic ends*. New York: Norton.

Whyte, M. K. (1978). *The status of women in preindustrial societies*. Princeton: Princeton University Press.

Wiggins, J. S. (2003). *Paradigms of personality assessment*. New York: Guilford.

Williams, B. (1994). Patient satisfactyion: A valid concept? *Social Science & Medicine, 38*(4), 509–516.

Williams, W. H., & Evans, J. J. (2003). *Biopsychosocial approaches in neurorehabilitation: Assessment and management of neuropsychiatric, mood and behavioural disorders*. Hove, UK: Psychology Press.

Wilson, E. O. (1975). *Sociobiology*. Belknap Press.

Wilson, E. O. (1998). *Consilience: The unity of knowledge*. New York: Knopf.

Wolpe, J. (1958). *Psychotherapy by reciprocal inhibition*. Stanford, CA: Stanford University Press.

Wood, A., & Joseph, S. (2007). Grand theories of personality cannot be integrated. *American Psychologist, 62*, 57–58. https://doi.org/10.1037/003-066x62.1.57.

Woodworth, R. S. (1921). *Psychology: A study of mental life*. New York: Henry Holt.

Wootton, D. (2015). *The invention of science: A new history of the scientific revolution*. New York: Harper-Collins.

World Health Organization. (1948). *Constitution of the world health organization*. Geneva, Switzerland: World Health Organization.

World Health Organization, (1978). *Primary health care report of the international conference on primary health care, Alma-Ata, USSR, 6–12 September, 1978*. Geneva, Switzerland: World Health Organization.

World Health Organization. (2000). *The world health report 2000*. Geneva, Switzerland: World Health Organization.

World Health Organization. (2008a). *Primary health care: Now more than ever*. Geneva, Switzerland: World Health Organization.

World Health Organization. (2008b). *The global burden of disease: 2004 update*. Geneva, Switzerland: World Health Organization.

World Health Organization. (2008c). *2008-2013 action plan for the global strategy for the prevention and control of noncommunicable diseases*. Geneva, Switzerland: World Health Organization. Retrieved from http://apps.who.int/iris/bitstream/10665/44009/1/9789241597418_eng.pdf.

World Health Organization. (2010). *Framework for action on interprofessional education and collaboration*. Geneva, Switzerland: World Health Organization.

World Health Organization. (2018). *People at the centre of care*. Retrieved from http://www.wpro.who.int/health_services/people_at_the_ centre_of_care/definition/en.

World Health Organization. (2019). *World Health Statistics 2019: Monitoring health for the SDGs, sustainable development goals*. Geneva: World Health Organization.

Wrangham, R. (2019). *The goodness paradox: The strange relationship between virtue and violence in human evolution*. New York: Pantheon Books.

Xu, J., Murphy, S. L., Kochanek, K. D., Bastian, B., & Arias, E. (July 26, 2018). Deaths: Final data for 2016. *National Vital Statistics Reports, 67*(5), 1–76.

Yakubu, A., & Mabogunje, O. A. (1993). Skin cancer in African albinos. *Acta Oncology, 32*, 621–622.

Yon, Y., Mikton, C. R., Gassoumis, Z. D., & Wilber, K. H. (2017). Elder abuse prevalence in community settings: A systematic review and meta-analysis. *Lancet Global Health, 5*(2), e147–156.

Zhang, T., & Meaney, M. J. (2010). Epigenetics and the environmental regulation of the genome and its function. *Annual Review of Psychology, 61*, 439–466. https://doi.org/10.1146/annurev.psych.60.110707.163625.

Zhang, Y., Qi, G., Park, J., & Chatterjee, N. (2018). Estimation of complex effect-size distributions using summary-level statistics from genome-wide association studies cross 32 complex traits. *Nature Genetics, 50*, 1318–1326.

Index

Note: Page numbers followed by "f" indicates figures, "t" indicates tables and "b" indicates boxes.

V

W

Y

9780128164266